Elizabeth Gundrey w
for many years befo
quality and value-fo
travel. Of all her bo
the most popular, re
enlarged editions, o

C000109898

What the press has said about
STAYING OFF THE BEATEN TRACK

'The best of the season's guidebooks to the
treasurehouse of rural accommodation in Britain
is Elizabeth Gundrey's *Staying Off the Beaten
Track*.' (*Financial Times*)

'Very accurate.' (*Law Society Gazette*)

And from other journals:

'Most travel guides all say the same thing. Not so
Elizabeth Gundrey's *Staying Off the Beaten
Track*, a hand-picked selection of original places
to stay.'

'A vividly personal yet immensely practical
selection of enjoyable places to stay.'

'The author's tastes are surely shared by many
wanting to find pleasing accommodation and
service without paying a fortune.'

'Elizabeth Gundrey's help will prove invaluable.'

'I have confidence in Elizabeth Gundrey's
recommendations.'

Pictured on the cover:

Low Murrah, west of Penrith, Cumbria
(see page 261)

STAYING
OFF THE
BEATEN TRACK

ELIZABETH GUNDREY

*A personal selection of moderately priced
inns, small hotels, farms and
country houses in England*

SIXTH EDITION
1987

This edition is published in
support of English Heritage
(see page 21)

ARROW BOOKS

To Andrew, with love

Arrow Books Limited
62–65 Chandos Place, London WC2N 4NW

A division of Century Hutchinson Ltd

London   Melbourne   Sydney   Auckland
Johannesburg and agencies
throughout the world

First published in Great Britain 1982
by Hamlyn Paperbacks
Second edition 1983
Third edition 1984
Fourth edition 1985
Fifth edition 1986
Arrow edition (Sixth edition) 1986

Set in Linotron Times by Tradespools Ltd, Frome,
Somerset
Printed and bound in Great Britain by
The Guernsey Press Co Ltd, Guernsey, C.I.

ISBN 0 09 949670 4

The author and publishers would like to thank
all those owners who allowed us to use their
drawings (additional line drawings by David
Mostyn, Peter Gregory, Matthew Doyle,
Nicole Tedder and Jeremy Ford).

Although every care has been taken to ensure
that all the information in this book is correct
and up-to-date, neither the author nor the
publishers can accept responsibility for details
which may have changed since the book went
to press.

CONTENTS

WHAT'S NEW THIS TIME?

This, the sixth, annual edition of *Staying Off the Beaten Track* has more entries than ever before: over 300.

★   There are many new entries for Dorset, Wiltshire, Hampshire, Somerset, Isle of Wight, Norfolk, East Sussex, Worcestershire and North Yorkshire in particular.

★   Pinpointing the whereabouts of houses is now easier: each has a cross-reference to the grid on the small map (page 26), which corresponds to the grid on Geographia's large-scale motoring map of England and Wales, available at bookshops.

★   A number of houses are offering early 'sampler' breaks coupled with summer holiday discounts (see page 14).

★   For the over-60s, free accommodation on Sunday nights is now offered at some houses (see individual entries).

★   Those houses that charge singles little or no more than half a couple have been indicated by the letter **S**.

★   A scenic two-week tour of the northern counties is described on pages 16–17.

★   Booking service (see page 18).

★   Each entry states the number of properties in the area at which you can use English Heritage membership (see page 21) for free admission.

★   There's more emphasis on imaginative breakfasts; vegetarian or wholefood options at dinner; above-average wine lists; cycle hire; 'no smoking' rooms; extra-firm mattresses; and the possibility of bridge fours being set up on request.

★   Several houses ordinarily closed in winter are willing to open up for house-parties of four to six friends (see text); others offer special terms for such group bookings.

★   Cooks or chefs are named.

★   And because 'heated' swimming-pools range from warm down to barely tepid, actual temperatures are given.

INTRODUCTION

A quiet treeless nook, with two green fields,
A liquid pool that glittered in the sun,
And one bare dwelling; one abode, no more!
It seemed the home of poverty and toil,
Though not of want: the little fields made green
By husbandry of many thrifty years,
Paid cheerful tribute to the moorland house.

Wordsworth

Not every entry in this book is quite so far off the beaten track as Blea Tarn (see page 72), the subject of the poem above. Some are even in town centres, but down byways a visitor might pass. The only common denominators are moderate price (well over half charge £8–£13 for bed-and-breakfast); assurance of a warm welcome and caring service; and individuality – the majority are the homes of owners, none of them alike, whose personality is clearly imprinted on the way the house is furnished, the style of hospitality, and the kind of cooking.

THE GREAT BRITISH BREAKFAST (OR THE GREAT BRITISH BORE?)

Increasingly, this individuality is evident even in the breakfasts. Although overseas visitors in particular regard a great plateful of bacon, eggs and all the trimmings as an event in itself, it can begin to pall if it appears unvaryingly, day after day, for a week or more – high in calories and cholesterol.

I'm delighted that, at places like Carnwethers, Font House, Old Forge, Ivy House, Pipps Ford (in particular), Preston Farm, Somerset House, Manor Farm Barn and The Stables, among others, there is a more imaginative approach. Along with 'full English breakfast' there are many other options to choose from.

Kedgeree, fishcakes and kidneys, three classics of the Victorian breakfast-table, seem to be making a comeback; black pudding, too. Hurray for mackerel or haddock served at several houses near the sea; and for genuine Craster kippers delivered from Northumberland, or Arbroath smokies from Scotland.

Eggs (free-range if you're lucky) may be offered to you en cocotte, coddled or baked as a change from the usual poached, fried or scrambled. Potato cakes make a change from fried bread; muffins or croissants from toast; home-made muesli from packet cereals. Several houses now offer a big choice of speciality coffees and teas (even rosehip or camomile). American-style pancakes or waffles, with real maple syrup, possets made with honey and cinnamon, and devilled mushrooms are among other imaginative options I've come across. And full marks for orange juice that is freshly squeezed, home-made bread and preserves, or a surprise like being offered whisky with your real Scottish porridge – properly made from oatmeal and not packet stuff.

OTHER TRENDS

You'll notice as you read this book that a number of small places (frequently in the vanguard of new ideas, while big hotels lag behind) offer imaginative vegetarian or wholefood dishes, often made from organically grown produce and stoneground whole-meal flour. 'No smoking' rooms are gaining ground. And cycles on loan make it easier to take a little exercise; while the provision of extra-firm mattresses or bed-boards recognizes the fact that these help aching backs.

Lest you think that a tendency to emphasize healthy living implies anything spartan, be assured that often these trends are noticeable at places where cooking and comfort are of the best.

As I make no claim to being a wine connoisseur, I recently had the wine lists of houses in my book vetted by a Master of Wine, more accustomed to scrutinizing those of the top hotels and restaurants in Britain. He was surprised at the overall excellence of what was on offer in many guest houses or small country hotels: 'Some very good bargains,' he commented. 'On the whole, I'm most impressed.'

It is not only the amenities at houses in this book that reflect changing trends, but also visitors' habits, too. More people are learning that spring and autumn are better times than summer for travelling in England. On 21 October 1985 (a still, dry and sunny day), *The Times* reported: 'The clear autumn has been a contrast to the wet, dreary summer, but neither is unusual in Britain.' Most houses now stay open until November, and some all through winter (equipping themselves with video films and Trivial Pursuit for the darkening evenings). Even those which close in winter are sometimes willing to open for a weekend house-party of four to six friends.

There is, however, still a disinclination among visitors to stay on Sunday nights (even when work on Monday does not compel a return home) and rooms are often vacant then. Some hotels in this book offer Sunday night's accommodation (not dinner) free to the over-60s if this is part of a three-night stay.

WHO READS *STAYING OFF THE BEATEN TRACK*?

I now get letters from as far afield as New Zealand or Texas, from globetrotting readers who plan entire tours of England around the places described in this book. And, by contrast, from the English who are, with its help, discovering corners of their own country they never previously knew; and a type of holiday they had never previously experienced. As one couple, like others, wrote: 'All our lives we have stayed at top-flight hotels but are now horrified at charges like £50–£70 for just bed-and-breakfast.' 'I have never before felt so much at home, at once, among complete strangers' (at Pipps Ford) is the kind of comment many make.

Businessmen use the book to find real home comforts when travelling in the course of their work; so do certain famous musicians and MPs, academics and royal equerries. Lynne Thompson (of The Coach House) wrote to me: 'I feel that if I stay here long enough most of the interesting people in the world will pass through my dining-room – this year we had air commodores and actresses, artists and archbishops, secretaries to Royals and a NATO general; publishers, international horse riders, orienteers, and a large party of ornithologists.

'Indonesians and Coptic Christians from Bengal, a Swiss art dealer and a Polish family, Anglican vicars and Israeli paratroopers, Scandinavians, Belgians, antipodean wanderers – the conversation between them is fascinating.

'One American, an irrigation expert with the World Health Organization, spent an evening being educated in the finer points of cricket by a prep school headmaster and a Group Captain of the Queen's Flight – I think it was possibly the high spot of his whole trip!'

Some readers tell me not only that they have stayed at half a dozen or more SOTBT houses but that they enjoy reading the book simply as 'armchair travellers'. To those who send me details of their own finds I am particularly grateful.

It is a pleasure to get letters saying that, after staying at places in this book, 'We're going home really rested – will return there again' or 'We made some good friends there'.

Equally, owners of places in this book regularly comment that readers of it are almost invariably 'such nice people', 'appreciative of what we have to offer', and so on. There are a few of the other kind. I rarely get complaints, and of these hardly any are justified. I have no time for the couple who – having left after failing to pay their bill in full, and been reminded of the 'oversight' – retaliated by writing to me with petty and trumped-up complaints about service. A trouble-maker who had been asked to leave did this too – and so did a woman who tried bringing two huge dogs into a no-dogs house. Then there are the visitors who let the bathwater overflow down the stairs (without apology), who gave offence to other guests, who conducted noisy husband-wife quarrels. Fortunately these types are few, but some long-suffering hosts have to endure in silence much more from visitors than ever visitors have to endure from them! I now make it a rule that *I will not take up complaints which have not been raised first with the hosts*, the majority of whom are positively eager to know of any lapse so that they can rectify it. One wrote: 'Please pass on comments good or bad as it helps us to improve (especially the bad ones, if any!).'

In addition to revisiting old entries from time to time, I keep in touch with all through a twice-yearly newsletter – a useful channel for ventilating readers' requests, suggesting more facilities, or drawing attention to minority needs (such as those of elderly or infirm travellers). The organizing of bridge fours – offered by several places in this edition – came about by this means, also the 'sampler breaks' mentioned on page 14, and the free Sundays for over-60s.

The majority of people write to praise. And often it is the little touches that they notice most appreciatively – the free tea on arrival, flowers in bedrooms, loan of maps to walkers, use of washing machine or hair drier. Such things add up to service of a really thoughtful and considerate kind, not found in large over-staffed hotels.

TO MAKE THE BEST USE OF THIS BOOK

Very full information is given about practical matters, but it is up to the reader to make use of this: for instance, there is no point in turning up with a dog or child in tow if the description does not say these are accepted; nor in expecting a garden, or alcoholic drinks, if these are not indicated.

I have visited almost every one myself, but in one or two cases I have relied on reports of friends whose standards I know to be the same as my own. I am indebted to my brother Walter Gundrey for several northern entries. I do not put in reports written by strangers (though recommendations for me to follow up are always very welcome); nor do I delegate the task to professional inspectors. Believing that ambience is far more important than statistics, I do not resort to symbols and abbreviations but describe each place (and its environs) as fully as I can, so that the reader may, I hope, get a true picture of what it is really like to stay there. The owner's personality and style, the kind of food that is served, seem to me so much more important than the number of bathrooms or the presence of an all-night porter.

Here are a dozen hints on getting what you personally really want.

1 It makes sense to **book well ahead:** many of these houses have few rooms.

2 It's best to stay at least 2–3 days: you cannot possibly appreciate an area if you only stay overnight (prices per night are often less, too, if you stay on).

3 Why stay in the famous and overcrowded places like Stratford-upon-Avon or York? Invariably there are pretty villages nearby... or, indeed, you can make for even more distant places which can be just as beautiful yet tourist-free.

4 I strongly recommend taking the trouble to get free booklets about the area before you set off (Tourist Board phone numbers are in the Contents list); and every habitual traveller should keep a copy of the booklet of town Tourist Information Centres issued free by the English Tourist Board (Thames Tower, Blacks Road, London W6).

Anyone touring England by car should have a good road atlas; and in addition I certainly recommend the AA's huge and beautifully produced volume *250 Tours of Britain* with detailed instructions for tours of discovery, some from 35 to 100 miles long, others simply day-trips (£15.95); or the Ordnance Survey's *Britain on Backroads,* equally handsome and with rather more emphasis on scenic byways both for long-distance journeys and for 60 local tours (£12.95).

5 When telephoning to book (3 minutes costs only 15p after 6 p.m. but don't phone at meal times or after 9 p.m.), it is helpful to make the following points: specify your needs exactly (e.g. double or twin beds; private bathroom if available; special diet; extra-firm mattress; preference for blankets or duvets; quiet aspect; etc.); say when you expect to arrive (some inns are closed until evening), and what meals you want; **ask how to find the house** and where to park. Check that ownership has not changed.
Check prices (inclusive of VAT and service) – those in this book are only approximate (they are quoted per person in a double room – singles may pay more – for one night). Rooms with bathrooms, four-posters, etc. usually cost more; longer or off-season stays may cost less per night.

6 Remember that, in particular, seaside resorts or other places suitable for children will be at their busiest (and dearest) in July–August and during half-term holidays (especially, in late May, which is also a bank holiday period). Other peak periods are, of course, Easter, Christmas, New Year and the bank holiday in late August. (The bank holiday in early May is not usually a peak, because it comes rather soon after Easter, but much depends on the weather.) There are local peaks, too (the Gold Cup races at Cheltenham or the regatta at Henley, for instance, are apt to fill hotels for miles around), and local troughs (Brighton, a conference centre, is least busy in high summer). You won't get much personal attention when hotels are full to bursting.

7 In holiday areas, travel on any day other than a summer Saturday if you can. Make ferry, Motorail or coach/train reservations well in advance if travelling at such periods.

8 Spring and autumn are, in my opinion, better periods for holidays. Weather can be excellent, colours of flowers or foliage superb, prices lower. Go to fruit-growing counties at blossom-time; areas with many gardens open to the public in spring (for azaleas) or June (for roses). Farms may have lambs then. Early

holidays in the Scillies, south coast and west can be idyllic. Woodland, mountains and moors come into their own during autumn, or even when snow falls: the seasons for birdwatching (migrant wildfowl) outdoors and log fires indoors. Some hotels and even farms offer special Christmas holidays; but, unless otherwise stated, those in this book will then be closed.

9 Single people may find more company in houses that have a shared dining-table, a bar, and no TV in the sitting-room. As my descriptions indicate, some owners mingle more with their guests than others do. Houses marked **S** charge singles little or no more than half a double.

10 Going abroad? Particularly if taking a morning flight from Gatwick, it is easy to find in this book inexpensive farms at which to stay the night before, where you can leave your car while away – transport to the airport being provided.

11 If you want absolute quiet, avoid any place that has a bar open to non-residents. Inns sometimes get extensions to their licensing hours for late private parties; and may lack quiet sitting-rooms.

12 At many places, you can dine or lunch without staying: see entries under 'meals'.

ECONOMIES

Well over half the places in this book charge **only £8–£13** for bed-and-breakfast. The rest, **£14–£16** (with a dozen a little higher). Two-thirds have bargain breaks or other discounts on offer, some exclusive to readers of this book. Only a third raise prices at the peak of summer. The cost of dinner is, in most cases, within the range **£5–£10**.

Families which pick establishments with plenty of games, swimming-pool, animals, etc., or that are near free museums, parks and walks, can save a lot on keeping youngsters entertained.

Inclusive terms for dinner, bed and breakfast (particularly for a week) can be much lower than those quoted here for these items taken separately. For short-notice bookings you may be able to get a reduction: no proprietor wants to have a room standing empty. This particularly applies to Sunday nights. Some hotels make a discount if you want only two courses from a three-course menu.

Give *ample* notice if you have to cancel. The law allows a hotelier to claim on you if your booked room remains unlet.

SAMPLER WEEKENDS

Certain hotels or houses have agreed to a new scheme which will help readers pick their summer holiday, and get a discount. It works like this. If you spend a couple of nights at one of them before Easter (to try out the accommodation and see what the area is like) and – before you leave – put down a deposit for a full holiday later (minimum, one week), you will be given a discount on the latter which may in some cases be as much as 20%. For precise details, ask the hotel of your choice. (Those participating in this offer are indicated in the text, after prices.)

Another interesting offer which some make: Sunday night's accommodation free to over-60s staying for three days.

SPECIAL NEEDS

Code letters after the names of hotels indicate which ones are (in alphabetical order) likely to prove suitable for families with *children* (**C**), *dogs* (**D**) or *handicapped people* (**H**); and for those who, being without a car, depend upon *public transport* (**PT**). (In the case of children, a minimum age is sometimes stipulated, in which case this has been indicated by a numeral: thus, **C**(5) means children over 5 are accepted.) **S** indicates those that charge singles no more, or only 10% more, than half a double (except, possibly, at peak periods). Some houses additionally have *self-catering* accommodation available (**S-C**); some accept visitors at *Christmas* (**X**), but do not necessarily provide Christmas meals. The symbol ✳ followed by a numeral indicates the number of English Heritage properties in the area free to members (see page 21).

In most cases, places that accept *children* (**C**) offer reduced rates and special meals. They may provide cots, high chairs and even baby-listening; or games and sports for older children. Please enquire when booking.

For *dogs* (**D**) a charge is rarely made, but often it is a stipulation that you must ask before bringing one; and the dog may have to sleep in your car, not the bedroom, or be banned from public rooms.

Handicapped people vary in their needs. Wherever I have used the code-letter **H**, this indicates that not only is there a ground floor bedroom and bathroom but that these, and doorways, have sufficient width for a wheelchair, and that steps are few. For precise details ask when booking.

It is not necessary to have a car in order to get off the beaten track because public transport is widely available: hotels indicated by the code **PT** have a rail station or coach stop within a reasonable distance, from which you can walk or take a taxi (quite a number of hosts will even pick you up, free, in their own car). The symbol **PT** further indicates that there are also some nearby buses to use for local sightseeing, but these may be few. Ask for details when booking.

PLEASE WRITE TO ME

Being a strictly one-woman show, without any large organization and its resources behind me, I particularly value readers' co-operation: that is, comments on places in this book, and recommendations of others worth consideration. (I am glad to hear from owners, too.) Use page 23 on which to write your comments or recommendations. **(If you want a reply, please enclose a stamped, addressed envelope.)**

Typical letter from a reader

It was a huge tonic to find places as you described them – almost as if one had been before and was returning to a favoured place, or on the recommendation of an old friend.

Marion Barker,
Teddington

And another

We have stayed at eight places in your book, and have never been disappointed. We have always been made to feel very welcome and comfortable, and have enjoyed excellent meals.

S. and D. Garner,
Stockport

A NORTHERN TOUR

In the last edition, I described a circular tour to take in England's twelve most popular 'sights', all in the south or centre: **Windsor**, **Oxford**, **Blenheim Palace**, **Warwick Castle**, **Stratford-upon-Avon**, **Bath**, **Salisbury Cathedral**, **Stonehenge**, **Broadlands** and **Beaulieu** (both near the New Forest), **Brighton**, **Leeds Castle** and **Hampton Court**: each with nearby accommodation described in this book.

Now for another circular tour, northward. (And going north you will find that, prices being lower, you could perhaps have 14 days' holiday for what would buy you only 12 further south.) The north has more spectacular scenery and National Parks; great mediaeval abbeys, castles and mansions; cathedral cities; and some splendours that are all its own, from the Lakes to Blackpool Tower, the Roman Wall and the mediaeval city of York itself – with Viking Centre, Railway Museum, castle (with museum) and of course York Minster. There are over eighty English Heritage historic monuments in the north.

Here is my own choice of itinerary, with suggestions about where to stay. Start with the **Peak District** (Derbyshire) for its rugged National Park scenery and Chatsworth (where to stay: *Highlow Hall*). Head north to **Bradford** in Yorkshire, a surprising city with world-famous photography museum, and the Brontës' village of Haworth nearby (*Old Hall*). From here you can also visit one of the north's most celebrated stately homes, Harewood. **Harrogate** is an elegant example of a spa resort, and from it York itself is within visiting distance (*Alexa House*). Then onwards to two other National Parks, the lovely **Yorkshire Dales** – don't miss Fountains Abbey nearby (you could stay at *Gunnarsgill*, *Howe Villa*, *Peat Gate* or *Spring End*), followed by the wild **North York Moors**, the coast beyond and Castle Howard (*Laskill*). The cathedral city of **Durham** comes next, and Beamish open-air museum (*Durham University* offers accommodation outside term-time); and then into Northumberland for, first, the **Northumberland National Park** and a spectacular coastline (*Horncastle*); followed by **Hadrian's Wall**, especially the Roman fort at Housesteads (*Holmhead*). Starting to turn south, the **Lake District National Park** in Cumbria comes next, mountains between the lakes (*Blea Tarn* or *Friar Hall*). **Blackpool**, Lancashire, has its celebrated Tower and pleasure beach (*Mains Hall* or *Singleton Lodge*). And finally (visiting Chester on the way), in Staffordshire are the quite outstanding leisure park and fine gardens of **Alton Towers** (*Onecote*).

Overseas visitors wanting to follow this scenic and varied route might do well to use Birmingham (or Manchester) international airport as their point of arrival; or pick it up from a north-east seaport served by car-ferries (Hull, Newcastle).

Please check prices before booking, and whether there has been any change of ownership (or cook!)

BOOKING SERVICE

For overseas visitors in particular, a booking service has been organised to save a lot of letter-writing or telephoning when planning a tour that involves stops at several places.

For a fee of £15 per person (children under 5 free), you will be sent a form on which to state your dates and your preferred stops and the maximum you wish to pay for bed-and-breakfast. When you have returned this form, reservations will be made for you.

As soon as you receive details of these reservations, you will need to confirm them by immediately sending a deposit to each place.

To use this service, please send £15 per person (non-returnable) with the following coupon to
SOTBT HOLIDAYS, ALSTON, CUMBRIA, CA9 3LG, ENGLAND
to arrive at least one month before you depart.

Name (capitals): ....

Address: ....

Date: ....

Please send me a booking-service form to complete. I enclose a non-returnable fee of £15 sterling (*sterling* cheque or bank draft, Eurocheque, traveller's cheque signed twice, etc.) *per adult.*

VOUCHERS WORTH £15

This voucher is worth £5 at any establishment starred in the list on pages 27–38 provided it is presented **ON ARRIVAL** and not later. It is valid throughout 1987. **FOR CONDITIONS OF USE, SEE OVER**.

This voucher is worth £5 at any establishment starred in the list on pages 27–38 provided it is presented **ON ARRIVAL** and not later. It is valid throughout 1987. **FOR CONDITIONS OF USE, SEE OVER**.

This voucher is worth £5 at any establishment starred in the list on pages 27–38 provided it is presented **ON ARRIVAL** and not later. It is valid throughout 1987. **FOR CONDITIONS OF USE, SEE OVER**.

OFFER OF NEXT EDITION

Using an out-of-date edition can lead to costly disappointments. A new edition appears every January, updated, with fresh entries added, some deleted and others revised. Make sure you are not using an out-of-date edition by sending a stamped self-addressed envelope to Explore England, Alston, Cumbria, CA9 3LG, for an order form (UK only) on which you can apply for the 1988 edition even before it reaches the shops. No need for a letter: just put SOTBT 1988 on top left corner of the envelope. **New in 1988:** Scotland. And many more entries for Yorkshire (especially the Dales), Derbyshire (the Peak District), Cambridgeshire (the wild Fens), Herefordshire, Gloucestershire (the Cotswolds).

What this voucher can be used for varies from one establishment to another. Some will accept it towards the cost of accommodation, for instance; others towards the cost of a meal for two; and at some it may buy a bottle of wine.

Please enquire at the establishment of your choice (1) what you can use the voucher for; (2) whether its validity is CONDITIONAL UPON A MINIMUM BOOKING (for example, it may be valid only if you stay for a specified number of days).

You may present only one voucher at any one establishment.

What this voucher can be used for varies from one establishment to another. Some will accept it towards the cost of accommodation, for instance; others towards the cost of a meal for two; and at some it may buy a bottle of wine.

Please enquire at the establishment of your choice (1) what you can use the voucher for; (2) whether its validity is CONDITIONAL UPON A MINIMUM BOOKING (for example, it may be valid only if you stay for a specified number of days).

You may present only one voucher at any one establishment.

What this voucher can be used for varies from one establishment to another. Some will accept it towards the cost of accommodation, for instance; others towards the cost of a meal for two; and at some it may buy a bottle of wine.

Please enquire at the establishment of your choice (1) what you can use the voucher for; (2) whether its validity is CONDITIONAL UPON A MINIMUM BOOKING (for example, it may be valid only if you stay for a specified number of days).

You may present only one voucher at any one establishment.

ENGLISH HERITAGE MEMBERSHIP

If you appreciate England's historic monuments, it's well worth joining a rather special 'club' by becoming a member of English Heritage – the organization set up in 1984 to look after over 350 of the country's great fortresses (such as Dover Castle), abbeys (Rievaulx in Yorkshire, for instance), Roman or prehistoric sites (most notably, Stonehenge) and other 'sights' as varied as Queen Victoria's magnificent country home on the Isle of Wight and windswept Hadrian's Wall stretching across the north.

Membership is a two-way benefit. What you receive is a membership card entitling you to visit English Heritage properties without payment – Hampton Court and the Tower of London, too; half-price admission to many buildings in Wales and Scotland; a beautifully produced quarterly magazine, with articles by experts, colour photographs, details of forthcoming events in English Heritage properties ranging from concerts to mediaeval jousts, book reviews, and even a children's page (children are enrolled in the junior section, Keep, with its own events, badges, etc.); an illustrated handbook describing all the sites, worth £2; a map of England showing where they all are; guided tours and talks exclusive to members, particularly where local branches flourish; and the offer of books and souvenirs by post, at special prices.

Throughout *Staying Off the Beaten Track,* I have indicated after the name of each hotel (by means of the symbol ✿) the number of places round about it to which your membership card will give you free entry. Others make no charge.

As to the benefit which English Heritage gets from your subscription, you will be helping it not only to preserve and maintain its present properties but to acquire others needing rescue. Further, English Heritage aids archaeological digs, historic gardens, the National Trust, museums and churches that are in need, windmills and other bygone industrial monuments. Its Education Service assists schools to teach children about their heritage.

To join, either call at an English Heritage property or fill in the coupon overleaf (IN CAPITALS) and post to English Heritage, Box 43, Ruislip, HA4 0XW. If applying for more than one person, please list full names (IN CAPITALS) on a separate sheet, with children's birth dates.

☐ **Individual:** £10.00 a year

☐ **Family groups:** £20.00 for two parents and all children under 16, who will be enrolled in KEEP. Each member receives an individual card.

☐ **Senior Citizen:** £6.00 for people qualifying for the State pension.

£   is enclosed*/may be debited to the credit card shown below.

*Cheques should be made payable to ENGLISH HERITAGE.

Access/Amex/
Barclaycard No   ☐☐☐☐☐☐☐☐☐☐☐☐☐☐☐☐☐☐☐

<u>Mr/Mrs/Ms</u> Initials   Surname _____

Address _____

                      Postcode
_____

When booking, or enquiring, please mention *Staying Off the Beaten Track* as your source of information

READER PARTICIPATION

1 It would be very helpful if you will let me know your opinion of places from this book at which you have stayed. Please post this to me at 19 Fitzjohns Avenue, London NW3 5JY (no phone calls please!).

Names of establishments   **Your comments**

More space overleaf

2 If you find other places you think I should visit, for possible inclusion in a future edition, please will you either send me their brochure or give your own description (including price and address).

Your name and address (*caps*) ....

....

....

The AA's *250 Tours of Britain* (described on pages 11–12) can be ordered from Explore England, Alston, Cumbria, CA9 3LG for £17.95 (sterling), delivered to any UK address.

REGIONAL LIST OF HOUSES IN THIS BOOK

The hotels and houses in this book appear in alphabetical order. For convenience in locating them, they are grouped in this list according to the areas covered by individual regional tourist boards (see map, page 26). On the left is the nearest town, with its map reference, followed by the house or hotel and its nearest village. You are advised to buy the Geographia touring map of England and Wales because the references are keyed to that map. Contact the appropriate tourist board for maps and booklets about each region (information about England as a whole is obtainable from the English Tourist Board: 01-846 9000).

★ **Establishments marked with a star will accept the discount vouchers from page 19. Other discounts to readers are described in the text.**

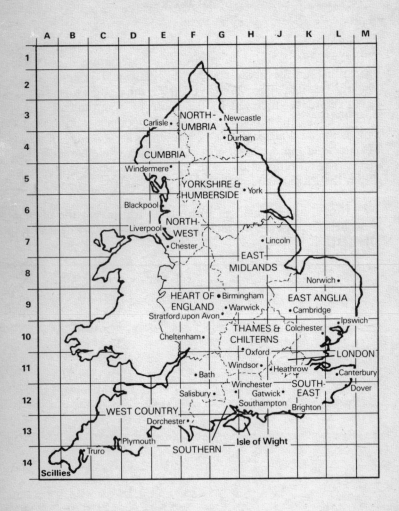

NORTH-UMBRIA

Carlisle • Newcastle

• Durham

CUMBRIA

Windermere •

YORKSHIRE & HUMBERSIDE

• York

Blackpool •

NORTH-WEST

Liverpool •

• Chester

• Lincoln

EAST MIDLANDS

Norwich •

HEART OF ENGLAND

• Birmingham

• Warwick

EAST ANGLIA

• Cambridge

Stratford upon Avon •

THAMES & CHILTERNS

Colchester •

Ipswich •

Cheltenham •

• Oxford

LONDON

• Windsor

• Heathrow

Canterbury •

• Bath

Winchester •

SOUTH-EAST

Salisbury •

Gatwick •

Dover •

Southampton

Brighton •

WEST COUNTRY

Dorchester •

• Plymouth

Isle of Wight

• Truro

SOUTHERN

Scillies

26

Including the counties of Sussex, Kent and Surrey.

Ashford, KENT (L.12)	Bell Inn, Smarden ★	61
Battle, EAST SUSSEX (K.12)	Little Hemingfold ★	256
Brighton, EAST SUSSEX (J.12)	Twenty-One	428
Canterbury, KENT (L.11)	Ebury Hotel ★	164
	Parkfield House, Selling ★	342
Chichester, WEST SUSSEX (G.12)	Easton House, Chidham ★	163
	White Barn, Bosham ★	457
	Whyke House ★	468
	Woodstock House, Charlton	476
Dorking, SURREY (J.12)	Bulmer Farm, Holmbury St Mary ★	81
	Crossways Farm, Abinger ★	145
East Grinstead, SURREY (J.12)	Chithurst Farm, Horne	98
Farnham, SURREY (H.12)	Trevena House Hotel ★	425
Gatwick, SURREY (J.12)	Hillands, Charlwood	223
Guildford, SURREY (G.12)	Clandon Manor Farm, East Clandon	103
	Drummond Arms, Albury	157
	Hazelgrove, East Clandon	105
Hailsham, EAST SUSSEX (K.12)	Cleavers Lyng, Herstmonceux	109
Hastings, EAST SUSSEX (K.12)	Fairlight Hall, Fairlight ★	171
	105 High Street	172
	The Russell, St Leonard's-on-Sea	379
Heathfield, EAST SUSSEX (K.12)	Little Byres, Dallington	254
Horsham, WEST SUSSEX (J.12)	Brookfield Farm, Plummers Plain ★	78
Lewes, EAST SUSSEX (J.12)	Deep Thatch Cottage, Rodmell	155
Maidstone, KENT (K.11)	Harrow Inn, Lenham ★	213
	Heavers, West Malling ★	217
	Moatenden Priory, Headcorn	279
Midhurst, WEST SUSSEX (G.12)	Redford Cottage, Redford	368

Petworth, WEST SUSSEX	Coldharbour Farm, Sutton	122
(G.12)	River Park Farm, Lodsworth	371
Rye, EAST SUSSEX	Cliff Farm, Iden Lock ★	420
(K.12)	Little Orchard ★	257
	Old Vicarage	259
	Swan Cottage	456
	Tighe Farm, Stone-in-Oxney	418
	Western House	454
Tenterden, KENT (K.12)	Little Hodgeham, Bethersden ★	442
	Verrall Cottage, High Halden ★	440
	West Cross House	448
Winchelsea, EAST	New Inn ★	296
SUSSEX (K.12)		
Worthing, WEST SUSSEX	Findon Farmhouse, Findon	174
(J.12)		

SOUTHERN *Southern Tourist Board: 0983 524343*

Including the counties of Hampshire, eastern Dorset and the Isle of Wight.

Bembridge, ISLE OF	Crab and Lobster Inn, Foreland	135
WIGHT (G.13)		
Bournemouth, DORSET	Cliff House	114
(G.13)	Mon Bijou Hotel	282
Brockenhurst,	Wide Lane Cottage	469
HAMPSHIRE (G.12)		
Petersfield, HAMPSHIRE	Barrow Hill Farm, Ramsdean	55
(H.12)	Cross Keys, East Meon	142
	Cumbers House, Rogate	148
Poole, DORSET (G.13)	Fairlight Hotel, Broadstone	189
	The Gables ★	187
Portsmouth, HAMPSHIRE	Fortitude Cottage ★	182
(H.13)		
Shanklin, ISLE OF WIGHT	Apse Manor	47
(G.13)	Cavendish House	92
	The Grange, Alverstone ★	48
	Osborne House Hotel	92

Southampton, HAMPSHIRE (G.12)	Walnut Cottage, Cadnam	445
Swanage, DORSET (G.13)	White Lodge	466
Ventnor, ISLE OF WIGHT (G.13)	Under Rock, Bonchurch ★	430
	Woody Bank, St Lawrence	478
Wareham, DORSET (F.13)	Old Granary	307
	1 The Quay	308
	Trent Vale Farmhouse, Hyde	423
Winchester, HAMPSHIRE (G.12)	Carbery, Stockbridge	88
	The Plough, Itchen Abbas	476
	Winnall Cottage Farm, Easton	475
Yarmouth, ISLE OF WIGHT (G.13)	George Hotel ★	195
	The Nodes, Old Totland ★	299
	Rockstone Cottage, Colwell Bay	301

WEST COUNTRY *West Country Tourist Board: 0392 76351*

Including the Isles of Scilly and the counties of Avon, Cornwall, Devon, western Dorset, Somerset and Wiltshire.

Ashburton, DEVON (D.13)	Bossell House, Buckfastleigh ★	75
	Wellpritton Farm, Holne ★	447
Bath, AVON (F.11)	Avonside, Limpley Stoke	51
	Charnwood House	330
	Oldfields	329
	The Orchard, Bathford	333
	Paradise House	340
	Somerset House ★	392
Bere Regis, DORSET (F.13)	Appletree Cottage ★	44
Bridport, DORSET (E.13)	Chimneys, Chideock ★	96
	Ilchester Arms, Symondsbury	98
	Innsacre Farmhouse Hotel, Shipton Gorge	236
	Manor Hotel, West Bexington ★	269
	Marquis of Lorne, Nettlecombe ★	273
	Roundham House Hotel ★	377
	Uploders Place, Uploders ★	433
Bristol, AVON (F.11)	Cameley Lodge, Temple Cloud	86

HEART OF ENGLAND

Heart of England Tourist Board:
0905 613132

Including the counties of Gloucestershire, Hereford & Worcester,
Shropshire, Staffordshire and Warwickshire.

(Banbury, OXON) (G.10)	Pond Cottage, Warmington, Warwickshire ★	355
Birmingham, WEST MIDLANDS (G.9)	Grimstock Hotel, Coleshill ★	205
Broadway, WORCS (G.10)	Mill Hay House	276
(Burford, OXON) (G.10)	Lamb Inn, Great Rissington, Gloucestershire ★	244
Cheltenham, GLOS (F.10)	Bouchers, Bentham	77
Evesham, WORCS (G.10)	The Croft, Ashton-under-Hill ★	138
Gloucester, GLOS (F.10)	Damsells Cross ★ and Damsells Lodge, Painswick	151
Hereford, HEREFORD (F.10)	The Steppes, Ullingswick ★	401
	Stone House Farm, Tillington ★	406
Kenilworth, WARKS (G.9)	Clarendon House Hotel ★	105
Leamington Spa, WARKS (G.9)	Lansdowne House	246
Ledbury, HEREFORD (F.10)	Butchers Arms, Woolhope ★	83
Leek, STAFFS (F.7)	Onecote Old Hall, Onecote	331
	White House, Grindon	332
Malvern, WORCS (F.10)	Holdfast Cottage Hotel, Welland ★	225
Northleach, GLOS (G.10)	Cotteswold House	132
	Windrush House, Hazleton ★	473
Ross-on-Wye, HEREFORD (F.10)	Ganarew House, Ganarew ★	191
Shipston-on-Stour, WARKS (G.10)	Longdon Manor, Darlingscott ★	259
	White Bear Inn	459
Southam, WARKS (G.9)	The Granary, Fenny Compton Wharf	199
	Snowford Hall, Hunningham	391

32

Stratford-upon-Avon, WARKS (G.9)	King's Lodge, Long Marston ★	243
	Loxley Farmhouse, Loxley ★	263
	Old Town House	319
	Sugarswell Farm, Shenington	409
Tetbury, GLOS (F.11)	The Gentle Gardener	193
Warwick, WARKS (G.9)	Ashleigh House, Henley-in-Arden ★	48
Whitney-on-Wye, HEREFORD (E.10)	Rhydspence Inn	373
Worcester, WORCS (F.9)	The Birche, Shelsey Beauchamp ★	63
	Duckswich House, Upton-on-Severn	158
	Forge Mill, Shelsey Beauchamp	180
	Leigh Court, Leigh	250
	Pool House Hotel, Upton-on-Severn	357
	Talbot Inn, Knightwick	413
	Upton House, Upton Snodsbury ★	437

THAMES & CHILTERNS   *Thames & Chilterns Tourist Board: 0235 22711*

Including the counties of Oxfordshire, Bedfordshire, Buckinghamshire, Berkshire and Hertfordshire.

Abingdon, OXON (G.11)	Fallowfields, Southmoor ★	173
Aylesbury, BUCKS (H.10)	Foxhill, Kingsey ★	184
Banbury, OXON (G.10)	Feldon House, Lower Brailes ★	413
	Swalcliffe Manor, Swalcliffe	411
Beaconsfield, BUCKS (H.11)	Old Jordans, Jordans	312
Burford, OXON (G.10)	Bay Tree Hotel	56
	Forest Gate, Milton-under-Wychwood	179
	Manor Farm Barn, Taynton ★	268
Faringdon, OXON (G.11)	Portwell House ★	358
Henley-on-Thames, OXON (H.11)	Turville Lodge, Turville Heath	427
Hungerford, BERKS (G.11)	Bear Hotel	72
	Blakeway Books	71
Newbury, BERKS (G.11)	Blue Boar, Chieveley ★	74

33

Oxford, OXON (H.10)	Chadlington House, Chadlington	93
	Old Inn, Black Bourton	310
Reading, BERKS (H.11)	Neals Farm, Wyfold	290
Thame, OXON (H.10)	Upper Green Farm, Towersey ★	435
Windsor, BERKS (H.11)	Christopher Hotel, Eton	100
Witney, OXON (G.10)	Morar Farm, Bampton ★	283
	Olde Farm, Minster Lovell	328
	University Farm, Bampton	285

EAST MIDLANDS   *East Midlands Tourist Board: 0522 31521*

Including the counties of Derbyshire (see also North-West), Leicestershire, Lincolnshire, Northamptonshire and Nottinghamshire.

Belper, DERBYSHIRE (G.8)	Shottle Hall Farm, Shottle ★	386
Boston, LINCS (J.8)	Georgian House, Sutterton	197
Bourne, LINCS (J.8)	Beaufort House	58
Corby, NORTHANTS (H.9)	Old Forge, Rockingham	305
Horncastle, LINCS (J.7)	White Hart Inn, Tetford	462
Kettering, NORTHANTS (H.9)	Dairy Farm, Cranford St Andrew	150
Lincoln, LINCS (H.7)	Carline Guest House	169
	Edward King House	167
	Village Farm, Sturton-by-Stow ★	442
Spalding, LINCS (J.8)	Guy Wells, Whaplode ★	208
	Hawkes House	214
Stamford, LINCS (J.8)	Corner Cottage (Hare and Hounds), Greatford	127
Uppingham, LEICS (H.9)	Pepperday Cottage, Barrowden ★	349

EAST ANGLIA   *East Anglia Tourist Board: 0473 822922*

Including the counties of Cambridgeshire, Essex, Norfolk and Suffolk.

Bury St Edmunds, SUFFOLK (K.9)	High Green House, Nowton ★	219
	Westley Hall, Westley ★	456

YORKSHIRE & HUMBERSIDE *Yorkshire & Humberside*
Tourist Board: 0904 707961

Ampleforth, NORTH YORKS (H.5)	Newton Grange Farm	249
Bradford, WEST YORKS (G.6)	Old Hall, Denholme	309
Harrogate, NORTH YORKS (G.5)	Alexa House	40
	Grassfield, Pateley Bridge ★	200
	Sportsman's Arms, Wath-in-Nidderdale	396
Helmsley, NORTH YORKS (H.5)	Laskill House Farm	248
Richmond, NORTH YORKS (G.4)	Gunnarsgill Hall, Gunnerside	206
	Howe Villa	233
	Old Vicarage, Muker	324
	Peat Gate Head, Low Row ★	346
	Spring End, Low Row	398
Skipton, WEST YORKS (F.5)	Unicorn Hotel ★	431

NORTH-WEST *North-West Tourist Board: 0204 591511*

Including the counties of Cheshire, Lancashire, Merseyside and the High Peak of Derbyshire.

Blackburn, LANCS (F.6)	Harrop Fold Farm, Clitheroe	211
	Mytton Fold Farm Hotel, Whalley ★	285
Blackpool, LANCS (E.6)	Mains Hall, Little Singleton ★	264
	Singleton Lodge Farm, Singleton	390
Lancaster, LANCS (E.5)	New Capernwray Farmhouse, Carnforth ★	294
Preston, LANCS (F.6)	Clay Lane Head Farm, Garstang ★	107
(Sheffield, WEST YORKS) (G.7)	Highlow Hall Farm, Hathersage, Derbyshire	221
Silverdale, LANCS (E.5)	Silverdale Hotel	388

NORTHUMBRIA   *Northumbria Tourist Board: 0632 817744*

Including the counties of Durham and Northumberland.

Alnwick,	New Moor House, Edlingham ★	297
NORTHUMBERLAND	West Ditchburn Farm, Eglingham	450
(G.2)		
(Coldstream,	Coach House, Crookham,	
SCOTLAND) (F.2)	Northumberland ★	116
Durham, CO. DURHAM	Durham University: Trevelyan	
(G.4)	College and St Aidan's College	160
Haltwhistle,	Holmhead, Greenhead ★	227
NORTHUMBERLAND		
(F.3)		
Hexham,	Bishopfield Farm, Allendale ★	67
NORTHUMBERLAND		
(F.3)		
Middleton-in-Teesdale,	Teesdale Hotel	415
CO. DURHAM (F.4)		
Morpeth,	Font House, Netherwitton	177
NORTHUMBERLAND		
(G.3)		
Newcastle-upon-Tyne,	Horncastle Farm, Kirkwhelpington	231
NORTHUMBERLAND		
(G.3)		
Rothbury,	Orchard House ★	334
NORTHUMBERLAND		
(G.2)		

CUMBRIA   *Cumbria Tourist Board: 09662 4444*

Ambleside (E.4)	Blea Tarn House, Little Langdale	72
Brampton (F.3)	New Bridge Hotel, Lanercost	292
Carlisle (E.3)	Hare and Hounds Inn, Talkin ★	209
Cockermouth (E.4)	Birk Bank Farm, Brandlingill	65
Millom (E.5)	Foldgate Farm, Bootle	175
	The Stables, Bootle	399

Penrith (F.4)	Low Murrah ★	261
	Prospect Hill Hotel, Kirkoswald ★	362
	The White House, Clifton	464
Tebay (F.4)	Gaisgill Farm, Gaisgill	189
Ulverston (E.5)	Appletree Holme, Blawith	45
Wigton (E.4)	Friar Hall Farm, Caldbeck ★	186

Please check prices before booking, and whether there has been any change of ownership (or cook!)

Abbey House, Church Street, Abbotsbury, west of Weymouth, Dorset, DT3 4JJ *Tel: 0305 871330*   **C D S X ⌗ 4**

Over a century before the Norman Conquest, one of Canute's followers founded an abbey here which flourished until it was broken up by Henry VIII. The remains of 14th-century walls surround (and, indeed, form part of) this historic house, reputedly once the monks' infirmary. New discoveries are constantly being unearthed by its owner, Mr Ross-Turner (a builder specializing in conservation projects): when I was there, the remains of the monastic watermill were being excavated.

From the house, one looks across a garden of smooth, terraced lawns with flowering scented shrubs, vineyard and old apple-trees alongside palms and eucalyptus. A screen of bamboos conceals the vegetable garden. Beyond lies a millpond, the largest tithe-barn in England (currently used to store reeds used by local thatchers), hills, and a glimpse of the sea. On one of the hilltops St Catherine's chapel dominates the skyline. It is an idyllic spot.

rear view

In the house, old plaster and paint have been removed, and an ancient 20-foot fireplace and mullion windows revealed. The big sitting-room has antiques and comfortable armchairs, and all around are slipware dishes or figures made by Mr Ross-Turner's father, who founded the local pottery.

Lindy Ross-Turner uses garden produce when cooking meals such as home-made soup, steak-and-kidney pie and meringues with raspberries. Or you can eat well in the village, at the Ilchester Arms.

In Abbotsbury there is a lot more to see – in particular, the unique swannery which originated when the monks 'farmed' swans for the table; and very lovely subtropical gardens, with a grove of huge pink and red camellias towering overhead. The mysterious Chesil Bank (18 miles of pebble ridge in the sea) is seen well from here; and the surrounding countryside is unspoilt, much of it protected by the National Trust. Weymouth, still a very traditional old resort, is well worth visiting; and so is the strange island of Portland from which comes the white Portland stone that has been exported all over the world.

The following facts have been supplied by the owners:

Bedrooms There are 5 rooms, which include singles, doubles and family rooms. Bed-and-breakfast costs from £12 (per person) including service and VAT; prices go up in high season. There are reductions for stays of 5 nights or more; and 'bargain breaks' as well.

Some if not all of the rooms have the following amenities: central heating; armchairs; views of sea, countryside or garden; choice of duvets or blankets; orthopaedic mattress or backboard; tea/coffee-making facilities; door keys. Breakfast in bed is available.

Meals The dinner menu is fixed price (£8). There is a choice of dishes on the menu, which consists of 3 courses and coffee. Dinner is served at 7 pm. Vegetarian or special diets can be prepared. Lunches and packed lunches can be provided; and snacks at other hours. Morning, afternoon or bedtime drinks (coffee, tea etc.) can be ordered for a charge. Non-residents are not admitted to the dining-room. Wine and other alcoholic drinks can be brought in.

Public rooms There are 2 sitting-rooms. The following are available in one or both of them: central heating, open fire, TV (colour), books, magazines, local guides and leaflets.

Surroundings The grounds consist of 1¾ acres of garden and vineyard, with clock golf and lawn bowls. These are available in the neighbourhood: tennis, golf, swimming, sea fishing.

Cars The nearest main road is the A35 from Dorchester to Bridport.

Languages spoken French.

Alexa House, 26 Ripon Road, Harrogate, North Yorkshire, HG2 2JJ *Tel: 0423 501988*　　　**C H PT S ♯12**

Dating from 1830, this house is typical of many such solidly built and handsome private homes which later became small hotels in Yorkshire's famous spa town. It has been furnished by Marilyn and Peter Bateson with an eye to their guests' comfort (generous armchairs in the bedrooms, for instance) more than to elegance.

In the cheerful dining-room, Marilyn serves traditional English meals – such as home-made soup, a roast with four vegetables and fruit pie. She recently uncovered a pink-and-white marble fire-place, and added silver chandeliers.

Behind the house are some small new rooms (very neatly designed) which are ideal not only for other visitors but also for disabled guests – with Sitz baths and grab-rails, for instance, and an emergency bell connected to the house. (Marilyn was once a teacher of physically handicapped children, and understands what is needed.) A recent addition is a ground-floor suite with its own sitting-room.

A clerical visitor wrote to Marilyn after his first stay: 'I have never fared better since I once spent a weekend at Balmoral. Both hostesses proved to be most charming and kind, but I think you have the edge over H.M. for you did not feel disposed to discuss my sermon with me.'

Elegant Harrogate is full of shops selling antiques and other luxuries. Its award-winning gardens and flowery parks are famous; it has a large, modern entertainments centre; and it is an ideal centre from which to explore the Yorkshire Dales and such famous sights as Fountains Abbey, Ripon Cathedral, Harewood House, Harlow Car gardens and, of course, the city of York.

Readers' comments: Every comfort, and super food. Courteous welcome, we had an excellent time – our stay surpassed all others. *And from Cyril Smith, MP:* Absolutely superb, better than a 4-star hotel, extremely comfortable.

41

The following facts have been supplied by the owners:

Bedrooms There are 12 rooms, which include singles, doubles and family rooms.
Bed-and-breakfast costs from £13.50 (per person in a double room) including
service and VAT; prices go up in high season. There are reductions for stays
of 7 nights or more; and 'bargain breaks' as well.

　　The rooms have the following amenities: central heating or electric heaters;
electric blankets, washbasin, shower, own bathroom and wc, shaver-point;
hair drier; radio, TV (colour), armchairs; choice of duvets or blankets; tea/
coffee-making facilities; door keys.

Meals The dinner menu is fixed price (£8). There is no choice of dishes on the fixed
menu, which consists of 3 courses and coffee. Dinner is served at 6.30 pm.
Special diets can be prepared. Packed lunches can be provided; and snacks at
other hours. Morning, afternoon or bedtime drinks (coffee, tea etc.) can be
ordered for a charge. Wine and other alcoholic drinks can be ordered.

Public rooms There is a sitting-room with central heating, gas fire, TV (colour),
books, magazines, local guides and leaflets, indoor games (such as chess,
draughts, cards and dominoes), record-player and records, bar. Maps on loan.

Surroundings There is a patio with chairs. Golf and swimming-pools are available
in the neighbourhood.

Cars The nearest main road is the A61 from Leeds to Ripon.

**Allens Farmhouse, Three Hammer Common, north-east of
Wroxham, Norfolk, NR12 8XW**　*Tel: 0692 630904*　　**C PT X ⌂8**

The furniture is the outstanding feature of this 18th-century
farmhouse, rescued from dilapidation by Peter Charlton. He
taught himself not only to design these beautifully proportioned
pieces but to make them by hand – from handsome, solid wood,
with silk-smooth finish. The staircase, too. One of the most
striking pieces is an almost throne-like chair, of mediaeval
simplicity: the oak came from an old kitchen door.

In the dining-room are a teak table and slat-back chairs,
furnishings in earthy colours and a brick inglenook with fire under
an iron hood (the old bread oven still survives). The sitting-room,
with another inglenook, has deep velvet chairs and shaggy carpet.
Guests are welcome to use the sun-room, too; or to sit on the
paved terrace overlooking the large and beautifully kept garden
with lily-pool, well paved paths winding among brilliant begonias
and geraniums.

Upstairs are light and immaculate bedrooms. The strawberry-
and-white family room with built-in pine furniture is particularly
popular because it overlooks the adjoining farm's activities.

Betty uses the garden's organically grown produce in her

cooking; and makes her own bread and preserves. Unless more exotic dishes are preferred, she sticks to traditional favourites like roast pork (served with four vegetables *and* Yorkshire pudding) and lemon meringue pie. As an alternative to the usual things, you can have haddock or kippers at breakfast.

For a description of this area, see page 242.

The following facts have been supplied by the owners:

Bedrooms There are 3 rooms, which include double and family rooms. Bed-and-breakfast costs from £9 (per person in a double room) including service and VAT.

Some if not all of the rooms have the following amenities: central heating; electric blankets, washbasin, shaver-point; armchairs; views of farmland and garden; choice of duvets or blankets; orthopaedic mattress or bed-board; tea/coffee-making facilities; door keys.

Meals The dinner menu is fixed price (£5.50) or à la carte. There is no choice of dishes on the fixed menu, which consists of 3 courses and coffee. Dinner is served at 6–8 pm. Vegetarian or special diets can be prepared. Lunches and packed lunches can be provided; and snacks at other hours. Morning, afternoon or bedtime drinks (coffee, tea etc) can be ordered – free. Non-residents are not admitted to the dining-room. Wine and other alcoholic drinks can be brought in.

Public rooms There is a sitting-room with central heating, open fire, TV (colour), books, magazines, local guides and leaflets, indoor games (such as cards, Monopoly, Scrabble etc.).

Surroundings The grounds consist of a garden.

Cars The nearest main road is the A1151 from Norwich to Stalham.

When booking, or enquiring, please mention *Staying Off the Beaten Track* as your source of information

43

Appletree Cottage, 12 Shitterton, Bere Regis, south of Blandford Forum, Dorset, BH20 7HU   *Tel: 0929 471686*   **C PT S ♯ 4**

This is a real Hansel-and-Gretel style cottage – thick cob (clay) walls and thatched roof, with honeysuckle clambering round the pink front door. It was built in the 17th century and was a tiny inn when the little lane outside was once a coaching road, and is now a listed building.

Inside, all ceilings are low, and walls slope. The breakfast-table is in the sitting-room which has silky patchwork cushions on the velvet armchairs gathered around the inglenook with log stove. The very modern bathroom (its chocolate-brown suite includes a bidet) is also on the ground floor. Bedrooms have sprigged wallpapers, beams and board doors – some overlooking the pretty garden with flagstone steps leading to the lawn. For evening meals, Beryl Wilson recommends two inns in the hamlet.

Bere is about half way between Poole and Dorchester, the environs of which are described elsewhere in this book. Lulworth Cove, T.E. Lawrence's cottage, Hardy country, good walks, pretty villages like Milton Abbas, a parachute club, seaside resorts and mellow old towns are all within easy reach.

rear view

The following facts have been supplied by the owners:

Bedrooms   There are 2 double or family rooms. Bed-and-breakfast costs from £9 (per person in a double room); prices go up in high season. There are reductions for stays of 3 nights or more.

One or both of the rooms have the following amenities: central heating; views of countryside or garden; duvets. Bedtime drinks (coffee, tea etc.) can be ordered for a charge.

44

Public rooms There is a sitting-room with central heating, open fire, TV (colour), local guides and leaflets, piano.

Surroundings These are available in the neighbourhood: parachuting (in the village), riding, fishing, golf.

Cars The nearest main road is the A35 from Dorchester to Poole.

Appletree Holme, Blawith, north of Ulverston, Cumbria, LA12 8EL   *Tel: 0229 85618*   C(10) ⌗2

Before coming to this isolated spot, Roy and Shirley Carlsen ran Leeming House on Ullswater, with a reputation for excellence which caused it to grow so big (staff of forty) that ultimately 'the nicest people could no longer afford our prices'.

So they sold up and bought a smallholding on the southern edge of the Lake District, and now have just a few rooms for visitors.

Although the house looks like many other lakeland farms outside, the once-neglected interior has been given a completely new life. Ceiling beams have been exposed, and a dry-stone fireplace with a copper hood put in, replacing a tiled monstrosity. The floor is of polished slate slabs, the staircase of oak, board doors are fastened by wrought-iron hinges and latches. Furnishing fabrics have a country look, carpets are thick, colours and lighting restful.

There is no staff. The Carlsens say, 'All we wanted to do was cook and be hosts' – and to tend the five acres with their hens, a few cows, and the fruit and vegetables which supply their kitchen.

Meals are served in a dining-room with a view to the far hills, and delicious food is brought to tables laid with silver and fine glass.

The three bedrooms are beautiful, and each has its own bathroom. In one, Roy has given his fancy free rein – the huge, circular bath has chandeliers to either side: a Barbara Cartland of a bathroom! The water is filtered direct from a mountain spring.

Coniston Water is near, and also Windermere. Beyond the market town of Ulverston lies the sandy expanse of Morecambe Bay. Historic Kendal is an easy drive in one direction, Furness Abbey and the fishing villages of the Cumbrian coast in the other. This part of the Lake District has its own character. Many buildings are of red sandstone, and the scenery is gentler: Duddon Valley is particularly pretty, with waterfalls, ferns and birch trees. Grange-over-Sands has the lakeland rose show in July.

There are plenty of notable houses to visit – Beatrix Potter, Ruskin and Wordsworth all knew the area well. You can watch hand-cut crystal being made, hunt for antiques or crafts, go to agricultural shows, or simply walk the fells.

Appletree guests have free use of certain Champneys health spa facilities nearby, such as swimming, Jacuzzi and water exercise classes.

The following facts have been supplied by the owners:

Bedrooms There are 3 rooms, which include doubles and family rooms. Bed-and-breakfast costs from £18 (per person in a double room) including service and VAT. There are special rates for longer stays.

All the rooms have the following amenities: central heating; washbasin, shower, own bathroom and wc, shaver-point; armchairs; views of countryside, farmland, garden; tea/coffee-making facilities. One has a bubble bath. There is an adjoining suite with its own patio.

Meals There is no choice of dishes on the menu (£12), which consists of 4 courses and coffee. Dinner is served when required. Special diets can be prepared. Packed lunches can be provided; and snacks at other hours. Morning, afternoon or bedtime drinks (coffee, tea etc.) can be ordered – for a charge. Wine and other alcoholic drinks can be ordered.

Public rooms There are 2 sitting-rooms. The following are available in one or both of them: central heating, open fire, colour TV, video recorder, books, magazines, local guides and leaflets, indoor games (such as Scrabble and cards), record-player and records.

Surroundings The grounds consist of garden, orchard and farmland. These are available in the neighbourhood: golf, fishing, birdwatching, boating, swimming.

Cars The nearest main road is the A5084 from Greenodd to Coniston.

Apse Manor, west of Shanklin, Isle of Wight, PO37 7PN
Tel: 0983 866651   **C(4) D H PT X ♯ 4**

Until recently, this fine Tudor mansion was a farmhouse but it has since been renovated – Suzanne Boynton will show you her albums of 'before' and 'after' pictures as you sit by the log fire blazing in a huge inglenook that was one of the features uncovered and restored. This is in a great room with coffered ceiling and stone-mullioned windows, the other end of which is used for dining (buttoned banquettes of cream velvet surround tables with lace over crimson cloths).

A corridor, still with a long row of bells to summon servants, leads to bedrooms which have flowery wallpapers and light colour schemes. The main entrance hall serves as a bar – you help yourself and write down what you have taken.

The choices at dinner by candlelight may include plaice goujons or home-made pâté to start with; pork cooked with cider, apples and cream; then perhaps crême caramel or profiteroles and cheeses. Suzanne, who used to do large-scale catering, says she much prefers cooking for smaller numbers to higher standards, often using produce (including eggs) straight from the garden.

The surroundings are attractive, from the flowerbeds by the drive, with cupid statues here and there, to the stone verandah with view of a stream below.

The resort of Shanklin, its sandy beaches and beautiful chine (ravine), are only a mile away; the picturesque village of Godshill and its smithy are in the opposite direction. As in many parts of the Island, there are plenty of well-marked footpaths for walkers; and a great many 'sights' to see in this part of the island are described under other entries.

The following facts have been supplied by the owners:

Bedrooms There are 6 rooms, which include doubles and family rooms. Bed-and-breakfast costs from £13 (per person in a double room) including service and VAT; prices go up in high season. There are reductions for stays of 2 nights or more; and 'bargain breaks' as well.

    The rooms have the following amenities: central heating; own bathroom and wc, shaver-point; radio, TV (colour), armchairs; views of countryside or garden; orthopaedic mattress; tea/coffee-making facilities; door keys. Breakfast in bed is available.

Meals The dinner menu is fixed price (£8) or à la carte. There is a choice of dishes on the fixed menu, which consists of 5 courses and coffee. Dinner is served at 6.45 pm. Vegetarian or special diets can be prepared. Lunches and packed lunches can be provided. Morning, afternoon or bedtime drinks (coffee, tea etc.) can be ordered. Wine and other alcoholic drinks can be ordered.

Public rooms There is a sitting-room with central heating, open fire, TV (colour), books, magazines, local guides and leaflets.

Surroundings The grounds consist of 2 acres of gardens.

Cars The nearest main road is the A3020 from Shanklin to Newport.

About a mile northward is **The Grange, Alverstone**; an immaculate guest house where Geraldine Watling provides good home cooking (tel: 0983 463729).

Ashleigh House, Whitley Hill, Henley-in-Arden, west of Warwick, Warwickshire, B95 5DL *Tel: 05642 2315* C(5) **D S ♯ 4**

This handsome Edwardian mansion, once the home of a Birmingham merchant, stands well back from the road, on top of a hill with fine views. Since Colin Eades, a retired accountant, took it over (together with his partner Francisco Garcia, who used to run a restaurant) it has been immaculately restored and filled with Edwardian – and earlier – antiques.

Francisco in particular enjoys spending time with visitors and giving them sound advice on where to go hunting for antiques in this area – also on where to dine in Henley or elsewhere.

Every bedroom is furnished in keeping with the style of this spacious, solid house and all the original features have been retained – shuttered bay windows, panelled doors, turned banisters, for example.

There is good walking country all around, an 18th-century canal for boats, historic Henley-in-Arden itself (it has the longest village street in England), Stratford-upon-Avon, great Warwick Castle, Birmingham, the National Exhibition Centre and all the countryside associated with Edith Holden's *Country Diary of an Edwardian Lady* (see page 106). And, at the end of a day's sightseeing there is the large garden in which to relax. The front brims with dahlias, geraniums and petunias; the back with fruit and vegetables for the table (with an old wind-pump to draw water from a deep spring). Peaches, grapes and melons flourish in the small conservatory.

The following facts have been supplied by the owners:

Bedrooms There are 7 rooms, which include singles, doubles and family rooms; and another 4 in a converted coach house. Bed-and-breakfast costs from £15 (per person in a double room) including service and VAT; prices go up in high season.

Some if not all of the rooms have the following amenities: central heating; shower, toilet, washbasin, shaver-point; TV (b & w), armchairs; views of countryside/farmland/garden; choice of duvets or blankets; door keys. Tea-making facilities on request.

Public rooms There is a sitting-room with central heating, TV (colour), books, magazines, local guides and leaflets.

Surroundings The grounds consist of over 1 acre of garden.

Cars The nearest main road is the A34 from Stratford to Birmingham.

Languages spoken Spanish, Portuguese, a little Italian and French.

Please check prices before booking, and whether there has been any change of ownership (or cook!)

Ashley House, The Esplanade, Fowey, Cornwall, PL23 1BD
Tel: 072683 2310   **C(5) D S ⌗ 3**

Like many former fishermen's cottages, this house is crammed in among others clinging to the cliffside: a place of narrow stairs and passageways, small rooms, and unexpected nooks. Downstairs, Mike Garland has put in pine panelling, with chintz-upholstered furniture; the dining-room, scarlet and white, has Windsor chairs. Local watercolours on the walls are for sale. Other rooms upstairs have harbour views glimpsed between houses.

Mike and his sister aim to cook anything his guests ask for – whether French cuisine or tripe-and-onions – if given enough notice. Otherwise, they may produce such a fixed-price meal as: kidneys with rice as a starter; roast lamb or local fish; a mousse; cheeses and good coffee.

Although Fowey is crowded in summer (especially during the regatta and powerboat races), Ashley House is a good choice out of season, for its very thick walls and huge logs ablaze under a copper hood make it snug.

My favourite bedroom, with rosebud wallpaper and fabrics, opens onto a roof patio overlooking the small walled garden and fish-pool. There are neat, pine-panelled bathrooms.

As to the attractions of Fowey, see page 272. Mike has his own 16-foot boat you can sail.

The following facts have been supplied by the owners:

Bedrooms There are 8 rooms, which include singles, doubles and family rooms. Bed-and-breakfast costs from £12 (per person in a double room) including service and VAT; prices go up in high season. There are reductions for stays of 3 nights or more; and 'bargain breaks' as well.

   Some if not all of the rooms have the following amenities: central heating or electric heaters; electric blankets, washbasin, shower, own bathroom and wc; views of sea or garden; balcony; choice of duvets or blankets; tea/coffee-making facilities; door keys. Breakfast in bed is available.

Meals The dinner menu is fixed price (about £6) or à la carte. There is a choice of dishes on the fixed menu, which consists of 3 courses and coffee. Dinner is served from 7 pm. Special diets can be prepared. Lunches and packed lunches can be provided; and snacks at other hours. Morning, afternoon or bedtime drinks (coffee, tea etc.) can be ordered for a charge. Non-residents are not usually admitted to the dining-room. Wine and other alcoholic drinks can be ordered.

Public rooms There are 2 sitting-rooms etc. The following are available in one or both of them: central heating, open fire, TV (b&w), books, magazines, local guides and leaflets, indoor games (such as draughts, cards, chess), record-player and records, bar.

Surroundings The grounds consist of a small garden. These are available in the neighbourhood: sailing, riding, windsurfing, diving, golf, fishing.

Cars The nearest main road is the A390 from St Austell to Liskeard.

Languages spoken French.

Avonside, Limpley Stoke, east of Bath, Wiltshire, BA3 6EX
Tel: 022122 2547   **C**(10) **PT S ♯ 5**

A typical English country house, built of honey-coloured Bath stone, the Challens' secluded home stands on the banks of the River Avon: walks along it (or the nearby Kennet and Avon Canal) are one of the attractions of staying in this very scenic area.

Ursula has furnished the sitting-room with tangerine or pale lime armchairs, oriental rugs and antiques that show up well against walls painted peach – on which hang many paintings by Peter who, after serving as a major in the Gurkhas, turned to a completely different career as an artist. Through the bay window is a serene view of the well-kept lawn and landscaped grounds.

Other rooms are equally pleasing, with attractive wallpapers and leafy views. The Challens treat visitors as if they were house guests, offering them pre-dinner drinks and wine (no extra charge). Typical of the kind of meal Ursula serves: avocado pâté; roast lamb with quince jelly and vegetables from the garden; a brûlée of brown sugar, cream and yogurt over raspberries.

Alternatively, visitors can go out to the excellent Nightingales restaurant in the village or to the Hop Pole Inn.

At Bradford-on-Avon several steep roads converge downhill to the mediaeval bridge with domed chapel on it. It takes time to discover all Bradford's handsome houses, Saxon church, vast tithe barn and old inns. Only a mile further is Bath (see page 341–2) and, northward, such other lovely spots as Corsham, Lacock (mediaeval abbey, and museum of photographic history) and the Chippenham-Calne area, described on pages 131–2. Malmesbury (on a hill almost surrounded by the River Avon) has its famous Norman abbey and handsome stone houses from the 17th and 18th centuries lining its streets and market square.

The following facts have been supplied by the owners:

Bedrooms There are 2 double rooms. Bed-and-breakfast costs from £12 (per person in a double room) including service and VAT; prices go up in high season. There are reductions for stays of 4 nights or more.

Both rooms have central heating and electric heaters; electric blankets, washbasin, shaver-point; armchairs; views of countryside and garden. Tea or breakfast in bed is available.

Meals The dinner menu is fixed price (£9). There is no choice of dishes on the fixed menu, which consists of 3 courses, wine and coffee. Dinner is served at 8 pm. Afternoon tea can be ordered, free. Non-residents are not admitted to the dining-room. Wine and other alcoholic drinks can be brought in.

Public rooms There is a sitting-room with central heating, open fire, books, magazines, local guides and maps, indoor games (such as backgammon, chess, bagatelle, cards), piano. Bridge can be arranged. Maps on loan.

Surroundings The grounds consist of 1½ acres of garden and orchard, with hard tennis court, croquet and coarse fishing. These are available in the neighbourhood: golf, racing, canoeing, Bath Sports Centre.

Cars The nearest main road is the A36 from Bath to Beckington.

Bank Cottage, Bryher, Isles of Scilly, TR23 0PR
Tel: 0720 22612   **C S**

Even a millionaire might have a long search before finding
somewhere to stay in quite such an idyllic situation as this little
guest house on Rushy Bay. Visitors here have a superb sandy
beach (right outside) virtually all to themselves: when I was there,
I encountered only one other couple on the golden, sunny sands.
And beyond it is one of England's most beautiful seascapes,
dotted with 22 islets.

Mac Mace works as a diver: sometimes diving for lobsters and
crabs or for archaeological finds, including Spanish doubloons, on
the many nearby wrecks; sometimes for sea urchins, the decorative shells of which are exported by the thousand. He and his wife
Tracy take a few guests in their cottage (built at least 300 years
ago, but with later additions). The rooms are simple, with low
ceilings and thick walls to keep winter's gales at bay. Bedrooms
are cheerful and bright, with fresh flowers; the sitting-room snug –
a stove is lit on chilly evenings.

Many visitors are content just to sit all day in the colourful
garden (facing south-west) to enjoy the view of the bay, sheltered
by the pink-flowered escallonia hedges; or they can accompany
Mac when he is setting nets or fishing. The sunsets are outstanding. A gate opens onto the beach, but although the climate is warm
here, the sea is not. There is a badminton lawn. The garden is at its
most colourful in early summer (fuchsias, flowering cherries, tulips
and arum lilies abound); the islets are best in late spring, when

they are smothered in pink sea-thrift and fresh green fronds of bracken.

Vegetables and loganberries are home-grown, rolls home-baked, eggs from their own hens. A typical meal cooked by Tracy may start with fish or fish pâté, followed by a roast or casserole. Tracy particularly enjoys making puddings like banana mousse or sherry trifle and her vegetarian meals are imaginative. Sometimes meals are served outdoors, using the granite barbecue.

There is rarely any rain in summer, and so, all along the wild tracks of the island, succulents and cacti flourish together with high, blue echiums from New Zealand and the Madeira geranium (magenta in colour, round and bushy).

Among other visitors to the island, you are likely to meet botanists, ornithologists (especially in autumn) and artists – and families renewing friendships year after year, for this is a place to which people come back repeatedly. It is ideal for little ones, as there are so many safe beaches and lanes; and island children quickly become friends with young visitors. For town children, this is a paradise of wild violets, bumblebees, pennyworts growing on the stone walls and lichens in a dozen colours. Boats take visitors to all the other Scilly islands, and to visit lighthouses, seal colonies, bird rocks or the gig races. Diving, boating and shark fishing can be arranged.

Visitors arriving by boat from St Mary's (see pages 90–91) are met and their baggage taken up for them by tractor or Landrover. The boats provide a service throughout winter (which can be mild and sunny, or with dramatic storms), but less frequently. Up to Easter, there are very few visitors; but even in summer Bryher is never crowded for there is only one hotel. Although 300 day-trippers may arrive in mid-morning, they rapidly disperse among the many lanes and footpaths in the hills.

Reader's comment: Wished we could stay for ever!

The following facts have been supplied by the owners:

Bedrooms There are 3 double or single rooms. Dinner, bed-and-breakfast costs from £15 (per person in a double room) including service and VAT; prices go up in high season.

Some if not all of the rooms have the following amenities: central heating or electric heaters; radio, colour TV, armchairs; washbasins and own bathroom; views of sea and garden; choice of duvets or blankets. Breakfast in bed is available.

Meals There is no choice of dishes on the fixed menu, which consists of 4 courses and coffee. Dinner is served at 6.30 pm. Special diets can be prepared. Lunches and packed lunches can be provided; and snacks at other hours. Morning, afternoon or bedtime drinks (coffee, tea etc.) can be ordered – free; soft drinks too. Non-residents are not admitted to the dining-room. Wine and other alcoholic drinks can be brought in.

Public rooms There is a sitting-room with open fire, colour TV, books, magazines, local guides and leaflets, indoor games (such as Scrabble, chess and other board games).

Surroundings The grounds consist of ½ acre of garden with badminton. These are available in the neighbourhood: table tennis, snooker, fishing (including shark fishing), diving and boating. Prawning nets provided.

Closed to visitors We are not open in winter.

Barrow Hill Farm, Ramsdean, west of Petersfield, Hampshire, GU32 1RW *Tel: 073087 340* **C(8) D S ⌗9**

A nearby hill with prehistoric burial-mound gives this beef and dairy farm its name. In the opposite direction it has a view of equally ancient Butser Hill, a windswept height well worth a visit.

The tile-hung house itself is beautifully furnished, with Victorian antiques shown at their best against well-chosen colour schemes and fabrics. The beamed sitting-rooms are divided by a see-through fireplace, and on the sills of the big windows all round is a profusion of pot-plants. Breakfast is served at a large oval table of mahogany in the dining-room.

Everything is immaculate, outside as well as in: from carefully trained roses climbing up flint walls to the smooth lawns where one can sit to enjoy the setting sun amid the scent of catmint or lavender. Old chimney-pots have been used for planting petunias and lobelias.

rear view

Mary Luff serves only breakfast, recommending local inns (or Langish House Hotel) for other meals, including those at East Meon, described on page 143.

Petersfield's 18th-century streets are pleasant; and all around are hills, woods and tranquil valleys of great beauty: a very agreeable area to explore by car or on foot. Jane Austen's home at Chewton and Gilbert White's at Selborne are only a few miles away. (There is more about this area on page 149.)

The following facts have been supplied by the owners:

Bedrooms There are 3 rooms, which include single and double rooms. Bed-and-breakfast costs from £10 (per person in a double room) including service and VAT; prices go up in high season. There are reductions for stays of 4 nights or more; and 'bargain breaks' as well.

Some if not all of the rooms have the following amenities: central heating or electric heaters; electric blankets, washbasin, shower, own bathroom and wc, shaver-point; radio, armchairs; views of countryside or garden; tea/coffee-making facilities; door keys. Breakfast in bed is available.

Public rooms There is a sitting-room with central heating, open fire, TV (colour), books, magazines, local guides and leaflets, indoor games (such as cards and Scrabble).

Surroundings The grounds consist of 300 acres of farmland.

Cars The nearest main road is the A272 from Petersfield to Winchester.

Closed to visitors We are not open between November and March.

Bay Tree Hotel, Sheep Street, Burford, Oxfordshire
Tel: 099382 3137   **D PT S X ♯ 5**

Not many hotels have the distinction of a noble memorial in the parish church. But the Bay Tree was originally the home of a Tudor magnate, and there he now lies, resplendent in marble.

This lovely old house of warm Cotswold stone is beautifully furnished with antiques, William Morris fabrics, deep leather armchairs around the great log fires (there are four of them in the various public rooms) and good paintings.

Everything is fresh and home-made (the hotel also owns Huffkins, round the corner, from which come chutneys and preserves, cakes and loaves, and the richest of Christmas puddings). The table d'hôte menu, cooked by chef Paul Evans, has a very wide choice of delicious and imaginative dishes. The bedrooms are pretty as well as comfortable. The Bay Tree is open all the year, including Christmas.

Burford itself is one of the most interesting Cotswold towns, with plenty of antiques and craft shops, bookshops and boutiques, small inns and cobbled byways, with the beautiful River Windrush flowing under an ancient bridge at the foot of the hill. Within easy reach are a great many other towns or villages of charm, beautiful landscapes (particularly, in my opinion, in autumn and winter), and typical Cotswold cottages everywhere. The elegant town of Cheltenham is near, and it is possible to go to a performance at the Royal Shakespeare Theatre at Stratford in an evening. There are bird gardens at Bourton-on-the-Water, a wildlife park near Burford itself. Oxford can be visited from here, and innumerable stately homes are tucked in among the hills and valleys.

Reader's comment: The food is a delight.

The following facts have been supplied by the owners:

Bedrooms There are 24 rooms, which include singles and doubles. Dinner, bed-and-breakfast ordinarily costs £34 but **to readers of this book the price is £25** (except on Fri.–Sat.), including VAT.

Some if not all of the rooms have the following amenities: central heating or electric heaters; washbasin, own bathroom and wc, shaver-point; armchairs; view of garden; good lighting for reading in bed. Breakfast in bed is available.

Meals There is a choice of dishes on the menu, which consists of 3 courses and coffee. Dinner is served from 7.30 pm. Special diets can be prepared. Lunches and/or packed lunches can be provided. Morning, afternoon or bedtime drinks (coffee, tea etc.) can be ordered for a charge. Wine and other alcoholic drinks can be ordered.

Public rooms There are 4 sitting-rooms, etc. The following are available in one or more of them: central heating, open fire, magazines, local guides and leaflets, piano, bar.

Surroundings The grounds consist of a large garden. These are available in the neighbourhood: tennis, golf.

Cars The nearest main road is the A40 from London to Wales

Beaufort House, 30 West Street, Bourne, south of Lincoln, PE10 9NE   *Tel: 0778 422609*   **C PT S X ⊞ 4**

I almost passed this by: a Victorian terraced house of no outstanding distinction when viewed from the road. But, as soon as I went inside, what a surprise! Imaginative interior design, and imaginative food too. The small hotel was originally run by Ann Moggan: when a bad back forced her to give it up, she took the trouble to demonstrate all her recipes, for a month, to her successor Paula Collins who, appreciating the style of the house, has every intention of continuing in the same way. Her husband, Richard, as a ship's captain has brought worldwide experience of hotels to bear on the addition of extra touches of comfort.

One steps into a sitting-room (with bar) where pine and cane furniture contrast with the scarlet Turkey carpet. Beyond this lies the dining-room, which has a pale mulberry Berber carpet and a room-divider created from an old church screen that was a lucky 'find'.

A fine Gothic-style staircase, blue-carpeted, leads upstairs to the bedrooms; my favourite is no.1: lace over a pink spread on the bed, grass-green carpet, pretty fireplace and mirror.

There is a lovely garden at the back (and a terrace where meals are served on summer evenings); three lawns with rustic seats succeed one another, divided by beds of heathers or bulbs, with acacias that bloom late in May.

Meals are imaginative. A house speciality is avocado filled with a cheese pâté and orange segments. You might choose game pie for a main course, then possibly chocolate pots with whisky or a raspberry-and-cinnamon flan, followed by cheeses.

Bourne itself is a small market town, well placed to visit Stamford (see page 128), magnificent Burghley House (horse trials are held there), Grantham (birthplace of Isaac Newton and Margaret Thatcher, it has a superb church and good local museum), Belton House (National Trust), Peterborough and Lincoln (for cathedrals, and for shopping), Sandringham and the north Norfolk coast, and Spalding (bulb country – see page 215). Forest and fens both lend themselves to walking, birdwatching and pleasant drives.

The following facts have been supplied by the owners:

Bedrooms There are 5 rooms, which include single, double and family rooms. Bed-and-breakfast costs from £12.50 (per person) including service and VAT. Prices go up in high season. There are reductions for stays of 7 nights, and 'bargain breaks'.

Some if not all of the rooms have the following amenities: central heating or electric heaters; washbasin, shower, own bath and wc, electric blankets, shaver-point; radio, phone, TV (b & w), armchairs; views of garden; tea/coffee-making facilities; door keys. Breakfast in bed is available.

Meals The dinner menu is fixed price (£4.25) or à la carte. There is a choice of dishes on the fixed menu, which consists of 3 courses and coffee. Dinner is served at 7 pm. Special diets can be prepared. Lunches and packed lunches can be provided; and snacks at other hours. Morning, afternoon or bedtime drinks (coffee, tea etc.) can be ordered for a charge. Wine and other alcoholic drinks can be ordered.

Public rooms There is a bar/sitting-room with central heating, books, magazines, local guides and leaflets, games such as Monopoly and dominoes.

Surroundings The grounds consist of ¼ acre garden. These are available in the neighbourhood: tennis, swimming, badminton, squash, water-sports, fishing, golf, riding.

Cars The nearest main road is the A15 from Lincoln to Peterborough.

Languages spoken French.

Credit cards accepted Access, Visa.

The Beehive, Osmington, east of Weymouth, Dorset, DT3 6EL
Tel: 0305 834095   C(5) **D PT S X ♯ 4**

Mary Kempe's father was Lord of the Manor at Osmington; and this little thatched stone cottage was the holiday home of her childhood. While the manorial lands passed into other hands, she was pursuing an academic career at the universities of Nairobi and London: the former accounts for the presence of African crafts in the old cottage, which is now her permanent home.

It is tucked away – in a pocket-handkerchief garden – up a steep lane leading to countryside of great beauty, with some lovely walks; while to the south fine coast scenery lies only a mile away (shingle beaches closest, sandy ones a little further).

The friendly sitting-room is a place of books and water-colours, lead-paned windows and old cretonne-covered sofas or chairs. Breakfast is served in the big, cork-floored kitchen warmed by a cosy stove (you can buy jars of Mary's home-made jams to take home). She produces imaginative dinners with many dishes based on traditional local recipes and produce – for instance, Martlemas (or Michaelmas) beef which is marinaded in wine and vinegar then rubbed with spices before being baked, or Wessex chicken in a cider sauce. Before this might come Dorset pâté or a soup of carrots or lentils; and after it apple hedgehog, blueberry pie or buttered oranges perhaps; then cheeses. (For those who want a simpler two-course menu the price is halved.) Or you can eat well at the Sunray Inn.

Birdwatchers go out from here to spend days at Radipole Lake, the Fleet or Studland nature reserve. Others tour the Thomas Hardy sites. Osmington, being roughly midway between Poole at one end of Dorset and Lyme Regis at the other, is a good centre from which to explore all parts of the county: see details elsewhere in this book.

Upstairs, among the cottage-style bedrooms (and bathroom decorated with African hippos), Mary has a large collection of maps and books on all aspects of Dorset history and wildlife, and is herself a willing fount of guidance on where to go.

The following facts have been supplied by the owner:

Bedrooms There are 4 rooms, which include single and double rooms. Bed-and-
    breakfast costs from £9 (per person in a double room) including service and

VAT; prices go up in high season. There are reductions for stays of 7 nights or more; and 'bargain breaks' as well. Sunday accommodation free to over-60s staying 3 days.

Some if not all of the rooms have the following amenities: central heating or electric heaters; washbasin, shaver-point; armchairs; views of countryside or garden; choice of duvets or blankets; bedboard; tea/coffee-making facilities; door keys.

Meals The dinner menu is fixed price (£7.50). There is no choice of dishes on the menu, which consists of 4 courses and coffee. Dinner is served at 7.30–8 pm. Vegetarian or special diets can be prepared. Packed lunches can be provided. Morning, afternoon or bedtime drinks (coffee, tea etc.) can be ordered free. Non-residents are not admitted to the dining-room. Wine and other alcoholic drinks can be brought in.

Public rooms There is a sitting-room with central heating, open fire, TV (colour), books, magazines, local guides and leaflets, indoor games (such as backgammon, cards, jigsaw puzzles), record-player and records. Bridge can be arranged.

Surroundings The grounds consist of a garden. These are available in the neighbourhood: golf, riding, windsurfing, fishing, swimming.

Cars The nearest main road is the A353 from Weymouth to Wareham.

Languages spoken Simple French.

Closed to visitors We are closed in January.

Bell Inn, Smarden, west of Ashford, Kent
Tel: 023377 283   C D S ♯15

Kent has innumerable picturesque old inns, but few can be more attractive than the 15th-century Bell. Facing an apple orchard and surrounded by a beer-garden, it has a façade of chequered brickwork overhung with scalloped tiles. Inside there are three bars, two with inglenook fires and all paved or brick-floored. Here one can eat very well, seated on oak settles or Windsor chairs under beams strung with hop-bines – and Ian Turner keeps nearly a dozen different kinds of real ale to sample.

Outdoors an iron spiral staircase, wreathed in honeysuckle, leads up to the bedrooms, still with the original board ceilings and white brick walls but immaculately furnished in soft colours. Visitors are provided with the wherewithal to make their own continental breakfast.

Three times a year, Morris dancers come to the Bell; and on the second Sunday in each month there is a gathering of vintage cars or of steam engines.

The following facts have been supplied by the owners:

Bedrooms There are 4 rooms, which include singles and doubles. Bed-and-breakfast costs from £10 (per person) including service and VAT; prices go up in high season. There are reductions for stays of 5 nights or more; and 'bargain breaks' as well.

   Some if not all of the rooms have the following amenities: electric heaters; TV, armchairs; views of countryside/farmland; tea/coffee-making facilities; door keys.

Meals The dinner menu is à la carte. Dinner is served from 6 pm. Special diets can be prepared. Lunches and packed lunches can be provided; and snacks at other hours. Wine and other alcoholic drinks can be ordered.

Public rooms The following are available in the bars: central heating, open fire, TV, books, magazines, local guides and leaflets, games (such as darts and bar-billiards).

Surroundings The grounds consist of 1 acre of garden.

Cars The nearest main road is the A274 from Maidstone to Headcorn.

Languages spoken A little French and German.

Bickleigh Cottage, Bickleigh, south of Tiverton, Devon, EX16 8RJ   *Tel: 088 45 230*   C(6) S ♯ 4

This very picturesque thatched cottage, built about 1640 and later extended, has been run as a guest-house by the same family for over 50 years. It stands on a road by the banks of the River Exe, with a foaming weir a few yards downstream: everyone's ideal of a typically Devonian beauty-spot.

   The rooms downstairs are full of antiques such as old chests and carved oak chairs, as well as a collection of blue glass and other interesting trifles including articles of Honiton lace made by Mrs Cochrane, which are for sale. The bedrooms (many with river views) are more simply furnished, though one has a four-poster bed. Outside is a pretty riverside garden with a fish-pool and glasshouses containing a collection of cacti and succulents.

Meals are of plain home cooking, a typical menu being smoked mackerel, roast lamb, pineapple meringue and cheeses.

The attractions of this area are described on page 230.

The following facts have been supplied by the owners:

Bedrooms There are 9 rooms, which include singles and doubles. Bed-and-breakfast costs from £12.50 (per person in a double room) including VAT. There are reductions for stays of 7 nights or more.

Some if not all of the rooms have the following amenities: central heating or electric heaters; washbasin, shower, own bathroom and wc, shaver-point; views of river and garden; tea/coffee-making facilities; door keys.

Meals The dinner menu is fixed price (£6.25). There is no choice of dishes on the fixed menu, which consists of 4 courses and coffee. Dinner is served at 7 pm. Packed lunches can be provided. Non-residents are not admitted to the dining-room. Wine and other alcoholic drinks can be brought in.

Public rooms There are 2 sitting-rooms etc. The following are available in one or both of them: central heating, TV (colour), books, magazines, local guides and leaflets.

Surroundings The grounds consist of a riverside garden. These are available in the neighbourhood: fishing, golf, riding.

Cars The nearest main road is the A396 from Exeter to Tiverton.

Closed to visitors We are not open from mid-October to April (or to Easter if in March).

The Birche, Shelsey Beauchamp, north-west of Worcester, WR6 6RD   *Tel: 08865 251*   C D ♯4

Previously a farm (from pre-Domesday until a decade ago), this elegant and beautifully sited house now belongs to an American manufacturing company with interests in Kidderminster (they originally bought it to accommodate their visiting directors). From the big bay window of its dining-room, yellow-curtained, one looks down to the private trout lake with Canada geese, cherry orchard beyond, and views of the Clee Hills. Green velvet chairs are drawn up to tables at which manageress Claire Sutherland (whose family farms nearby) supervises the serving of meals, which must be pre-booked. There is much emphasis on local produce – salmon, home-grown vegetables and herbs, even the horseradish which accompanies the roast sirloin. Claire records regulars' favourite dishes – from the avocado mousse with prawns or the chicken terrine through to jam rolypoly or crême-de-menthe ice cream.

In the sitting-room, William Morris armchairs cluster around the inglenook fire in a beamed and white-walled room where there are always big vases filled with fresh flowers. The bedrooms are especially attractive and original. I particularly liked one which had a chocolate carpet, grass-cloth walls, scalloped bedspread and cushioned seats in the bay window overlooking the lake. At no greater price, one can book a suite with rosy bedheads, duvets and valances contrasting with the celadon carpet; in the matching sitting-room is a fire, alcoves with flowers, and even a cooking-corner in which to produce your own snack meals. This, too, has window seats and lake view.

The Birche is ideally placed for visiting the cathedral cities of Worcester and Hereford, Malvern spa and hills, historic Ludlow and Bewdley, the Wyre Forest and the River Severn.

The following facts have been supplied by the owners:

Bedrooms There are 3 rooms, which include single, double and family rooms. Bed-and-breakfast costs from £18 (per person in a double room) including service and VAT. There are reductions for stays of 4 nights or more; and 'bargain breaks' as well. **10% discount to readers of this book**.

    The rooms have central heating or electric heaters; washbasin, shower or own bathroom and wc, shaver-point; radio, TV (colour), phone, armchairs; views of countryside or garden; choice of duvets or blankets; bed-board; tea/coffee-making facilities on request; door keys. Breakfast in bed is available.

Meals The dinner menu is fixed price (from £10.50). There is no choice of dishes on the menu, which consists of 4 courses and coffee. Dinner is served at 7.30 pm. Vegetarian or special diets can be prepared. Lunches and packed lunches can be provided; and snacks at other hours. Morning, afternoon or bedtime drinks (coffee, tea etc.) can be ordered for a charge. Wine and other alcoholic drinks can be ordered.

Public rooms There is a sitting-room with central heating, open fire, TV (colour), books, magazines, local guides and leaflets, indoor games (such as cards and chess), record-player and records on request; bar.

Surroundings The grounds consist of 35 acres of cherry orchards; with trout fishing. These are available in the neighbourhood: shooting, fishing, hunting, riding, tennis, squash.

Cars The nearest main road is the A443 from Worcester to Tenbury Wells.

Languages spoken A little French.

Credit cards accepted Visa, Amex.

Birk Bank Farm, south of Cockermouth, Cumbria
Booking service: 0498 81563   **C(5) ♯ 6**

In a broad valley to the north of the Lake District is this very typical lakeland farm, lying at the end of a long track which winds through a sloping field of sheep, with rooks cawing overhead. It is a cluster of big, grey stone buildings with high arches, built in the 16th century, at the heart of a 125-acre farm where sheep and beef-cattle are reared. A tiny paved garden separates the farmhouse from the yard.

The house is kept immaculate inside and out: everything is light and bright. Guests eat together at two tables, in the dining-room with beamed ceiling and a garden view. Plain, home cooking: dinner might consist of soup made from home-grown vegetables, beef or chicken, fresh fruit salad, cheese and coffee or tea. Bread is home-baked. Biscuits with bedtime drinks are home-made.

There is nothing exceptional in the style of Birk Bank, but guests are comfortable and well-fed – and they keep returning for walking or pony-trekking holidays.

The ancient town of Cockermouth is at the north of the Lake District, perhaps the most dramatic part. Beyond lie plains, as far as the Solway Firth, with Scotland in sight and some of the most dramatic sunsets in England. In the vicinity are wild Ennerdale, with one of the most beautiful expanses of water in the Lake District, a tarn full of trout, and Loweswater, the northernmost of the lakes. There is plenty of mountain scenery up to Cockermouth, with its castle ruins and one of Wordsworth's houses, and (going south-east) over on the coast is the picturesque, sadly neglected old port of Maryport, with a small museum of fishing and lifeboat history; Whitehaven, which is more active; and St Bees headland – a 300-foot cliff of red sandstone where seabirds congregate. The best seasons are perhaps spring – green and lush, with Wordsworth's daffodils appearing – or autumn, when the colours are at their most brilliant.

Among several lakes within easy driving distance are Crummock Water with a 100-foot waterfall beside it and Bassenthwaite Lake with a view of Skiddaw. Good food can be found at the Pheasant Inn. The lake is frequented by migrant birds in the autumn. Keswick, surrounded by good walking country, has been described as a mecca for poets and artists because it is such a beautiful town, with a particularly interesting museum. Carlisle has several outstanding buildings to visit, including its ancient cathedral and the museum housed in a Jacobean mansion, Tullie House. A golf course and swimming-pool are within a short drive.

Readers' comments: Spotless, very comfortable, food excellent. Ideally situated. Cannot praise enough, more than happy.

The following facts have been supplied by the owners:

Bedrooms There are 3 double rooms. Dinner, bed-and-breakfast costs from £12.50 (per person) including service and VAT. Reductions for 2 nights or more.
Some if not all of the rooms have the following amenities: electric blankets; shaver-point; views of countryside, farmland, garden.

Meals The dinner menu consists of 4 courses and coffee. Dinner is served at 6.30 pm. Special diets can be prepared. Morning or bedtime drinks (coffee, tea etc.) are provided – the latter free. Non-residents are not admitted to the dining-room. Wine and other alcoholic drinks can be brought in.

Public rooms There is a sitting-room with open fire, colour TV, books, magazines, local guides and leaflets, indoor games (such as dominoes, cards and draughts).

Cars The nearest main road is the A5086 from Cockermouth to Egremont.

Closed to visitors We are not open in winter.

Bishopfield, Allendale, south of Hexham, Northumberland, NE47 9EJ *Tel: 043483 248* **C(12) D PT S ✿15**

Built in 1740, this stone farmhouse with clematis growing up its walls stands in 200 acres through which the River Allen runs (with trout for guests to fish, a small deer park, and nature reserve). There are views of the fields, with cows and their calves, from the guests' sitting-room on the first floor. This is a big room with crackling fire on a stone hearth, a huge pink sofa, long velvet curtains, and paintings done by a local lady in her eighties. In one corner, a decorative spiral staircase of white ironwork leads to the floor above.

Kathy Fairless serves good, homely meals – soups with cream and croûtons, fish brought direct from the North Sea, and fresh fruit salad for example. Guests eat by candlelight and log fire, with silver and Minton china. Sometimes, shooting-parties take the house, when hot lunches with good wines are carried to the grouse moors. And one of the breakfast options is haggis!

Bedrooms have individuality: for instance, a blue-and-white four-poster in one; patchwork quilts in another; Laura Ashley fabrics and attractive Victorian furniture in them all. Although there is central heating, it is possible to have a coal fire in your bedroom: a rare treat. On the stairs are many watercolours by Kathy, and elsewhere a display of decorated eggs – a hobby of her mother, who sometimes demonstrates this craft to visitors.

Outside there is plenty to see and do. One can swim in river pools, give a hand with haymaking or herding the cattle, pony-trek, enjoy a barbecue on fine evenings, or just sit idle in the sunken rock garden with pool. There's a special celebration at New Year. One of the most interesting parts is the farmyard, where a huge smelting pot has been turned into a well-head, apples from the orchard are laid out on a wall to ripen in the sun, and there is an ancient barn beneath the lichen-covered slates of which a drama was acted out over two centuries ago. When clearing the hay-loft a few years back, an old muzzle-loading pistol was found. Experts identified it as a Jacobite pistol, and connected it with the tradition that a rebel on the run had been arrested at Bishopfield after the rising of 1745. Presumably he was hiding among the hay.

Allendale is Catherine Cookson's country. She lives nearby and many of her Mallen stories are set here. It is one of the loveliest parts of the north country, wild and rocky, in parts comparable with some Swiss scenery. Allen Banks, where two rivers converge, is a beauty spot. Not far off is the Killhope pass (nearly two thousand feet high) with a great wheel once used for crushing ore when these hills were mined for lead. In Allendale town, on every New Year's Eve costumed 'guizers' parade with blazing tar-barrels on their heads – vestige of a half-forgotten pagan fire-rite. At Hexham is a great Norman abbey, well worth visiting, and a lively market every Tuesday. The Roman Wall, Kielder Forest with its vast landscaped reservoir, and the Scottish borders are not far off.

The following facts have been supplied by the owners:

Bedrooms There are 9 rooms, which include single and double rooms. Bed-and-breakfast costs from £12 (per person) including service and VAT; prices go up in high season. A barn is being converted to provide more bedrooms (with bathrooms) and a sitting-room.

Some if not all of the rooms have the following amenities: central heating or electric heaters; electric blankets, washbasin, shower, own bathroom and wc, shaver-point; colour TV, armchairs; views of countryside/farmland/garden; choice of duvets or blankets; tea/coffee-making facilities; door keys; phones. Other extras: drinks in bedrooms, ice-maker, clothes-drying.

Meals The dinner menu is fixed price (£6). There is a choice of dishes on the menu, which consists of 3 courses and coffee. Dinner is served at 6.30 pm. Special diets can be prepared. No dinners on Fridays. Cream teas. Lunches and packed lunches can be provided; and snacks at other hours. Non-residents are not admitted to the dining-room. Wine and other alcoholic drinks can be ordered.

Public rooms There are 2 sitting-rooms with central heating, open fire, TV, books, magazines, local guides and leaflets, indoor games (such as cards, Scrabble, dominoes etc.) and snooker. Bridge can be arranged.

Surroundings The grounds consist of 200 acres of farm and woodlands. These are available in the neighbourhood: riding school, golf, bowls, tennis, swimming, squash, trout and salmon fishing, clay-pigeon shooting.

Cars The nearest main road is the A69 from Newcastle to Carlisle.

Closed to visitors We are not open in January and February except for house-party bookings and a New Year celebration.

Blackwater Hotel, Church Road, West Mersea, north-east of Chelmsford, Essex, CO5 8QH   *Tel: 0206 38 3338*   **C D PT X ♯3**

The coastline here is a wilderness of creeks, islets and estuaries made colourful by the sails of small boats. A causeway now connects Mersea to the mainland, yet it still has the feel of an island with an identity all its own. There are Roman, Saxon and Norman remains – and, of course, the beds of Colchester oysters still flourish as they have done for centuries. Visitors go there, too, for all the usual seaside pleasures, for golf, sea-angling or for riding and walking. At nearby Fingringhoe Wick is an outstanding bird reserve, with hides alongside its lakes.

Down a quiet side-street is the creeper-covered Blackwater Hotel. Downstairs, beams and scarlet gingham tablecloths, copper pans and strings of onions, give the dining-room the informal air of a French bistro – these touches are Monique Chapleo's style. Here and in the small sitting-room with its tub chairs there are bowls of roses and pinks. All the bedrooms are very neat and fresh: wallpaper, curtains and bedspreads in matching sprigged patterns; bedheads of cane. Outside is a lawn with seats.

The food cooked by chef Roudesli is excellent, and the wine list is good. One might start with mushrooms champenoises or local seafood, to be followed by rabbit pie or guinea fowl in Marsala sauce and a pudding such as profiteroles or lemon tart. There is a bamboo-and-chintz coffee-room that serves snacks.

Although so near London, there are plenty of rural rides in this part of Essex, and many sights to see within a few miles – such as the timbered village of Coggeshall (with Paycockes, a National Trust house, and antique shops), the historic city of Colchester founded by the Romans before London (castle, museums, old churches, ancient byways and zoo), St Osyth's Priory and East Bergholt (Constable country). Maldon is very near – an old port still frequented by the great sailing-barges.

Readers' comments: Charming hostess, excellent dinner and breakfast superb. Excellent cuisine.

The following facts have been supplied by the owners:

Bedrooms There are 7 rooms, which include singles, doubles and family rooms. Bed-and-breakfast costs from £15 (per person in a double room) including service and VAT. There are reductions for stays of 7 nights or more; and 'bargain breaks' as well. Sampler breaks (see page 14).

    Some if not all of the rooms have the following amenities: central heating or electric heaters; shower, own bathroom and wc, shaver-point; TV (b & w), armchairs; tea/coffee-making facilities; door keys. Breakfast in bed is available.

Meals The dinner menu is à la carte. Dinner is served at 7–10 pm. Special diets can be prepared. Lunches and packed lunches can be provided; and snacks at other hours. Morning, afternoon or bedtime drinks (coffee, tea etc.) can be ordered. Wine and other alcoholic drinks can be ordered.

Public rooms There is a sitting-room with central heating, open fire, books, magazines, local guides and leaflets. Also bar.

Blakeway Books, 13 Bridge Street, Hungerford, Berkshire, RG17 0EH   *Tel: 0488 83581*   C PT S X ♯5

What bliss! To live above a well-stocked bookshop (history and literature are the specialities) *and* with a view of the Kennet and Avon Canal just outside – colourful narrowboats and ducks on the water, mediaeval black-and-white houses on the opposite bank.

The Blakeways' home and shop are in an attractive Georgian house. Its breakfast-room has handsome furniture, china displayed in an alcove, and interesting pictures. Upstairs, bedrooms have flowery wallpapers and attractive paintings; and there is a sitting-room with large armchairs.

Picturesque Hungerford is famous for its scores of antique shops (many open even on Sundays). Nearby are the windswept heights of the Berkshire Downs where racehorses train, and you can walk along the prehistoric Ridgeway Path. The sites of Iron Age forts or burial mounds dot the area. The Kennet valley is in complete contrast – fertile meadows with birch and oak woods beyond, a great area for birdwatchers. The villages here have flint-and-brick cottages roofed with thatch. In and around both Lambourn and Newbury are historic buildings (the latter has a theatre in a converted watermill), stately homes and pretty villages. Yet all this is little more than an hour from London.

The following facts have been supplied by the owners:

Bedrooms There are 2 single or double rooms. Bed-and-breakfast costs from £8 (per person) including service and VAT.
   One or both rooms have the following amenities: electric heaters; washbasin, shaver-point; armchairs; views of countryside; tea/coffee-making facilities; door keys. Breakfast in bed is available.

Public rooms There is a sitting-room with heating, TV (b & w), books, magazines, local guides and leaflets, indoor games (such as Scrabble, cards), record-player and records.

Surroundings Fishing and hang-gliding are available in the neighbourhood.

Cars The nearest main road is the A4 from London to Bristol.

Only breakfast is served by Mrs Blakeway, but nearby is the **Bear Hotel** (tel: 0488 82512), a historic coaching inn celebrated for its gastronomic menus; it also has good bar snacks. (There's also excellent accommodation here, including a lovely four-poster bedroom – with weekend 'bargain breaks' all year round.)

Blea Tarn House, Little Langdale, Ambleside, Cumbria
Booking service: 0498 81563   **D S ♯ 5**

'A home it seemed of poverty and toil', said Wordsworth of Blea Tarn House, but it does not seem at all like that any more, for it is warm and cosy and prettily decorated, with an open fire in the corner of the guests' sitting-cum-dining room. Just off it is Sheila's kitchen, for she likes to talk to her guests while she prepares, as it might be, egg mayonnaise, roast beef, and apple or lemon-meringue pie. She serves classic country dishes, always with two vegetables (usually fresh, occasionally frozen, but never tinned) and two sorts of potatoes. In summer, there will be more in the way of salads, and in cooler weather hotpots and cobblers.

Upstairs, the bedrooms are small, but they are quaint and pretty, and they give some good views.

This is the very heart of the Lake District, for Blea Tarn House sits on its own, high above the Langdales, Great and Little, amid the scenery which has made the area such a draw for centuries – rugged and colourful, and punctuated by famous peaks. Reached by a narrow and twisting road, this is a popular beauty-spot, but it is never excessively crowded with the sightseers who can sometimes detract from such places. From the late afternoon onwards the peace and quiet are unbroken – there is not even a television set in the house.

A field away from the house is the tarn (small lake) from which it takes its name, where you can bathe or fish. Within a few miles are some of the Lake District's best known villages – Grasmere, Hawkshead, Ambleside, Coniston – and on the other side of Windermere the elaborate National Park Visitor Centre at Brockhole.

Readers' comments: Comfortable atmosphere, friendliness, good food.

The following facts have been supplied by the owners:

Bedrooms There are 3 double rooms. Dinner, bed-and-breakfast costs £15 (per person) including service and VAT.
Some if not all of the rooms have the following amenities: central heating; washbasin, shaver-point; views of farmland/garden; choice of duvets or blankets; door keys.

Meals There is no choice of dishes on the fixed menu, which consists of 3 courses and coffee. Dinner is served at 6.30 pm. Lunches and packed lunches can be provided. Morning or bedtime drinks (coffee, tea etc.) can be ordered for a charge. Non-residents are not admitted to the dining-room. Wine and other alcoholic drinks can be brought in.

Public rooms There is a sitting-room with open fire, books, magazines, local guides and leaflets.

Surroundings These are available in the neighbourhood: fishing, swimming, rock climbing.

Cars The nearest main road goes from Ambleside to Coniston.

Blue Boar, North Heath, near Chieveley, north of Newbury, Berkshire, RG16 8UE *Tel: 0635 248236* **C(10) H PT ⌗5**

This is an 'olde worlde' inn – thatch, whitewash, lattice windows and roses outside; carved oak settles, low beams and tobacco-coloured walls within. It was built in Tudor times, but the stone boar which gave it its name was brought here a century later by Cromwell (who had looted it from Ripley Castle in Yorkshire). On 27 October 1644, he stayed at the inn before fighting the Battle of Newbury, and presumably (like modern guests who forget their shavers or slippers) accidentally left the boar behind when he moved on – to a defeat, as it turned out.

There are three bars, each with dining tables (one of the inglenooks which no longer has a fire is used as a dining recess). Here you can eat steaks, salmon and other traditional fare – or, more adventurously, garlic mussels or deep-fried Camembert for a starter, and venison in wine or chicken breast stuffed with shellfish as a main course.

Noel Morton, formerly a pilot, has converted buildings at the back into very attractive modern bedrooms, decorated in restful colours: pale buff velvet has been used for bedheads, toning with sepia prints that decorate the walls. These rooms open onto a small garden and patio with chairs.

North Heath, just off the M4, is a useful place for a stopover en route to Wales. A few miles to the north is Wantage, a place of cobbled ways and old houses with a good local museum; and beyond it Faringdon (described elsewhere) in the Vale of White Horse, and the Berkshire Downs. To the south lies Newbury, woodlands, lovely Kennet Valley, and Hungerford, celebrated for its innumerable antique shops. Thatched cottages, streams, windmills, long-distance footpaths, prehistoric sites, watercress beds and undisturbed villages all give this area (so near to London) great charm.

The following facts have been supplied by the owners:

Bedrooms There are 16 rooms, which include singles, doubles and family rooms. Bed-and-breakfast costs from £14 (per person in a double room) including service and VAT; prices go up in high season. There are reductions for stays of 2 nights or more; and 'bargain breaks' as well. Sunday accommodation free to over-60s staying 3 days.

 The rooms have the following amenities: central heating; shower or own bathroom and wc, shaver-point; TV (colour), phone, armchairs; views of countryside or garden; orthopaedic mattress; tea/coffee-making facilities; door keys.

Meals The dinner menu is à la carte. Dinner is served at 7 pm. Vegetarian or special diets can be prepared. Lunches and packed lunches can be provided; and snacks at other hours. Morning, afternoon or bedtime drinks (coffee, tea etc.) can be ordered for a charge. Wine and other alcoholic drinks can be ordered.

Public rooms There is a sitting-room with central heating, open fire, TV, books, magazines, local guides and leaflets.

Surroundings The grounds consist of 5 acres of open land. The following games or sports are available in the grounds: tug-o'-war, claypigeon shooting, riding. These are available in the neighbourhood: riding, racing, ballooning, rough shooting, tennis, badminton, golf.

Cars The nearest main road is the M4 from London to the west.

Languages spoken A little French.

Credit cards accepted Visa, Access.

Bossell House, Plymouth Road, Buckfastleigh, south of Ashburton, Devon, TQ11 0DG *Tel: 03644 3294* **C D H PT S X ⌗3**

Redecorating and the putting down of new carpets were in progress when I visited Bossell House, which is run by Sylvia and Eric Bottell with their daughter Melanie and son-in-law chef (Malcolm Wright). It is a mansion with tower, built by a wealthy woollen-mill owner in 1835. A large glass-walled dining-room was later added from which to enjoy views of the big garden (it has one of the tallest monkey-puzzle trees in Britain, a Canadian redwood and other specimen trees). The Bottells had decades of brambles and weeds to clear before they could plant flowers and vegetables. When not in the large, bay-windowed sitting-room or the damask-papered bar-lounge, guests can sit at tables with sunshades on the paved terrace outside. There is also a snug cellar bar with games.

Bedrooms are spacious, with antique or old-fashioned furniture, velvet bedheads and striped duvets.

There is also simpler accommodation (much used by fishing parties) in a coach house.

A wide choice is offered on the table d'hôte menu. Malcolm cooks such popular dishes as trout with almonds, haddock in prawn sauce, roast chicken or beef stroganoff – all sauces are home-made, and many vegetables home-grown.

From Buckfastleigh one can readily visit Torquay and its sandy bays, Dartmoor, the River Dart (with river trips from Totnes to Dartmouth), a steam railway, Buckfast Abbey, Paignton zoo, Plymouth, Exeter and many picturesque fishing ports on the south coast of Devon.

The following facts have been supplied by the owners:

Bedrooms There are 17 rooms, which include singles, doubles and family rooms. Bed-and-breakfast costs from £14.50 (per person in a double room) including service and VAT. Out of season, there are reductions for stays of 2 nights or more and 'bargain breaks' as well. Sampler breaks (see page 14).

Some if not all of the rooms have the following amenities: central heating or electric heaters; electric blankets, washbasin, shower, own bathroom and wc, shaver-point; radio, TV (colour, with video), phone, armchairs; views of countryside, farmland, garden; choice of duvets or blankets; tea/coffee-making facilities; door keys. Breakfast in bed is available, and bed-boards.

Meals The dinner menu is fixed price (£8) or à la carte. There is a choice of dishes on the fixed menu, which consists of 3 courses and coffee. Dinner is served from 6.30 pm. Special diets can be prepared. Lunches and packed lunches can be provided; and snacks at other hours. Morning, afternoon or bedtime drinks (coffee, tea etc.) can be ordered for a charge. Wine and other alcoholic drinks can be ordered.

Public rooms There are 2 sitting-rooms with central heating, TV (colour), books, magazines, local guides and leaflets, indoor games (such as Scrabble, Trivial Pursuit, cards, Monopoly etc.), piano, bars.

Surroundings The grounds consist of 3 acres of garden. The following games or sports are available in the grounds: tennis, bowls, outdoor badminton, tennis trainer, croquet. These are available in the neighbourhood: swimming, tennis, riding.

Cars The nearest main road is the A38 from Exeter to Plymouth.

Languages spoken French.

Credit cards accepted Visa, Access.

Bouchers, Bentham, south of Cheltenham, Gloucestershire, GL51 5TZ   *Tel: 0452 862373*   C(5) **D PT S ♯5**

Once a farmhouse, Bouchers is still surrounded by hayfields just beyond the garden, where rock doves fly across the lawns and rose-beds to a graceful weeping willow. A sundial on one wall declares the date of the house, 1661, and of the old cider-house which is now the workshop of Mr Daniels (he is a carpenter).

Inside all is immaculate and very comfortable, and you will get a warm welcome from Mrs Daniels as you step through the front door straight into the big U-shaped living-room. Here plenty of velvet armchairs are grouped round the hearth where an open fire crackles in winter, and a grandfather clock ticks the time away. Round the other side of the U is the dining-room, for breakfast only (visitors eat other meals at the Cross Hands Inn nearby or at one of the innumerable restaurants in Cheltenham, which is also near).

77

The Gloucester area is described on pages 152–3. Bentham, on the edge of the Cotswolds, is close to the route south to Bath. Gloucester with its cathedral, historic Cirencester (don't miss the Roman museum) and the Forest of Dean are all within easy reach.

The following facts have been supplied by the owners:

Bedrooms There are 2 double rooms. Bed-and-breakfast costs £8 (per person) including service.
  The rooms have central heating; washbasin, shaver-point; views of countryside/farmland/garden.
Public rooms There is a sitting-room with central heating, open fire, TV (colour), books, magazines, local guides and leaflets.
Surroundings The grounds consist of an acre of garden.
Cars The nearest main road is the A46 from Cheltenham to Bath.

Brookfield Farm, Plummers Plain, Horsham, West Sussex, RH13 6LO   *Tel: 0403 76568*   **C D H PT X #1**

Although this modernized farmhouse in the Sussex Weald is now virtually a guest-house, it is on a very real farm with hundreds of acres of sheep and cattle. The owner is John Christian who is well known on TV and radio farming programmes, but much of its popularity is due to its manageress, Carole. Born just down the road, John lectures on farming and travels widely to study farm methods overseas; and his sons, living nearby, are farmers too. Like many farmers he is sociable, and loves to talk to his guests about farming and the local area – it's his way of relaxing after a strenuous day's work.

When I arrived, from my bedroom window I saw him mowing the lawn which slopes down to the lake – and then running up an American flag on one of the flagpoles (a tribute he often pays to overseas visitors is to fly their national flag). Beyond lay fields and woods. As twilight fell, the only sound was the baaing of lambs.

On the white walls of the beamed dining-room, made cheerful by scarlet lampshades and cushions, is a huge collection of old plates. Guests usually share tables for a meal of generous home cooking. The picture windows that look out onto the lawn slide right back on warm evenings, and there is a paved terrace with seats and lighting outside. Inside is a copper-topped bar.

The sitting-room has sofas and armchairs of ample dimensions, lots of personal bits and pieces, and an open fire for chilly nights.

There is one bedroom and bathroom on the ground floor for those who find stairs difficult.

John occasionally organizes a barbecue or barn dance, celebrates Christmas and New Year (fireworks!), and sometimes takes visitors on a tour of the neighbourhood's many old inns (though he doesn't drink himself) or to see a local cattle-market in action. Adjoining the house is a games room (with bar billiards, darts, video games and so forth); children can ride the donkey; there are pedal-boats and a canoe on the lake (and a watersplash into it); and croquet on the lawn, as well as children's slides and swings, and a golf-driving range. A new indoor swimming-pool is being constructed. A small King Charles' spaniel bosses Boris (the huge boxer) under the beady eye of 30-year-old Adam, a grey she-parrot.

Walkers can make for St Leonards Forest. Some of the most popular sights of Sussex and Kent are within motoring distance, including Arundel (castle), Chichester (cathedral), Chartwell (Churchill's house), Hever (stately home), and the gardens of Nymans and Leonardslee.

Gatwick Airport is near, and visitors can be collected from there by car. Some people going on holiday abroad spend a night at Brookfield first and then leave their car here, at far less cost than using an airport car park.

The following facts have been supplied by the owners:

Bedrooms There are 16 rooms, which include singles, doubles and family rooms. Bed-and-breakfast costs from £13.75 (per person in a double room), including VAT. There are reductions for stays of 7 nights or more; and 'bargain breaks' as well.

Some if not all of the rooms have the following amenities: central heating or electric heaters; washbasin, shower, own bathroom, shaver-point; radio, colour TV, armchairs; views of countryside, farmland, garden; choice of duvets or blankets; tea/coffee-making facilities; door keys. Breakfast in bed is available. Sampler breaks (see page 14) and, out of season, free Sunday accommodation for over-60s staying 3 days.

Meals The dinner menu is fixed price (£7.50) or à la carte. There is a choice of dishes on the fixed menu, which consists of 3 courses and coffee. Dinner is served at 6.15 pm. Special diets can be prepared. Packed lunches can be provided. Morning, afternoon or bedtime drinks (coffee, tea etc.) can be ordered – for a charge. Wine and other alcoholic drinks can be ordered.

Public rooms There are 2 sitting-rooms, etc. The following are available in one or both of them: central heating, open fire, colour TV, books, magazines, local guides and leaflets, indoor games (such as billiards, cards, darts and Star Wars), an organ, record-player and records, sauna and gym. Bridge can be arranged.

Surroundings The grounds consist of garden and lake (with fishing, swimming and boats, croquet, golf-driving), farmland and forest. These are available in the neighbourhood: golf, riding. Conducted car tours arranged.

Cars The nearest main road is the A281 from Horsham to Brighton.

Buckinghamshire Arms, Blickling, south of Cromer, Norfolk, NR11 6NF   *Tel: 0263 732133*   **C D PT ⌗8**

From your bed you may see over the high wall that surrounds Blickling Hall and enjoy a fine view of this great mansion and its handsome gardens, one of the National Trust's most outstanding properties.

The Buckinghamshire Arms, run by Nigel Elliott, is a 17th-century inn (almost as old as the Hall itself) in a rural setting. The bars are truly traditional: one is a snug and the other amply furnished with oak seats and bar. In the dining-room, which has a tiled floor, flowers and candle-lamps stand on the sprigged cloth of each table.

Up stairs lined with 'Spy' cartoons are some of the most attractive bedrooms in this book: two with a view of Blickling Hall, another with lattice-paned windows overlooking a lawn and pantiled barn. Four-poster beds are complemented by good colour schemes – brown-and-white, or mulberry and dark green, or light and sprigged – with armchairs from which to enjoy the scenery.

There are good bar snacks daily, and the dining-room provides more ambitious meals, with choices at every course. One might select, for example, seafood pâté or watercress soup and then perhaps duckling with peach-and-brandy sauce or crab mornay, followed by a choice of puddings or cheeses.

Close by is the historic market town of Aylsham: strolling among its old houses, inns and shops is a pleasure. Also near are Norwich, the coast, wild marshes frequented by birds, the Broads, and more great houses or pretty villages.

The following facts have been supplied by the owners:

Bedrooms There are 4 rooms, which include single, double and family rooms. Bed-and-breakfast costs from £20 (per person in a double room) including VAT; prices go up in high season. There are substantial reductions for stays of 2 nights or more; and 'bargain breaks' as well.

Some if not all of the rooms have the following amenities: central heating or electric heaters; washbasin, shaver-point; TV (colour), armchairs; views of countryside or garden; tea/coffee-making facilities; door keys. Breakfast in bed is available.

Meals The dinner menu is fixed price (£12.50) or à la carte. There is a choice of dishes on the fixed menu, which consists of 3 courses and coffee. Dinner is served from 7.30 pm. Vegetarian or special diets can be prepared. Lunches and packed lunches can be provided; and snacks at other hours. Morning, afternoon or bedtime drinks (coffee, tea etc.) can be ordered for a charge. Wine and other alcoholic drinks can be ordered.

Surroundings The grounds consist of 2 acres of lawn and play area with swings and slides.

Cars The nearest main road is the A147 from Cromer to Norwich.

Bulmer Farm, Holmbury St Mary, south of Dorking, Surrey, RH5 6LG   *Tel: 0306 730210*   C(12) **D S X #1**

In the folds of Surrey's high North Downs (most of which are so scenic that they are in National Trust protection) a number of very picturesque villages lie hidden, and Holmbury is one. Near the centre stands Bulmer Farm, built about 1680. One steps straight into the large dining-room, and through this to an attractive sitting-room – a room of pink walls and old beams, chairs covered in cretonne patterned with pink poppies, logs crackling in front of the cherubs and harps of an old iron fireback in the inglenook. It opens onto the large garden.

Upstairs are attractive bedrooms with immaculate paintwork and cottage-style furnishings.

Outdoors (where chickens run free among the old rickstones, a Dutch barn is crammed with hay, and cows shelter in an ancient byre, the tiles of its long, wobbly roof softened with moss) is a small farm shop from which you can take home Bulmer's own vegetables or eggs, lettuces from the glasshouses, local honey or Gill Hill's home-made marmalade. David will show you the lake he created a few years ago, now a haven for herons, kingfishers, Canada geese, snipe and other wildfowl.

Bed-and-breakfast only, but the area is full of inns offering good meals.

Some tourists find this a good area in which to stay while visiting London – train day-tickets cost only £3 or so, and the journey takes three-quarters of an hour (from Dorking).

The surrounding area of woodland and hills is one of the finest beauty-spots near the capital, truly rural, and dotted with stately homes to visit, footpaths to follow, historic churches and villages with craft shops, trout farms, antiques and the like. Dorking and Guildford (the latter with castle ruins, river trips and a good theatre) are each well worth a day's visit. The Royal Horticultural Society's gardens at Wisley are near, too.

Reader's comments: One's every wish is catered for. So warm and friendly.

The following facts have been supplied by the owners:

Bedrooms There are 3 double rooms. Bed-and-breakfast costs from £9 (per person in a double room) including service and VAT.
    Some if not all of the rooms have the following amenities: central heating or electric heaters; washbasin, shower, shaver-point; views of countryside, farmland, garden; tea/coffee-making facilities; door keys.

Public rooms There is a sitting-room with open fire, TV (colour), books, magazines, local guides and leaflets, indoor games (such as Scrabble), record-player and records.

Surroundings The grounds consist of 2 acres of garden plus 30 acres farm. These are available in the neighbourhood: squash, tennis, swimming, golf, badminton.

Cars The nearest main road is the A25 from Dorking to Guildford.

Languages spoken A little German.

Closed to visitors We are not open in December and January.

Butchers Arms, Woolhope, south-west of Ledbury, Herefordshire, HR1 4RF   *Tel: 043277 281*   **S X ♯3**

The sun streamed down from a clear blue sky onto the paved garden where I was lunching; a small stream clattered by and birds were singing. Yet it was mid-November!

The half-timbered Butchers Arms, which dates back to the 14th century, stands among fields and woods far from any other building. Nevertheless its excellence is well known to scores of people who, though they live some distance away, beat a path to its door; and the bar was crowded. Even the snacks are outstanding, and the small restaurant is of gourmet standard. Breakfasts too are excellent.

Hospitable Mary Bailey, previously a computer programmer who took over the inn only a few years ago, has built up a wide repertoire of rather unusual dishes to complement the straightforward Herefordshire beef steaks which are also served. From a wide selection one might, for instance, choose fried clams or a terrine made from tongue, chicken-livers and brandy to start with; while main courses often include rabbit-and-bacon pie, pigeon with juniper berries and beef Bourguignonne. Vegetarian dishes are imaginative.

In the bar, where an open fire crackles, you must duck your head to avoid low beams. As to the dining-room and bedrooms, these are furnished simply but with comfort, but there is no sitting-room.

Woolhope is in the middle of a particularly scenic area: the Wye Valley and Symonds Yat are only a few miles away; so are the attractive old towns of Ross-on-Wye, Ledbury and Hereford with its fine cathedral. The Welsh borders, Black Mountains, Forest of Dean and Malvern Hills attract walkers as well as those who enjoy touring by car along traffic-free lanes. Go in late autumn if you want to see a blaze of copper and gold foliage everywhere.

Readers' comments: Pleasant comfortable room; excellent staff; food extremely good. One of the nicest holidays in years. Excellent value.

The following facts have been supplied by the owners:

Bedrooms There are 3 double or single rooms. Bed-and-breakfast costs from £13.50 (per person) including service and VAT. There are reductions for stays of 7 nights or more; and 'bargain breaks' as well.

The rooms have central heating; electric blankets, washbasin, shaver-point; TV (b & w), armchairs; views of countryside/farmland; choice of duvets or blankets; tea/coffee-making facilities; door keys; fruit.

Meals The dinner menu is à la carte. Dinner is served from 7.30–9.00 pm on Wednesdays to Saturdays only. Special diets can be prepared. No smoking. Lunches and packed lunches can be provided. Wine and other alcoholic drinks can be ordered. Bar snacks on all days.

Public rooms There is a lounge bar (open during licensed hours only), with central heating and open fire. Books, magazines, local guides and leaflets, indoor games (such as cards, dominoes, solitaire).

Surroundings The grounds consist of a patio garden.

Cars The nearest main road is the A438 from Hereford to Ledbury.

Buttons Green Farm, Cockfield, north of Lavenham, Suffolk, IP3 OJF *Tel: 0284 828229* **C D PT S ♯4**

Behind a big duckpond and masses of roses stands an apricot-coloured house built around 1400, the centre of an 80-acre farm of grain and beet fields. A serious fire a few years ago revealed all sorts of hidden architectural features – mullioned windows and a Tudor fireplace upstairs – all now restored.

In the sitting-room, with large sash windows on two sides, a pale carpet and silky wallpaper make a light background to the antiques and velvet armchairs grouped round a big log fire. In one window is an epiphyllium which annually produces over 80 huge pink blooms. The dining-room has a log-burning stove in the brick inglenook, and leather-seated chairs are drawn up at a big oak table. Here Mrs Slater serves meals with plenty of home-grown or home-made produce, crisp bread from the local bakery, her own chutneys and marmalade. Among her most popular starters are asparagus mousse and home-made pâté. A chicken or other roast may follow and then, for instance, chocolate soufflé or raspberries and cream.

Twisting stairs lead to big beamed bedrooms with sloping floors, which Mrs Slater has furnished attractively with flowery fabrics, pot-plants and good pieces of old furniture.

In every way this is a wonderfully relaxing house to which to return, tired at the end of a day's sightseeing.

The farm is only a few minutes from Lavenham, one of the county's show villages – very beautiful (but, in summer, often very crowded), with a guildhall owned by the National Trust and a spectacular church. Still further south, in beautiful countryside threaded by rivers with old bridges and water-meadows, are such other historic villages as Bures (where St Edmund was crowned King of East Anglia in 855), pretty Kersey, full of colourful half-timbered cottages, and Nayland. Within easy reach are places described elsewhere in this book: Bury St Edmunds, Sudbury, 'Constable country' (Dedham, East Bergholt, Flatford Mill). Made rich by wool, Suffolk farmers of the Middle Ages put their money into building churches for every village, many of almost cathedral-like magnificence.

The following facts have been supplied by the owners:

Bedrooms There are 3 rooms, which include single, double and family rooms. Bed-and-breakfast costs from £10 (per person in a double room) including service and VAT; prices go up in high season.

Some if not all of the rooms have the following amenities: electric heaters; washbasin, own bathroom and wc, shaver-point; TV (colour), armchairs; views of countryside/farmland/garden; choice of duvets or blankets; tea/coffee-making facilities.

Meals The dinner menu is fixed price (£5). There is no choice of dishes on the menu, which consists of 3 courses and coffee. Dinner is served at 6.30 pm. Special diets can be prepared. Morning, afternoon or bedtime drinks (coffee, tea etc.) can be ordered for a charge. Non-residents are not admitted to the dining-room. Wine and other alcoholic drinks can be brought in.

Public rooms There is a sitting-room with open fire, TV (colour), books, magazines, local guides and leaflets.

Surroundings The grounds consist of ½ acre garden, and farmland.

Cars The nearest main road is the A1141 from Lavenham to Bury St Edmunds.

Closed to visitors We are not open from November until April.

Cameley Lodge, Temple Cloud, south of Bristol, Avon
Tel: 0761 52790   **C(6) PT S S-C ⚹5**

A huge, stone barn in a superb setting was converted a few years ago into an extremely comfortable guest-house, run by John Harris whose parents own the farm on which it stands. It was built three hundred years ago for hay. Now it has a big sitting-room with bar and log fire, and an airy dining-room with windows overlooking the trout lake below, which is shared by swans, ducks and anglers. The conversion has been done with style: a red pantiled roof was put on, lattice windows inserted and panelled wood doors hung. Above are pleasantly furnished bedrooms, some with lake views and some looking towards the 13th-century church which stands close by.

Unexpectedly, Cameley Lodge is often quite full midweek but not at weekends – for Bristol businessmen find it a quiet place in which to confer, where they can offer business guests good fishing afterwards. Meals are based on local produce served in generous quantities (a whole 2lb trout may be offered as one serving). As a starter there might be prawn-and-apple cocktail or kidneys in brandy, before such a main course as suprême of chicken with a Madeira-and-peach sauce. Residents pay 10% less than other visitors who come to dinner.

This is a very scenic area. The limestone Mendip Hills vary from wild ridges to gently rounded foothills, with drystone walls. Caves and gorges (at Cheddar and Wookey, in particular) add to their interest; and the stone, of course, means villages are as beautiful as many in the Cotswolds. The cathedral city of Wells is the region's greatest jewel; but Bristol now is very well worth visiting – its ancient quays restored, many good restaurants and theatres (the Welsh National Opera Company comes here), fine mediaeval church, and Brunel's SS *Great Britain* to visit.

The following facts have been supplied by the owners:

Bedrooms There are 4 rooms, which include single, double and family rooms. Bed-and-breakfast costs from £12.50 (per person in a double room) including service and VAT.

Some if not all of the rooms have the following amenities: central heating or electric heaters; washbasin, shower, own bathroom and wc, shaver-point; TV (b & w), phone, armchairs; views of countryside/lake/farmland/garden; tea/coffee-making facilities; door keys. Breakfast in bed is available.

Meals The dinner menu is à la carte. Dinner is served at 7 pm. Special diets can be prepared. Lunches and packed lunches can be provided; and snacks at other hours. Morning, afternoon or bedtime drinks (coffee, tea etc.) can be ordered for a charge. Wine and other alcoholic drinks can be ordered.

Public rooms There are 2 sitting-rooms etc. The following are available in one or both of them: central heating, open fire, books, magazines, local guides and leaflets, bar.

Surroundings The grounds consist of 60 acres of trout lake and farmland. Golf and riding are available in the neighbourhood.

Cars The nearest main road is the A37 from Bristol to Wells and Shepton Mallet.

Credit cards accepted Access, Visa, Amex.

Carbery, Stockbridge, west of Winchester, Hampshire, SO20 6EZ *Tel: 0264 810771* **C PT S ⌗11**

Unexpectedly, Ann and Philip Hooper's Georgian house (on the main road to Salisbury and the west country) encloses an L-shaped swimming-pool heated to 80°F in summer – with a paddling end and slide for children: the kind of amenity one usually finds only in large hotels. This is backed by flint-walled terraces and steps (with a small fountain among the rock plants) leading up to lawns and a badminton court which overlook the famous River Test, where anglers fish for trout.

You enter through a games-cum-reception room at the back. Beyond this are a dining-room with blue-and-white gingham cloths on the tables, where simple meals are served – such as home-made soup, roasts or (of course) trout, and sponge puddings – a television-room with cretonne chairs, and another sitting-room. Everything is very spick-and-span. Of the bedrooms, no.5, and several singles are among the nicest as they overlook the pool and garden or river, not the road.

Apart from being a good stopover when travelling between London and Devon, Carbery is an excellent base from which to explore two cathedral cities (Winchester and Salisbury), the New Forest and the sea coast beyond.

The following facts have been supplied by the owners:

Bedrooms There are 6 rooms, which include single, double and family rooms. Bed-and-breakfast costs from £12.50 (per person) including service and VAT.
Some if not all of the rooms have the following amenities: central heating; washbasin, shaver-point; armchairs; views of countryside or garden; door keys.

Meals The dinner menu is fixed price (£6). There is no choice of dishes on the menu, which consists of 3 courses and coffee. Dinner is served at 7 pm. Packed lunches can be provided; and snacks at other hours. Morning, afternoon or bedtime drinks (coffee, tea etc.) can be ordered for a charge. Non-residents are not admitted to the dining-room. Wine and other alcoholic drinks can be ordered.

Public rooms There are 2 sitting-rooms etc. The following are available in one or both of them: central heating, TV (colour), books, magazines, local guides and leaflets, indoor games (such as darts, pool, board games, children's football), piano.

Surroundings The grounds consist of an acre of landscaped gardens, with swimming-pool and badminton court. These are available in the neighbourhood: riding, golf, fishing.

Cars The nearest main road is the A30 from London to Exeter.

Carnwethers, Pelistry Bay, St Mary's, Isles of Scilly, TR21 0NX
Tel: 0720 22415   C S

St Mary's, the principal island in the Scillies, is only three miles long. Even its centre of action, Hugh Town, can hardly be called busy by mainland standards (though it does receive tides of day-visitors during high summer), and so it is easy to find any number of unfrequented coves or beaches within a mere quarter of an hour or so from Hugh Town. Pelistry Bay is one of these – sheltered from wind, calm and unspoilt. Around it are pines and ferns, coastal footpaths and nature trails.

Carnwethers is more than an ordinary guest-house (and a very good one, at that): it is also a centre for marine studies. Its owner is Roy Graham, well known in the island and beyond as an underwater explorer and photographer, and a marine archae-ologist – with 30 years in the Navy before he came here. Even non-experts appreciate his library of books on maritime subjects (wrecks, shipping, fish, wildlife, boats) and his immense knowledge of Scillonian history and ecology. His illustrated lectures in St Mary's twice a week should not be missed. He has assembled a number of videos about the islands which he shows to visitors, and can advise on boating or diving.

As to the house itself, this was once a farmhouse, but has been modernized. It is still surrounded by fields. Every room is as neat as a new pin. There is a bar and lengthy list of good value wines, a heated 30-foot swimming-pool within sight of the sea itself but sheltered by granite walls and flowering shrubs, solarium, sauna, games room (for table tennis, darts, pool, etc.) and croquet lawn.

Meal times fit in with the times of the buses that take visitors into Hugh Town for evening events: not cinemas and night clubs, but slide shows which are usually packed out, concerts and the pubs.

Local produce is much used by Joyce for meals: fish (obviously), new potatoes, free-range eggs, home-grown vegetables and home-made marmalade, for example. A typical meal might comprise soup (not home-made) or fruit juice, roast turkey, and rolypoly pudding or fudge cake. Breakfasts include options like kedgeree and kippers. The dining-room has hanging plants, a stove for cold days and views of the fields with cows, flowers or potatoes in them according to season. Here and in the sitting-room, there are pictures of ships and seascapes. Bedrooms, too, are agreeably decorated; colours are pretty, cupboards have louvred pine doors, and each has at least its own shower.

The main attractions of the Scillies are their unspoilt beauty, mild climate, low rainfall and pure air. Storms are brief, sunny days long. Visitors to St Mary's get about on foot, by bus, and with hired cars or cycles (no cars on the other islands, which are reached by boats that regularly ply to and fro: see pages 54 and 119–20). Of course, the superb scenery and the solitude are the biggest attractions on all the islands; but in St Mary's, the main island, there are other things of interest: prehistoric villages and burial chambers; old fortifications and watch-tower; a clifftop golf course with arguably the most beautiful setting in England; boat-building, pottery and other crafts to watch (or learn); streams and pools, rocks and islets to explore; subtropical flowers growing wild, butterflies, and rare birds that excite the ornithologists. The excellent local museum tells the story of the innumerable wrecks in these waters and of the latest discoveries by underwater archaeologists diving to them. There is the lifeboat station to visit, and weekly races of gigs (a type of rowing-boat peculiar to the Scillies). Penninis Head is infinitely more beautiful than Land's End: just one of the many memorable walks around the varied coastline. Nearly every kind of sea sport, of course; and fish that go straight from sea to saucepan. Day-trips to each of the other islands are well worth taking. Among these, Tresco is world-famous for its romantic gardens planted with subtropical flowers from every continent; it contains an outdoor museum of ships' figureheads.

rear view

The following facts have been supplied by the owners:

Bedrooms There are 10 rooms, which include singles, doubles and family rooms. Bed-and-breakfast costs from £12 (per person) including service and VAT; prices go up in high season. There are special discounts for payment in advance and for rail/helicopter packages: these offer very big savings.

Some if not all of the rooms have the following amenities: central heating or electric heaters; electric blankets, washbasin, shower, own bathroom and wc, shaver-point; armchairs; views of sea, countryside, farmland, garden; choice of duvets or blankets; tea/coffee-making facilities; radio; hair drier; door keys. Bed-boards available and (for a charge) TV.

Meals The dinner menu is fixed price (£7). There is usually a choice of dishes on the menu, which consists of 4 courses and coffee. Dinner is served at 6.30 pm. Packed lunches can be provided. Bedtime hot drinks can be ordered. Non-residents are not admitted to the dining-room. Wine and other alcoholic drinks can be ordered. No smoking.

Public rooms There are 2 sitting-rooms. The following are available in one or both of them: central heating, colour TV, books, magazines, local guides and leaflets. Bridge can be arranged.

Surroundings The grounds consist of ½ acre of lawns, shrubs, heated pool (75°), etc. The following games or sports are available in the grounds: croquet, putting, pool table, darts, table tennis. These are available in the neighbourhood: golf, fishing, cycle hire, sub aqua, squash, windsurfing, birdwatching.

Closed to guests We are not open in winter.

Nearby is **Carn Vean** (tel: 0720 22462) in a pleasant setting of lawn and trees. Here Laurel Deason provides inexpensive accommodation and meals, as well as running a tea-garden.

Cavendish House, Eastmount Road, Shanklin, Isle of Wight, PO37 6DN   *Tel: 0983 862460*   **PT ♯4**

Although this resort is full of hotels, I had difficulty in finding any with really attractive rooms. Lesley Peters' home is an exception. She has furnished the large Victorian rooms with style – Laura Ashley fabrics and well-chosen colour schemes complementing good antiques. She has made the most of handsome architectural features (for instance, picking out in blue the plasterwork vine of one ceiling and filling an old tiled fireplace with pot-plants). Every room has a table and chairs for breakfast, as there is no dining-room. For dinner, Lesley recommends Small's, a French brasserie; or you can take the nearby lift to the foot of the cliff and **Osborne House Hotel** where, after an excellent help-yourself buffet, prepared by Mike Hogarth, you can sit on the flowery, grass-enclosed verandah facing the sea.

The following facts have been supplied by the owners:

Bedrooms   There are 3 double rooms. Bed-and-breakfast costs from £12.50 (per person in a double room) including service and VAT; prices go up in high season. There are reductions for stays of 7 nights or more; and 'bargain breaks' as well.

The rooms have central heating; shower or own bathroom and wc, shaver-point; radio, TV (colour), armchairs; local guides and leaflets; tea/coffee-making facilities; door keys. Breakfast in bed is available.

Surroundings These are available in the neighbourhood: tennis, riding, swimming, squash.

Cars The nearest main road runs from Shanklin to Ryde and Newport.

Languages spoken French, Spanish.

Credit cards accepted Access, Visa.

Closed to visitors We are not open between December and Easter.

Chadlington House, Chadlington, north-west of Oxford, Oxfordshire, OX7 34Z *Tel: 060 876 437* C(2) **D PT S** ⚏3

Peter and Rita Oxford, after many years of running a city hotel (in Oxford), decided they wanted a life in the country, and so they bought this many-gabled house (once the home of a judge). Although parts of it are far older, it is mostly typical late-Victorian – with much detailing of the period still intact (arches, brass handles on panelled doors, moulded ceilings and turned oak banisters). Parquet, brass stair-rods and coal-scuttles shine like the breastplate of righteousness, and in the main sitting-room a coal fire blazes cheerfully when the weather is cold. (On more than one occasion, guests have had snowball matches outside.) There is a quiet corner for card-players.

The house was very run-down when the Oxfords took it over, and all the new plumbing, wallpaper, paintwork, tiling and double-glazing has been done by Peter himself – to a higher standard than some professionals achieve.

Bedrooms are spacious and provided with capacious wing armchairs, generous storage and thick carpets. Really big windows (with far views beyond pastures where sheep or cows graze) make them light and cheerful.

Jane Hinchcliffe does the cooking. A typical meal might be home-made cauliflower soup, roast beef and baked apples (with alternative choices at each course). Often vegetables are home-grown.

The garden consists of lawns, flowerbeds and big old trees (mostly cypresses and sycamores). Apples are espaliered against the old brick wall at one end, and there is a barbecue which is used for grilling steaks on summer nights if guests prefer this to dining indoors.

This peaceful part of the Cotswolds, not greatly frequented by tourists, has very fine views across the Evenlode valley. All the famous beauty spots are within easy motoring distance – as are Oxford's colleges and Woodstock with Blenheim Palace. Burford and Banbury are two other interesting historic towns with good restaurants and tempting shops. Stratford-upon-Avon and the Royal Shakespeare Theatre are accessible, too.

Readers' comments: Have not enjoyed a hotel so much for over 20 years. Excellent food and accommodation, very friendly. Excellent value – have visited it twice. Very pleasant and relaxing.

The following facts have been supplied by the owners:

Bedrooms There are 12 rooms, which include singles, doubles and family rooms. Bed-and-breakfast costs from £19 (per person) including VAT; prices go up in high season. There are reductions for stays of 3 nights or more; and 'bargain breaks' as well as reductions for pensioners (except in high season). **10% discount to visitors showing this copy of *Staying Off the Beaten Track*.** Sampler breaks (see page 14).

Some if not all of the rooms have the following amenities: central heating or electric heaters; electric blankets, washbasin, shower, own bathroom and wc, shaver-point; radio, TV, armchairs; views of countryside, farmland, garden; tea/coffee-making facilities; door keys.

Meals The dinner menu is fixed price (£9.50) or à la carte. There is a choice of dishes on the fixed menu, which consists of 3 courses and coffee. Dinner is served at 7.30 pm. Special diets can be prepared. Lunches or packed lunches can be provided; and snacks at other hours. Morning, afternoon or bedtime drinks (coffee, tea etc.) can be ordered – for a charge. Wine and other alcoholic drinks can be ordered.

Public rooms There are 2 sitting-rooms. The following are available in one or both of them: central heating, open fire, colour TV, books, magazines, local guides

94

and leaflets, indoor games (such as Monopoly, Mastermind, draughts and cards) and a bar. Bridge can be arranged.

Surroundings The grounds consist of an acre of garden, with Aunt Sally, swingball etc. These are available in the neighbourhood: tennis, swimming, riding.

Cars The nearest main road is the A34 from Oxford to Stratford-upon-Avon.

Credit cards accepted Visa, Access.

Closed to visitors We are not open in December and January except for house-parties of friends.

Cherrybrook, Two Bridges, north-east of Yelverton, Devon, PL20 6SP   *Tel: 0822 88260*   **C D S ⚏3**

High up and right in the middle of Dartmoor, this little hotel is full of character. It was built by a friend of the Prince Regent when he acquired farming rights on the moor, and many of the old features are still to be seen – low-beamed ceilings and thick stone walls (now painted white). What was once a cowshed is now a sitting-room, with rugs on floors made of polished slate. On the walls, John Reynolds has hung old peat-digging tools and a pair of Canadian snow shoes (still awaiting sufficient snow to make them useful). There is a log stove and, tucked away at one end, a small bar. Pewter mugs hang from a beam; Susan's spinning-wheel stands ready for use.

Bedrooms are pleasantly furnished, with leafy views and no sound louder than the baaing of sheep. Every room is immaculate, and paintwork throughout is pristine. I particularly appreciated the huge armchairs facing the big windows of bedroom no.2.

This remote house generates its own electricity, pumps its own pure spring water – and has no TV. Truly 'away from it all'!

95

There are always choices at each course of dinner, from which one might perhaps choose mushroom soup, chicken casseroled in cider, chocolate sponge and then cheese. Vegetables and eggs are home-produced.

As to sightseeing, apart from the moor itself (a National Park) and all its villages, National Trust houses and gardens, nature reserves and guided walks (of one to six hours), it is possible to visit both north and south coasts of Devon as well as the historic cities of Plymouth and Exeter. Occasionally special holidays are offered with walks laid on, or visits to National Trust houses.

The following facts have been supplied by the owners:

Bedrooms There are 8 rooms, which include singles, doubles and family rooms. Bed-and-breakfast costs from £15 (per person in a double room) including service and VAT. There are reductions for stays of 3 nights or more; and 'bargain breaks' as well. Sampler breaks (see page 14).

    Some if not all of the rooms have the following amenities: central heating; electric blankets, washbasin, own bathroom and wc, shaver-point; armchairs; views of countryside, farmland, garden; tea/coffee-making facilities; door keys.

Meals The dinner menu is fixed price (about £8). There is a choice of dishes on the fixed menu, which consists of 4 courses and coffee. Dinner is served at 7.30 pm. Special diets can be prepared. Packed lunches can be provided; and snacks at other hours. Afternoon or bedtime drinks (coffee, tea etc.) can be ordered for a charge. Wine and other alcoholic drinks can be ordered.

Public rooms There is a sitting-room with central heating, open fire, books, magazines, local guides and leaflets, indoor games (such as chess, Monopoly, Scrabble etc.), bar.

Surroundings The grounds consist of 4 acres of newly planted trees and shrubs. There are 3 golf courses within 10 miles.

Cars The nearest main road is the A38 from Exeter to Plymouth.

Chimneys, Chideock, west of Bridport, Dorset, DT6 6JH
Tel: 029789 368   **C PT ⌗3**

This pretty thatched cottage in its old-fashioned garden is on the road from Georgian Bridport to the historic town of Lyme Regis. Built in the 17th century, the guest-house has been furnished in keeping with its age. The bedrooms are pretty (the ones at the back are quiet, front ones are double-glazed), the sitting-room and bar beamed and with log fires in winter. One bedroom has a four-poster, and several are beamed.

For dinner you might get a home-made soup, pork chop in

orange sauce, ice cream made with Cointreau, cheese, Rombouts coffee (and free liqueur), on a table with lace cloth, cut glass and Royal Worcester china. For breakfast, try the coddled eggs.

Mr and Mrs Hardy lend visitors Ordnance Survey maps and give advice. For example, they can tell you where to find fossils easily plucked from the Blue Lias clay (they lend fossil-hunting hammers), or where the best walks are on clifftops or through valleys – and if you want a lift back at the end of a walk, they are willing to come and fetch you in their car. They also show a film of Dorset.

Chideock itself is a very pretty village of thatched cottages, in a fold of the west Dorset hills designated an 'area of outstanding natural beauty'. The sea is close and much of the coastline hereabouts belongs to the National Trust. Within a short distance are Lyme Regis, Charmouth, Abbotsbury (swannery and sub-tropical gardens), Chesil Beach, Portland and Weymouth – all on the coast. Among the hills and vales, the farmlands and streams, are Sherborne (castle and abbey), Cerne Abbas (abbey and the giant cut in the chalk hills nearly two thousand years ago) and Beaminster (Georgian houses).

Readers' comments: Beautifully appointed house, historic without detracting from 20th-century comforts, comfortable, friendly, good food. Very helpful and pleasant, well prepared food but not too exotic. Charming house and owners. A delight; meal was exceptionally good value, owners have warmth and humour.

The following facts have been supplied by the owners:

Bedrooms There are 6 rooms, which include double and family rooms. Bed-and-breakfast costs from £12 (per person in a double room) including service and VAT. There are reductions for stays of 3 nights or more, and 'bargain breaks' as well.

Most rooms have the following amenities: central heating or electric heaters; electric blankets, washbasin, shaver-point; views of countryside, farmland, garden; choice of duvets or blankets; hair drier; tea/coffee-making facilities; door keys. Continental breakfast in bed is available. Some rooms have bathroom or shower. Laundering facilities available. No smoking.

Meals The dinner menu is fixed price (£7). There is some choice of dishes on the menu, which consists of 4 courses and coffee with liqueur. Dinner is served at 7.30 pm. Special diets can be prepared. Morning, afternoon or bedtime drinks (coffee, tea etc.) can be ordered – for a charge – and vacuum flasks can be filled. Non-residents are catered for only by prior arrangement. Wine and other alcoholic drinks can be supplied. No smoking.

Public rooms There is a sitting-room with central heating, log fire, colour TV and video, books, magazines, local guides and leaflets, and indoor games (such as cards, chess, Scrabble, jigsaw puzles, backgammon, etc.). Maps on loan. There is also a bar with log fire.

Surroundings The grounds consist of a garden. These are available in the neighbourhood: riding, sea-fishing, windsurfing, golf and swimming.

Cars The nearest main road is the A35 from Dorchester to Exeter. Car washing and vacuuming facilities free.

In the nearby village of picturesque Symondsbury is the mediaeval **Ilchester Arms** (tel: 0308 22600) where Bill and Caroline Wiscombe have built up a reputation for very good food, with a few bedrooms available.

Chithurst Farm, Horne, north of East Grinstead, Surrey, RH6 9JU   *Tel: 034284 2487*   C S ⌗8

Despite being so near Gatwick (and even London is only 35 minutes from the nearest rail station), this farm seems truly remote, reached by a long and winding lane. Built in the 16th century, it has tile-hung walls of mellow red brick against which the japonica flowers in spring.

Inside are low beams and a twisting staircase leading to simple but spacious bedrooms. These have double-glazing so that the sound of Gatwick's aircraft (numerous only in summer) is not disturbing, with air-conditioners providing fresh air. In the visitors' sitting/dining-room, armchairs and a rocking-chair are grouped around a huge inglenook fireplace (with log stove), its original spit-rack still in place.

Visitors are welcome to watch cows being milked, and even to help feed baby lambs sometimes. This is a good area for walking in the North Downs. There are several stately homes, gardens, and bird or wildlife parks nearby. Even Brighton in one direction, and the Kentish Weald in the other, are soon reached. Nearby, several old towns like Horsham and Dorking are worth exploring.

Some people stay at the farm before flying from Gatwick, and if necessary Mrs Tucker will produce very early breakfasts. A nearby garage will house your car, with free transport (24 hours a day) to and from the airport – where parking would cost you far more.

Mrs Tucker does not provide evening meals, but has a list of recommended local restaurants etc. which do. Chithurst Farm is remarkably good value for this area.

The following facts have been supplied by the owners:

Bedrooms There are 3 rooms, which include single, double and family rooms. Bed-and-breakfast costs from £10 (per person) including service and VAT; prices go up in high season. There are reductions for stays of 7 nights or more.

   Some if not all of the rooms have the following amenities: central heating or electric heaters; electric blankets, shaver-point; armchairs; views of countryside, farmland, garden; choice of duvets or blankets; tea/coffee-making facilities. Morning, afternoon or bedtime drinks (coffee, tea etc.) can be ordered for a charge.

Public rooms There is a sitting-room with central heating, open fire, TV (colour), books, magazines, local guides and leaflets.

Surroundings The grounds consist of a garden and 80 acres of farmland. These are available in the neighbourhood: golf, fishing, leisure centre. Bicycles available for hire.

Cars The nearest main road is the A264 from East Grinstead to Crawley.

Languages spoken Limited French.

Closed to visitors We are not open from October to Easter.

Christopher Hotel, Eton, near Windsor, Berkshire, SL4 6AN
Tel: 07538 52359   **C D H PT X ✿2**

It is easy to pass this by without noticing it, for although the inn itself is right on the old High Street of Eton, the accommodation is at the back – built round what was an old cobbled coachyard in the days when this was a posting inn.

Each room is self-contained – almost like a mini-cottage in a terrace. The furnishings are immaculate and the carpets deep – everything very simple, fresh and agreeable. The where-withal is provided to make your own continental breakfast and there is a refrigerator; it is possible to use the room for other snack meals. Full breakfast is extra. Everything is of high quality, with a great deal of attention paid by Ronald and Barbara France to comfort and convenience.

Near the entrance is a tiled patio with wooden tables, over-looked by upper bedrooms reached via a flowery balcony; but all activity here ends at 11.30. The far end is quieter.

In its 300-year-old history, the Christopher has received varied comments, from 'How great I used to think anybody just landed at the Christopher' (Horace Walpole, 1746) to 'The cause of much evil and temptation' (said by a rather later headmaster of Eton). Part that became a baby-wear shop, patronized by Queen Mary, is now a bar with traditional brews of beer on tap. In the adjoining inn is a restaurant.

Eton College and its ancient chapel are, of course, the greatest attractions in the immediate vicinity, but Windsor is just across the bridge. Eton High Street is full of antique shops, restaurants and bistros. Windsor, its castle, park and theatre are too famous to need describing. The whole of the Thames Valley is very beautiful here, best explored by boat to Henley or Marlow; and within easy reach are Ascot, the lovely Chiltern hills (at their best in autumn, perhaps, when the beech leaves turn copper) with historic towns and villages, Milton's cottage, Penn and Gray associations. This is a good area in which to go hunting for antiques, and it's close to Heathrow airport.

Reader's comment: A good choice – well done, The Christopher!
£55.

The following facts have been supplied by the owners:

Bedrooms There are 24 rooms, which include singles, doubles and family rooms. Bed-and-breakfast costs from £17.80 (per person in a double room) including service and VAT. (A third bed in a double room costs only £5.)

The rooms have the following amenities: central heating; washbasin, shower, wc, shaver-point; radio, colour TV, phone; tea/coffee-making facilities, toaster, refrigerator; trouser press; hair drier; door keys. Family rooms have a bidet, too. Launderette available.

Meals The dinner menu is fixed price (£12) or à la carte. The fixed menu consists of 3 courses and coffee. Lunches can be provided. There are two bars, one for residents only.

Surroundings The grounds consist of a meadow leading down to the river.

Cars The nearest main road is the M4 (Eton exit).

Church House, Grittleton, north of Chippenham, Wiltshire, SN14 6AP   *Tel: 0249 782562*   C(12) X #7

This little-known but very beautiful village lies just off the M4 midway between London and Wales: a cluster of elegant houses, a great Tudor mansion and church, all built from golden Cotswold limestone.

Church House began life in 1740 as a huge rectory, which it took six servants to run. Around it are lawns with immense copper beeches (floodlit at night), an orchard, fields of sheep and a swimming-pool, well heated in summer – as well as a walled vegetable and fruit garden which provides organic produce for the kitchen, where Anna Moore (cordon bleu trained) produces imaginative meals for her guests. A typical menu might comprise sorrel soup, chicken in a creamy apricot-and-curry mayonnaise, a tart of fresh peaches, English cheeses, fruit and wine (included in the price). Anna, who used to be a nurse, can also cater for special dietary needs.

She and her family treat all visitors as house guests. If you want to meet Grittleton people, she will invite some to dinner – a local historian, for example – and she often escorts overseas visitors on sightseeing tours. Some she takes to the Royal Shakespeare Theatre (Stratford is 1½ hours away), with a champagne picnic supper on the banks of the Avon afterwards. The Moores are a musical family, and occasionally arrange music evenings – there is one huge room with a grand piano used for this purpose.

The house, a listed building, has handsome and finely proportioned rooms. In the yellow sitting-room (which has an immense bay window overlooking the garden) are antique furniture, interesting paintings and a large log stove – often with Fergus, an Irish wolf-hound, snoozing in front of it. The dining-room is equally handsome: raspberry walls, an Adam fireplace of inlaid marble and, on the long mahogany table, silver candelabra and Victorian Spode Copeland china. The most impressive architectural feature is the graceful staircase that curves its way up to the second floor, where the guest rooms are (and also a kitchen equipped with facilities for making tea etc. at any hour). These bedrooms are furnished with antiques and curtains of heavy green silk; and Anna provides each with such extras as fruit, mineral water and a daily newspaper.

There is an immense amount to see and do in the neighbourhood. Close by is Badminton (celebrated for the annual horse-trials, attended by the royal family); Bath is only 12 miles away; and the many historic (and prehistoric) sites of Wiltshire are all around. Both the west country and the Cotswolds are accessible from Grittleton.

The following facts have been supplied by the owners:

Bedrooms There are 4 rooms, which include single, double and family rooms. Bed-and-breakfast costs from £14 (per person in a double room) including service and VAT. There are reductions for stays of 8 nights or more; and winter 'bargain breaks' as well. Sampler breaks (see page 14).

    Some if not all of the rooms have the following amenities: central heating; own bathroom and wc, shaver-point; radio, armchairs; views of countryside or garden; choice of duvets or blankets; bed-board; tea/coffee-making facilities; door keys. Breakfast in bed is available.

Meals The dinner menu is fixed price (£8.50). There is no choice of dishes on the fixed menu, which consists of 4 courses, wine and coffee. Dinner is served at 8 pm. Vegetarian or special diets can be prepared. Lunches and packed lunches can be provided; and snacks at other hours. Morning, afternoon or bedtime drinks (coffee, tea etc.) can be ordered for a charge. Wine and other alcoholic drinks can be brought in.

Public rooms There are 2 sitting-rooms etc. The following are available in one or both of them: central heating, open fire, TV (colour), books, magazines, local guides and leaflets, indoor games (such as chess, darts, indoor boules, table skittles), piano, record-player and records. There is a sun-bed.

Surroundings The grounds consist of 11 acres of lawns and pasture. The following games or sports are available in the grounds: croquet, trampoline, swimming-pool (80°). These are available in the neighbourhood: riding and bicycling.

Cars The nearest main road is the M4 from London to Wales.

Languages spoken French.

Clandon Manor Farm, Back Lane, East Clandon, east of Guildford, Surrey, GU4 7SA *Tel: 0483 222357 and 222765*   C(12) PT ⌗3

When financial disaster struck Sir Freddie Laker, this immaculately kept farm was one of the properties he had to sell. Its purchaser, surprisingly, was Sally Grahame, who hitherto had led a typically Kensington life as an interior designer. But inside Sally the townee there was clearly a country-girl struggling to get out, and she took to this life like one of her newly-acquired ducks to water.

Clandon is only half an hour from the outskirts of London – yet it feels as if it were a hundred miles away, so deeply rural is the peace. On the farm are a hundred cattle; innumerable pigs, free-range chickens, geese, Khaki Campbell ducks and rabbits; and fifty horses. The horses include some pale mink-coloured Norwegian Fiords, rare in this country, with manes of black-and-white – velvety to stroke, gentle and at their superb best when pulling the bottle-green brougham (built in Paris about 1890) which Sally hires out for weddings and suchlike, complete with green-uniformed coachman and groom.

The black-and-white beamed cottage which contains guests' bedrooms (simply but prettily furnished, with flowery or striped duvets in pastel colours) is surrounded by lawn, farmyard and flint barns hung with baskets of geraniums and often crammed with hay, oats or barley. Mrs Haines, wife of Sally's farm manager, comes in to cook breakfast. For other meals, most visitors go to the Queen's Head which is right opposite the farm.

East Clandon, itself a very lovely old village, is well placed for exploring the many others hidden in the folds of the North Downs – much of the landscape protected by the National Trust which also owns a large number of the stately homes near here. These include Hatchlands, Polesden Lacey, Clandon Park and Loseley House. Beauty-spots (many accessible to motorists as well as walkers) have great variety; the spectacular summit of Box Hill, the woods of Leith Hill, the blue Silent Pool near Albury, the watercress beds (and clock with automaton) at Abinger Hammer, riverside villages such as Shere, Ranmore Common (National Trust), the Royal Horticultural Gardens at Wisley, trips on the River Wey at Guildford (castle, theatre and old byways too), the coaching town of Dorking (good antique and craft shops here), and much more. And all so very close to London!

The following facts have been supplied by the owners:

Bedrooms There are 3 rooms, which include double and family rooms. Bed-and-breakfast costs from £8.50 (per person in a double room) including VAT.
Some if not all of the rooms have the following amenities: central heating; TV (colour), armchairs; views of farmland or garden; door keys. Breakfast in bed is available.

Public rooms There is a small sitting-room with central heating, TV (colour), books, magazines, local guides and leaflets.

Surroundings The grounds consist of 300 acres of farmland. These are available in

104

the neighbourhood: tennis (Wimbledon), skating, Sandown, Kempton and Ascot races.

Cars The nearest main road is the A246 from Leatherhead to Guildford.
Languages spoken A little French.

Also in this area is **Hazelgrove**, a comfortable and well-kept 'twenties house with lovely garden and sun-room, on the road to Leatherhead. Mrs Green can provide snack meals as well as breakfast. (Tel: 048 65 4467.)

Clarendon House Hotel, Kenilworth, Warwickshire, CV18 1LZ
Tel: 0926 57668   **D PT S** (weekends) **X ♯4**

Built well before Elizabeth I came to the throne, this old inn has yielded up many surprises during successive improvements: most recently, the discovery (in what is now one of the bars) of a 35-foot well, its mossy depths now open to view.

Bearded owner Martyn Lea (part-time pilot and sea diver) does all the conversion work himself, aided only by a teenage lad and Sadie, his Old English sheepdog. When I visited, he was busy creating more bedrooms further along the labyrinth of corridors (reputedly haunted) and laying out a huge garden.

In the oldest part, the very ancient cruck construction (possibly dating back to 1430, Henry VI's reign) is exposed: that is, an actual oak tree with forked trunk supporting the roof.

The bedrooms differ in style, the prettiest having a net-draped four-poster and beamed ceiling. In the sitting and dining-rooms, cherry-red upholstery, white walls and dark oak predominate. The dining-room has Martyn's large collection of antique maps, and items of Cromwellian armour – a reminder that Roundhead troops were quartered here during the Civil Wars and the siege of Kenilworth Castle (the imposing ruins of which overlook a lovely green, thatched cottages, and the spot where Raleigh is said to have planted the very first potatoes which he introduced here from America).

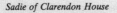

Sadie of Clarendon House

As to the food, there is a very wide à la carte choice. Chef Peter Williams specializes not only in beef, cooked in a dozen different ways, but game (hare, pigeons, venison, pheasant, grouse, partridge or wild duck – depending on the season), always well marinaded with different flavours before being cooked. There is also a good choice of vegetarian dishes. In the bars the range of drinks includes several real ales and a number of malt whiskies.

The old part of Kenilworth forms a most lovely town, full of architectural and historic interest. Within a few miles are Coventry Cathedral, Warwick Castle and gracious Leamington Spa. A little further: Stratford-upon-Avon and Charlecote (National Trust). A 70-mile round trip from Kenilworth takes in Stratford, the Cotswolds and Warwick.

I was pleased to find that in every bedroom Mike Stoddart, the house manager, had placed a copy of my booklet, 'The Countryside of the Edwardian Lady', which is a guide to the Solihull byways (north-west of Kenilworth) where Edith Holden sketched wild flowers for *The Country Diary of an Edwardian Lady*. The area is part of what was once Shakespeare's Forest of Arden and here, too, there are National Trust mansions, mediaeval churches, country and canalside walks, woodlands and meandering rivers.

Readers' comments: Excellent service. Truly memorable; charming and comfortable rooms; more enjoyable than a 5-star hotel. Service and staff excellent; very friendly.

The following facts have been supplied by the owners:

Bedrooms There are 33 rooms, which include singles and doubles. Bed-and-breakfast costs from £18 (per person in a double room) including service and VAT. There are reductions for stays of 2 nights or more during late summer; and 'bargain breaks' as well. Sunday night free to over-60s staying 3 days. Sampler breaks (see page 14). Special rates for singles at weekends.

    Some if not all of the rooms have the following amenities: central heating; washbasin, shower, own bathroom and wc, shaver-point; radio, TV (colour), video films, phone, armchairs; view of garden; door keys; tea/coffee-making facilities. Breakfast in bed is available, and bed-boards. Free laundering facilities; hair drier and curlers available.

Meals The dinner menu is fixed price (£9.50) or à la carte. There is a choice of dishes on the fixed menu, which consists of 4 courses and coffee. Dinner is served from 7 pm. Special diets can be prepared. Lunches and packed lunches can be provided; and snacks at other hours. Morning, afternoon or bedtime drinks (coffee, tea etc.) can be ordered for a charge. Wine and other alcoholic drinks can be ordered.

Public rooms There are 2 sitting-rooms etc. The following are available in one or both of them: central heating, TV (colour), books, magazines, local guides and leaflets, cards and games. Maps on loan.

Surroundings These are available in the neighbourhood: swimming, golf, riding, tennis, bowls, flying, football, rugby, squash, cycle hire.

Cars The nearest main road is the A452 from Birmingham's National Exhibition Centre to Leamington Spa.

Credit cards accepted Access, Visa.

Clay Lane Head Farm, Cabus, Garstang, north of Preston, Lancashire, PR3 1WL   *Tel: 09952 3132*   **C D PT S**

Though hardly off the beaten track – it stands on the A6 – Clay Lane Head Farm could easily be missed as one sped by, on the way to or from Scotland or the west country. It would be a good place to break a long journey, though it deserves more than a brief overnight visit, for both the house and the surroundings have much to offer.

The stone house, which is more characterful than it appears to be from the outside, is basically 16th century, and some of the internal walls are of plastered reeds. It is a rambling, beamy old place, full of family antiques and Victoriana, with a book-lined sitting-room to sprawl in (it has a log fire); and it has not been clinically modernized. The rooms face away from the main road.

Mrs Higginson, a pharmacist, dispenses good food home-made from fresh ingredients, including plenty of cream from the Jersey cow. There are goats too, and ponies for children to ride; and though this is no longer a working dairy farm, there are cattle and sheep on the land. In the barn, antiques and crafts are on sale.

The immediate surroundings are not exciting, but there is good reason to investigate the hinterland – notably the Trough of Bowland, which is like a miniature Lake District without the lakes. The steep, heather-covered hills here are excellent for walking and picnicking, and there are picturesque stone villages and mansions to visit. One such is Browsholme Hall, a little-altered Jacobean house still in the possession of the family which provided the hereditary Bowbearer of Bowland. Historic towns such as Lancaster and Clitheroe are not far, and the Lake District and the resorts of the Lancashire coast are within an easy day-trip.

The following facts have been supplied by the owners:

Bedrooms There are 3 rooms, which include single, double and family rooms. Bed-and-breakfast costs from £8.50 (per person in a double room) including service and VAT. There are reductions for stays of 7 nights or more. Sampler breaks (see page 14).

   Some if not all of the rooms have the following amenities: electric heaters; electric blankets, washbasin, shaver-point; armchairs; views of countryside, farmland, garden; choice of duvets or blankets; door keys.

Meals The dinner menu is fixed price (£5). There is no choice of dishes on the menu, which consists of 4 courses and coffee. Dinner is served at 6.30 pm. Special diets can be prepared. Morning, afternoon or bedtime drinks (coffee, tea etc.) can be ordered free. Non-residents are not admitted to the dining-room. Wine and other alcoholic drinks can be brought in.

Public rooms There are 2 sitting-rooms etc. The following are available in one or both of them: open fire, TV (colour), books, magazines, local guides and leaflets, indoor games (such as chess, Monopoly, Scrabble, cards, dominoes), piano, record-player and records.

Surroundings The grounds consist of 30 acres of fields and garden. Riding is available. These are available in the neighbourhood: fishing, tennis, swimming. Maps and cycles on loan.

Cars The nearest main road is the A6 from Preston to Lancaster.

Languages spoken French.

Cleavers Lyng, Herstmonceux, east of Hailsham, East Sussex, BN27 1QJ *Tel: 0323 833131* **C D PT S #3**

Many centuries ago this was a yeoman's house – with a tile-hung exterior typical of Sussex, and an interior given character by beams, and an inglenook fireplace in the dining-room. Marylin Holden and her sons have been running it for many years as a small hotel, and often have visitors to nearby Herstmonceux Castle – its beautiful gardens and moat can be seen in summer.

The bedrooms are prettily furnished, and have views of the garden and its apple-trees with the far distant hills beyond.

Good, plain meals are cooked (home-made soups, steak-and-kidney pie and so forth), with home-made preserves on sale. Cream teas are served in the garden during summer and by a log fire in winter. All cakes and bread are home-made. On Sundays there is always a traditional lunch with a choice of two roasts. The unusual name means a woodcutter's (cleaver's) hill by a marsh (lyng).

Herstmonceux village is the centre of Sussex trug-making (trugs are traditional garden baskets made from slats of willow), one of many pretty Downland villages around here. It is an area in which valleys alternate with wooded ridges that have panoramic views when the leaves thin out. Many craftsmen work here and wrought iron is a local speciality.

Reader's comment: Very welcoming.

The following facts have been supplied by the owners:

Bedrooms There are 8 rooms, which include singles and doubles. Bed-and-breakfast costs from £11.25 (per person), including VAT; prices go up in high season. There are reductions for stays of 7 nights or more; and winter 'bargain breaks' as well.

   Some if not all of the rooms have the following amenities: central heating; washbasin, shaver-point; armchairs; views of countryside, farmland, garden; balcony; door keys. Breakfast in bed is available.

Meals The dinner menu is fixed price (£4.50) or à la carte. There is a choice of dishes on the fixed menu, which consists of 3 courses and coffee. Dinner is served at 7 pm. Special diets can be prepared. Lunches and packed lunches can be provided; and snacks at other hours. Morning, afternoon or bedtime drinks (coffee, tea etc.) can be ordered for a charge. Non-residents are admitted to the dining-room for lunch and tea only. Wine and other alcoholic drinks can be ordered.

Public rooms There is a sitting-room with central heating, colour TV, books, magazines, local guides and leaflets, indoor games (such as chess and draughts).

Surroundings The grounds consist of an acre of gardens with play area. These are available in the neighbourhood: squash, tennis, golf, riding.

Cars The nearest main road is the A271 from Horsebridge to Bexhill.

The Cleeve, Hawkcombe, Porlock, west of Minehead, Somerset, TA24 8QW   *Tel: 0643 862351*   **C D S ✴3**

Little Porlock attracts many visitors to its narrow streets, but The Cleeve is sited five minutes' walk away from all that, within its own four acres of woodland. The Victorian house perches on a hillside, facing south and sheltered from any wind. A steep drive up to it passes banks smothered with thousands of daffodils in spring, lavender and fuchsias later on; up at the top, from the terrace, lawn or wide windows there are fine, open views to the distant hills. The Fentons fell immediately in love with it all when, on Pip's retiring early from his work as a professional engineer in Bath, they came househunting here a few years ago. The best bedroom from which to enjoy the views is no. 3 (there are windows on three sides). With luck you might see Exmoor deer who trespass in the garden and eat the roses.

   Furnishings and food are both homely in style. Many visitors dine in Porlock's restaurants (such as Lapsewood or Cross Lane House) but for those who prefer to stay in, Thelma cooks such meals as soup (not always home-made), roasts and (Pip's favourites) bread-and-butter pudding or 'mediaeval tart' in which mincemeat combines with apples and sherry.

At the Ship Inn, Southey wrote a poem to Porlock ('thy verdant vale so fair to sight, thy lofty hills with fern and furse so brown . . .'). There are fine sea views at Porlock Weir, along the coast (the road to Lynton and the little harbour at Lynmouth is one of the steepest in England), and inland to wild Exmoor, its pretty villages (such as Parracombe, Brendon and Dunster) and wooded valleys. Visit the cliffs at Heddon's Mouth. From Exford there's a strenuous walk to high Dunkery Beacon.

The following facts have been supplied by the owners:

Bedrooms There are 5 rooms, which include single, double and family rooms. Bed-and-breakfast costs from £8.50 (per person) including service and VAT; prices go up in high season. There are reductions for stays of 7 nights or more.

Some if not all of the rooms have the following amenities: central heating; electric blankets, washbasin, shower, own bathroom and wc, shaver-point; armchairs; views of countryside or garden; orthopaedic mattress or backboard; tea/coffee-making facilities; door keys.

Meals The dinner menu is fixed price (£5). There is no choice of dishes on the menu, which consists of 3 courses and coffee. Dinner is served at 7 pm. Vegetarian diets can be prepared. Packed lunches can be provided. Non-residents are not admitted to the dining-room. Wine and other alcoholic drinks can be brought in.

Public rooms There is a sitting-room with central heating, TV (colour), books, magazines, local guides and leaflets, indoor games (such as Scrabble, Sorry, Monopoly etc.).

Surroundings The grounds consist of 4 acres of woodland, terraces and lawn. These are available in the neighbourhood: tennis, bowls, riding.

Cars The nearest main road is the A39 from Bridgwater to Barnstaple.

Closed to visitors We are not open between November and February.

Just outside Porlock is **Terrells Cottage** (tel: 0643 862638), built by a doctor in the 'twenties and now run by the Plumbs as a small hotel in a lovely garden. 'Very good ... excellent cooking', said a reader who described himself as 'a fussy Swiss'. (Sampler breaks, see page 14).

Cley Mill, Cley-next-the-Sea, east of Cromer, Norfolk, NR25 7NN
Tel: 0263 740209   **C D PT S-C ♯8**

On the enthusiastic recommendation of a friend, I made my way to this most unusual of guest-houses – not, in fact, next to the sea (for centuries of silting up followed by land reclamation has left Cley a little way inland) but overlooking a rivulet winding its way through salt marshes where cattle graze and the only sound is the wind in the reeds.

Once Cley was a principal port of East Anglia, and great ships came to collect wool – and flour from the mediaeval windmill (the present structure dates from the 18th century). Milling ceased in 1921, since when generations of the Blount family have lived in it: one of the most celebrated visitors was the Duchess of Bedford who learned to fly when she was about seventy, and was lost flying at sea in 1937.

Only a few years ago, it was completely renovated, and the rooms are excellent. One enters through the dining-room – beams overhead, board floor with rugs – for which oak chairs and sideboard were specially made locally. The circular sitting-room has big armchairs around the brick fireplace, where Toby jugs are arranged, and window-seats overlooking the marshes. Upstairs, bedrooms are named according to the original purpose which they served: for instance, in the Wheat Chamber flour was sifted; in the Stone Room above it the flour was ground. Lace bedspreads and wild flower curtains contrast with brick walls, now painted white, and soft green carpet. One room has a balcony running all round the mill, with views on one side to Blakeney Harbour and on the other to the pantiled roofs and chimney pots of Cley, its flint gables and its walls with hollyhocks peering over the top. Higher still are observation and information rooms, with telescope.

The Mill is run by Carolyn Hederman, who produces such meals as roast lamb or pheasant, or fish with Hollandaise sauce; followed by something like lemon soufflé or chocolate mousse. Her own liking is for nouvelle cuisine dishes, but she is prepared to adapt to her guests' tastes. Much produce is local; eggs are from her own hens.

Occasionally, experts run short courses here – in birdwatching (Cley has a bird sanctuary), landscape painting or calligraphy, for instance.

Cley is in the centre of the north Norfolk coast; a shoreline of cliffs and sands now officially protected for its beauty and its wildlife. Inland are woods, heath and pretty villages of flint walls or (eastward) red carr stone, with inns where crab salads are as common as ham sandwiches. The National Trust owns a number of stately homes which, along with castles and almost cathedral-like churches, innumerable craft studios and wildlife reserves, provide plenty of opportunities for sightseeing. Blakeney's water-front is always lively with boats; Cromer is a family seaside resort in the old-fashioned style.

The following facts have been supplied by the owners:

Bedrooms There are 4 rooms, which include single, double and family rooms. Bed-and-breakfast costs from £12.75 (per person in a double room) including service and VAT; prices go up in high season. There are reductions for stays of 2 nights or more; and 'bargain breaks' as well.

Some if not all of the rooms have the following amenities: central heating; washbasin, shower, own bathroom and wc, shaver-point; armchairs; views of sea and countryside; balcony; choice of duvets or blankets; tea/coffee-making facilities on request; door keys.

Meals The dinner menu is fixed price (£8). There is a choice of dishes on the menu, which consists of 3 courses and coffee. Dinner is served at 7–9 pm. Vegetarian or special diets can be prepared. Lunches and packed lunches can be provided; and snacks at other hours. Morning, afternoon or bedtime drinks (coffee, tea etc.) can be ordered free. Wine and other alcoholic drinks can be brought in.

Public rooms There is a sitting-room with central heating, open fire, TV (colour), books, magazines, local guides and leaflets; indoor games (such as table tennis, darts, Scrabble, etc.).

Surroundings These are available in the neighbourhood: swimming, riding, golf.

Cars The nearest main road is the A149 from Wells to Cromer.

Cliff House, Alumhurst Road, Westbourne, Bournemouth, Dorset   *Tel: 0202 763003*   **C(7) H PT S X ♯6**

It is rare for a small hotel like this to get the top grading of the English Tourist Board (meaning that its rooms have all the amenities usually associated only with grand hotels). But there is even more to Cliff House than this.

When disability made it hard for Alex to go on running a big hotel, the Clarks bought this small one instead (then a run-down house), converted it to their own exacting standards, and – with Letty now doing most of the physical work involved – run it as a private hotel well above the Bournemouth average.

It has one of the best sites in the area, on a clifftop with far views (which can be enjoyed from chairs in the tiny garden), and close by lovely Alum Chine – a flowery ravine cut through the chalk by a small stream on its way down to the sea. From here you can walk along the promenade to Bournemouth Pier and the city centre. In the opposite direction are glades of pines and sweet chestnuts; and groves of rhododendrons that bloom in May.

The hotel is exceptionally comfortable, and its menus very varied. From a choice of starters one might have home-made soup or cod in parsley sauce or pâté, perhaps to be followed by braised steak. But it is the puddings which are the real stars of the show. To peep into the huge refrigerator beforehand is like looking into an Aladdin's cave of cream-decorated gâteaux and roulades and mousses: definitely not a fit sight for slimmers. For those who can still manage it, there will then be cheese with celery.

Being himself disabled, Alex has a particular concern for anyone who has difficulty getting about (there is, for instance, a lift). The majority of the guests are over 50. He makes everyone feel welcome, and regularly puts on a slide show about Bournemouth and its environs as well as giving personal advice about local sightseeing.

Bedrooms are very spacious, comfortable and – like everything about the house – immaculate. Some have balconies from which to enjoy the sea views, but these cost a little bit more. Their furniture was made – to very high standards – by the disabled community living in Alamein village, near Alton. The spacious sitting-room is furnished in similar taste to other rooms. Huge fringed velvet chairs are grouped around mock-onyx coffee tables on a pink floral carpet; and on two sides are bay windows looking out to sea.

For a description of the Bournemouth area, see pages 282–3.

Readers' comments: Excellent in every way. Very friendly.

The following facts have been supplied by the owners:

Bedrooms There are 11 rooms, which include singles, doubles and family rooms. Bed-and-breakfast costs from £15.50 (per person) including service and VAT; prices go up in high season. There are reductions for stays of 7 days or more except in high summer; and 'bargain breaks' as well in spring and autumn.

Some if not all of the rooms have the following amenities: central heating; washbasin, shower, own bathroom and wc, shaver-point; TV (colour), armchairs; views of sea, balcony; tea/coffee-making facilities; door keys.

Meals The dinner menu is fixed price (£6). There is a choice of dishes on the fixed menu, which consists of 5 courses and coffee. Dinner is served at 6 pm.

Packed lunches can be provided; and snacks at other hours. Morning, afternoon or bedtime drinks (coffee, tea etc.) can be ordered for a charge. Non-residents are not admitted to the dining-room. Wine and other alcoholic drinks can be ordered.

Public rooms There are 2 sitting-rooms (and a snooker room). The following are available in one or both of them: central heating, books, magazines, local guides and leaflets, indoor games (such as Scrabble and cards).

Surroundings These are available in the neighbourhood: golf, riding, tennis, fishing, bowls.

Closed to visitors We are not open from November to March, except for Christmas.

115

Coach House, Crookham, Cornhill-on-Tweed, east of Coldstream (Scotland), Northumberland, TD12 4TD
Tel: 089082 293   **C D H PT S S-C X #3**

This is almost on the border of Scotland – and very close to the site of Flodden Field, where in 1513 Henry VIII's armies slaughtered the King of Scotland and 10,000 of his followers: the very last mediaeval battle with knights wearing armour, and swords or arrows the principal weapons. Each August there is a tremendously emotive spectacle commemorating it, with 200 horsemen bearing down at a canter after being led by the Coldstream Guards across the old bridge at Coldstream. A piper plays that tragic lament for the fallen, 'The Flower of the Forest'.

The Coach House is a group of several old farm buildings forming a square around a courtyard which traps the sun. What was the coach house itself is now a highly individual sitting-room, with lofty beamed ceiling and great arched windows where there used to be doors for the carriages. One looks onto an orchard. Colours are light and cheerful, and for winter use there is a log fire in an enormous brick fireplace. The dining-room was once a smithy and the forge still stands at one end.

An old stone house is now used as an annexe, particularly suitable for families who would like the use of its kitchen to prepare children's meals (which means that very little is charged for their accommodation) and its games room. It has panelled doors of stripped pine, pointed 'gothick' windows, beams, an old Victorian kitchen-range, and an immensely high attic bedroom where you can see how the old rafters were fastened with wood pegs.

In the main part, some of the ground-floor bedrooms look onto paddocks where goats graze. All are light and airy, with interesting paintings and a file of leaflets on the many local places worth visiting. Two have airing-cupboards and fridges which guests find useful for a variety of purposes (baby's feeds, dog's meat, insulin or soft drinks).

The owner, Lynne Thompson, used to travel a great deal when she was a singer, and so has a lot of practical ideas about what travellers need – disabled travellers in particular. When converting the buildings, she had doorways made wide enough for wheel-chairs, and unnecessary steps eliminated. She has a stack of information about local sights accessible by wheelchair. Even clothes cupboards and bathrooms have been designed for ease of access.

This is the place to come for good, wholesome food. Porridge is properly made from pinhead oatmeal, and breakfast includes bacon from an Edinburgh smokery, beef sausages from a local butcher, and free-range eggs. Other breakfast alternatives are 'home-toasted grains' (oats, coconut, honey), rhubarb compôte, and home-made jams (apricot and almond, rhubarb and orange and damson cheese, for instance). For dinner, she may prepare a choice of six starters (pâtés, soups, quiche); a roast or casserole; puddings like lemon meringue pie or almond ice cream with damson sauce; cheese and coffee. Steak, pheasant and salmon are often served, and garden produce.

This is a fascinating area to visit. Across the border are Scotland's ancient abbey towns (Jedburgh, Melrose, Kelso, Dry-burgh). The Pennine Way ends near here, Kirk Yetholm is a famous gipsy centre, and in the Border mill towns cashmere and other woollies can be had for less than half the price charged in city shops. It's an area of wide open spaces and blue skies, breezy but hardly ever rainy. Historic Berwick-on-Tweed and the spectacular Northumbrian coast are accessible; the Cheviot Hills lie to the south.

Readers' comments: Very friendly and welcoming, exceptionally well organized; most impressed. Warm and friendly owner; professional efficiency. A great success! Wonderful.

The following facts have been supplied by the owner:

Bedrooms There are 11 rooms, which include singles, doubles and family rooms. Bed-and-breakfast costs from £12 (per person) including service and VAT.
   Some if not all of the rooms have the following amenities: central heating or electric heaters; electric blankets, washbasin, shower, own bathroom and wc, shaver-point; armchairs; views of countryside, farmland, garden; choice of duvets or blankets; tea/coffee-making facilities; door keys. Breakfast in bed is available, also orthopaedic mattresses. Clothes washing facilities available.

Meals The dinner menu is fixed price (£7.50). There is a choice of starters on the menu, which consists of 4 courses and coffee. Dinner is served at 7.30 pm. Special diets can be prepared. Tea with home-made cakes is free on the day of arrival. Non-residents are not admitted to the dining-room. Wine and other alcoholic drinks can be brought in. Occasional barbecues.

Public rooms There are 3 sitting-rooms etc. The following are available in one or more of them: central heating, open fire, colour TV, books, magazines, local guides and leaflets, indoor games (such as Monopoly, cards, dominoes, jigsaws), record-player and records, darts, table tennis. Also a billiards room.

Surroundings The grounds consist of paddock, orchard and fields. These are available in the neighbourhood: private salmon and trout-fishing, riding and golf. Escorted riding available.

Cars The nearest main road is the A697 from Morpeth to Coldstream.

Closed to visitors We are not open in winter (except for Christmas).

Coastguards, St Agnes, Isles of Scilly, TR22 0PL
Tel: 0720 22373   **C D S**

There are very few coastguards living in the many coastguard cottages still left around the shores of England: electronic surveillance has taken over from the man with the spyglass. Needless to say, such cottages were always well sited for sea views – on coasts where high seas and jagged rocks make spectacular scenery, but are hazards for ships, where coves and inlets were an attraction to smugglers.

One such group of cottages stands on a high point of St Agnes, a little island in the Scillies so unspoilt that there are no cars, no hotel, no commercialism at all. It is a paradise for those who want nothing more than sunshine early or late in the year, wild flowers, walks, birdwatching, going about in boats and perfect peace; a place where children can roam freely.

Wendy and Danny Hicks live in one of these cottages, with a couple of rooms for guests. They have furnished the rooms simply but attractively, with interesting objects around. The sitting-room has a William Morris sofa and brown tweed curtains, polished board floors, many books on the shelves and an open fire for chilly evenings. The pieces of iron-studded furniture are from Curaçao where Danny's father was a mining engineer. The collection of old bottles (from inkwells to flasks that contained sheep-cures) are mostly local finds. As in all Scillonian homes, there are flowers in every room – and children's drawings, framed. Danny makes ship models sold in London's West End galleries (you can watch him at work in his studio at the bottom of the little garden).

The food is all of a very good, homely style: bread is home-baked, soups home-made, clotted cream is from a friendly neighbourhood cow, fish (of course) straight out of the sea, and new potatoes from the fields around. For breakfast, you may be offered (among more conventional things) a big grilled mackerel.

Visitors reach St Agnes via St Mary's (see pages 90–91) from which boats take them in 15 minutes to the little quay at St Agnes. (Mrs Hicks will supply all the times etc. for getting to the Scillies by rail and boat or helicopter.) Luggage is conveyed for them up the steep track that leads to the few cottages; past the Turk's Head inn (for a really succulent Cornish pasty, pause here!) and past Rose Cottage, one of two houses which serve Cornish cream teas and light lunches. Whatever track you follow, there is a superlative view at every turn. This is a great place for birdwatchers, particularly in autumn when rare migrants arrive. But even at other times it is a pleasure to watch the red-legged turnstones, for instance, scuttling like busy mice among the rock-pools on the shore. Around the lighthouse (built in 1680) are fields from which daffodils and narcissi are sent early in the year to mainland florists. There are strange rock formations and islets, deserted sandy coves and pools, a simple church (built from money raised by salvaging a wreck), and – a mystery – the centuries-old Troy Town maze by a remote cliff edge. Altogether, one of the last places of true wilderness left in England.

The following facts have been supplied by the owner:

Bedrooms There are 2 rooms, a double and a family room. Bed-and-breakfast and evening meal costs £16 (per person) including service (no VAT). **Discounts are offered to readers of this book, except in high summer.**
   The rooms have electric blankets and views of sea. Laundering facilities available.

Meals There is no choice of dishes on the fixed menu, which consists of 4 courses and coffee. Dinner is served at 6.30 pm. Special diets can be prepared. Packed lunches can be provided. Morning, afternoon or bedtime drinks (coffee, tea etc.) can be ordered – free. Non-residents are not admitted to the dining-room. Wine and other alcoholic drinks can be brought in.

Public rooms There is a dining/sitting-room with open fire, books, local guides and leaflets, box games.

Surroundings The grounds consist of a small garden. These are available in the neighbourhood: tennis, rock fishing, swimming – and you can join in island cricket.

Closed to visitors We are not open in winter.

Cobblers, South Creake, north-east of Fakenham, Norfolk, NR21 9PF   *Tel: 032879 200*   **D S ♯8**

The mainly 18th-century buildings of Cobblers (flint and brick, with pantiled roofs) form a U-shape, enclosing a particularly pretty little garden that comes as a surprise when one turns in from the main road. Arches and hanging baskets of flowers surround the lawn and a sun-trapping patio, stone hounds guard a lily-pool (lit up at night), there are tubs of marigolds, and one can open a narrow wrought-iron gate to watch trout and ducks in the clear stream flowing by – the River Burn.

Ian Dow put aside his apron to greet me (it was his silver-polishing day), a rubicund host formerly a theatrical production manager – hence the many theatrical designs, photographs and posters around the house. The small sitting/dining-room is crammed with other interesting objects – from samplers and old jigsaw pictures to portraits of his Scottish ancestors. Here his wife Mardi serves generous meals that may comprise, for instance, avocado with smoked trout, followed by duck or another roast, and home-made ice creams or soufflés, then cheeses. The table is laid with blue-and-gold china, damask napkins and Victorian silver; sherry before and wine with the meal are included.

The bedrooms are attractively furnished with, for instance, both furniture and walls painted dark billiardcloth green to contrast with the shaggy rust carpet in one room; ivy trellis paper in another which has fabrics striped in cobalt blue and white.

South Creake is centrally placed for enjoying many of Norfolk's contrasting areas – the scenic coast lies six miles north; there are bird reserves; several great houses lie near (Oxburgh, Blickling, Felbrigg – all National Trust – and also Holkham, Houghton and royal Sandringham). Walsingham with its two shrines is a pictur-esque town. Both Norwich and King's Lynn are within easy reach, as well as several pleasant coastal resorts and the lavender fields at Heacham.

The following facts have been supplied by the owners:

Bedrooms　There are 2 rooms, a single and a double. Bed-and-breakfast costs from £13 per person.
　　　One or both of the rooms have the following amenities: central heating and electric heaters; washbasin, shower, own wc, shaver-point; views of garden; tea/coffee-making facilities; door keys.

Meals　The dinner menu is fixed price (£7.50). There is no choice of dishes on the fixed menu, which consists of 4 courses and coffee. Dinner is served at 7.30 pm. Wine and other alcoholic drinks can be brought in, but sherry and wine are included in the price.

Public rooms There is a sitting-room with central heating, open fire, TV (colour), books, magazines, local guides and leaflets.

Surroundings The grounds consist of a garden. These are available in the neighbourhood: riding, sailing, golf, tennis and swimming.

Cars The nearest main road is the A148 from Cromer to King's Lynn.

A little further east is Docking, where Margaret Robinson caters inexpensively for bed-and-breakfast guests in her immaculate 18th-century cottage, **Holland House** (tel: 04858 295), with peaceful garden.

Coldharbour Farm, Sutton, south-east of Petworth, West Sussex, RH20 1PR *Tel: 07987 200* **C(10) ♯5**

Nowhere could feel more off the beaten track than this, even though London is only 60 miles away.

A seemingly endless lane, trees arching overhead, winds its way through folds in the South Downs until at the end of the trail one suddenly arrives at this large, black-and-white farmhouse, built in 1665. There is an attractive brick terrace outside with chairs and tubs of flowers, and a fine view towards the hills: the walkers' South Downs Way is only a quarter-hour away. At one side, is a large and well-tended garden with a herbaceous border running the length of a fine flint wall.

Within, there are large, low bedrooms in pretty colours, furnished with antiques; a little beamed sitting-room opening onto

the garden; and a dining-room with refectory table, rush chairs and grandfather clock. Here Mrs Shiner serves dinners – two courses only. She cooks such things as pork with a sauce of wine, tomatoes and onions, and pavlovas made with fresh peaches. Vegetables in great variety come from her garden.

'Coldharbour' is an ancient term for an overnight camp without cover: very different from today's comforts!

As to sightseeing, the sea is only 12 miles away; and walks, long or short, are one of the greatest attractions of the area – as well as the many stately houses (Petworth, Uppark, Goodwood, Arundel Castle etc.).

Reader's comment: Very good food.

The following facts have been supplied by the owners:

Bedrooms There are 3 twin-bedded rooms. Dinner, bed-and-breakfast costs from £18 (per person) including service and VAT. There are reductions for stays of 7 nights or more.
   Some if not all of the rooms have the following amenities: central heating or electric heaters; washbasin, own bathroom and wc, shaver-point; armchairs; views of countryside/farmland/garden; tea/coffee-making facilities.

Meals There is no choice of dishes on the fixed menu, which consists of 2 courses and coffee. Dinner is served at 7.30 pm. Packed lunches can be provided. Morning or afternoon drinks (coffee, tea etc.) can be ordered for a charge. Non-residents are not admitted to the dining-room. Wine and other alcoholic drinks can be brought in.

Public rooms There is a sitting-room with central heating, TV (colour), video recorder, books, magazines, local guides and leaflets.

Surroundings The grounds consist of an acre of garden and 160 acres of farmland. Swimming-pool and riding are available in the neighbourhood.

Cars The nearest main road is the A285 from Petworth to Chichester.

Closed to visitors We are not open from November to March except for house-parties of friends.

College Farmhouse, Thompson, north of Thetford, Norfolk, IP24 1QG   *Tel: 095383 318*   C(7) S ⌗6

Over six centuries ago, colleges (meaning residential communities) of some half-dozen priests were established in various parts of East Anglia, to serve local communities. This house was built for one of them. When these colleges were (like the monasteries) disbanded by Henry VIII, it became a private house: the new owner had his coat-of-arms put above the main fireplace.

Later, carved oak panelling with fluted pilasters was put into the dining-room; a second storey was added in 1700; and then all manner of Victorian or later accretions followed. These last William and Lavender Garnier have gradually removed, revealing forgotten fireplaces and beams masked by hardboard. A tremendous task; and when they took over, the only running water was from leaks in the roof. The house is therefore full of curious architectural features – Gothic windows blocked up, walls (some three feet thick) with odd curves, steps up and down.

The Garniers have collected together interesting pieces of furniture and some ancestral portraits of their own (including a great-grandfather who took part in the first Oxford and Cambridge boat-race, and selected dark blue as Oxford's now famous colour). Bedrooms have pleasing fabrics – brilliant nasturtiums on the bed of one room, for instance; yellow linen bedheads in another white-panelled room – and in one the basin is set in a thick, handsome plank of polished elm. Each bedroom has armchairs and TV, as there is no sitting-room for guests' use.

Outside, a lovely old garden slopes down to eel ponds, and flint walls make a perfect background to the roses, herbaceous borders and great copper-beech.

Breakfast is the only meal served, but there is good inn food at the thatched Chequers, a mile away.

Thompson is in an attractive, leafy part of Norfolk, where the landscape undulates and villages are pretty. There are varied options for day-outings – from the very beautiful Norfolk coast to

Cambridge, from Norwich and the Broads to Bury St Edmunds (described elsewhere in this book). Breckland is an area of heath and meres, with little population now but a considerable history (explained in Thetford's museum, in a Tudor house). Visit Brandon to see the variety of ways flints are used in building; and Grimes Graves where prehistoric man mined the chalk to find these, for use as tools and weapons. Caste Acre lies within Norman earthworks (the priory remains are impressive); near Denver is an unusual windmill, and the 15th-century, moated Oxburgh Hall; Thetford's architecture begins with Saxon remains and the riverside walks here are particularly attractive.

The following facts have been supplied by the owners:

Bedrooms There are 4 rooms, which include single and double rooms. Bed-and-breakfast costs from £9.50 (per person in a double room) including service and VAT.

  The rooms have the following amenities: central heating and electric heaters; electric blankets, shaver-point; TV (colour), armchairs; views of countryside/farmland/garden; bed-board on request. Morning, afternoon or bedtime drinks (coffee, tea etc.) can be ordered free.

Surroundings The grounds include 3 acres of garden.

Cars The nearest main road is the A1075 from Thetford to Watton.

Languages spoken 'School' French and German.

Coombe Farmhouse, Widegates, east of Looe, Cornwall, PL13 1QN   *Tel: 05034 223*   **C D H ⌗3**

Built in similar style to an Indian hill station, and on a marvellous site with a sea view between hills, this 'twenties house had long been coveted by Alexander Low who used to bring his family regularly to Looe for holidays. When at last it came up for sale, it had deteriorated into a seedy guest-house, gaudily decorated, with barbed wire and a cow-field outside. But within a year he and Sally transformed it and its grounds, and every year sees still further improvements (a swimming-pool and a stone-walled games room for snooker and table tennis are the most recent).

  Alex frequents sale-rooms to find additions to the already rich array of antiques, paintings and interesting objects with which he has filled the house. Some, like the collection of fans, are family heirlooms.

  The dining-room extends into a glassed-in verandah from which there are views of terraced lawns where peacocks roam, and of a pond (one of several) frequented by ducks and coots. Elsewhere white goats, geese and ponies graze, there are woods with rhododendrons, and camellias grow wild.

All rooms have an abundance of pot-plants, flowers are put on each green-clothed dining table and in each bedroom, and on cool nights log fires crackle on two hearths: all part of the considerable attention to detail which has made this place so special.

My bedroom (like several, very big indeed) opened straight onto the garden. Others upstairs have armchairs or, in one case, a big sofa from which to enjoy the view. All are very comfortably furnished, and with thick carpets.

As a professional photographer and one-time picture editor of the *Telegraph* magazine, Alex used to travel a lot and knows what makes guests feel truly at home. They are welcome to take picnic lunches into the garden, for instance; and to help themselves to drinks, writing down in a book what they have had.

A typical dinner prepared by Sally may comprise something like home-made soup, roast duck and a fruit sponge accompanied by Cornish clotted cream – freshly cooked from local produce, and served in generous quantities.

As to sightseeing, there are twenty mansions and gardens within motoring distance, plenty of coast or moorland walks and river trips, a wide choice of sandy bays or coves, and such special attractions as a monkey sanctuary and another for seals. There is a huge choice of unusual museums or exhibitions: mechanical music, miniature villages, smuggling, steam rail, air history, mining, shire horses, local history, tropical birds, historic pottery and much more.

The following facts have been supplied by the owners:

Bedrooms There are 8 rooms, which include singles, doubles and family rooms. Bed-and-breakfast costs from £10 (per person in a double room) including service and VAT; prices go up in high season. There are reductions for stays of 7 nights or more for families; and 'bargain breaks' as well.

Some if not all of the rooms have the following amenities: central heating or electric heaters; washbasin, shower, own bathroom and wc, shaver-point; armchairs; views of sea, countryside, farmland, garden; door keys.

Meals The dinner menu is fixed price (£7.50). There is no choice of dishes on the fixed menu, which consists of 4 courses and coffee. Dinner is served at 7–7.30 pm. Special diets can be prepared. Lunches and packed lunches can be provided; and snacks at other hours. Morning, afternoon or bedtime drinks (coffee, tea etc.) can be ordered for a charge. Wine and other alcoholic drinks can be ordered.

Public rooms There is a sitting-room with central heating, open fire, TV (colour), books, magazines, local guides and leaflets. Also a games room with snooker, table tennis, cards, Trivial Pursuit, chess, video films.

Surroundings The grounds consist of 10 acres of lawns, meadows, woods and ponds. The following games or sports are available in the grounds: croquet, swingball, swimming-pool (73° in summer) and ample space for football, cricket etc. These are available in the neighbourhood: golf, fishing, tennis, riding, water-skiing, bowling, putting.

Cars The nearest main road is the B3253 from Hessenford to Looe.

Languages spoken French.

Closed to visitors We are not open between November and February.

Corner Cottage (Hare and Hounds), Greatford, north of Stamford, Lincolnshire, PE9 4QA *Tel: 077836 332* **C(10) S ⊞6**

This pretty 18th-century cottage of golden stone belongs to Peter and Valerie Wilkins who run the Hare and Hounds Inn almost opposite: one breakfasts in the cottage, and eats other meals (excellent bar food – such as a 1¼ lb sole straight from the coast) in the inn itself.

The village is well worth a stopover. A stream trickles its way through the centre; and in the garden of each cottage is an immense crown or similar symbol, filled with flowers – the work of a local eccentric who made these from concrete in the 1930s.

Corner Cottage has been furnished for visitors to a very high standard indeed. On the ground floor is a new, upholstered suite on a deep 'sculptured' carpet, facing a brick fireplace for which logs are supplied. At the opposite end is the lace-clothed breakfast table. An open-tread pine staircase leads to excellent bedrooms: the most romantic one, in pink-and-white, has a broderie anglaise drape over the head of the brass bed; and an oval bath as well as a shower.

This part of the country is perhaps at its best in spring when the scudding clouds in blue skies are reflected in the many dykes that drain the land, and the fields of the bulb-growing districts (described elsewhere) are brilliant with daffodils or tulips – road verges too. Villages of stone and thatch are picturesque, and this is an outstanding area for gardeners who want to go home laden with purchases from the many nurseries. People who use the port of Harwich, or the M11 motorway, are now discovering its previously rather overlooked delights. As to nearby Stamford, this is one of England's jewels: a mediaeval stone town almost intact, as lovely as any in the Cotswolds yet far less tourist-ridden. The cathedral cities of Lincoln and Peterborough are easily reached from here. Good level walking country, too – and with churches of almost cathedral-like splendour dotted about, comparable with the famous ones of East Anglia. The vast lake of Rutland Water can also be visited from here.

The following facts have been supplied by the owners:

Bedrooms There are 3 rooms, which include a single and doubles. Bed-and-breakfast costs from £10 (per person) including service and VAT.

Some if not all of the rooms have the following amenities: central heating; washbasin, shower, own bathroom and wc, shaver-point; views of countryside, farmland, garden; choice of duvets or blankets; tea/coffee-making facilities; hair drier and curlers; door keys.

Meals The dinner menu is à la carte. Dinner is served at 7–9 pm; and snacks at other hours. Wine and other alcoholic drinks can be ordered.

Public rooms There is a sitting-room with central heating, open fire, TV (colour), books, magazines, local guides and leaflets.

Surroundings The grounds consist of a garden. These are available in the neighbourhood: leisure centre, water-sports centre.

Cars The nearest main road is the A16 from Stamford to Market Deeping.

Cott Inn, Dartington, north of Totnes, Devon, TQ9 6HE
Tel: 0803 863777   **C D PT X ⌗4**

This long, low inn with roses rambling over whitewashed walls and a thatched roof looks almost too good to be true: a once-upon-a-time kind of place. It was built in 1320, by a laborious method called cob, for which no one has time these days but which has withstood six centuries and looks like standing for another six. Cob walls are immensely thick, built up painstakingly from one lump of clay upon another, each layer left to dry before the next is added. The thick, uneven walls not only give the inn character but keep it warm in winter and cool in summer. The stone-flagged bars and dining-room, with oak settles, have low-beamed ceilings, and there are great fireplaces for logs.

Bedrooms are pretty, comfortable and, mostly, quiet. Lunch is selected from hot and cold dishes on a buffet, but dinner is served

at table: salmon, duck, steaks and other local produce. The Cott is now run by Steve Culverhouse whose career in catering began there twenty years ago.

The Cott is a good staging-post on the long journey to Cornwall, or for a holiday in one of England's most beautiful regions – south Devon. There is much to see and do in the area but the beauty of the countryside and coast are what make it so outstanding (and its mild climate, with an early spring each year). Many streams run down to coves and creeks, and the country lanes are always going up hills and down valleys as they wind between banks full of wild flowers, visiting sleepy villages on the way. To the north lies wild Dartmoor. For those who want them, resorts like Torquay and Plymouth (with its naval dockyard and its *Mayflower* associations) are easily reached, as well as many smaller towns: Totnes (with historic streets), Brixham (fishing harbour), Dartmouth (old quays), Slapton Ley (waterfowl reserve) and Salcombe (for sailing). Dartington Hall, only a few minutes from the Cott, is an outstandingly beautiful mediaeval mansion in lovely gardens. A number of musical and artistic enterprises are connected with it: crafts (glass, furniture, weaving). The boat trips from Totnes to Dartmouth are particularly well worth taking.

Reader's comments: Excellent meals, will go again.

The following facts have been supplied by the owners:

Bedrooms There are 6 double rooms. Bed-and-breakfast costs £18.50 (per person in a double room) including VAT, but there are reductions for stays of 3 nights.

All the rooms have the following amenities; electric heaters; washbasin, shaver-point; armchairs; views of garden; door keys. Breakfast in bed is available.

Meals The dinner menu is £10 or à la carte. Dinner is served from 7 pm. Special diets can be prepared. Lunches and/or packed lunches can be provided; and snacks at other hours. Morning, afternoon, or bedtime drinks (coffee, tea etc.) can be ordered – for a charge. Wine and other alcoholic drinks can be ordered.

Public rooms There is a sitting-room with central heating, colour TV, books, magazines, local guides and leaflets, and a bar.

Surroundings The grounds consist of a large garden. These are available in the neighbourhood: golf, tennis, swimming, fishing, riding.

Cars The nearest main road is the A385 from Totnes to Plymouth.

The Cottage, Westbrook, Bromham, south-east of Chippenham, Wiltshire, SN15 2EE   *Tel: 0380 850255*   **C D H S-C X ⌗7**

Converted stables, weatherboarded and pantiled, provide the accommodation here, in a quiet hamlet once the home of Thomas Moore, the Irish poet. The adjoining mediaeval cottage was originally a coaching inn.

Inside, the roof beams are still visible. The bedrooms have been furnished in keeping with the style of the building and Gloria Steed has added such decorative touches as patchwork cushions and pincushions which she made herself. Through the bedroom windows one can sometimes see deer and rabbits, with a distant landscape created by Capability Brown in the 18th century.

At breakfast (in a room with rough white walls, small William Morris armchairs and beautifully arranged flowers) there will be, in addition to the usual things, home-made muesli and some very special jams from France. For other meals, Gloria can show you a selection of menus from all the inns and restaurants within a few miles (I ate very well at the Lysley Arms). Occasionally she invites guests to a family barbecue in the garden.

This is very lovely walking country, and with lots of sightseeing possibilities too (Lacock, Devizes, Avebury and Bath are all within a few miles; and Bowood House is close – an Adam building in superb grounds, with lake and cascade). Chippenham and Calne are historic market towns, with fine churches and other buildings of golden stone. Castle Combe is a much-photographed village in a dramatic setting – woods above it, stream through it, mellow stone cottages and fan-vaulted church. This part of Wiltshire is very rustic but with fine limestone houses built in the centuries when wool brought wealth. Riverside pastures contrast

131

with hills and wooded dells. (There is more about the county in other entries.)

The following facts have been supplied by the owners:

Bedrooms There are 5 double rooms. Bed-and-breakfast costs from £12.50 (per person in a double room) including service and VAT. Sampler breaks (see page 14).

    Some if not all of the rooms have the following amenities: central heating or electric heaters; electric blankets, washbasin, shower, own bathroom and wc, shaver-point; TV (b&w), armchairs; views of countryside or garden; choice of duvets or blankets; orthopaedic mattress or bed-board; tea/coffee-making facilities; door keys.

Public rooms There are 2 sitting/breakfast-rooms. The following are available in one or both of them: central heating, open fire, TV (colour), books, magazines, local guides and leaflets.

Surroundings The grounds consist of 2 acres of garden and paddock with 9-hole putting and badminton. These are available in the neighbourhood: riding, fishing, golf, swimming.

Cars The nearest main road is the A3102 from Calne to Melksham.

Cotteswold House, The Square, Northleach, Gloucestershire, GL54 3EG *Tel: 0451 60493* **PT S ♯5**

This is not strictly 'off the beaten track', being in the centre of the historic little town, but now that heavy traffic has been diverted, Northleach is – even though on the A40 London-to-Wales road – quite a quiet place. The house has tremendous character, after

132

being carefully restored by Mrs Powell a few years ago. Zigzagging passages lead to roomy bedrooms with rugged stone walls and low oak beams now exposed. She has furnished all the rooms with good carpets and folkweave or similar fabrics. Guests breakfast in a dining-room with oak furniture, including a vast carved chest, and can use the large sitting-room and its comfortable yellow armchairs – big and velvety. There are plenty of good places for dinner within a few yards, such as The Country Friends and the Union Inn.

Northleach and its environs are described on page 474.

The following facts have been supplied by the owners:

Bedrooms There are 4 rooms, which include single, double and family rooms. Bed-and-breakfast costs from £10.75 (per person in a double room) including service and VAT; prices go up in high season. There are reductions for stays of 4 nights or more.

    Some if not all of the rooms have the following amenities: central heating; shaver-point; door keys.

Public rooms There is a sitting-room with central heating, TV (colour), books, magazines, local guides and leaflets.

Cars The nearest main road is the A40 from Fishguard to London.

―――――――――――

Cove House, Ashton Keynes, north-west of Swindon, Wiltshire, SN6 6NS *Tel: 0285 861221* **C D S ⌗7**

The narrow trickle running through this little village is in fact the infant Thames; you can walk right to its source from here. All around is a chain of large pools (originally gravel-diggings) now known as the Cotswold Water Park, which more or less encloses Ashton Keynes as if it were an island: birdwatchers come here to view the waterfowl.

Here Peter and Elizabeth Hartland live in one half of a 17th-century manor house (with later alterations) surrounded by a particularly lovely and secluded garden which has a succession of lawns (one for badminton and another for putting) and a paved carriage-yard with barbecue beside its lily-pool. One of its previous owners was Puritan John Richmond who had a part in founding Taunton, Massachusetts.

Indoors is a large, friendly sitting-room; a dining-room that has interesting wallpaper, antiques and huge heirloom paintings; and

Elizabeth's lovely flower arrangements everywhere. A feature in the small library is an alcove lined with a large-scale, illuminated map of the area. Here Peter keeps a collection of packs for visitors, each full of carefully compiled information about day outings in different directions (to Malmesbury, Bath, Cirencester etc.); and his own 'good food guide' to local eating-places. Yet another sitting-room, upstairs, is for TV.

Bedrooms have individuality – one green-and-white sprigged; another full of roses; while a third (turquoise, with brass bed-heads) has an unusual domed ceiling. Flowers and fruit are usually present.

Elizabeth uses garden produce for meals, at which the Hartlands dine with their guests. You might start with gazpacho or home-made pâté, perhaps; to be followed by a roast or salmon mayonnaise and then perhaps fruit sorbets or rhubarb-and-orange pudding.

Ashton Keynes is on the edge of the Cotswolds. Among other sightseeing possibilities the following are within an easy drive: Cheltenham, Oxford, Stonehenge and Avebury, Bath, Stratford-upon-Avon, Marlborough, Faringdon – all described elsewhere in this book.

The following facts have been supplied by the owners:

Bedrooms There are 4 rooms, which include single, double and family rooms. Bed-and-breakfast costs from £11 (per person) including service and VAT. There are reductions for stays of 7 nights or more; and 'bargain breaks' as well. Sunday accommodation free to over-60s staying 3 days.

Some if not all of the rooms have the following amenities: central heating or electric heaters; electric blankets, washbasin, shower, own bathroom and wc, shaver-point; radio, TV (colour or b&w), armchairs; views of garden; choice of duvets or blankets; bed-board; tea/coffee-making facilities.

Meals The dinner menu is fixed price (£8). There is no choice of dishes on the menu, which consists of 3 courses and coffee. Dinner is served at 7.30 pm. Morning, afternoon or bedtime drinks (coffee, tea etc.) can be ordered for a charge. Garden fruit free (when available) for picnics. Wine and other alcoholic drinks can be brought in.

Public rooms There are 2 sitting-rooms. The following are available in one or both of them: central heating, open fire, TV (colour), books, magazines, local guides and leaflets, indoor games (such as chess, draughts, Cluedo, backgammon). Videos of local attractions. Maps on loan.

Surroundings The grounds consist of 1¼ acres of garden, with clock golf and badminton for children. These are available in the neighbourhood: tennis, squash, riding and windsurfing.

Cars The nearest main road is the A419 from Swindon to Cirencester.

Languages spoken A little German and French.

Crab and Lobster Inn, Foreland, east of Bembridge, Isle of Wight
Tel: 098387 2244   **C PT S X**

This old inn perched on a clifftop provides simple accommodation and spectacular views over the Channel. David Hill will tell you the inn was not named after the plentiful local shellfish but a New Zealand shrub (Puniceus) which has flowers that look like crab or lobster claws and which grows by its walls. Before he took over the inn he used to have the job of advising hotels on their wine, so naturally his are good value. Good straightforward food – big lobsters straight from the sea (at dinner served 'Thermidor' or 'Auld Reekie'). The breakfasts are of heroic proportions.

The inn started in 1810 as tea-rooms, but one day the clifftop garden fell into the sea. The dining-room, with big windows and red checked tablecloths, is a jolly place hung with nets, glass floats and wicker lobster-pots; its walls are white-painted boards, and there are pot-plants everywhere. Adjoining it is a bar with casks of sherry, peach and apricot wine, mead and scrumpy alongside more conventional drinks.

Outside are the weatherboarded watchtower of the coastguards who keep a careful eye on the reef below, footpaths along the cliff-top or down to the sands, and, out in the sea, the enormous old Nab Tower that was built in Southampton and towed to its site in the days when French invasion was feared, later to be used for suspending anti-submarine nets across the approaches to the Solent. David and the coastguards who frequent the bar are full of anecdotes about such local oddities, and about some of his past visitors ('we get prince and pauper here'), who have included the French Ambassador on one occasion, and Edward Heath with the crew of *Morning Cloud* on another. The inn is very busy in high summer.

Bembridge itself is an interesting little place with a lifeboat house open to the public, sailing harbour and a particularly good maritime museum. Coast and rolling countryside are equally lovely here. Although it is at the east end of the island where most of the resorts are, it is not difficult to get to the wilder west end (see page 196). There is a lot to visit here: many stately homes, fossils around Sandown (visit the geology museum to identify your finds), a first-rate wildlife park, botanical gardens with an intriguing museum of smuggling, Queen Victoria's house outside the sailing centre of Cowes, beautiful Blackgang Chine with one lovely garden after another, a centre with dozens of craftsmen at work, Carisbrooke Castle (where Charles I was imprisoned), the light-house of St Catherine's Point (open to the public), vineyards, picturesque Godshill (the church is worth the uphill stroll) and bird gardens.

Readers' comments: Food excellent; service most attentive.

The following facts have been supplied by the owners:

Bedrooms There are 5 rooms, which include singles, doubles and family rooms.
Bed-and-breakfast costs from £9.50 (per person) including VAT. There are reductions for stays of 7 nights or more.
Some if not all of the rooms have the following amenities: central heating or electric heaters; washbasins, shower, shaver-point; radio, armchairs; views of sea, countryside, farmland; tea/coffee-making facilities; door keys.
Meals The dinner menu is à la carte. Dinner is served from 7 pm. Lunches and/or packed lunches can be provided; and snacks at other hours. Morning,

afternoon or bedtime drinks (coffee, tea etc.) can be ordered – for a charge. Wine and other alcoholic drinks can be ordered.

Public rooms Apart from the bars, there is a sitting-room with TV and sea views.

Surroundings The grounds consist of clifftop and beach. These are available in the neighbourhood: riding, sailing, golf.

Cars The nearest main road is the A3055 from Ryde to Shanklin.

Criterion Hotel, Cawsand, west of Plymouth (Devon), Cornwall, PL10 1PD   *Tel: 0752 822244*   **C D PT S X ♯6**

Inconspicuous when seen from the narrow street, this little hotel occupies one of the most intriguing sites of any in this book. Originally three fishermen's cottages, it is built not just on but into the vertical cliffs behind Cawsand Bay, which faces the historic waters of Plymouth Sound. One descends from the dining-room to a cellar lounge below, and to yet another cellar (the bar) below that: each with verandah hanging over the sea and steps down to what is, at low tide, a private beach of golden sand (perfect for a pre-breakfast swim). The sea here is so clear you can watch the fish swim, while not far off all the shipping going to the dockyard at Plymouth passes by.

The rooms have been furnished in keeping with the old stone buildings, their low ceilings and boarded doors, narrow and twisting corridors. I particularly liked bedroom no. 2 which has a window seat from which to enjoy the sea view. There are model ships about, local artists' paintings (for sale) and a large number of Victorian dolls beautifully dressed by Mrs Kidd, for she loves

137

sewing as much as cooking – some of these, too, are for sale. She bakes the hotel's bread and cakes, as well as cooking such meals as bouillabaisse, beef Bourguignonne (served with interesting vegetables) and queen of puddings (accompanied by Cornish clotted cream), with cheese and coffee to follow.

Cawsand (though so easy to reach by ferry from Plymouth) is a place most tourists pass by, and so it has not been ruined like Polperro, for instance. The shops sell good pottery not trashy souvenirs, and there is no vandalism. The peninsula on which it stands is a pretty area; beyond it lies Plymouth and south Devon in one direction (see pages 338–9) and the Looe area in the other (see page 337).

The following facts have been supplied by the owners:

Bedrooms There are 8 rooms, which include singles, doubles and family rooms. Bed-and-breakfast costs from £13.50 (per person in a double room) including service and VAT. There are reductions for stays of 3 nights or more; and 'bargain breaks' as well. Sampler breaks (see page 14).

Some if not all of the rooms have the following amenities: electric heaters; electric blankets, washbasin, own shower and wc, shaver-point; radio, TV (colour), armchairs; views of sea; balcony; choice of duvets or blankets; door keys. Breakfast in bed is available, also laundering facilities.

Meals The dinner menu is fixed price (£9.50). There is a choice of dishes on the fixed menu, which consists of 3 courses and coffee. Dinner is served at 7.30 pm. Special diets can be prepared. Lunches and packed lunches can be provided; and snacks at other hours. Morning, afternoon or bedtime drinks (coffee, tea etc.) can be ordered for a charge. Wine and other alcoholic drinks can be ordered.

Public rooms There is a sitting-room with central heating, TV (colour), books, magazines, local guides and leaflets, board games etc., record-player and records, bar (with a range of malt whiskies). Maps on loan.

Surroundings These are available in the neighbourhood: fishing, water sports, golf, riding.

Cars The nearest main road is the A38 from Bodmin to Bristol and beyond.

The Croft, off Cottons Lane, Ashton-under-Hill, south of Evesham, Worcestershire, WR11 6SS *Tel: 0386 881641*   C(7) PT S ⬚4

The hill under which Ashton lies is Bredon Hill – it suddenly rises to nearly 1000 feet in an otherwise gentle landscape of placid rivers, apple orchards and pastures where cows graze. Prehistoric and Roman earthworks contrast with a great mediaeval tithe barn (National Trust), castellated 'Gothick' folly and pretty villages.

Vigorous walkers can see eight counties from the summit (some say fourteen on a clear day). Around it is a spring Apple Blossom Trail, well signposted by the AA.

Tucked away at the hill's foot is The Croft, a stone-and-brick house on a sloping grassy site where the Langridges have planted willows, conifers and flowering shrubs.

The stone-walled sitting-room has a velvet-covered suite grouped around the log stove. Upstairs are simple but pleasantly furnished bedrooms, one with a view from the bed of distant Broadway Hill; one, up a twisting stairway, is tucked under the eaves – a quaint attic room of tiny windows and exposed beams.

Usually Betty provides only bed-and-breakfast: other meals are by special arrangement (or you can eat well at a nearby village inn, The Star).

Ashton is surrounded by lovely countryside and interesting places to visit (many described in other entries in this book): the Vale of Evesham, the River Avon (boat trips available), historic and elegant Evesham with its market and its Almonry museum, a number of historic houses and gardens, cathedrals and abbeys, the showpiece village of Broadway (crowded in summer), Malvern (spa town) and Pershore – famous for its plums as well as its historic buildings. The Wychavon Way for walkers is near.

The following facts have been supplied by the owners:

Bedrooms There are 3 rooms, which include single and double rooms. Bed-and-breakfast costs from £8 (per person) including service and VAT. There are reductions for stays of 2 nights or more; and 'bargain breaks' as well.

Some if not all of the rooms have the following amenities: central heating or electric heaters; electric blankets, washbasin, armchairs; views of countryside or garden.

Meals The dinner menu is fixed price (£5). There is no choice of dishes on the menu, which consists of 3 courses and coffee. Dinner is served at 7 pm. Morning, afternoon or bedtime drinks (coffee, tea etc.) can be ordered free. Non-residents are not admitted to the dining-room. Wine and other alcoholic drinks can be brought in.

Public rooms There is a sitting-room with central heating, wood stove, TV (colour), books, magazines, local guides and leaflets, indoor games (such as Scrabble, Monopoly, Sorry, etc.).

Surroundings The grounds consist of 12 acres of garden and orchard. These are available in the neighbourhood: golf, tennis.

Cars The nearest main road is the A435 from Evesham to Cheltenham.

Closed to visitors We are not open in January.

Crookwood Watermill, Stert, south-east of Devizes, Wiltshire, SN10 3JA   *Tel: 0380 2985*   **S ♯5**

There has been a watermill here since Saxon times but the present pantiled building, carefully restored by Elliott Herod-Taylor (a semi-retired vet), dates from about 1850. Though the mill-race is now partly filled with rushes, and the wheel awaits replacement, the mill's other surroundings have changed little through the centuries.

One finds it at the end of a very long winding track, amid pastures where Elliott's Jersey cows graze, the Wiltshire hills making a lovely backdrop to the scene. Close by is a thatched farmhouse, home of Elliott's son; and around the mill periwinkles and pansies grow.

The four floors of the mill have been converted into comfortable rooms, though still with the old joists exposed – and, in the sitting-room, the hopper down which the wheat was once fed to the turning stones that ground it into flour. One of the millstones now serves as the hearth for a log stove. On the board walls are hunting prints and bookshelves; antiques and cretonne sofas furnish the room.

The one letting bedroom above is small but sufficient. Guests eat in the kitchen/dining-room downstairs, with the family. Denise (a wildlife expert, connected with the award-winning Devizes Museum) cooks organic produce from the farm: asparagus, pheasant, lamb, veal and pork, honey and jams, free-range eggs; above all, she uses the dairy products of the Jersey herd (not only thick cream to go with crêpes or mousses, strawberries or raspberries, but also fruit yogurts, cottage cheese and – made by her French daughter-in-law – *fromage frais*). These are also on sale.

Birdwatchers like staying at the mill in order to spot the buzzards, curlews, owls and woodpeckers which abound in this peaceful place. Denise, who participates in the national Flora Mapping Scheme, can point out all kinds of wild flowers. Visitors are also welcome to watch milking or the cream-separator at work.

Devizes has pleasant Georgian houses round its market square. It stands at one end of the lovely Vale of Pewsey, with Salisbury Plain to the south. This is an area of contrasts: unspoilt chalk downs, prehistoric remains, river valleys, prairie-sized wheatfields, high views, boat trips, wildlife walks along the Kennet and Avon Canal, markets, museums, stately homes such as Longleat, villages of thatched cottages – it is a place that deserves a long stay.

The following facts have been supplied by the owners:

Bedrooms There is 1 double room. Bed-and-breakfast costs from £10 (per person) including service and VAT. There are reductions for stays of 3 nights or more. The room has central heating; TV (b&w), armchair; choice of duvets or blankets; door key. Breakfast in bed is available.

Meals The dinner menu is fixed price (£4.50). There is a choice of dishes on the fixed menu, which consists of 3 courses and coffee. Dinner is served when required. Vegetarian diets can be prepared. Morning, afternoon or bedtime drinks (coffee, tea etc.) can be ordered free. Non-residents are not admitted to the dining-room. Wine and other alcoholic drinks can be brought in.

Public rooms There is a family sitting-room with open fire, TV (colour), books, magazines, local guides and leaflets. Bridge can be arranged.

Surroundings The grounds consist of 76 acres of dairy farmland. These are available in the neighbourhood: riding, swimming (open air).

Cars The nearest main road is the A342 from Devizes to Upavon.

Languages spoken French.

Cross Keys, The Cross, East Meon, west of Petersfield, Hampshire, GU32 1NN *Tel: 0730 87251* **C**(5) **S ⌗9**

In one of Hampshire's most beautiful villages, through which a trout river threads its way, is a lane where three 17th-century cottages have been united to make a very attractive family home for the young Mackinlays. The River Meon cuts across their large garden, stepping-stones and a little bridge leading from one half to the other where there is a croquet lawn (big enough for the annual village fête to be held here): a lovely scene, with hills beyond, to contemplate from wicker chairs on the paved terrace.

rear view

Bedrooms are pleasantly furnished – crochet bedspread, rose prints and antique furniture, for instance. The informal sitting-room has an alcove of coronation and other mugs facing the leaded windows, with handsome chairs of turquoise leather, brass-studded, around a table where Rachel serves breakfast. For other

142

meals, there are two historic inns close by – The George (where I chose an excellent game pie from their bar snacks) and the Izaak Walton, of *Compleat Angler* fame.

This green valley amid the South Downs has churches that go back to Saxon times, flint-walled houses, and prehistoric burial mounds. To the south are woodlands, remnants of the once-great Forest of Bere, and then comes Portsmouth Harbour. Despite heavy traffic on roads into the port, this is well worth a visit – to see Nelson's *Victory*, Henry VIII's *Mary Rose* and his Southsea Castle, Victorian forts up on the hills and Norman Portchester Castle down by the waterfront. There are boat trips and ferries to the Isle of Wight; excellent museums (don't miss the Royal Marines one); Dicken's birthplace; much ceremonial on 'Navy Days'; and waterfowl on the wilder shores of the two natural harbours here. Queen Elizabeth Forest contrasts with all this (drive to Georgian Buriton, up Butser Hill, or visit the recreated Iron Age village). There's a mediaeval palace at Bishop's Waltham. Hambledon has a vineyard, Hayling Island sandy beaches, West Meon church the grave of Lord (of Lord's Cricket Ground) and walls that are a superb example of the flint-knapper's craft. Northward lies the Itchen Valley, see pages 475–6.

The following facts have been supplied by the owners:

Bedrooms There are 2 rooms, single and double. Bed-and-breakfast costs from £9 (per person in a double room) including service and VAT; prices go up in high season.

One or both of the rooms have: central heating, electric heaters; own bathroom and wc; armchairs; views of countryside and garden; door keys.

Surroundings The grounds consist of 5 acres of lawns and a river.

Cars The nearest main road is the A272 from Petersfield to Winchester.

Languages spoken French.

Closed to visitors We are not open between November and January.

Crosskeys, Hilgay, south of King's Lynn, Norfolk, PE38 0LN
Tel: 0366 387777   **C PT ♯4**

Long ago, this riverside house was an inn, beside a ford across the pretty River Wissey (it now has a bridge).

When it was taken over by Joan and William Lamb after he left the RAF, it was derelict: they themselves executed the transformation into an impeccably converted small hotel, with garden.

One steps straight into a small, rustic bar with copper tables, beyond which is the beamed dining-room (where Joan serves such meals as home-made soup, chicken chasseur and fruit tart with cream, for example). The bedrooms are quite outstanding for such an unpretentious little hotel: beautiful wallpapers, four-posters in two, and armchairs from which to enjoy views of river or garden (or to watch TV). I liked no. 3 best. A ground-floor suite of two rooms and bathroom would be ideal for families: children are delighted by the sight of ducks and boats on the river a few yards away and ponies grazing right outside.

The area immediately around is rather flat, but soon one comes to the very fine beech and oak forest around Thetford (itself well worth a visit). Historic King's Lynn and Bury St Edmunds, the superb north coast of Norfolk, Ely, Cambridge and Newmarket are all within a short drive; Norwich and the Norfolk Broads a little further.

The following facts have been supplied by the owners:

Bedrooms There are 5 rooms, which include double and family rooms. Bed-and-breakfast costs from £16.20 (per person in a double room) including service and VAT. There are 'bargain breaks'.

    The rooms have the following amenities: central heating; own bathroom and wc, shaver-point; radio, TV (colour), armchairs; views of countryside and river; choice of duvets or blankets; tea/coffee-making facilities; door keys.

Meals The dinner menu is fixed price (£6.50) or à la carte. There is a choice of dishes on the fixed menu, which consists of 3 courses and coffee. Dinner is served from 7 pm. Vegetarian or special diets can be prepared, and packed lunches can be provided. Morning, afternoon or bedtime drinks (coffee, tea etc.) can be ordered for a charge. Wine and other alcoholic drinks can be ordered.

Public rooms There is a sitting-room with central heating, books, magazines, local guides and leaflets, and a bar.

Surroundings The grounds consist of ⅔ acre of garden. Golf is available in the neighbourhood.

Cars The nearest main road is the A10 from Ely to King's Lynn.

Closed to visitors We are not open from mid December to mid January.

Crossways Farm, Abinger, south-west of Dorking, Surrey, RH5 6PZ *Tel: 0306 730173* **C PT S ▦1**

Meredith's *Diana of the Crossways* (one of those books everyone has heard of and few have read) took its title from this historic building of unusual architectural interest.

One steps through the arched door in a high wall to find a small, enclosed garden with a flagged path leading to the wide front door of the house. In its façade decorative brickwork combines with local sandstone, and Dutch-style arches curve over the small-paned windows. There is an immense chimney-stack towering above – 30 feet in circumference. But the most striking feature of all is the great oak staircase inside, its two flights leading up to large, beamed bedrooms, simply but comfortably furnished; the banisters and newels handsomely carved.

The house has had many owners since it was built about 1620. For the last quarter-century, the Hughes family have farmed here, producing beef and corn. Mrs Hughes serves homely farmhouse meals (like Irish stew, fish pie, roast chicken etc.) usually with garden vegetables; or you can eat outstandingly well at, for instance, nearby Wootton Hatch.

Crossways is attractive to many people: walkers, because both the Pilgrims' Way and the Greensand Way are near (and you need no car – buses can be picked up only yards away); continental visitors, because it is a good half-way stop en route to the west country or to Wales; people making for Gatwick, because the

Guildford-Gatwick-Brighton coach stops only a few steps from the door. And for Londoners, it's an ideal weekend retreat: a drive of only half an hour or so.

For more about this area, see page 82.

The following facts have been supplied by the owners:

Bedrooms There are 3 rooms, which include single, double and family rooms. Bed-and-breakfast costs from £9 (per person in a double room) including service and VAT. There are reductions for stays of 5 nights or more.
Some if not all of the rooms have the following amenities: electric heaters; electric blankets, washbasin; armchairs; views of countryside/farmland/garden; choice of duvets or blankets; tea/coffee-making facilities; door keys. Hair drier and laundering facilities available.

Meals The dinner menu is fixed price (£5). There is no choice of dishes on the fixed menu, which consists of 3 courses and coffee. Dinner is served at 7 pm. Lunches and packed lunches can be provided. Wine and other alcoholic drinks can be brought in.

Public rooms There is a sitting-room with wood burner, TV (colour), books, magazines, local guides and leaflets, indoor games (such as board games, puzzles, cards). Maps and gumboots on loan.

Surroundings The grounds consist of a garden with croquet and putting. These are available in the neighbourhood: riding, golf, tennis, swimming, squash.

Cars The nearest main road is the A25 from Guildford to Dorking.

Closed to visitors We are not open from November to mid March except for house-parties of friends.

Crown Inn, Downham Market, south of King's Lynn, Norfolk, PE38 9DH   *Tel: 0366 382322*   C(14) PT ♯4

The unassuming and small façade of this inn, facing the market square, gives no hint of what lies behind. The 17th-century building straggles far back, and when you pass under the high arch (built for coaches) you come first to the bars and beyond them to what were once a considerable range of stables – since converted by Geoffrey Wareham into restaurant and kitchens, with rooms above: black-and-white pantiled buildings, with hanging baskets of flowers. These were once yeomanry barracks.

The bar is more or less as it has been for the last century or so – oak-panelled, jugs hanging from its beams, a brick hearth at each end. The bar is made from sherry casks, and on the walls are wartime photographs of the famous Pathfinders air squadron who, based nearby, used this bar as their 'local'. Below are cellars that

146

date from the time when there stood here a monastic lodge for visitors to the nearby priory (long gone).

The stable restaurant has been discreetly converted: floors and walls are of brick, solid elm tables stand in each former loose-box. A young chef works in full view at one end, cooking charcoal-grilled steaks or chops, for instance. Gâteaux, pâtés and everything else are made in the kitchens. A house speciality is Humble Pie (filled with sausage meat, potatoes and cheese). Breakfasts are served elsewhere – in a low-beamed Dickensian parlour, beyond which are two very handsome Jacobean staircases leading to the bedrooms (and a residents' sitting-room). These are spacious and furnished to a much higher standard than is usual in country inns: most have beautiful bathrooms en-suite, fully tiled.

From Downham Market one can tour north Norfolk. Royal Sandringham is a few miles in one direction, Ely cathedral in the other. The King's Lynn area is described on page 144.

The following facts have been supplied by the owners:

Bedrooms There are 10 rooms, which include single and double rooms. Bed-and-breakfast costs from £12 (per person in a double room) including service and VAT. There are 'bargain breaks'.

Some if not all of the rooms have the following amenities: central heating; washbasin, shower, own bathroom and wc, shaver-point; TV (colour), phone, armchairs; tea/coffee-making facilities; door keys.

Meals The dinner menu is à la carte. Dinner is served from 6–10 pm. Vegetarian or special diets can be prepared. Lunches and packed lunches can be provided; and snacks at other hours. Morning, afternoon or bedtime drinks (coffee, tea etc.) are free. Wine and other alcoholic drinks can be ordered.

Surroundings These are available in the neighbourhood: fishing, swimming, sailing, golf, squash, tennis.
Cars The nearest main road is the A10 from Ely to King's Lynn.
Credit cards accepted Most.

Cumbers House, Rogate, east of Petersfield, Hampshire, GU31 5EJ *Tel: 073080 401* C(10) **PT S** ⌗**9**

A large woodland garden screens this comfortable brick house from the road, and beyond are fine downland views. Every bedroom is spacious, has large casement windows, and is pleasantly furnished – for instance, white bedspreads and curtains contrasting with coral walls and chair-covers, flowers and bowls of pot-pourri on handsome mahogany or walnut furniture. In the green-and-grey sitting-room, there are pretty trifles around: ivory-framed miniatures, pots of velvety gloxinias or delicate streptocarpus, old china. Guests are welcome to play on the mellow and well-tuned Schiedmeyer, and to pass idle hours on the swing-seat in the garden, surrounded by varied firs, catalpa, magnolia and a fruitful fig-tree, chatting with Jon Aslett, who used to be in the Gurkhas. From the surrounding woods a deer occasionally wanders in, to be chased away by the tiny but ever-vigilant Licky, a Lancashire heeler.

Mrs Aslett is an excellent cook and produces imaginative meals – for instance, cucumber soup, Normandy chicken (with a creamy

rear view

148

apple sauce) and chocolate-brandy mousse. Bread is home-baked; eggs and honey are home-produced, too. Breakfast options include home-made fishcakes.

Non-smokers preferred.

Apart from the Georgian towns of Petersfield and Midhurst, both very near, Rogate is within a short drive of Chichester (cathedral, theatre, harbour, Roman palace); Petworth and Uppark, stately homes belonging to the National Trust; Broadlands (the Mountbatten home); Arundel (castle, river trips, antiques market, three museums, wildfowl trust); and even Portsmouth (for HMS *Victory* and Henry VIII's *Mary Rose*) and Brighton (the Regency Pavilion). There is polo to be watched at Midhurst; racing at Goodwood.

Readers' comments: Full of praise – maximum stars! Thoroughly enjoyed the welcome, and the cooking. Delightfully warm welcome, pretty rooms, delicious food, a great deal of trouble taken for our comfort. Excellent value.

The following facts have been supplied by the owners:

Bedrooms There are 3 rooms, which include a single and doubles. Bed-and-breakfast costs from £12 (per person) including service and VAT; prices go up in high season.
  Some if not all of the rooms have the following amenities: central heating or electric heaters; electric blankets, washbasin, shower, own bathroom and wc, shaver-point; radio, TV (colour), armchairs; views of countryside or garden, tea/coffee-making facilities. Breakfast in bed is available; and bed-boards, hair drier, iron.

Meals The dinner menu is fixed price (£7) or à la carte. There is a choice of dishes on the menu, which consists of 3 courses, wine and coffee. Dinner is served at 7.30 pm. Special diets can be prepared. Morning, afternoon or bedtime drinks (coffee, tea etc.) can be ordered for a charge. Non-residents are not admitted to the dining-room. Wine and other alcoholic drinks can be brought in.

Public rooms There is a sitting-room with central heating, open fire, TV (colour), books, magazines, local guides and leaflets, indoor games (such as Scrabble, Monopoly, cards etc.), piano.

Surroundings The grounds consist of 3½ acres of woodland, lawns etc. Badminton and croquet. Tennis is available in the neighbourhood. Cycle on loan, also maps and gumboots.

Cars The nearest main road is the A272 from Midhurst to Petersfield.

**Dairy Farm, Cranford St Andrew, east of Kettering,
Northamptonshire, NN14 4AQ**   *Tel: 053678 273*   **C S X ⌗7**

This is not in fact a dairy farm but arable and sheep. Its name
derives from the old dairy (now the dining-room) around which
the manor house was built, in 1610. It is a fine building with
mullioned lattice windows in limestone walls and a thatched roof.
Its noble chimney-stacks, finials on the gables, dormer windows
and dignified porch give it great character. In the grounds stands a
circular stone dovecote (mediaeval) with unique rotating ladder
inside, used for collecting the birds from the 400 pigeonholes that
line it.

Audrey and John Clarke have hung old family portraits in the
hall and sitting-room, and furnished the house with things like an
oak dresser, chests and ladderback chairs that are in keeping with
it.

Meals consist of straightforward home cooking – soups, roasts,
fruit pies – using fruit and vegetables from the garden. Mrs Clarke
also does a cordon bleu menu, which costs a little more and has to
be ordered ahead.

Visitors enjoy local walks (beside a willow-fringed stream,
across-country, or simply to the Woolpack Inn). This is good
cycling country, too. Sightseeing possibilities include Burleigh
House, Rockingham Castle, the mediaeval stone town of Stamford, Althorp (home of the Princess of Wales's father), Lamport
and Kirby Halls, Peterborough Cathedral, Cambridge, Uppingham and Oundle; and at Kettering, Wicksteed Park is an ideal

place to take children. Oundle is as attractive as many old Cotswold towns, for the local stone is the same, but much less frequented by tourists. The buildings of its famous public school are like an Oxford college. One can take boat trips on the River Nene, and visit watermills and a country park just on the outskirts. For more about this area, see page 306.

The following facts have been supplied by the owners:

Bedrooms There are 3 rooms, which include single, double and family rooms. Dinner, bed-and-breakfast costs £16.50 (per person in a double room) including service and VAT. There are reductions for stays of 4 nights or more.
   Some if not all of the rooms have the following amenities: central heating or electric heaters; electric blankets, washbasin, own bathroom and wc, shaver-point; radio, TV, armchairs; views of countryside/farmland/garden; door keys. Breakfast in bed is available.

Meals The dinner menu is fixed price (£4.50) or à la carte. There is no choice of dishes on the fixed menu, which consists of 3 courses and coffee. Dinner is served at 7 pm. Special diets can be prepared. Lunches and packed lunches can be provided; and snacks at other hours. Morning, afternoon or bedtime drinks (coffee, tea etc.) can be ordered for a charge. Non-residents are not admitted to the dining-room. Wine and other alcoholic drinks can be brought in.

Public rooms There is a sitting-room with central heating, open fire, TV (colour), books, magazines, local guides and leaflets, record-player and records.

Surroundings The grounds consist of a garden with croquet.

Cars The nearest main road is the A604 from Kettering to Cambridge.

Damsells Cross and Damsells Lodge, The Park, Painswick, south of Gloucester, Gloucestershire, GL6 6SR
Tel: 0452 813197 (Cross) and 0452 813777 (Lodge)
D H S S-C PT ⌘6

Mrs Pointer and Mrs Cooke are sisters, living in houses next to one another. The first is a stone mansion in traditional Cotswold style (mullioned windows with leaded panes, solid oak doors that have iron fittings which were specially made by a local blacksmith, wide corridors and elegant arches indoors), and the second is a smaller but still very comfortable house, originally the lodge to the mansion. Both are in a peaceful rural lane and have truly spectacular views from every window. The Lodge has a small garden of lawns, stone terrace and flowering shrubs; Damsells Cross is surrounded by (at the front) a sunken garden with drystone walls and stone troughs of flowers and (at the back) terraces and a swimming-pool, all against a backdrop of fine trees. At both only breakfast is provided – guests eat dinner at the nearby Royal William or in one of Painswick's restaurants.

At the big house, Mrs Pointer has chosen very pretty fabrics for the large bedrooms – lacy bedspreads, or white flower-sprigged ones matching the wallpaper. Breakfast is eaten at a big table of figured mahogany in a bay window which overlooks the garden, its swimming-pool and the leafy view beyond.

Mrs Cooke is a welcoming hostess who soon makes friends with her visitors (they sometimes end up playing piano duets with her!). She has made the Lodge immaculate and very comfortable. The huge sitting-room has windows on three sides, and a big log stove. Everywhere there are thick carpets and good furniture (even the bathroom is pretty luxurious). In my view, the best bedroom is one separate from the house: it is in a one-floor garden cottage, with huge sliding windows through which to step straight onto the lawn or to view the distant hills while still in bed and ideal for anyone who finds stairs difficult.

In the Middle Ages, Painswick village was once a wealthy wool town, as its fine stone houses and great church testify. It is famous for its 99 enormous yews, centuries-old, clipped into arches or other neat shapes, and for its fine peal of twelve bells. The ideal time to visit is in late September, when the annual yew-clipping takes place, with children dancing and singing in a circle round the churchyard. To the north lies the cathedral city of Gloucester, and to the south the wooded Cotswold hills, with particularly spectacular views from Minchinhampton and Rodborough Commons (National Trust land). Go west for the Severn estuary with its throngs of seabirds and geese. Also in the area are Slimbridge Wildfowl Trust, Westonbirt Arboretum, Badminton House (a Palladian mansion, where the Queen is often seen at the spring horse trials), 12th-century Berkeley Castle in its lovely grounds, and a village named Paradise, with its pub the Adam-and-Eve.

Readers' comments: Mrs Pointer is a delightful hostess – good breakfast, lovely garden.

The following information relates to Damsells Cross:

Bedrooms There are 2 rooms, which include single, double or family rooms. Bed-and-breakfast costs from £12.50 (per person in a double room) including service and VAT; prices go up in high season.
   Some if not all of the rooms have the following amenities: central heating or gas heaters; electric blankets, washbasin, shower, shaver-point; radio, TV (colour), armchairs; views of countryside, farmland, garden; choice of duvets or blankets; tea/coffee-making facilities; door keys. Breakfast in bed is available.

Public rooms There is a sitting-room with central heating, open fire, TV (colour), books, magazines, local guides and leaflets.

Surroundings The grounds consist of 5 acres of garden with tennis court and unheated swimming-pool.

Cars The nearest main road is the A46 from Stroud to Cheltenham.

Dedham Hall, Dedham, north of Colchester, Essex CO7 6AD
Tel: 0206 323027　　**H PT ☼4**

Set back from the village, beyond a large green (where sheep graze) and a big duckpond, stands this lovely old house, with a wide-spreading magnolia tree in front of it and gardens all around. Wisteria and clematis clamber up its pink walls. Just beyond the pantiled barns and the lawns, spangled with daffodils in spring, is Dedham's fine mediaeval church.

   When the Slingos moved here there was an immense amount to do. The house, which developed in stages from the 14th to 17th centuries, had once been the miller's house and a bakery (the watermill itself is being turned into flats). Now it is elegantly furnished with antiques, decorated in lovely colours and filled with flowers from the garden. Every room, from the beamed hall to the

153

carpeted and wallpapered bathroom, is attractive. In the sitting-room, a log fire is lit on chilly evenings.

The food in the beamed dining-room is very good; home-grown vegetables are served and home-made bread. A typical dinner might consist of avocado and walnut mousse, outstandingly good roast beef with Yorkshire pudding, and meringues. Home-made jam, chutneys and honey are on sale.

Picturesque Dedham is, of course, celebrated for its Constable connection. The painter's great-great-grandson still lives here, and it was he who advised William Slingo when he decided to start offering art holidays at Dedham Hall. A 15th-century barn has been converted into a studio (and opposite is another converted into a bedroom suite suitable for disabled visitors). Some courses last a week, others for only a few days, with tutors who are experts in landscape, flower or portrait painting.

The valley of the River Stour is one of the most beautiful in England, still much as it was when Constable painted landscapes here, and well provided with footpaths. His Flatford Mill is only two miles away from Dedham. Among many picturesque villages just across the Suffolk border, mediaeval Lavenham and Kersey are perhaps the most famous. The sea is only a half-hour away in the opposite direction; and the Romano-Norman city of Colchester is close.

Reader's comment: Most enjoyable.

The following facts have been supplied by the owners:

Bedrooms There are 12 rooms, which include singles, doubles and family rooms. Bed-and-breakfast costs from £13.50 (per person in a double room) including service and VAT. There are reductions for stays of 7 nights or more.

Some if not all of the rooms have the following amenities: central heating or electric heaters; electric blankets, washbasin, shower, own bathroom and wc, shaver-point; armchairs; views of countryside, lake, farmland, garden; choice of duvets or blankets; tea/coffee-making facilities; door keys.

Meals The dinner menu is fixed price (£9.50). There is no choice of dishes on the fixed menu, which consists of 3 courses and coffee. Dinner is served at 7.30 pm. Special diets can be prepared. Non-residents are not usually admitted to the dining-room. Wine and other alcoholic drinks can be ordered.

Public rooms There are 2 sitting-rooms etc. The following are available in one or both of them: central heating, open fire, TV (colour), video recorder, books, magazines, local guides and leaflets, indoor games (such as Scrabble, Ludo and cards), piano, bar. Bridge can be arranged.

Surroundings The grounds consist of 6 acres of garden and paddock, with croquet. These are available in the neighbourhood: golf, fishing, riding.

Cars The nearest main road is the A12 from Ipswich to Chelmsford.

Closed to visitors We are not open mid-December to end-February.

For bed-and-breakfast only, **Upper Park** (tel: 0206 323197) at Dedham is excellent. It is full of family heirlooms, paintings and beautiful furnishings. (One can dine at Dedham Hall, by arrangement, or at the Marlborough Head in the middle of Dedham, for instance.) Mrs Watson and her daughter are immensely attentive to visitors' every need.

Deep Thatch Cottage, Rodmell, south of Lewes, East Sussex, BN7 3HF *Tel: 0273 477865* **C PT S X ⌗3**

The Frasers' weatherboarded and thatched cottage, with small lattice-paned windows, is in a delightful South Downs village near the River Ouse. Their guests often include archaeologists working at Lewes Castle (who have told them that parts of the cottage date from the 12th century), or literary historians who come for the Virginia Woolf connection: she lived in Rodmell (her house, now in the care of the National Trust, is open to the public) and ended her troubled life in the Ouse. Some older villagers still remember her.

The dining-room (which has pine furniture and a folk-weave rug) opens onto a large south-facing garden with high trees surrounding its winding lawn. In the deep-carpeted sitting-room, antiques and a big sofa face the log fire. Upstairs, every bedroom (low beamed and with board doors) enjoys a garden view; some have appliqué or patchwork bedspreads.

Bernadette, who used to run a restaurant in Brighton, cooks such things as individual pies (steak-and-kidney, chicken-and-mushroom), or fresh local fish, with garden vegetables; followed perhaps by lemon meringue tart or garden raspberries and cream (two courses only, but plentiful second helpings and unlimited coffee).

rear view

She willingly meets people arriving from the continent at Newhaven, or at Lewes station (London is only 50 minutes away); who thereafter walk the Downs or go sightseeing by local bus, to historic Lewes and beyond. She also welcomes people who choose this placid spot for a stay-put convalescence (there is a downstairs bedroom).

Rodmell itself has an excellent pub and a Norman church worth visiting. It lies close to the least spoilt area of this part of the coast, about which much more has been written under other entries.

The following facts have been supplied by the owners:

Bedrooms There are 4 rooms, which include single, double and family rooms. Bed-and-breakfast costs from £15 (per person) including service and VAT; prices go up in high season. There are reductions for stays of 7 nights or more; and 'bargain breaks' as well.

Some if not all of the rooms have the following amenities: central heating; electric blankets, own bathroom and wc, shaver-point; TV (colour), armchairs; views of garden; tea/coffee-making facilities; door keys. Breakfast in bed is available.

Meals The dinner menu is fixed price (£5). There is no choice of dishes on the fixed menu, which consists of 2 courses and coffee. Dinner is served when it suits guests. Vegetarian or special diets can be prepared. Lunches and packed lunches can be provided; and snacks at other hours. Morning, afternoon or bedtime drinks (coffee, tea etc.) can be ordered free. Non-residents are not admitted to the dining-room. Wine and other alcoholic drinks can be brought in.

Public rooms There is a sitting-room with central heating, open fire, TV (colour), books, magazines, local guides and leaflets.

Surroundings The grounds consist of a garden.

Cars The nearest main road is the A7 from Lewes to Newhaven.

Drummond Arms, Albury, east of Guildford, Surrey, GU5 9AG
Tel: 048 641 2039   **D PT ♯3**

The crowning jewel of this country inn is a fast-flowing stream (the Tillingbourne) which runs among the willows at the end of its secluded garden, enclosed by beech hedges and yews. It is surrounded by woods where pigeons coo.

The bedroom which has the best views of the garden is no. 7. All are spacious and well-carpeted, with armchairs, TV and pleasant colour schemes chosen by Mrs Ranson.

Downstairs, there is a formal dining-room, but I preferred to eat in the more convivial atmosphere of the bar (traditionally furnished with tapestry seats, pewter and Toby jugs) where the so-called snacks are excellent and inexpensive: braised liver, for instance, and perfectly cooked fruit pies.

Albury is tucked away in one of the most scenic parts of the high Surrey Downs, with the famous viewpoint of Newlands Corner nearby, the brilliantly blue Silent Pool, picturesque Shere village and its stream, a celebrated blacksmith-automaton striking the hours at Abinger Hammer, National Trust woodlands, and – along the pretty little River Tillingbourne – trout farms and watercress beds. The historic towns of Guildford and Dorking are described elsewhere.

Albury itself is an interesting village: many of its small cottages have immense, ornate chimneys copied from those at Hampton Court. Drummond is a family name of the Duke of Northumberland, local landowner. Parts of the local mansion, Albury Park (which he owns), are open to the public, and in its grounds – originally landscaped by John Evelyn – are two contrasting churches of historic interest.

The following facts have been supplied by the owners:

Bedrooms There are 7 rooms, which include single and double rooms. Bed-and-breakfast costs from £13 (per person in a double room) including service and VAT.

Some if not all of the rooms have the following amenities: central heating; washbasin, own bathroom and wc, shaver-point; radio, TV (colour), armchairs; views of garden; choice of duvets or blankets; orthopaedic mattress; tea/coffee-making facilities; door keys.

Meals The dinner menu is à la carte. Dinner is served from 7.30 pm. Vegetarian or special diets can be prepared. Lunches and packed lunches can be provided. Wine and other alcoholic drinks can be ordered.

Surroundings The grounds consist of a lawn. These are available in the neighbourhood: riding, fishing.

Cars The nearest main road is the A25 from Dorking to Guildford.

Languages spoken French, Spanish, Italian.

Credit cards accepted Diners Club, Amex, Visa, Access.

Duckswich House, Welland Road, Upton-on-Severn, south of Worcester, WR8 0QW *Tel: 06846 2145* **C D H S ⌗4**

Oliver Messel had a hand in the design of this lovely house which, though built as late as 1952, has a distinctly 'thirties look in some of its detail – and in colour-schemes with shell pink, shades of beige or pale greens predominating. It could be the setting for a Noel Coward play.

The long sitting-room has scalloped alcoves for china, and French doors opening onto a stone terrace with wrought-iron balustrade, from which one can step down to the lawns of a landscaped garden and its lake beyond. Some of the fittings in the house – such as mirror-glass light switches and elaborate drapes – are like those which Messel used when designing interiors at The Dorchester.

Bedrooms are spacious, with pretty bedheads and wallpapers. Christine Smithson has added good paintings and prints, with ewers of flowers everywhere.

In the dining-room are a very fine yew table, shield-back chairs and a built-in sideboard of palest walnut. Here Christine serves such meals as salmon mousse with prawns, beef olives and orange/lemon charlotte. Artichokes, asparagus and other vegetables are home-grown.

For a description of the Upton area, see page 357.

The following facts have been supplied by the owners:

Bedrooms There are 8 rooms, which include single, double and family rooms. Bed-and-breakfast costs from £12.50 (per person) including service and VAT; prices go up in high season. There are reductions for stays of 2 nights or more; and 'bargain breaks' as well.

    Some if not all of the rooms have the following amenities: central heating or electric heaters; electric blankets, washbasin, shower, own bathroom and wc, shaver-point; armchairs; views of countryside or garden; choice of duvets or blankets; tea/coffee-making facilities; door keys. Breakfast in bed is available.

Meals The dinner menu is fixed price (£10.50). There is no choice of dishes on the menu, which consists of 3 courses and coffee. Dinner is served at 7–7.30 pm. Vegetarian or special diets can be prepared. Lunches and packed lunches can be provided; and snacks at other hours. Morning, afternoon or bedtime drinks (coffee, tea etc.) can be ordered for a charge. Non-residents are not admitted to the dining-room. Wine and other alcoholic drinks can be ordered or brought in.

159

Public rooms There are 2 sitting-rooms etc. The following are available in one or both of them: central heating, open fire, TV (colour), books, magazines, local guides and leaflets, indoor games (such as chess, draughts, etc.), piano, record-player and records; bar.

Surroundings The grounds consist of 6½ acres of gardens, with tennis and croquet. These are available in the neighbourhood: riding, fishing, river boats.

Cars The nearest main road is the A38 from Upton to Worcester.

Durham University: Trevelyan College and St Aidan's College, Elvet Hill Road, Durham, DH1 3LN *Tel: 0385 61133 (Trevelyan); 0385 65011 (St Aidan's)* C H(only St Aidan's) **PT S ⊞11**

Unlike some newer universities, which were built at a distance from any town, the colleges of Durham are within a short walk of the city centre. Two which provide accommodation for visitors are very economical and pleasant bases from which to explore this enjoyable city.

The accommodation is available to visitors only during university vacations (which fortunately coincide with the main holiday periods); and it is mostly in single rooms, with some twin-bedded ones but no doubles. Trevelyan College has won an award for its accommodation.

St Aidan's (see picture) and Trevelyan College share a park-like site with other colleges, where there are lots of trees and shrubs (and very convenient parking). Both are good examples of the architecture of the great expansion in universities which took place in the 1960s – the first by Sir Basil Spence and the second by Stillman & Eastwick-Field.

In both, the bedrooms are off narrow corridors which follow a roughly circular path round the building. All have washbasins, and bathrooms are close. There are also small pantries for preparing hot drinks, and coin-operated washing machines. These are available to visitors, as are plenty of sitting-rooms and such facilities as tennis courts (at St Aidan's), television room, bar, and pool table. A public golf course and squash courts are nearby. Most of the rooms have views of grass and trees. Those at Trevelyan College are not all rectangular in shape, and at both the windows are angled to give a pleasant feeling of privacy. Furnishings are light and modern.

Visitors are served in the dining-hall, with the tables arranged in groups. The hall at St Aidan's, with one of Sir Basil Spence's characteristic barrel-vaulted roofs, gives a splendid view of the cathedral and city through tall windows. At Trevelyan College, the impressive windowless hall is hung with big modern paintings.

Breakfast is the standard English one, but other meals (lunches are available) are an improvement over much institutional food. At St Aidan's, dinner cooked by Mr Park might consist of French onion soup, chicken chasseur and chocolate mousse. At Trevelyan College the menu might be hors d'oeuvres, entrecôte Bourguignonne with parmentier potatoes and salsify, and strawberry syllabub (cooked by Barry Fitzpatrick).

Minutes away from the colleges is the university's Oriental Museum, a priceless collection. The centre of Durham City is about a quarter of an hour's walk (or there are buses from a stop near the colleges).

Durham, among cathedral cities, bears comparison with York, and it has been less self-consciously preserved. The cathedral, probably the grandest Norman building in Europe, dominates it, with the castle alongside. They stand high in a tight loop of the Wear (along which there is a riverside path), surrounded by picturesque streets, some quiet and some bustling. There are good booksellers and other shops for browsing, including an interesting covered market.

There is plenty of scope for excursions, to Lindisfarne and the sandy Northumbrian coast, to the undervalued countryside of County Durham, or down into Yorkshire along the A1.

Note: many universities offer comparable accommodation. For a full list write to British Universities Accommodation Consortium (SOTBT), c/o The University, Nottingham.

The following facts have been supplied by the Bursars:

St Aidan's (Bursar: Cmdr. Bull)

Bedrooms There are 320 rooms, which include single and twin-bedded rooms. Bed-and-breakfast costs £10 (per person) including service and VAT. There are reductions for stays of 5 nights or more; and special offers for a full week's board.

Some if not all of the rooms have the following amenities: central heating; washbasin; armchairs; views of garden; balcony; tea/coffee-making facilities; door keys.

Meals The dinner menu is fixed price (£6). There is no choice of dishes on the fixed menu, which consists of 4 courses and coffee. Dinner is served at 6.30 pm. Special diets can be prepared. Lunches and packed lunches can be provided. Morning, afternoon or bedtime drinks (coffee, tea etc.) are available from vending machine or from pantry for a charge. Non-residents are not admitted to the dining-room. Wine and other alcoholic drinks can be ordered.

Public rooms There are 2 sitting-rooms etc. The following are available in one or both of them: central heating, TV, local guides and leaflets, piano, bar.

Surroundings The grounds consist of 2 acres of landscaped gardens. The following games or sports are available in the grounds: tennis, croquet. Golf is available in the neighbourhood.

Cars The nearest main road is the A1050 from Durham to Darlington.

Languages spoken French.

Closed to visitors We are not open from October to late March and late April to early July.

Trevelyan College (Bursar: Lt. Col. D. A. Brown)

Bedrooms There are 276 rooms, which include single and twin-bedded rooms. Bed-and-breakfast costs from £8.25 (per person in a double room) including service and VAT. Sampler breaks available (see page 14).

All rooms have the following amenities: central heating; washbasin; shaver-point; armchairs; views of countryside, garden; choice of duvets or blankets; tea/coffee-making facilities; door keys.

Meals The dinner menu is fixed price (£4.75). There is no choice of dishes on the fixed menu, which consists of 3 courses and coffee. Dinner is served at 6.30 pm. Special diets can be prepared. Lunches and packed lunches can be provided; and snacks at other hours. Morning or afternoon drinks (coffee, tea etc.) can be ordered for a charge. Wine and other alcoholic drinks can be ordered or brought in.

Public rooms There are 5 sitting-rooms etc. The following are available in one or more of them: central heating, TV, books, magazines, local guides and leaflets, indoor games (such as table tennis, cards), piano, bar.

Surroundings The grounds consist of 9 acres of park, with tennis. These are available in the neighbourhood: tennis, squash, golf, swimming, boating.

Cars The nearest main road is the A1.

Closed to visitors We are not open at the following periods: mid Jan to mid March; mid April to end of June.

Easton House, Chidham, west of Chichester, West Sussex, PO18 8TF *Tel: 0243 572514*   **C D PT S ⌗5**

Every corner of this Tudor house has been filled by Mary Hartley with unusual furniture and trifles. A modern white-and-red poppy wallpaper contrasts with old beams, oriental rugs with stone-flagged floor, scarlet folkweave curtains with antique chandeliers. Jim Hartley collects mirrors (Spanish, art deco, rococo – every conceivable kind) and pictures of cats; Mary makes patchwork; guests play on the Bechstein if so inclined. It's a free-and-easy atmosphere, a house full of character, and fun. Even the bathrooms are pretty, with delicately sprigged wallpapers.

Although this is only a bed-and-breakfast house (one can dine well in Chichester, particularly at Thompson's, or in the waterfront inns of Bosham), visitors are welcome to linger in the comfortable lime-green sitting-room with its log stove (where tea is served on arrival); or in the garden, under the shade of magnolia and walnut trees.

Peaceful Chidham looks across an inlet to ancient Bosham, one of the most picturesque sailing villages on the winding shores of Chichester's lovely natural harbour (with boat trips): very popular and therefore very crowded in high summer. Chichester itself is near. It has a mediaeval cathedral, Georgian houses and a festival theatre of considerable renown.

Wherever you drive or walk there is fine scenery; and plenty of interesting sights within a few miles – such as the Weald &

Downland Open-Air Museum (acres of ancient buildings recon-structed), the huge Roman palace of Fishbourne, a brass-rubbing centre in Chichester and crafts complex in Bosham (which also has an open-air theatre), fine gardens at West Dean, a fascinating 'live' museum of mechanical music (organs, pianolas etc.), military aircraft at Tangmere, rose nursery at Apuldram, Kingley Vale nature reserve and Chilsdown vineyard.

The Arundel-Petworth area, too, is close, described elsewhere in this book.

Readers' comments: Peaceful house with great character, very reasonably priced.

The following facts have been supplied by the owners:

Bedrooms There are 3 rooms, which include double and family rooms. Bed-and-breakfast costs from £10.50 (per person) including service.
    Some if not all of the rooms have the following amenities: central heating or electric heaters; washbasin, shower, own bathroom and wc, shaver-point; armchairs; views of sea, countryside, farmland, garden; tea/coffee-making facilities; also laundering, hair drier and electric blankets.
Public rooms There is a sitting-room with central heating, open fire, TV (colour), books, magazines, local guides and leaflets, indoor games (such as Monopoly, Scrabble etc. and jigsaws), piano. Maps on loan.
Surroundings The grounds consist of a garden. These are available in the neighbourhood: sailing, golf, tennis.
Cars The nearest main road is the A27 from Chichester to Portsmouth.
Languages spoken French and German.

Ebury Hotel, New Dover Road, Canterbury, Kent, CT1 3DX
Tel: 0227 68433   C D H PT S-C ⏾15

This is a very big Victorian mansion (run by Jane and Anthony Mason), set back from a main road out of Canterbury, with an acre of garden at the rear. The food and furnishings are conven-tional, with much emphasis on comfort and space. The sitting-room is huge and, like the other rooms, immaculately kept. There is an indoor swimming-pool.

As to dinner, there are four choices at each course – mainly classic dishes like salmon mayonnaise, steak Bercy or roast duck, cooked by Joseph Keyes.

The city centre is within walking distance: its attractions are described on page 343. The Ebury Hotel, being on the road to

Dover, is a useful place to stay before or after a ferry-crossing to the continent – or as a base from which to explore the historic south Kent coast, the Cinque Ports, Dover Castle and Dover's famous Roman 'Painted House' or the Kent countryside, the garden of England.

The following facts have been supplied by the owners:

Bedrooms There are 15 rooms, which include single, double and family rooms. Bed-and-breakfast costs from £18 (per person in a double room) including VAT. There are reductions for stays of 2 nights or more; and 'bargain breaks' as well. **A 10% discount is offered to readers of this book.**

All of the rooms have the following amenities: central heating or electric heaters; washbasin, shower, own bathroom and wc, shaver-point; colour TV, phone, armchairs; garden view; choice of duvets or blankets; door keys. Continental breakfast in bed is available.

Meals The dinner menu is fixed price (£8.50) or à la carte. There is a choice of dishes on the menu, which consists of 3 courses and coffee. Dinner is served from 7 pm. Special diets can be prepared. Lunches and packed lunches can be provided; and snacks at other hours. Morning, afternoon or bedtime drinks (coffee, tea etc.) can be ordered for a charge. Wine and other alcoholic drinks can be ordered.

Public rooms There is a sitting-room, with central heating, open fire, colour TV, books, magazines, local guides and leaflets and a bar. Swimming-pool (82°).

Surroundings The grounds consist of 2 acres of lawn. These are available in the neighbourhood: golf, fishing, squash, tennis.

Cars The nearest main road is the A2 from London to Dover.

Edgehill Hotel, Hadleigh, Suffolk, IP7 5AP
Tel: 0473 822458   **C D PT ⌗4**

Hadleigh, once a rich wool town, went through bad times but is now prospering again. As a result, its very lengthy High Street is full of shops enjoying a new life as wine bars, antique shops and so forth. It is a street of colourful façades, gables, pargetting (decorative plasterwork), overhanging bay windows, carved wood details, ornamental porches and fanlights over the doors. Behind lie meadows and a river.

One of the High Street's many fine buildings to have been rejuvenated recently is a Tudor house with Georgian façade which is now this private hotel. Rodney Rolfe, formerly the manager of a motor dealer's, took over Edgehill Hotel in 1976 and began to convert it. The well-proportioned rooms have been furnished in good taste, and attractive wallpapers chosen for each one. In all the spacious bedrooms there are thick-pile carpets and good furniture. The large sitting-room has glass doors opening onto the walled garden, and on cold days there is a blazing fire.

Angela Rolfe, previously a teacher, and her mother do all the cooking and use home-grown raspberries, strawberries, vegetables and other produce from the kitchen garden. She serves home-made soup, roasts and 'good, old-fashioned puddings' like plum duff, rice or bread-and-butter pudding. She is not only a good cook, but makes and sells crafts.

This is a good base from which to explore the very pretty countryside and villages nearby, and such well-known beauty-spots as mediaeval Lavenham, Dedham, Woodbridge on the Deben estuary, Kersey, Long Melford and many others. There are stately homes to visit nearby and the castle at Colchester.

The following facts have been supplied by the owners:

Bedrooms There are 6 rooms, which include single, double and family rooms. Bed-and-breakfast costs from £14 (per person in a double room) including service and VAT. There are reductions for stays of 5 nights or more; and winter weekend 'bargain breaks' as well. Sunday accommodation free to over-60s staying 3 days. Sampler breaks (see page 14).

Some if not all of the rooms have the following amenities: central heating, double glazing; washbasin, shower, own bathroom and wc, shaver-point; TV, armchairs; door keys. Breakfast in bed is available; also hair drier and laundering.

Meals The dinner menu is fixed price (£7.50). There is no choice of main course on the fixed menu, which consists of 3 courses and coffee. Dinner is served at 7 pm. Special diets can be prepared. Packed lunches can be provided; and snacks at other hours. Morning, afternoon or bedtime drinks (coffee, tea etc.) can be ordered for a charge. Wine and other alcoholic drinks can be ordered.

Public rooms There is a sitting room with central heating, open fire, colour TV, books, magazines, local guides and leaflets, indoor games.

Surroundings The grounds consist of a walled flower garden and a vegetable garden.

Cars The nearest main road is the A12 from London to Ipswich.

Edward King House, Old Palace, Lincoln, LN2 1PU
Tel: 0522 28778   **C PT S ⌗4**

This is one of my most interesting finds, named for the bishop who in 1888 enlarged it from a small 18th-century building (adjoining the mediaeval ruins of the original bishop's palace) to its present dimensions.

Its situation is superb. High up, some of its bedroom windows – and its garden – overlook the city roofs below; while those on the other side have an unsurpassed view of Lincoln Cathedral, floodlit at night, which looms up right above the house.

The premises are sometimes used for clerical gatherings, or as accommodation during the city's quarterly Assizes; so you may find it full of bishops or barristers at certain times – and what you get for dinner (served in a separate room from that used for such conference participants) will depend on what they are eating: a homely set meal, or a sophisticated à la carte to choose from, with price varying accordingly. Meals are served only when a conference is on. At other times you may dine in one of Lincoln's many restaurants.

The two dining-rooms are handsome. Details like grey-and-white panelling with alcoves and gilt-framed mirrors in one, for instance; in the other, the navy tablecloths and sprigged napkins contrast with red damask walls on which portraits of bishops hang. There are flowers on every table.

An unusual staircase under an oval ceiling leads up to a primrose-and-white sitting-room dedicated to one of Lincoln's sons, Australian explorer Matthew Flinders, whose wife's botanical drawings decorate the walls. (By chance, the present warden of the house is Australian.) Pretty bergère armchairs stand around, complemented by well chosen lamps and cushions.

Unusual and varied fireplaces are a particular feature throughout the house, including the conference room where you can sometimes visit art exhibitions. And a long stone passageway takes you to the 15th-century buttery, now used as a chapel, of the original palace: it has a fine coffered and painted ceiling.

Bedrooms are immaculate. Sprigged fabrics and papers give them a cottagey look.

(When phoning to book, ask for Margaret Mitchell.)

Lincoln is one of England's finest old cities. The cathedral and castle perch on a 200-foot ridge; narrow streets of mediaeval houses wind downhill from these. There is a Roman gateway, unique in that traffic still passes through it, and others built in the Middle Ages or Tudor period. There's a boating marina, a mediaeval bridge with premises on it, and all around contrasting countryside – flat fens, the rolling Wolds, a sandy coastline and fine churches in old villages, all best appreciated after visiting the Museum of Lincolnshire Life (in Lincoln).

The following facts have been supplied by the owners:

Bedrooms There are 18 rooms, which include single, double and family rooms. Bed-and-breakfast costs from £10.50 (per person in a double room) including service and VAT; prices go up in high season.

Some if not all of the rooms have the following amenities: electric heaters; washbasin; armchairs; views of cathedral or of garden; choice of duvets or blankets; tea/coffee-making facilities; door keys.

Meals The dinner menu is fixed price (£4.50). There is no choice of dishes on the fixed menu, which consists of 3 courses and coffee. Dinner is served at 6.30 or 7 pm. Special diets can be prepared. Lunches and packed lunches can be provided; and snacks at other hours. Morning, afternoon or bedtime drinks (coffee, tea etc.) can be ordered for a charge. Wine and other alcoholic drinks can be ordered.

Public rooms There are 2 sitting-rooms etc. The following are available in one or both of them: central heating, TV (colour), books, magazines, local guides and leaflets, piano, record-player and records, bar.

Surroundings The grounds consist of a garden.

Cars The nearest main road is the A15 from Lincoln to Peterborough.

Languages spoken French.

A modern alternative 5 minutes from the centre is **Carline Guest House** (tel: 0522 30422) which is kept in immaculate and comfortable style by John Pritchard. Bed-and-breakfast only – unusually well-equipped rooms.

Etchilhampton House, Etchilhampton, south-east of Devizes, Wiltshire, SN10 3JH   *Tel: 0380 2927*   **C D ♯5**

This gracious house (surrounded by lawns, fine trees and the herbaceous borders of a walled garden) was built by a local merchant in the 18th century. Now it is the home of Priscilla and Michael Maude, both widely travelled. Priscilla used to work in the British embassies of Rome and Paris, there developing a taste for the arts (she is now an organizer of the local Decorative and Fine Arts Society).

In the green-and-white dining-room with garden view, there is 18th-century mahogany furniture – but only seersucker table-cloths. Here are served (if pre-booked) such traditional meals as melon, chicken casserole, and a pavlova or fruit pie, perhaps. There is a coral sitting-room with alcoves full of books; and from the big hall a fine staircase rises to spacious bedrooms – their large sash windows have garden views. Flowery wallpapers (even in a bathroom) and simple furniture predominate.

rear view

Guests are welcome to use the garden, the croquet lawn, tennis court and heated covered swimming-pool. The best view of the wisteria-covered house is from the back: to one side of the door, with pretty fanlight under its arch, is a great wall-sundial ('I only tell ye sunnie hours'). At the side of the house is a sunken rose-garden, brick-paved.

Visitors staying here (only 2 hours from London) find the local scenery delightful, but can go further afield to visit Bath, Longleat and other stately homes, prehistoric Avebury and Stonehenge, Salisbury Cathedral and even (just in Wales) Chepstow Castle and the Wye Valley. This is good cycling and walking country (with views of the famous white horses carved into the chalky downs), and one can go on the historic Kennet and Avon Canal.

The following facts have been supplied by the owners:

Bedrooms There are 4 rooms, which include single, double and family rooms. Bed-and-breakfast costs from £10 (per person in a double room) including service and VAT.

Some if not all of the rooms have the following amenities: electric heaters; washbasin; radio, TV, armchairs; views of countryside and garden; choice of duvets or blankets; tea/coffee-making facilities; door keys.

Meals The dinner menu is fixed price (£7). There is no choice of dishes on the menu, which consists of 4 courses and coffee. Dinner is served at 7.30 pm. Morning, afternoon or bedtime drinks (coffee, tea etc.) can be ordered free. Wine and other alcoholic drinks can be brought in.

Public rooms There are 2 sitting-rooms etc. The following are available in one or both of them: open fire, TV, books, magazines, local guides and leaflets, indoor games (such as cards, Bagatelle, board games), piano.

Surroundings The grounds consist of 8 acres of garden and paddock, with tennis, croquet and heated (75°) swimming-pool. Golf and riding are available in the neighbourhood.

Cars The nearest main road is the A342 from Devizes to Andover.

Languages spoken French, German, Italian.

Fairlight Hall, Fairlight, east of Hastings, East Sussex, TN35 5DR
Tel: 0424 813145   C(7) **D** S-C ♯3

This is an extraordinary building in a spectacular setting, which enjoys quiet. A mock-castle, it was built in 1853 by a local magnate who surrounded it with grass terraces from which to enjoy the sea view across to France and with sequoias and other stately trees. In May, rhododendrons flanking the long drive come into bloom. Close by are clifftop walks, sandy coves, Fairlight Glen and other beauty-spots in Hastings' country park.

171

The Hall is now divided between two generations of the Crowson family. Visitors are accommodated in the north wing's huge rooms. The furnishings are comfortable rather than elegant; every room and corridor is close-fitted with good carpet; paint-work and wallpaper are fresh; central heating effective even in these high-ceilinged rooms (it helps that some walls are three feet thick). There are two sea-view dining-rooms, which means that a family may have the exclusive use of one. Because Mrs Crowson runs the wing single-handed she uses convenience foods as well as local produce; but keeps a list of local restaurants for those who wish to dine well elsewhere.

The resort of Hastings is only three miles away: its old town, fishing quarter, clifftop castle remains and labyrinth of caves are the most interesting parts. In the other direction are the pictur-esque mediaeval towns of Winchelsea (see page 296) and Rye (page 258).

Readers' comments: Service, furnishings, comfort of the highest quality. Friendly and helpful. Delightfully peaceful. Excellent value. Memorable holiday: marvellous place, wonderful scenery.

The following facts have been supplied by the owners:

Bedrooms There are 4 rooms, which include single, double and family rooms. Bed-and-breakfast costs from £11 (per person in a double room) including VAT. There are reductions for stays of 7 nights or more.
  Some if not all of the rooms have the following amenities: central heating or electric heaters; electric blankets, washbasin, shaver-point; armchairs; views of sea, countryside, farmland, garden; tea/coffee-making facilities; door keys; orthopaedic mattresses.

Meals The dinner menu is fixed price (£5.50). There is some choice of dishes on the menu, which consists of 3 courses. Dinner is served at 7 pm. Morning, afternoon or bedtime drinks (coffee, tea etc.) can be ordered for a charge. Non-residents are not admitted to the dining-room. Wine and other alcoholic drinks can be brought in.

Public rooms There is a sitting-room with central heating, TV (colour), books, magazines, local guides and leaflets, indoor games (such as Scrabble, chess, draughts and cards).

Surroundings The grounds consist of lawns and woodland. These are available in the neighbourhood: riding, golf, tennis.

Cars The nearest main road is the A259 from Folkestone.

Languages spoken French.

In the picturesque old town area of Hastings, Dorothea and Stanley Pelling (at **105 High Street**) take bed-and-breakfast guests in their attractive little Tudor house. At the back, a tiny garden (all steps and terraces, clinging to the steep hillside) is an afternoon suntrap. Plenty of nearby restaurants; excellent fish-and-chips at the Blue Dolphin. (Tel: 0424 424894.)

Fallowfields, Southmoor, west of Abingdon, Oxfordshire, OX13 3BH   *Tel: 0865 820416*   **C**(10) **D H PT ⚹3**

Once the Begum Aga Khan lived in this attractive country house surrounded by a large garden with croquet, heated swimming-pool and stone barns. A big lawn with spreading trees separates the house from the road to Abingdon.

Now Mrs Crowther runs it as a small hotel, every room full of her own decorative touches and with great emphasis on comfort and space. One bed is a king-size four-poster. Typical of Mrs Crowther's attention to detail: the bedroom tea-trays are renewed both morning and evening. She provides imaginative meals – on the night when I stayed, avocado mousse was followed by chicken in a creamy mango-and-pimento sauce and a huge array of puddings, and then cheese. Most vegetables and fruit are home-grown, including unusual things like fennel and lovage for soup.

Alison not only paints but makes (for sale) dried flower arrangements and pot-pourri.

From Fallowfields (only an hour from London or Heathrow) it is easy to visit Oxford, Stratford, Bath, the Cotswolds and – less well known but full of scenic and historic interest – the lovely Vale of the White Horse, Berkshire (see page 359).

The following facts have been supplied by the owners:

Bedrooms There are 4 rooms, which include single, double and family rooms. Bed-and-breakfast costs from £14.50 (per person in a double room) including service and VAT.

Some if not all of the rooms have the following amenities: central heating or electric heaters; electric blankets, washbasin, shower, own bathroom and wc, shaver-point; radio, TV (colour), armchairs; views of countryside, farmland, garden; tea/coffee-making facilities; door keys.

Meals The dinner menu is fixed price (from £11) or à la carte. There is a choice of dishes on the menu, which consists of 4 courses and coffee. Dinner is served at 8 pm. Special diets can be prepared. Packed lunches can be provided; and snacks at other hours. Morning, afternoon or bedtime drinks (coffee, tea etc.) can be ordered for a charge. Non-residents are not admitted to the dining-room. Wine and other alcoholic drinks can be ordered.

Public rooms There are 2 sitting-rooms etc. The following are available in one or both of them: central heating, open fire, TV (colour), video recorder, books, magazines, local guides and leaflets, indoor games (such as Scrabble, cards etc.), piano, record-player and records, bar.

Surroundings The grounds consist of 12 acres of paddocks (with sheep and horses) and garden. The following are available in the grounds: table tennis, croquet, swimming-pool (70°), hard tennis court. These are available in the neighbourhood: fishing, windsurfing, water skiing, riding, golf, leisure centre.

Cars The nearest main road is the A420 from Oxford to Swindon.

Closed to visitors We are not open from October to Easter except for house-parties of friends.

Findon Farmhouse, Findon, north of Worthing, West Sussex, BN14 0TF *Tel: 090671 3469* **C D PT ⌗3**

The farm lands were long ago built on, but this elegant Georgian house survives almost intact (except for two doors, which Elisabeth Russell aims to replace). Anyone who appreciates fine architecture would love the gracious staircase curving up under the circular ceiling, with an unusual oval window at the top; the pretty fluted fire-surround in the sitting/dining-room; the sash windows deepset between white panelled shutters; egg-and-dart mouldings around the ceilings; the fanlight over the front door.

Elisabeth has chosen attractive fabrics and colours (peach for the stair walls, avocado in the sitting-room); and everywhere are good paintings, books and objects.

Many of her visitors are walkers tramping the nearby South Downs Way. They usually dine at one of Findon's many restaurants or inns. (The coach from London stops next door, incidentally.)

174

Findon is a pretty village with three racing stables, and Goodwood, Cowdray and other race meetings are in the vicinity. Historic Cissbury Ring (Iron Age fort) is nearby on the South Downs, and the country is excellent for walking or riding. Findon is also well placed for visiting good theatres (at Brighton and Chichester) and opera at Glyndebourne. The south coast is close, and there are many pretty villages or stately homes to visit.

The following facts have been supplied by the owners:

Bedrooms There are 2 rooms, usable as single, double or family rooms. Bed-and-breakfast costs from £13 (per person in a double room) including service and VAT; prices go up in high season.

One or both rooms have the following amenities: central heating or electric heaters; electric blankets; TV (b & w), armchairs; choice of duvets or blankets; door keys. Breakfast in bed is available.

Meals Lunches and packed lunches can be provided; and snacks at other hours. Morning, afternoon or bedtime drinks (coffee, tea etc.) can be ordered for a charge. Non-residents are not admitted to the dining-room.

Public rooms There is a sitting-room with central heating, open fire, TV (colour), books, magazines, local guides and leaflets, indoor games (such as Scrabble, backgammon and cards), record-player and records.

Surroundings These are available in the neighbourhood: tennis, riding, swimming.

Cars The nearest main road is the A24 from Worthing to Horsham.

Foldgate Farm, Bootle Village, near Millom, Cumbria
Booking service: 0498 81563   **C PT S X ♯2**

A real Cumbrian farm, and well outside the main tourist areas, it covers 90 acres on which are kept Swaledale and Herdwick sheep as well as some cattle. The approach to the farm is through a cobbled courtyard, with a great stone byre and stables at one side, Muscovy ducks perching on a dry-stone wall, and sundry old iron pots and kettles filled with stonecrop, London pride or primroses. A stream slips quietly by. Pat, the sheepdog, comes bounding out to greet visitors.

The rooms have old furniture, and hooked rag rugs are everywhere. Guests sometimes eat with the family, by a dresser where mugs hang, the clothes airer suspended overhead and a grandfather clock ticking in one corner. There are bacon-hooks in the ceiling, old horn-handled shepherds' crooks stacked in the hall, and a bright coal fire in the evenings.

Mary does most of the talking as she serves guests a proper farmhouse meal, and her husband is glad to tell visitors about his sheep and all the local goings-on – guests are welcome to watch the life of the farm, and to join in at haymaking time in July or August.

You'll get real country fare here: Cumberland sausage, 'tatie pot', plum pudding with rum sauce, farm duckling, Herdwick lamb or mutton, rum butter on bread, currant cake with tea on arrival and at bedtime, and jams made from local blueberries, pears or marrow and ginger. There are free-range eggs for breakfast. This is a thoroughly unpretentious, homely and friendly place to stay – but not for those who want everything shiny as a new pin.

As to the countryside around, there are the moors of Corney Fell close by and roads winding up and down, with sea views.

See also pages 400–401.

176

The following facts have been supplied by the owners:

Bedrooms There are 3 rooms, which include single, double and family rooms. Dinner, bed-and-breakfast costs from £13.50 (per person), including service and VAT. There are reductions for stays of 2 nights or more.

    Some if not all of the rooms have the following amenities: electric heaters; electric blankets, shaver-point; armchairs; views of countryside or garden; tea/coffee-making facilities. Clothes washing free.

Meals The dinner menu is fixed price (£3.75) and consists of 4 courses and coffee. Dinner is served at 6 pm. Special diets can be prepared. Lunches or packed lunches can be provided. Bedtime drinks (coffee, tea etc). can be ordered free. Wine and other alcoholic drinks can be brought in.

Public rooms There is a sitting-room with open fire, colour TV, books, magazines, local guides and leaflets, playing cards. Maps on loan.

Surroundings The grounds consist of about 90 acres of farmland. These are available in the neighbourhood: pony trekking and fishing in the stream for brown trout.

Cars The nearest main road is the A595 from Broughton to Whitehaven.

Font House, Netherwitton, north of Morpeth, Northumberland
Tel: 067 072 668   **C D ⌗10**

Nearly every piece of furniture in Font House is a collector's item – not surprisingly, since Pat Burn is in the antiques trade – and there are books in almost every room, too. All the bedrooms have their own bathrooms, and one (with four-poster bed) a dressing-room as well. The 18th-century house is tucked away in its own gardens. At the front, in part of what may once have been the village green, stand a stone cross and the old village well. Behind are a bordered lawn and a paddock which is full of daffodils in the spring, and beyond that is the river which gives the house its name.

Mrs Burn is a keen cook. She specializes in English and French provincial food, though on some nights the meal might be Italian all through. On an English night, the menu might consist of salmon and cucumber quiche, roast beef, trifle and Stilton. The next morning, as she is no believer in unvaried egg-and-bacon breakfasts, you might get kedgeree, croissants or Craster kippers; ramekins, potato cakes, speciality teas and coddled eggs.

Northumberland is a county of great estates, and Netherwitton – no more than a hamlet really – is an estate village, neat and tidy as all such places are. Another nearby estate is Wallington Hall, once the home of the Trevelyan family and now the largest estate owned by the National Trust. The mansion – basically 17th century but with many interesting later features – has a very large park and a beautiful walled garden. Another nearby National Trust mansion is Cragside, built for Lord Armstrong (the armaments magnate) and the first house in the world to be lighted by electricity. Further away is the Northumbrian coast, with miles of deserted sandy beaches, famous ruined castles, and the Farne islands.

The following facts have been supplied by the owners:

Bedrooms There are 3 rooms, which include single, double and family rooms. Bed-and-breakfast costs from £12.50 (per person in a double room) including service and VAT; prices go up in high season. There are reductions for stays of 4 nights or more. Sunday night free to over-60s staying 3 days.

 Some if not all of the rooms have the following amenities: central heating or electric heaters; electric blankets, washbasin, shower, own bathroom and wc, shaver-point; armchairs; views of countryside, farmland, garden; tea/coffee-making facilities; door keys.

Meals The dinner menu is fixed price (£10). There is no choice of dishes on the fixed menu, which consists of 3 courses and coffee. Dinner is served at 7–7.30 pm. Lunches and packed lunches can be provided. Morning, afternoon or bedtime drinks (coffee, tea etc.) can be ordered for a charge. Wine and other alcoholic drinks can be ordered.

Public rooms There are 2 sitting-rooms. The following are available in one or both of them: central heating, open fire, books, magazines, local guides and leaflets, indoor games (such as Scrabble, cards and dominoes), record-player and records.

Surroundings The grounds consist of 3 acres of gardens and paddock by river. These are available in the neighbourhood: riding, swimming, tennis.

Cars The nearest main road is the A1 from Newcastle to Berwick.

Closed to visitors We are not open from mid October to end of April.

178

Forest Gate, Frog Lane, Milton-under-Wychwood, north of Burford, Oxfordshire, OX7 6TL   *Tel: 0993 830357*
C(5) D PT S-C ⌗5

'It's an ugly house!' insists Wilhelmina Church, but I found her home full of character – its Victorian builder gave it turrets, stained glass and even a goblin on the roof. Its surroundings are quiet but undistinguished (recently built houses face it). What, however, does make it very special is the high standard and exceptional comfort of the spacious bedrooms. I particularly liked one in which rosebud fabrics and pink velvet bedheads contrast with the thick grass-green carpet, white walls and simple stripped-pine doors. There are first-floor sitting-room with stone-mullioned bay window, chairs on the lawn, and a modern scarlet-tiled kitchen which guests are welcome to use at any hour when they want to make tea or coffee. A one-time hotelier, Wilhelmina is a mine of information about local sightseeing. Bed-and-breakfast only: most guests dine in the bar of the Shaven Crown for £3 or so, where I found the so-called 'snacks' are of almost gourmet standard. For information about the area see page 57.

Readers' comments: Such a friendly, happy atmosphere, breakfast beautifully served... Scent of pot-pourri and flowers in the bedrooms.

The following facts have been supplied by the owners:

Bedrooms There are 4 rooms, which include single, double and family rooms. Bed-and-breakfast costs from £10 (per person in a double room) including service and VAT.

179

Some if not all of the rooms have the following amenities: central heating and electric heaters; washbasin, shower, own bathroom and wc, shaver-point; armchairs; tea/coffee-making facilities; views of countryside and garden; duvets or blankets; door keys. Breakfast in bed is available.

Public rooms There are 2 sitting-rooms etc. The following are available in one or both of them: central heating, open fire, TV (colour), books, magazines, local guides and leaflets.

Surroundings The grounds consist of ½ acre of garden. Tennis and golf available locally.

Cars The nearest main roads are the A40 from Oxford to Cheltenham and A361 from Burford to Chipping Norton.

Languages spoken Dutch, German, French, Italian.

Forge Mill, Shelsley Beauchamp, north-west of Worcester, WR6 6RR   *Tel: 08865 461*   C(5) S ⌗4

Julian and Sue Dolman (both solicitors) bought what was virtually a jungle, and have transformed both garden and 18th-century house into one of the most delightful places to stay described in this book.

Long ago, the Teme (one of Britain's prettiest rivers) was a centre for the hand-forging of iron – smelting, with furnaces served by water-powered bellows, took place nearby; and at this spot agricultural implements were hammered into shape. All long gone.

One enters Forge Mill through the kitchen, in what was once a worker's cottage. Hop-bines are strung along the old beams. It was here that the Dolmans uncovered, during restoration work, the exit of a tunnel from a great house nearby, supposedly used by Royalists on the run during the Civil War: just one of their many discoveries.

Here breakfast is served (the jams are home-made); by pre-arrangement only, dinners can be ordered which might include pheasant casserole or lamb with apricot stuffing, perhaps followed by garden raspberries and cream.

There's a big sitting-room furnished in soft blues, and with hydrangea fabrics on sofa and chairs. A great brick fireplace, with slate hearth, stretches the width of the beamed room. Through French doors one can stroll out to a garden with a series of kingcup pools among rocks, brick paths, and a croquet lawn. Seven hives of bees produce honey for the table.

The dining-room has antiques and interesting paintings (the rest of the house has these, too), Sue's embroideries, Royal Worcester china and good silver.

Upstairs under the roof beams is a sitting-hall (with either TV or a fine view to enjoy) dominated by a portrait of one of Marie Antoinette's ladies-in-waiting, who shared her fate on the guillotine.

There's much more, too. A children's playroom. A pool and grounds that draw birdwatchers to view kingfishers and herons; little owls, buzzards and woodpeckers. The collections of glass-paintings and of Dr Syntax prints. And the witch hole. ('The *what*?' Julian will tell you!)

As to the bedrooms, these are of the same standard as the rest. In one, very fresh-looking Laura Ashley fabrics (white plus cherries) with pine built-in furniture. By contrast, a mauve room with silky patchwork in pastel colours and a Seychelles batik the Dolmans brought back from their honeymoon.

Worcestershire has a tremendous amount to see. Fine scenery, historic buildings (including churches), hill walks, waterside dairy-farms, a magnificent cathedral in Worcester itself, hop fields and orchards, woods, and 'sights' which include Elgar's birthplace (Broadheath), an outdoor museum of salvaged ancient buildings (at Avoncroft), the Royal Worcester porcelain museum and factory (bargains to be had!) and a variety of stately homes. River trips, the Three Choirs festival and delightful villages or towns (like Abberley, Bewdley, Chaddesley Corbett, Feckenham,

Ombersley, Stourport-on-Severn and Tenbury Wells) make this a good centre for a week-long holiday.

The following facts have been supplied by the owners:

Bedrooms There are 2 double rooms. Bed-and-breakfast costs from £10.50 (per person) including service and VAT; prices go up in high season. There are reductions for stays of 3 nights or more.

One or both of the rooms have the following amenities: central heating or electric heaters; washbasin, shower, own bathroom and wc, shaver-point; radio, armchairs; views of countryside and garden; tea/coffee-making facilities.

Meals The dinner menu is fixed price (£4). There is no choice of dishes on the menu, which consists of 2 courses and coffee. Dinner is served at 7 pm. Vegetarian or special diets can be prepared. Lunches and packed lunches can be provided; and snacks at other hours. Morning, afternoon or bedtime drinks (coffee, tea etc.) can be ordered – free. Non-residents are not admitted to the dining-room. Wine and other alcoholic drinks can be brought in.

Public rooms There is a sitting-room with central heating, open fire, TV (colour), books, magazines, local guides and leaflets; indoor games (such as Scrabble, Boggle, Trivial Pursuit, Monopoly and cards), piano, record-player and records.

Surroundings The grounds consist of 2 acres of garden (with croquet) and paddocks; river fishing.

Cars The nearest main road is the A44 from Worcester to Leominster.

Languages spoken French, Portuguese.

Fortitude Cottage, 51 Broad Street, Old Portsmouth, Hampshire, PO1 2JD   *Tel: 0705 823748*   **C D H PT ▢8**

Carol Harbeck's little cottage – one room piled on top of another – backs onto her mother's (also a guest-house), with a flowery little courtyard and fountain between the two. Hers is named for the Fortitude Inn, which was once here; itself named for HMS *Fortitude*, a ship-of-war which ended its days as a prison hulk in the harbour – overlooked by the big bay window of Carol's first-floor sitting-room. This is Portsmouth's most historic area. From here, Richard Lionheart embarked for the Crusades, Henry V for Agincourt, and the first settlers for Australia. It's a place of ramparts and bastions, quaint buildings and byways, much coming-and-going of ships and little boats.

All the rooms in the cottage are prettily furnished – even the bathroom; and Carol (who serves only bed-and-breakfast) can recommend a dozen good eating-places nearby. Handy as a stopover for people using Portsmouth's port, Fortitude Cottage

182

deserves a longer stay. For Portsmouth (and its adjoining Regency resort, Southsea) have so much to offer: HMS *Victory*, the *Mary Rose*, the Royal Navy's museum and that of the Marines, cathedral and historic garrison church, Henry VIII's Southsea Castle, the sands of nearby Hayling Island and the wild places of Chichester Harbour, clifftop Victorian forts, Roman/Norman Portchester Castle, submarine museum at Gosport, a big new leisure centre, other museums (including Dickens' birthplace), the Searchlight Tattoo every September, trips to the Isle of Wight, and a fine downland countryside to explore inland.

The following facts have been supplied by the owners:

Bedrooms There are 3 rooms, which include single, double and family rooms. Bed-and-breakfast costs from £10 (per person in a double room) including service and VAT. There are reductions for stays of 4 nights or more.

    Some if not all of the rooms have the following amenities: central heating; washbasin, shower, own bathroom and wc, shaver-point; TV (b&w); views of sea; choice of duvets or blankets; tea/coffee-making facilities; door keys.

Cars The nearest main road is the A3 to London.

Languages spoken German.

**Foxhill, Kingsey, south-west of Aylesbury, Buckinghamshire,
HP17 8LZ**   *Tel: 0844 291650*   **C(5) S ⌗4**

The first impression is delightful: a sparkling white house beyond
green lawns where Muscovy ducks waddle with their young
towards a pool crossed by an arching stone bridge. The gnarled
remains of an immense 500-year-old elm tree stand beside the
drive.

The interior is just as attractive. The house having been the
home of an architect, Nick Hooper, and his family for many years,
it is not surprising that its modernization was done with imagina-
tion, and with care to respect its 17th-century origins. In the hall,
floored with polished red quarry-tiles, a wrought-iron staircase
leads up to bedrooms with beamed ceilings, attractive wallpapers
and rugs, and restful colour schemes. Board doors have the
original iron latches. The breakfast-room (which also serves as a
sitting-room) has brown gingham tablecloths and rush-seated
chairs. Here Mary-Joyce – a warm, gentle hostess – serves only
breakfast, recommending for other meals plenty of inns and
restaurants in the ancient market town of Thame, only a few
minutes away.

At the back of the house is a large garden with heated
swimming-pool beyond which the Hoopers' black-faced sheep
graze, against a distant view of the Chiltern Hills.

Thame is a lively place in autumn when the mile-long market

place at its heart is filled with stalls for the annual fair, but quiet at other times; and beyond it lie all the attractions of Oxfordshire described elsewhere in this book. In west Buckinghamshire, too, there is plenty – from the wooded hills of the Chilterns down into the fertile Vale of Aylesbury. Early in the year there are bluebells and cherry blossom; in autumn the beechwoods blaze with colour; always, there are glades and mossy banks to discover.

The centre of Aylesbury is picturesque, threaded with pathways and courtyards to explore on foot (one of the many inns, the King's Head, belongs to the National Trust). Of many villages worth visiting, go to Long Crendon not only for its lovely bridge, the river and rose-covered cottages but for two 15th-century houses (one belonged to Catherine of Aragon and is now owned by the National Trust). At Waddesdon is the Rothschild mansion, looking like a French château (also National Trust property); at Upper Wichendon, high up, a dramatic view of the Thames; Cuxham, in good walking country, has a stream through the middle.

All these are very near. Visitors staying for some time can also from here explore Oxford, West Wycombe, old Amersham, Henley and other Thames-side towns (even Windsor), and any number of castles, stately homes, museums etc. London is only an hour away.

Readers' comments: Wonderfully kind hosts, lovely home, top of our list!

The following facts have been supplied by the owners:

Bedrooms There are 3 rooms, which include double and family rooms. Bed-and-breakfast costs £11 (per person) including service and VAT.
   Some if not all of the rooms have the following amenities: central heating; washbasin, shower, shaver-point; armchairs; views of countryside, farmland, garden.

Public rooms There is a sitting-room with central heating, TV (colour), books, magazines, local guides and leaflets.

Surroundings The grounds consist of 3½ acres of garden and paddock, with heated (75°) swimming-pool and tennis. Riding and golf are available in the neighbourhood.

Cars The nearest main road is the A4129 from Princes Risborough to Thame.

Closed to visitors We are not open from December to February.

Friar Hall Farm, Caldbeck, south of Wigton, Cumbria
Booking service: 0498 81563　　**C S ♯5**

As the name suggests, this farmhouse has a long history. The Prior of Carlisle built a hospital here, which was dissolved in the reign of King John. The 12th-century part of the house was once the monks' refectory (hence the name 'hall'), with the hospital proper next door.

Today it is the centre of a 140-acre sheep and dairy farm. Caldbeck Fells rise up above the village where John Peel was born and is buried (the little churchyard is right opposite Friar Hall, across a tiny humpback stone bridge spanning a tumbling stream with a weir). The Blencathra foot-hounds still roam these fells in winter, just as they once did with John Peel – but now hang-gliders go up there too.

Guests use a snug sitting/dining-room with big leather armchairs, crimson velvet curtains and, on wintry evenings, logs blazing in a fireplace made of greenish Buttermere slate, casting a flicker on the gleaming brass fire-irons. The ceiling is beamed, the walls are thick.

All the bedrooms look across the tiny garden and the stream to the far hills beyond, and to a sky of scudding clouds when the wind blows. Fresh paint and light colours make them attractive; carpets are good; colour schemes simple (pink-and-white, or green-sprigged).

Dorothy serves typical farmhouse fare, using plenty of home-grown vegetables and other produce for dishes such as egg mayonnaise, roast lamb and fruit pies with cream.

Caldbeck is one of the Lake District's prettiest villages, with a pond (used by Muscovy ducks), the John Peel Inn, and a Wesleyan chapel carved with the reminder, 'Remember NOW thy creator'. The approach from the north is particularly lovely, driving across a heath with gorse towards a view of a green valley, with bracken-coloured hills beyond.

Apart from all the obvious attractions of the area, visitors often enjoy going to the October auctions (in Wigton) of horses and Shetland ponies, although the spectacle of foals being separated from the mares can be distressing.

The following facts have been supplied by the owners:

Bedrooms There are 3 rooms, usable as single, double and family rooms. Bed-and-breakfast costs from £9.75 (per person in a double room) including service and VAT. There are reductions for stays of 5 nights or more.
   Some if not all of the rooms have the following amenities: central heating or electric heaters; electric blankets, washbasin, shaver-point; armchairs; views of countryside, farmland, garden; choice of duvets or blankets; door keys.

Meals The dinner menu is fixed price (£5.25). There is no choice of dishes on the fixed menu, which consists of 3 courses and coffee. Dinner is served at 6 pm. Special diets can be prepared. Bedtime drinks (coffee, tea etc.) can be ordered for a charge. Non-residents are not admitted to the dining-room. Wine and other alcoholic drinks can be brought in.

Public rooms There is a sitting-room with open fire, TV (colour), books, magazines, local guides and leaflets.

Surroundings These are available in the neighbourhood: tennis and bowls.

Cars The nearest main road is the A595 from Carlisle to Cockermouth.

The Gables, 19 Forest Road, Branksome Park, east of Poole, Dorset, BH13 6DH   *Tel: 0202 760949*   **C**(3) **D PT S ⌗6**

Much of Branksome was once a large, private estate and its wide, leafy avenues still retain something of past dignity. Yet the popular, golden beaches are within a pleasant stroll of The Gables, through a valley of pine trees where a stream tumbles down to the sea.

The Gables was built as a mansion for an Edwardian lady of means, and many of the original details survive – the mahogany staircase and fire-surrounds, the art nouveau finger-plates on the doors, the pillared verandah overlooking a smooth lawn where croquet or golf balls click and evening sunlight casts long shadows from the pine or yew trees. The big bay window of the dining-room and most bedroom windows have a view of the garden, where squirrels are so bold that they come to drink at the bird-bath just outside.

Mrs Lowbridge's tables are laid with flowers and candles for dinner, which may consist of soup, roast pork, apple pie with ice cream, cheese and coffee, for example.

The rooms are spotless, the bedrooms not elegant but comfortable. Families wanting a traditional seaside holiday away from the razzmatazz of the front come here; and so, of course, do people who enjoy sailing in Poole's lovely natural harbour – in the grounds there is room to park not only cars but boat-trailers too.

Poole is full of historic interest, especially around its quay with the ancient homes of merchants and seamen, and old warehouses. There is also any amount of things to do or see: waterfront inns, good restaurants and shops, a fine aquarium, a rock and gem centre, craft workshops, boat-trips, lovely parks and lakes, a lifeboat display, three exceptionally well-designed museums (historical and maritime exhibits), wildlife, a country park, arts centre and opportunities for learning every conceivable sport on, by, or under the water. In Poole harbour is the National Trust's Brownsea Island, for wildlife and an open-air theatre. Compton Acre's gardens are exceptional – one leading into another, on a hillside, in a variety of styles (Italian, Japanese etc.). From Sandbanks a car-ferry takes you to Shell Bay, lovely Studland, Swanage, the Purbeck hills and the coast (see page 467).

The following facts have been supplied by the owners:

Bedrooms There are 12 rooms, which include double and family rooms. Bed-and-breakfast costs £13.80 (per person), including service and VAT. There are reductions for stays of 3 nights or more, and further reductions for stays of 7 nights.

Some if not all of the rooms have the following amenities: central heating or electric heaters; washbasin, shower, own bathroom and wc, shaver-point; armchairs; views of countryside, garden; door keys. Breakfast in bed is available.

Meals The dinner menu is fixed price (£4.95). There is some choice of dishes on the menu, which consists of 4 courses and coffee. Dinner is served at 6 pm. Special diets can be prepared. Lunches and/or packed lunches can be provided; and snacks at other hours. Morning, afternoon or bedtime drinks (coffee, tea etc.) can be ordered for a charge. Non-residents are not admitted to the dining-room. Wine and other alcoholic drinks can be ordered.

Public rooms There are 2 sitting-rooms etc. The following are available in one or both of them: open fire, colour TV, books, magazines, local guides and leaflets, indoor games (such as chess, draughts, dominoes, cards etc.) piano, record-player and records, and a bar. (Piped music too, alas!) Table tennis and badminton available.

Surroundings The grounds consist of an acre of gardens and a putting green. These are available in the neighbourhood: tennis, bowling, sailing and golf.

Cars The nearest main road is the A35 from Bournemouth to Poole.

Closed to visitors We are not open in winter.

For very comfortable accommodation and good food, but in a somewhat less attractive setting, there is the **Fairlight Hotel** at Broadstone, run by Brian Marshall (tel: 0202 694316). Golf course within yards.

Gaisgill Farm, west of Tebay, Cumbria
Booking service: 0498 81563   C(7) **D S X ⌗6**

People who zip along the M6 to Scotland miss a lot that is just a little way off the highway – like the long stone village of Tebay with the River Lune's gorge to the south of it. Nearby is Gaisgill with the 18th-century farmhouse of a shepherd.

The huge living-room with low-beamed ceiling, odd nooks and windows set deep in thick stone walls, is welcoming even in winter – with comfortable armchairs and sofas grouped around a blazing fire at one end and two big dining-tables at the other, with patchwork place-mats and small bowls of flowers. A grandfather clock tick-tocks slowly.

The patchwork is Joyce's; during winter she keeps busy on this and other needlework, sold to summer visitors. The Afghan rugs and cushion-covers are hers too; and she was teaching herself to spin while I was there – appropriately, for a shepherd's wife.

Among the antique furniture, the books and records, is a huge display of silver trophies and another of colourful rosettes – awards won by Alan and his dogs in innumerable sheepdog trials. If you want to see the trials in action, August is the time to go.

Although Alan has sheep on his own nine acres, he is largely occupied in training other farmers in the handling of their border collies. His father was a celebrated shepherd who went sheepdog trialling from his teens until he died at 82. And so was his grandfather, who sold his farm to Beatrix Potter (High Sawrey, not far away, now a National Trust property).

This is walking country, and Joyce cooks generous meals for appetites sharpened by the fells: home-made soups followed by a roast, for example, and then an array of help-yourself puddings (perfect pastry!) and cheeses.

After dinner, there are those fireside armchairs; while Alan, wearing a sweater his wife has spun and knitted, may reminisce about 'the worst spring in memory' when the force of the wind drove sheep before it and fifty were dug out of just one snowdrift, with hundreds more perishing; or he may explain the mysteries of 'gimmer hogs' and 'shearlings'. And then – a warm and comfortable bedroom.

The whole area around here is one of great beauty, from rugged crags and the ruins of Shap Abbey to valleys and fells full of wildlife. The motorway quickly whisks one on to Carlisle, the Lake District lies on the other side, and there are all the lovely villages and moors of the North Pennines to explore on the way to Alston. Eastwards, the Yorkshire Dales are surprisingly close; or Barnard Castle and the great Bowes Museum will provide a day's excursion.

Readers' comments: Charming house, lovely people – hospitality itself. Superb food. The best we have stayed at; a lovely position. Super atmosphere.

The following facts have been supplied by the owners:

Bedrooms There are 3 rooms, which include single, double and family rooms. Bed-and-breakfast costs from £9.25 (per person in a double room), including service and VAT.

Some if not all of the rooms have the following amenities: central heating or electric heaters; washbasin, shaver-point; armchairs; views of countryside, farmland, garden; door keys.

Meals The dinner menu is fixed price (£5). There is no choice of main dish on the menu, which consists of 3 courses and coffee. Dinner is served at 7.30 pm. Packed lunches can be provided; and snacks at other hours. Bedtime drinks (coffee, tea etc.) are available free. Wine and other alcoholic drinks can be brought in.

Public rooms There is a sitting-room with central heating, open fire, colour TV, books, magazines, local guides and leaflets, record-player and records.

Surroundings The grounds consist of a garden and farmland. Fishing is available in the neighbourhood.

Cars The nearest main roads are the M6 and the A685 from Kendal to Brough.

Ganarew House, Ganarew, west of Ross-on-Wye, Herefordshire, NP5 3SS *Tel: 0600 890442* **C D PT S ⌗3**

Perched upon a hillside with superb, leafy views from every window, Ganarew House feels as if it is miles from anywhere and yet a main road runs close by, hidden in the valley. It is a fine Victorian mansion of reddish sandstone with good details typical of its period – panelled doors, a handsome staircase, decorative ceiling mouldings and so forth. Elaine and Brian Stockwell, who turned it into a hotel some years ago, have redecorated it with care to preserve its character: no shrill colours, for instance, but tranquil tones and good furniture. Carpets are thick, armchairs deep, all rooms spacious and comfortable.

The large sitting-room is particularly attractive for anybody who wants a relaxing place in which to stay, reading or writing. Large chesterfields flank the log fire. Outside, the small garden has (in autumn) clusters of mistletoe among the red crab-apples. A great bay window with velvet seats looks out over and beyond the garden to the far hills of the Forest of Dean. The colours of autumn are reflected in the room itself: apricot walls, copper carpet and brown upholstery.

In the Wedgwood-blue dining-room (the colour of the walls is echoed in the Royal Doulton china too), truly exceptional meals are served – exceptional not only in the standard of Elaine Stockwell's cooking but also in 'her imaginative recipes (and notwithstanding the moderate price, the servings are on a heroic scale). A typical dinner – with several choices at each course – might comprise a starter such as melon-and-pear in a dressing of cream and tarragon, or a home-made terrine; superb Hereford-shire roast beef, or local trout in a sauce of horseradish and yogurt – with five vegetables, perfectly cooked; and such puddings as a soufflé of coffee and brandy or a meringue-and-nut confection; followed by a selection of cheeses and coffee.

The bedrooms are not only attractively furnished but roomy as well, and they have showers or else carpeted bathrooms which are unusually spacious. Throughout, the atmosphere is one of ease and of quiet welcome.

As to the environs, the whole area is one of scenic and historic interest: not only the Forest of Dean but also the Malvern Hills are within sight and offer good walks – as do the Black Mountains and the Wye Valley. Some people come for the cathedrals (Gloucester, Hereford, Worcester), Tintern Abbey, stately homes, and the ancient streets of Chepstow or Monmouth. Others are attracted by the fishing or golf (six courses within a half-hour drive). There's a lot to interest steam railway enthusiasts. Bristol and Cardiff (historic port, folk museums etc.) are both only 45 minutes away, and there are prehistoric remains and half-a-dozen castles to see.

Readers' comments: The best weekend of our lives; very good. Thoroughly enjoyed it. Excellent: food lovely, warm and friendly atmosphere. Food and accommodation superb.

The following facts have been supplied by the owners:

Bedrooms There are 10 rooms, which include single, double and family rooms. Dinner, bed-and-breakfast costs from £24 (per person) including service and VAT; prices go up in high season. There are reductions for stays of 7 nights or more; and 'bargain breaks' as well. Sunday night free to over-60s, staying 3 days (in winter).
  Some if not all of the rooms have the following amenities: central heating; washbasin, shower, own bathroom, bidet and wc, shaver-point; radio, colour TV, armchairs; views of countryside, farmland, garden; orthopaedic mattress; choice of duvets or blankets; tea/coffee-making facilities; door keys. Breakfast in bed is available.

Meals There is a choice of dishes on the fixed menu, which consists of 3 courses and coffee. Dinner is served at 7.30 pm. Special diets can be prepared. Lunches or packed lunches can be provided; and snacks at other hours. Morning, afternoon or bedtime drinks (coffee, tea etc.) can be ordered for a charge. Wine and other alcoholic drinks can be ordered.

Public rooms There are 2 sitting-rooms. The following are available in one or both of them: central heating, open fire, colour TV, books, magazines, local guides and leaflets and a bar.

Surroundings The grounds consist of a 2-acre garden. These are available in the neighbourhood: golf, squash, badminton, swimming, riding, canoeing and pony trekking.

Cars The nearest main road is the A40 from Monmouth to Ross-on-Wye.

The Gentle Gardener, Long Street, Tetbury, Gloucestershire, GL8 8AA   *Tel: 0666 52884*   **C D PT ⌗6**

This is an example of a town-centre house which nevertheless has some peaceful bedrooms overlooking the courtyards and garden at the back. It was once an inn with a different name. A lucky find (now used as the new sign outside) depicts a monk at work in the garden, and it was this that inspired the present name.

Walk through the big archway by which coaches used to enter and you are in a courtyard with tables, hanging pots of roses and an old pump. Beyond this lies a stone-walled garden with gnarled apple trees trained to make a green tunnel, and nearly a hundred rose bushes. There is still a skittle alley here.

Malcolm McClellan's hotel is celebrated for its food, cooked by Lynne Kimber. There is always a wide choice of original dishes at each course – things like smoked haddock roulade with cheese or avocado sorbet and a fruity salad to start with; chicken breast stuffed with spinach and pine kernels or pork fillet with Stilton and walnut sauce as a main course; and equally unusual puddings. Wines are good value. Meals are served in a simple but characterful dining-room decorated with old garden tools, dried flowers and seedheads. There is also a conventional lounge bar, and a wine-bar. Breakfasts are varied and include unusual choices such as kedgeree.

Bedrooms are pretty and the residents' sitting-room upstairs has handsome armchairs grouped around the stone grate where a fire burns in cold weather.

Tetbury is a lovely Cotswold market town, near the homes of Princess Anne and of the Prince of Wales, the abbey town of Malmesbury, historic Cirencester with its Roman and mediaeval antiquities and the Severn Valley area described on pages 152–3. It's an excellent place in which to hunt for antiques, visit vineyards, watch cattle-markets in progress or tour some of England's finest scenery.

The following facts have been supplied by the owners:

Bedrooms There are 19 rooms, which include single, double and family rooms. Dinner, bed-and-breakfast usually costs £28.50 (per person in a double room) including VAT, but there are reductions for stays of 2 nights or more; and 'bargain breaks' as well. **10% discount to readers showing a copy of this book**.

Some if not all of the rooms have the following amenities: central heating; bathroom or washbasin, shaver-point; radio, armchairs; views of garden; door keys. Breakfast in bed is available.

Meals There is a choice of dishes on the fixed menu, which consists of 3 courses and coffee. Dinner is served from 7.30–9.45 pm. Special diets can be prepared.

Lunches and packed lunches can be provided; and snacks at other hours. Morning, afternoon or bedtime drinks (coffee, tea etc.) can be ordered for a charge. Wine and other alcoholic drinks can be ordered.

Public rooms There is a sitting-room with central heating, open fire, music centre, books, magazines, local guides and leaflets, indoor games (such as chess and cards).

Surroundings The grounds consist of ¾ acre of garden, with skittles. Golf, riding, fishing, squash and tennis are available in the neighbourhood.

Cars The nearest main road is the A433 from Bath and Bristol to Cirencester.

Languages spoken French, German, Italian.

Credit cards accepted Visa, Diners Club, Access, Amex.

George Hotel, Yarmouth, Isle of Wight
Tel: 0983 760331   **C D H PT S X ⌗4**

This is a fine old hotel with its own tiny shell-strewn beach at the end of its garden. It adjoins the castle that was built by Henry VIII. The furnishing of the main panelled rooms has been done with style, and in character with the period of the house (1648). In fine weather, meals are often served on a paved terrace between lawn and sea, or in a glass-enclosed terrace adjoining the house. Nearby is the jetty from which ferries to the mainland come and go, making it easy to visit Lymington, Beaulieu and adjoining parts of Hampshire such as the New Forest.

The George is very much a family affair, run by Liz and John Amies. The traditional English food is cooked from fresh produce, fish and local game, and served on Rosita china. Sometimes dinners are served by candlelight and there is Gershwin on piano and bass.

The bedrooms (some with superb views of the Solent and its shipping) are comfortable, but modestly furnished (though sheets are of Irish linen). One was slept in by Charles II, for this was the house of Admiral Sir Robert Holmes, to whom the king gave the governorship of the island in return for services rendered to the Royalist cause. He was little better than a pirate. In the church is a grandiose marble statue with his head: this (plus sculptor) had been on its way to France – a part-finished statue of Louis XIV – when Sir Robert seized it and had it completed in his own likeness.

Yarmouth is the prettiest town on the island, with many 17th- and 18th-century buildings, and it is a sailing centre, too. It is at the west end of the island, close to the wilder and most beautiful parts where Tennyson lived and which are to a large extent preserved by the National Trust. Alum Bay (of the multicoloured sands and the chair-lift) and the Needles are nearby. An old fort on a spectacular site overlooking the Needles has recently been restored and opened to the public; Newtown (old despite its name) is a disused harbour, with a famous bird reserve. The area has superb downland scenery, cliffs, sandy beaches, pretty villages of thatched cottages, suntrap bays, many stately houses, wild flowers, gardens, sailing and other water-sports. There are all kinds of other interesting things to do – a windmill and a watermill to visit, Gatcombe House with a collection of costumes, potteries, a glassworks, Fort Victoria country park, Tennyson's house (now a grand hotel), a vineyard, a working museum of timbercraft, steam trains, a Roman mosaic, and (in nearly every month) flower shows, regattas and other frolics – mainly towards the east of the island. There is more about the Isle of Wight under other entries.

Readers' comments: Welcoming. Beautifully sited, good food, very comfortable.

The following facts have been supplied by the owners:

Bedrooms There are 20 rooms, which include single, double and family rooms.
Bed-and-breakfast costs from £14 (per person). There are reductions for stays
of 7 nights or more; and winter 'bargain breaks' as well.

    Some if not all of the rooms have the following amenities: central heating;
washbasin, own bathroom and wc, shaver-point; radio, TV, armchairs; views
of sea, garden; balcony; door keys. Breakfast in bed available. Sunday
accommodation free to over-60s staying 3 days. Sampler breaks (see page 14).

Meals The dinner menu is fixed price (£9) or à la carte. There is a choice of dishes
on the fixed menu, which consists of 3 courses and coffee. Dinner is served at
7.30–9.15 pm. Special diets can be prepared. Lunches and packed lunches can
be provided; and snacks at other hours. Morning, afternoon or bedtime drinks
(coffee, tea etc.) can be ordered for a charge. Wine and other alcoholic drinks
can be ordered.

Public rooms There are 3 sitting-rooms etc. The following are available in one or
more of them: central heating, open fire, books, magazines, local guides and
leaflets, indoor games (such as Scrabble, chess, Ludo), piano and a bar.

Surroundings The grounds consist of a ¾ acre garden by the sea. These are
available in the neighbourhood: sailing, fishing, riding, windsurfing and golf.

Cars The nearest main road is the A3054 from Freshwater to Newport.

Credit cards accepted Access, Visa, Diners Club, Amex.

**Georgian House, Sutterton, south of Boston, Lincolnshire,
PE20 2JH**   *Tel: 0205 460 763*   **C PT S ⌗4**

Marion and John Edgoose had only just finished redecorating and
furnishing when I visited. Everything throughout was spotless and
of the best quality: they have set themselves high standards.

Much had to be done to remove modern accretions and restore this 18th-century house, in the course of which they uncovered a colossal inglenook (now with log fire) and brick alcoves. Walls are thick and doorways low.

The sitting-room has a 'chinoiserie' look, due to the chintz on the sofas and an oriental firescreen. In the dining-room, tulip tablecloths match the wallpaper. Elsewhere, Marion has bird-of-paradise or honeysuckle wallpapers. Several bedrooms have particularly fine antique beds; one also has a chaise longue. Because the road outside is busy, each room has double-glazing.

Marion provides a choice of dishes at dinner – cooking traditional English favourites like home-made soup, roast beef with Yorkshire pudding, and lemon meringue pie.

Although parts of Lincolnshire can be flat and rather monotonous, its coast and nature reserves make it a great place for birdwatchers; and the peaceful, uncommercialized countryside is dotted with spectacular churches, and windmills. The nearby town of Boston is of great interest for its connection with the Pilgrim Fathers, its noble church and its pork butchers: Lincolnshire prides itself on its sausages, pies and haslett – a kind of meat loaf made from pork. One can go home loaded with such things, as well as fresh vegetables, fruit and flowers from the glasshouses and the fields.

The following facts have been supplied by the owners:

Bedrooms There are 3 rooms, which include double and family rooms. Bed-and-breakfast costs from £11 (per person in a double room) including service and VAT. There are reductions for stays of 4 nights or more; and 'bargain breaks' as well.

Some if not all of the rooms have the following amenities: central heating or electric heaters; electric blankets, washbasin, shower, own bathroom and wc, shaver-point; armchairs; views of countryside/farmland/garden; choice of duvets or blankets; tea/coffee-making facilities; door keys.

Meals The dinner menu is fixed price (from £4) or à la carte. There is a choice of dishes on the fixed menu, which consists of 3 courses and coffee. Dinner is served from 7 pm. Special diets can be prepared. Lunches and packed lunches can be provided; and snacks at other hours. Morning, afternoon or bedtime drinks (coffee, tea etc.) can be ordered free. Non-residents are not admitted to the dining-room. Wine and other alcoholic drinks can be ordered.

Public rooms There is a sitting-room with central heating, open fire, TV (colour), books, magazines, local guides and leaflets, indoor games (such as Scrabble and cards), piano, record-player and records.

Surroundings The grounds consist of a garden. These are available in the neighbourhood: tennis, squash, swimming, bowls.

The Granary, Fenny Compton Wharf, south of Southam, Warwickshire, CV33 0XE   *Tel: 029577 214*   D S ⌗6

On the banks of the Oxford Canal, where colourful narrow boats pass by, the Cotterills – local farming people – recently inherited a derelict 18th-century warehouse, and completely modernized it to make a new home for themselves (upstairs) and rooms for guests (on the ground floor). Everything indoors has been very neatly done, with pale colours predominating, while the garden outside is (though only a few years old) beautifully landscaped, rock plants and flowering shrubs grouped round a smooth lawn where one may sit to watch the boats glide by. All around are fields. Dinner can be had at the waterside George & Dragon near the house, or at other restaurants (June Cotterill gives guests a list).

The hamlet is close to where three counties meet, Warwickshire, Oxfordshire and Northamptonshire. Favourite day-trips for visitors include Coventry Cathedral, Northampton, the colleges of Oxford, Stratford-upon-Avon, Warwick Castle, the Cotswolds and the fruitful vale of Evesham.

The following facts have been supplied by the owners:

Bedrooms There are 3 double rooms. Bed-and-breakfast costs from £10 (per person) including service and VAT; prices go up in high season.

The rooms have the following amenities: central heating; washbasin, shower and wc, shaver-point; radio, armchairs; views of countryside, farmland, garden; choice of duvets or blankets; tea/coffee-making facilities; door keys.

Meals Lunches and packed lunches can be provided; and snacks at other hours.

Public rooms There is a sitting/dining-room with central heating, TV, books, magazines, local guides and leaflets, indoor games (such as cards and Scrabble).

Surroundings The grounds consist of 4 acres, with garden. Fishing and riding are available in the neighbourhood.

Cars The nearest main road is the A423 from Coventry to Banbury.

Grassfield, Pateley Bridge, north of Harrogate, North Yorkshire, HG3 5HL *Tel: 0423 711412* **C(5) D PT S ⌗12**

This country house is set back from the road, in its own gardens: it is a handsome Georgian building surrounded by lawns and trees. All the rooms are spacious and comfortably furnished; and Marguerite MacLellan studies her visitors' interests – for example, providing birdwatching and photography magazines, and suggesting local walks. There is a tranquil and informal atmosphere.

Meals are prepared from home-grown vegetables and local produce wherever possible, including free-range eggs and Nidderdale lamb. A typical menu: local smoked trout pâté, baked ham with honey glaze, apple strudel and cream. There is a wide selection of wines.

Pateley Bridge is an interesting small town (in 1982 it won the award for Europe's best floral village), with a number of good shops, set on a junction of several roads, which makes it a fine centre from which to go sightseeing. Grassfield is in the heart of Nidderdale, a place of crags, glens and pastures. A number of Yorkshire's most historic towns are within easy reach: Harrogate (elegant spa), Ripon (cathedral and market), Skipton (castle), for example. There are many pretty villages, particularly in nearby Wharfedale. Fountains Abbey is probably the most spectacular sight in the neighbourhood but there there are many other abbeys and castles too, caverns and strange rock formations, rivers and lakes, interesting shops, old inns, nature trails and much else. But it is the beauty of the landscape that brings most people here.

Readers' comments: Charming people, and we enjoyed all that you said we would. Food wholesome and fresh. Peace, comfort, excellent home cooking, unflagging individual attention to one's needs. A very high standard of service. All you said, and better! Exceedingly comfortable; food delicious. Owners welcoming and helpful.

The following facts have been supplied by the owners:

Bedrooms There are 9 rooms, which include single, double and family rooms. Bed-and-breakfast costs from £14.50 (per person in a double room) including service and VAT. There are reductions for stays of 3 nights or more. Sampler breaks (see page 14).

All the rooms have the following amenities: central heating; electric blankets, washbasin, shaver-point; armchairs; views of countryside or garden; choice of duvets or blankets; tea/coffee-making facilities; door keys. Some have private bathrooms. Breakfast in bed is available, also bed-boards, hair drier and TV.

Meals The dinner menu is fixed price (£8) and consists of 3 courses. Dinner is served at 7 pm. Special diets can be prepared. Packed lunches can be provided. Morning, afternoon or bedtime drinks (coffee, tea etc.) can be ordered for a charge. Wine and other alcoholic drinks can be ordered by residents.

Public rooms There are 3 sitting-rooms etc. The following are available in one or more of them: central heating, open fire, colour TV, books, magazines, local guides and leaflets, indoor games (such as Scrabble and Monopoly) and a bar. Bridge can be arranged. Gumboots and maps on loan.

Surroundings The grounds consist of 4 acres of lawns, woodlands and flower beds. These are available in the neighbourhood: riding, birdwatching, fishing (trout and coarse), canoeing, golf.
Cars The nearest main road is the A1 from London to Scotland.
Closed to guests We are not open in winter.

Greenings, 43 Fourth Avenue, Frinton-on-Sea, Essex, CO13 9DY
Tel: 02556 77379   **C(5) PT**

Once, starched nannies wheeling expensive prams were almost a symbol of sedate Frinton – a seaside resort still unspoilt by the clamour of commercialism. In one of its nicest avenues – wide grassy verges, flowering trees, and well-tended gardens all along it – stands a detached house built early this century, and now run as a small hotel by Ann Tooby (previously a City broker) and her husband (a graphic artist whose work adorns many of the walls).

Every room is immaculate, with polished wood floors and shining paintwork. The Wedgwood blue dining-room has a small bar; from the big velvet armchairs of the sitting-room, one looks into the garden, secluded by tall trees. Bedrooms are spacious, well-furnished and with thick carpets. The brown-and-peach family room is particularly well arranged, for the children's beds are separated (in a sunny verandah room) from the parents'.

At every meal there is a choice of courses. For example, a typical dinner might comprise mushrooms provençale, lamb casseroled in burgundy and several kinds of pudding.

202

At the end of the avenue are clifftop lawns, pretty public gardens and a view of Walton on Naze piers – below lies the long, clean, safe beach. Peaceful Frinton is also a good place from which to go touring: Mrs Tooby has worked out half a dozen different itineraries for guests, which she has marked on maps for their use. There are tennis, windsurfing and golf in the neighbourhood.

The following facts have been supplied by the owners:

Bedrooms There are 7 rooms, which include double and family rooms. Bed-and-breakfast costs from £11 (per person in a double room) including VAT; prices go up in high season. There are reductions for stays of 7 nights or more; and 'bargain breaks' as well. Sampler breaks (see page 14).

All rooms have the following amenities: central heating; own bathroom and wc, shaver-point; radio, armchairs; tea/coffee-making facilities; door keys.

Meals The dinner menu is fixed price (£7). There is a choice of dishes on the fixed menu, which consists of 3 courses. Dinner is served at 7–8 pm. Special diets can be prepared. Non-residents are not admitted to the dining-room unless invited by guests. Wine and other alcoholic drinks can be ordered.

Public rooms There is a sitting-room with central heating, TV (colour), books, magazines, local guides and leaflets, indoor games, bar.

Cars The nearest main road is the A133 from Colchester to Clacton.

Credit cards accepted Access, Visa.

Closed to visitors We are not open in December and January.

Grey Gables, Norwich Road, near Cawston, south of Cromer, Norfolk, NR10 4EY   *Tel: 0603 871259*   **C D ♯7**

Every year James and Rosalind Snaith travel in Europe looking for interesting new wines and recipes to add to their repertoire, for this former rectory is no ordinary guest-house. There is a choice of a three-course dinner or five-course feast that may include, after an hors d'oeuvres, creamed salmon or Italian bean soup, chicken Wellington with apricots in puff pastry, or fillet steak with Marsala sauce, choux filled with lemon curd and cream, and then cheeses. Vegetables come from the garden.

They have rung the changes on blue-and-beige colour schemes in nearly every room from the Victorian-style sitting-room and up the elegant mahogany staircase to the bedrooms. Dinner is eaten also at mahogany tables with velvet-upholstered chairs; silver, rosy Royal Albert china and candles make it an elegant occasion. I was looking at a needlework sampler made by Rosalind's great-aunt in the 'twenties when her mother told me embroidery had been a family tradition through at least four generations of craftswomen ('We never buy anything if we can embroider it ourselves!'): Rosalind herself continues it.

My favourite bedroom is no.1: pretty fireplace, big bay windows overlooking the semi-wild garden, blue-and-white flowery duvet on the king-size bed which has a buttoned bedhead.

(This part of Norfolk, between Cromer and Norwich, has been described under other entries.)

The following facts have been supplied by the owners:

Bedrooms There are 4 rooms, which include single, double and family rooms. Bed-and-breakfast costs from £14 (per person in a double room) including service and VAT; prices go up in high season. There are reductions for stays of 7 nights or more for full board; and 'bargain breaks' as well.

Some if not all of the rooms have the following amenities: central heating; washbasin, own bathroom and wc, shaver-point; radio, TV (colour), armchairs; views of countryside or garden; tea/coffee-making facilities; door keys.

Meals The dinner menu is fixed price (from £7). There is a choice of dishes on the fixed menu, which consists of 3 courses and coffee. Dinner is served from 7 pm. Vegetarian or special diets can be prepared. Lunches and packed lunches can be provided; and snacks at other hours. Morning or afternoon drinks (coffee, tea etc.) can be ordered for a charge. Wine and other alcoholic drinks can be ordered.

Public rooms There is a sitting-room with central heating, open fire, books, magazines, local guides and leaflets.

Surroundings The grounds consist of 4 acres of formal and semi-wild gardens, orchard and paddock. Lawn tennis.

Cars The nearest main road is the A140 from Norwich to Cromer.

Languages spoken French.

Grimstock Hotel, Gilson Road, Water Orton, Coleshill, east of Birmingham, West Midlands, B46 1AS
Tel: 0675 62369   **C H D PT X ♯4**

Ron Hughes, a master builder, bought this Edwardian country house only a few years ago with little idea of turning it into a hotel – but as well as restoring it throughout he has gradually added more and more rooms to let, so popular has it proved. No wonder, for it is a rural retreat in an otherwise very industrial area – Birmingham's tower blocks, electricity pylons and the motorway are close (yet, once you are in the leafy grounds of Grimstock House, easily forgotten). A useful place to know if you have to go to the National Exhibition Centre or Birmingham international airport, for example; or for a stopover when tackling the long haul on the M6 to or from Scotland. Coventry is near; and the countryside between is 'Edwardian Lady' territory (see page 106).

Everything indoors is solid and comfortable – armchairs are huge, most rooms spacious. The food, too, is conventional fare (steaks, salmon, chicken à la crême, for instance), carefully cooked by Garry Hack and in generous proportions. After dinner, one can sit on a summer evening by the pool with fountain at the front, or among the old apple trees at the back.

The following facts have been supplied by the owners:

Bedrooms There are 19 rooms, which include single, double and family rooms. **To readers of this book only**, bed-and-breakfast costs from £16.50 (per person in a double room) including service and VAT; prices go up in high season. There are reductions for stays of 10 nights or more.

Some if not all of the rooms have the following amenities: central heating or electric heaters; washbasin, shower, own bathroom and wc, shaver-point; radio, TV (colour), phone, armchairs; views of countryside, farmland, garden; choice of duvets or blankets; tea/coffee-making facilities; door keys. Breakfast in bed is available.

Meals The dinner menu is fixed price (£5.75) or à la carte. There is a choice of dishes on the fixed menu, which consists of 3 courses and coffee. Dinner is served at 6.30 pm. Special diets can be prepared. Lunches and packed lunches can be provided; and snacks at other hours. Morning, afternoon or bedtime drinks (coffee, tea etc.) can be ordered for a charge. Wine and other alcoholic drinks can be ordered.

Public rooms There are 2 sitting-rooms etc. The following are available in one or both of them: central heating, TV (colour), books, magazines, local guides and leaflets, piano, bar.

Surroundings The grounds consist of 2½ acres of gardens. These are available in the neighbourhood: badminton, squash, the National Golf Centre.

Cars The nearest main road is the A446 from Warwick to Lichfield.

Credit cards accepted Access, Visa.

Gunnarsgill Hall, Gunnerside, west of Richmond, North Yorkshire, DL11 6LA *Tel: 0748 86213* C S ⌗9

The main room here, a huge beamed space like the nave of a church, with mullioned and latticed windows, was a schoolroom 130 years ago. One end is now a studio, for Ken and Lesley Jones are respectively a silversmith and a painter. In the middle is the dining area, with an oak settle, elm tables, and farmhouse chairs. At the far end, under a gallery, the floor is covered with oriental rugs; and comfortable armchairs face a log fire.

Leslie, who loves cooking, prefers to use organically grown produce, and she has a network of local suppliers of fresh vegetables and eggs and a butcher who knows the quality of meat she insists on. You might perhaps choose soup made from local artichokes; chicken stuffed with pâté and mushrooms (served in a wine-and-garlic sauce); and pears in red wine (with chocolate-and-brandy sauce) – plus farm cheeses and coffee. Breakfasts are imaginative, and so are the vegetarian menus.

It is Ken's and Lesley's paintings that hang on the white-painted walls of the old schoolroom, where she and Ken can sometimes offer courses in enamelling as well as silverwork and painting.

At one side of the building, in what was the schoolmaster's home, are the bedrooms, furnished mostly with stripped pine and cotton prints. All give views of Gunnerside Gill, in which tumbles

206

a tributary of the River Swale that you can follow on foot to its source.

The house is reached by a narrow lane alongside the gill from Gunnerside, one of the picturesque stone villages which are a feature of Swaledale. Waterfalls, woodlands, streams, fells and the ruins of old lead mines give the area its distinctive character. There is plenty more to see: ancient churches and abbeys, prehistoric remains, strange geological formations (including crags and caves).

The following facts have been supplied by the owners:

Bedrooms There are 3 rooms, which include single, double and family rooms. Dinner, bed-and-breakfast costs from £19.50 (per person in a double room) including service and VAT; prices go up in high season. There are reductions for stays of 7 nights or more; and 'bargain breaks' as well.

Some if not all of the rooms have the following amenities: central heating or electric heaters; electric blankets, washbasin, own bathroom, shaver-point; views of countryside/farmland/garden; choice of duvets or blankets; tea/coffee-making facilities.

Meals The dinner menu is fixed price (£8.50). There is only a choice of starters on the fixed menu, which consists of 4 courses and coffee. Dinner is served at 6.30 pm. Special diets can be prepared. Lunches and packed lunches can be provided. Bedtime drinks (coffee, tea etc.) can be ordered free. Non-residents are not admitted to the dining-room. Wine and other drinks can be ordered.

Public rooms There are 2 sitting areas. The following are available in one or both of them: central heating, open fire, TV, books, magazines, local guides and leaflets, indoor games (such as chess, Scrabble, Monopoly, dominoes etc.), record-player and records.

Surroundings The grounds consist of a garden. Trout fishing is available in the neighbourhood.

Cars The nearest main road is the A1 from London to Scotland.

Guy Wells, Whaplode, east of Spalding, Lincolnshire, PE12 6TZ
Tel: 0406 22239   **C D PT S ♯4**

Springs in the land around this Queen Anne house are what gave it its name. It is in a lovely and secluded position, surrounded by a traditional garden, trees, and beyond that the fens. The Thompsons have daffodil and tulip fields as well as glasshouses where they cultivate geraniums, fuchsias and cyclamens.

The interior of the house is full of imaginative touches – like the addition of an alcove with domed top and scallop-edged shelves to one side of the brick hearth where a log stove stands. Raspberry velvet tub chairs contrast with homely stripped-pine doors. And there is no sound louder than a slow-ticking clock or the purr of their voluptuous cat.

Hall and staircase are pretty (with sprigged wallpaper, prints and bouquets of flowerheads dried by Anne), leading to the bedrooms – one of which is huge, with antique bedhead and an old cedar chest, while another has a mural painted by the Thompsons' daughter when she was 15 (she is now a music student). The best one of all has a spread with tucks and pink ribbons, chaise longue, and windows on two sides. One has a four-poster.

Visitors who choose Guy Wells do so in order to explore the superb churches of the county, to enjoy its bird life or the spring flowers, for the easy cycling (it's a level area) or just for the peace.

And for Anne's wholefood cooking (using their own vegetables and eggs). She makes all her own pâtés, soups, quiches or ratatouille for starters; a traditional roast or casserole may follow;

even ice cream is home-made, and puddings like raspberry pavlova, cheesecake or (a speciality I found delectable) a crême brulée in which yogurt combines with cream as a topping to brandied grapes. (Non-smokers preferred.)

From Whaplode, one can easily explore most of Lincolnshire and much of Cambridgeshire, too – Peterborough, in particular, is worth a day for its cathedral, river trips, local museums and shopping centre – all described elsewhere.

The following facts have been supplied by the owners:

Bedrooms There are 3 rooms, which include single, double and family rooms. Bed-and-breakfast costs from £10 (per person) including service and VAT; prices go up in high season. There are reductions for stays of 7 nights or more; and 'bargain breaks' as well.

 Some if not all of the rooms have the following amenities: central heating or electric heaters; electric blankets, washbasin, shower and wc, shaver-point; armchairs; views of countryside/farmland/garden; choice of duvets or blankets; door keys.

Meals The dinner menu is fixed price (£6.50) or à la carte. There is a choice of dishes on the fixed menu, which consists of 3 courses and coffee. Dinner is served at 7.30 pm. Special diets can be prepared. Lunches and packed lunches can be provided; and snacks at other hours. Morning, afternoon or bedtime drinks (coffee, tea etc.) can be ordered free. Wine and other alcoholic drinks can be brought in.

Public rooms There is a sitting-room with central heating, open fire, TV (colour), books, magazines, local guides and leaflets, indoor games (such as cards, Scrabble etc.).

Surroundings The grounds consist of 1½ acres of landscaped gardens, with tennis. These are available in the neighbourhood: swimming-pool, coarse fishing, squash and tennis.

Cars The nearest main road is the A151 from Spalding to Holbeach.

Hare and Hounds Inn, Talkin, east of Carlisle, Cumbria, CA8 1LE   *Tel: 06977 3456*   C PT S-C ⌗8

You could easily pass by this unassuming little inn in the middle of a quiet village – but there is more to it than meets the eye. Even the public bar is a bit different from the average, with wainy-edged yew tables made by the owner, logs in stone fireplaces at each end, and over the bar itself (where Theakston beer and draught cider are served) heraldic panels of stained glass.

Tucked away behind all this are peaceful, beamed bedrooms, and a farm-cottage annexe, quite attractively furnished and with pretty duvets on the beds. One has a four-poster.

The owner is Les Stewart, formerly design and export director of Wetheralls until a takeover. He discovered the 200-year-old Hare and Hounds in a run-down state, and decided to give it a new life. Now it has a reputation for good, simple meals served in the bar at modest prices – fillet steaks and jacket potatoes with a variety of fillings, for instance. The breakfasts are interesting, with a selection that even includes black pudding and a variety of waffles to choose from. There is a separate family room, still with the old black-leaded kitchen range and brass fender, where children's menus are served. When the inn is crowded service may be slow. Sometimes trout and salmon are available.

Talkin itself is situated in an interesting part of the country, surrounded by fells that are popular with walkers and near a large, unspoilt tarn with various water-sports. Hadrian's Wall is quite near: the most interesting parts at this end of it are the Banks Burn stretch and the fort at Birdoswald. The Scottish border-country and the Lake District are easily reached, too, and the beautiful Eden Valley lies to the south. Brampton is an old market town; Alston and the city of Carlisle are not far. Talkin used to be a stopping-place for monks making their way to Lanercost Priory: part of it is in ruins, but the very lovely nave is still used as a church and what was the guests' solar is a village hall. In the locality are a hand-loom weaver and a potter, a working water mill and fine gardens at Corby Castle.

Readers' comments: Much impressed by the welcome and hospitality. Have stayed repeatedly, and food is better than ever.

The following facts have been supplied by the owner:

Bedrooms There are 4 rooms, which include single, double and family rooms. Bed-and-breakfast costs from £11 (per person in a double room), including VAT. There are reductions for stays of 4 nights or more. Sunday accommodation free to over-60s staying 3 days. Sampler breaks (see page 14).

Some if not all of the rooms have the following amenities: central heating or electric heaters; electric blankets, washbasin, shower, own bathroom and wc, shaver-point; armchairs; views of countryside and farmland; choice of duvets or blankets; tea/coffee-making facilities; door keys. Breakfast in bed available.

Meals The dinner menu is fixed price (£6.50); or bar food. There is a choice of dishes on the fixed menu, which consists of 3 courses and coffee. Dinner is served at 7–9 pm. Lunches and/or packed lunches can be provided; and snacks at other hours. Morning, afternoon or bedtime drinks (coffee, tea etc.) can be ordered free. Wine and other alcoholic drinks can be ordered. Vegetarians catered for.

Public rooms There are 4 sitting-rooms etc. The following are available in one or more of them: central heating, open fire, colour TV, books, magazines, local guides and leaflets, indoor games (such as darts and dominoes), and a bar.

Surroundings The grounds consist of a beer garden. These are available in the neighbourhood: riding, swimming, fishing, boating, golf, birdwatching, windsurfing lessons.

Cars The nearest main road is the A69 from Carlisle to Brampton.

Harrop Fold Farm, Bolton-by-Bowland, Clitheroe, north of Blackburn, Lancashire, BB7 4PJ   *Tel: 02007 600*   **S X**

Though a working farm, Harrop Fold is hardly typical, for it is not every Lancashire farmhouse that offers haute cuisine by a trained chef or accommodation to vie with that of a luxury hotel.

It is in the Trough of Bowland, one of north Lancashire's beauty-spots, at the end of a long turning off one of the narrow lanes which wind up and down through this expanse of heather-covered hills. Originally 17th century, the house has the typical long shape of the area (reputedly Norse in origin) and is little changed externally. Internally, however, though there are plenty of gnarled wooden lintels and the like, it is very luxurious. The bedrooms, full of frills and furbelows, mostly have private bathrooms and television sets – one has an extra-large double bed. The public areas, enthusiastically decorated and furnished, flow into each other the length of the ground floor. One sitting area, where there is a bar, has a big open fire, and there is another upstairs.

Harrop Fold is run by two generations of the Wood family. One of the sons (the other runs the farm) is the chef; he did part of his training at Miller Howe, a Lake District hotel famous for its cooking. He it is who accounts for the presence on the menu of 'Andrew's Special', a mushroom-and-prawn first course. Main dishes might include pheasant or trout among a wide choice, for local fish and game are made much of here. Some revived historical dishes often appear – salmagundi, for example – and there are always enterprising vegetarian choices.

Prices include afternoon tea buffet; morning coffee; fruit and wine in your bedroom on arrival.

Though the emphasis at Harrop Fold is on self-indulgence, walkers and anglers are encouraged. In fact, the owners have made special arrangements for fishing; and they are prepared to send a car for guests at the end of a long walk. For motorists, they have prepared a book of suggested rides which can be borrowed for the day. There are sights to visit quite near (castles, mansions, beauty-spots) or further afield, the Brontë country and Blackpool.

The following facts have been supplied by the owners:

Bedrooms There are 8 bedrooms which include singles and doubles. Bed-and-breakfast costs from £14.50 (per person in a double room) including afternoon tea, service and VAT. There are reductions for stays of 2 nights or more. Sunday accommodation free to over-60s staying 3 days.

All rooms have the following amenities: central heating; bathrooms with bath or shower; TV (colour), armchairs; views of countryside and farmland; choice of duvets or blankets; tea/coffee-making facilities; door keys. Breakfast in bed is available, and video films.

Meals The dinner menu can be either fixed price (£10) or à la carte. There is a choice of dishes on the fixed menu, which consists of 3 courses and coffee. Dinner is served at 7.30–8.45 pm. Special diets can be prepared. Packed lunches can be provided. Wine and other alcoholic drinks can be ordered.

Public room There are 2 lounges with central heating, open fire, books, magazines, local guides and leaflets, indoor games (Scrabble, cards and chess). Also a bar. Bridge can be arranged.

Surroundings The grounds consist of 280 acres of farmland. These are available in the neighbourhood: golf, swimming, riding, hotel fishing.

Cars The nearest main road is the A59 from Preston to Skipton.

Credit cards accepted Access, Visa.

Harrow Inn, Warren Street, Lenham, south of Maidstone, Kent, ME17 2ED   *Tel: 0622 858727*   C PT ⌗ 9

Being so close to the A20 and not far from the M2, this is a convenient place for a stopover on the way to Dover or other parts of the Kent coast – and handy for visiting Canterbury, too. It is now rather more of a hotel than an inn, having recently been modernized by Mark Watson to a very high standard.

Beyond the large, comfortable bar is a spacious private sitting-room for residents – very pretty with flowery chintzes, pink curtains, white walls and a log stove. Bedrooms are equipped with Stag furniture, leafy curtains on wood poles and nice details like brass or wrought-iron fittings on the solid wood doors. Outside are rustic seats in a garden that has views of the quiet fields around.

Local produce (including game) and vegetarian dishes feature on menus which include such options as spinach and Stilton soup, pheasant stuffed with grapes, and hazelnut meringues. Bar food, too, is imaginative.

The countryside around here is very beautiful indeed, with small lanes twisting among the hills, ancient churches, and unspoilt inns (the Carpenters Arms at nearby Eastling is one of my favourites). Apart from all the famous places (Canterbury, historic Faversham, Chilham Castle, Whitstable of oyster fame, etc.), one can soon reach Sittingbourne for its Dolphin sailing-barge centre and its steam railway; the Isle of Sheppey (with Sheerness port, ancient Minster abbey and strange byways such as Harty); the Swale bird reserve; Conyer (more sailing-barges, and the Ship Inn); and other creeks and inlets on the north Kent coast – an area of great fascination, largely bypassed by tourists.

The following facts have been supplied by the owners:

Bedrooms There are 6 rooms, which include single, double and family rooms. Bed-and-breakfast costs from £14 (per person in a double room) including VAT. There are reductions for stays of 7 nights or more; and 'bargain breaks' as well.

    The rooms have the following amenities: central heating; washbasin, shower, own bathroom and wc, shaver-point; radio; views of countryside, farmland, garden; tea/coffee-making facilities; door keys. Continental breakfast in bed is available.

Meals The dinner menu is fixed price (£10.50). There is a choice of dishes on the fixed menu, which consists of 4 courses and coffee. Dinner is served at 7.30–9 pm. Special diets can be prepared. Lunches and packed lunches can be provided; and snacks at other hours. Morning, afternoon or bedtime drinks (coffee, tea etc.) can be ordered for a charge. Wine and other alcoholic drinks can be ordered.

Public rooms There is a sitting-room with central heating, open fire, TV (colour), books, magazines, local guides and leaflets. (No smoking.) Also a bar.

Surroundings The grounds consist of 1½ acres of garden and paddock. Cycles for hire.

Cars The nearest main road is the A20 from London to Dover.

Credit cards accepted Access, Visa.

———————————

Hawkes House, 34 London Road, Spalding, Lincolnshire, PE11 2TE *Tel: 0775 4661* **C D PT S-C ♯4**

A classical town-house (built in 1695, overlooking the river), this is the home of artist Hilldred Harman. It was up this river that the interior panelling came – imported from Norway. Hilldred has had it painted in attractive colours (apricot and grey in the sitting-room, for instance, complemented by grey corduroy curtains), on which she hangs her own paintings of local views – many for sale.

The dining-room has country-style curtains and tablecloths, and overlooks the garden. A very lovely staircase rises to the first-floor bedrooms, above which are self-catering rooms.

Guests are welcome to sit among the 250 roses in the brick-walled garden at the back, or in the revolving summerhouse. Many choose to dine out in Spalding (Hilldred recommends Isobel's Pantry, a thatched house just a little way along the river) but, by pre-arrangement, a meal can be provided – such as home-made soup, roast local pork and lemon sorbet. Spicy Lincolnshire sausages are a breakfast treat.

Spalding is a rather Dutch-style town, much of it 18th century, at the heart of the bulb-fields which bring in visitors every spring. The whole area is crowded during the May tulip-parade when elaborate floats progress through the streets (a way of using up the millions of flowerheads which have to be discarded in the course of propagating bulbs). At any time of year, however, gardeners find the area well worth visiting, particularly for the vast Springfields Gardens and glasshouses. Boston and Stamford, too, which are described elsewhere, are interesting places to visit.

The following facts have been supplied by the owners:

Bedrooms There are 2 double or family rooms. Bed-and-breakfast costs from £9.50 (per person in a double room) including service and VAT; prices go up in high season.

    The rooms have central heating and gas heaters; washbasin, shaver-point; armchairs; views of garden; choice of duvets or blankets; door keys. Breakfast in bed is available.

Meals The dinner menu is fixed price (£6.50) or à la carte. There is no choice of dishes on the fixed menu, which consists of 3 courses and coffee and must be booked in advance. Dinner is served at 7 pm. Special diets can be prepared. Packed lunches can be provided; and snacks at other hours. Morning, afternoon or bedtime drinks (coffee, tea etc.) can be ordered for a charge.

Public rooms There is a sitting-room with central heating, TV (colour), books, magazines, local guides and leaflets.

Surroundings The grounds consist of a garden. These are available in the neighbourhood: tennis, bowls, swimming-pool, squash, golf, sailing (river), fishing.

Cars The nearest main road is the A16 from Stamford to Grimsby.

Closed to visitors We are not open outside summer (except for self-catering).

Hawks Hill, Great Witchingham, north-west of Norwich, Norfolk, NR9 5QS *Tel: 0603 872552* **C**(10) **D X ⌗7**

Being right next to the Norfolk Wildlife Park, guests at this elegant 17th-century house of mellow brick can glimpse herons and other birds flying free around one of the park's willow-fringed pools.

The house has its own lovely surroundings: at the front, a cobbled and paved forecourt with stone troughs of colourful busy-Lizzies, and at the back a very big rose garden and lawn with interesting features – circular paving around a sundial, honeysuckle climbing up old apple trees, flint walls incorporating here a tiled niche and there the head of a Roman warrior.

Inside is a large, beamed sitting/dining-room with a stove on the brick hearth, handsome Turkey-red curtains and an open-tread staircase leading up to bedrooms with pretty fabrics. There are interesting paintings, and small treasures collected from all over the world.

Patricia Wayre serves meals based on her own or local produce. For instance, a prawn-and-haddock savoury may be followed by pheasant or leg of Norfolk lamb with garden vegetables, and then perhaps lemon pudding or a meringue bombe with strawberries.

The adjoining wildlife park (40 acres) deserves repeated visits to see its huge collection of European species living in nearly natural conditions: otters, seals, waterfowl, owls and much else (more exotic species include apes and bison); with freedom to picnic or for children to run about. Norwich and its cathedral are only 14 miles away and there are plenty of stately homes, seaside beaches, mediaeval villages, museums or castles, bird reserves and boating centres to explore.

rear view

The following facts have been supplied by the owners:

Bedrooms There are 2 rooms, a single and a double. Bed-and-breakfast costs from £10 (per person in a double room), no VAT or service charge. Sampler breaks (see page 14).

   The rooms have central heating and electric heaters; electric blankets, washbasin, own bathroom and wc, shaver-point; radio, armchairs; views of countryside and garden; orthopaedic mattress; tea/coffee-making facilities. Breakfast in bed is available, also clothes washing, and hair drier.

Meals The dinner menu is fixed price (£6.50). There is no choice of dishes on the menu, which consists of 3 courses and coffee. Dinner is served at anytime. Vegetarian or special diets can be prepared. Packed lunches can be provided; and snacks at other hours. Morning, afternoon or bedtime drinks (coffee, tea etc.) can be ordered for a charge. Non-residents are not admitted to the dining-room.

Public rooms There is a sitting-room with central heating, open fire, TV (colour), books, magazines, local guides and leaflets, maps on loan, record-player and records.

Surroundings The grounds consist of an acre of garden.

Cars The nearest main road is the A1067 from Norwich to Fakenham.

Heavers, Ryarsh, West Malling, west of Maidstone, Kent, ME19 5JU   *Tel: 0732 842074*   **C D PT S ⌗9**

Perched on a hilltop, this red brick farmhouse with dormer windows in the roof and clematis around the porch is at the heart of a smallholding which provides much of the produce that Jean Edwards (once a health visitor) enjoys cooking for her guests. Until a few decades ago, the old house was occupied by generations of the same farming family which built it in the 17th century. All around are country lanes, fields, woodlands and two long-distance footpaths – the North Downs Way and the Weald Way.

The sitting-room has very comfortable armchairs grouped around the brick hearth (stacked with logs), which still has the old bread oven alongside. It's a cosy room, with the soothing sound of a clock ticking, Gem (the Edwards' Jack Russell terrier) snoozing on the hearth, a collection of china pigs, good books and, in autumn, a vast wood bowl of Kentish cobnuts to dip into.

Jean enjoys cooking a wide repertoire of dishes (whenever she and her husband travel in the wine regions of France, she always returns with new recipes). She bakes her own bread; honey, eggs, blackberries, vegetables, geese and lamb are home-produced.

Beamed bedrooms with white-boarded, latched doors are prettily furnished with Laura Ashley fabrics and attractive colour schemes (pink- or blue-and-white, or moss-green with red-and-white). The Edwards have collected stuffed birds and maps for the walls, and pot-plants for every window sill. Through the windows are views of the Downs or of the garden which, even in winter, is colourful with witch hazel, holly berries and winter-flowering cherry trees. There's an old pump in it, a swing-seat on the brick patio, and a children's swing.

Although only an hour from south London, this is a good centre from which to explore rural Kent, the mediaeval bridges of the upper Medway, and any number of castles – Allington, Leeds, Rochester – and historic buildings – Boughton Monchelsea house, the friary at Aylesford, Sissinghurst with its famous gardens, the Archbishop's Palace at Maidstone. There's county cricket, boating and sailing, and a famous collection of carriages at Maidstone. But the scenery is the main thing: hills, orchards, streams, hop-gardens with the conical oast houses, half-timbered cottages, picturesque villages like Loose (a stream threads its way among the houses). West Malling itself is largely Georgian, with Norman remains; while Mereworth has an unusual classical church.

Reader's comment: Very good indeed.

The following facts have been supplied by the owners:

Bedrooms There are 3 double rooms. Bed-and-breakfast costs from £10 (per person in a double room) including service and VAT; prices go up in high season. There are reductions for stays of 7 nights or more. Sampler breaks (see page 14).

Some if not all of the rooms have the following amenities: central heating; electric blankets, washbasin, shaver-point; armchairs; views of countryside, farmland, garden; choice of duvets or blankets. Breakfast in bed is available.

Meals The dinner menu is fixed price (£8). There is no choice of dishes on the fixed menu, which consists of 3 courses and coffee. Dinner is served at 7.30 pm. Special diets can be prepared. Packed lunches can be provided; and snacks at other hours. Morning, afternoon or bedtime drinks (coffee, tea etc.) can be ordered free. Non-residents are not admitted to the dining-room. Wine and other alcoholic drinks can be brought in.

Public rooms There is a sitting-room with central heating, open fire, TV (colour), books, magazines, local guides and leaflets, indoor games (such as cards and board games), piano, record-player and records.

Surroundings The grounds consist of 5 acres of field and a large garden. Golf, swimming and riding are available in the neighbourhood.

Cars The nearest main road is the A20 from London to Maidstone.

Languages spoken French.

High Green House, Nowton, south of Bury St Edmunds, Suffolk, IP29 2LZ *Tel: 0284 86293* **C D H PT S X ⌗ 4**

Part Tudor and part Victorian, this delightful house is truly secluded – surrounded by brimming herbaceous borders, a paddock of geese and an old well, with wheat fields beyond. There are a lily pool (it is all that remains of a moat), troughs of begonias and fuchsias, and, where only the great frame of a mediaeval barn survives, Rosemary Thew has created a suntrap in which to sit, training scented roses and wisteria over the timbers, and placing wood seats to face the rural view.

The interior of the house is full of nooks and crannies, cabinets of old china and glass, antique furniture and low beams. There are oriel and mullioned windows, a brick fireplace, and wrought-iron hinges on bedroom doors. Some bedrooms are small and simple; but one has a four-poster, windows on three sides, a carved chest and a cheval mirror with painted flowers. Miss Thew (who worked with physically handicapped people until her retirement) has also provided two downstairs bedrooms ideal for disabled people.

She enjoys cooking (and grows fruit, asparagus etc. for the kitchen). The sort of dinner she serves can comprise a chicken vol-au-vent as a starter, then a roast joint, profiteroles and cheese. She is a genial, informal lady with whom one immediately feels at home; and, because she was formerly clerk to the local council, she is a mine of information about the area (and its people).

Bury and its environs are described on page 457.

Readers' comments: Warm welcome and excellent food. Wonderful welcome; most tranquil house.

The following facts have been supplied by the owners:

Bedrooms There are 6 rooms, which include single, double and family rooms. Bed-and-breakfast costs from £9.50 (per person in a double room) including service and VAT; prices go up in high season. There are reductions for stays of 7 nights or more; and 'bargain breaks' as well. Sunday accommodation free to over-60s staying 3 days.

  Some if not all of the rooms have the following amenities: central heating or electric heaters; washbasin, shower, own bathroom, shaver-point; radio, TV (colour or b&w); views of countryside, farmland, garden; choice of duvets or blankets; tea/coffee-making facilities; door keys. Breakfast in bed available. Hair drier, laundering, and orthopaedic mattress or bed-board available.

Meals The dinner menu is fixed price (£5). There is no choice of dishes on the menu, which consists of 4 courses, wine and coffee. Dinner is served from 7.30

220

pm. Special diets can be prepared. Non-residents are not admitted to the dining-room. Wine and other alcoholic drinks can be brought in. Tea free.

Public rooms There is a sitting-room with central heating, open fire, TV (colour), books, magazines, local guides and leaflets. Maps on loan.

Surroundings The grounds consist of one acre of garden.

Cars The nearest main road is the A134 from Bury St Edmunds to Sudbury.

Languages spoken German.

Highlow Hall Farm, near Hathersage, west of Sheffield (Yorkshire), Derbyshire, S30 JAX
Tel: 0433 50393   **C D S ♯ 5**

At the heart of this huge farm (raising sheep and cattle) is a castellated stone manor-house of considerable historic interest – complete with not one but four ghost stories. It is one of several similar ones in the Peak District built by a 16th-century farmer for each of his sons: his name, Eyre, is now famous because Charlotte Brontë, who stayed at Hathersage vicarage, took it for her heroine Jane Eyre. (And in the locality was a house which had burned down with, reputedly, a madwoman in it – inspiration for Thorn-field Hall.) In the square porch is a massive front door with old iron studs and hinges; the windows have stone mullions and small panes; and above the rugged walls of gritstone is a roof of dark stone slates. It is as if the house grew out of the land itself, for this is the northern (or 'dark') part of the Peak District – solid millstone grit, in contrast to 'white' limestone peaks further south.

The sitting-room was added in Georgian times, so it has large sash windows with views of the far moors, where the Wains' sheep graze, rising to slopes brilliant with heather in September and rusty bracken in October. The house is 800 feet above sea level (its name derives from 'high hlaw', meaning 'high hill'). Deep, velvety chairs are grouped round a blazing fire on cold days. Adjoining is the dining-room, with comfortably upholstered chairs around each table. Bed-and-breakfast only.

Bedrooms are roomy and comfortable, some with ancient stonework and all with fine views – not another building is in sight. One may wake in autumn to frost-sugared grass and grazing sheep; and, beyond a line of graceful pines, peaks rosy in the sun.

Margaret Wain will show you the most ancient part of the house (unused at present): the huge stone-flagged hall with great oak staircase. This was once the kitchen, and it still has an old stone sink, stone cheese-press, refectory table and ancient chest. She also has a big family Bible in which the Wain family's genealogy is traced back to 1322.

Many visitors come here simply for the scenery and the peace; but there are plenty of places worth visiting (and, of course, glorious walks – the Pennine Way starts in the Peak District). There are the Blue John caverns, stately homes such as Chatsworth and Haddon Hall, the summer 'well dressing' ceremonies in the many historic villages, interesting old towns such as Buxton and Bakewell, and the city of Sheffield – a great deal more than just an industrial centre (its art gallery, cathedral and theatre are all good, and it has a working 'industrial hamlet' open to visitors).

In hilly Buxton are plenty of interesting places to visit. In its heyday as a spa it emulated Bath, so there are splendid Georgian crescents and squares, a superb Assembly Room (now housing the library) and flowery parks through which the River Wye bubbles its way. A century later, further notable buildings went up – the glass pavilion for subtropical gardens, concert hall and (recently restored to all its glory) the opera house. Each July or August Buxton holds an international festival of opera, music and drama.

There are sheepdog trials and agricultural shows, open days at Losehill Hall (where country crafts are demonstrated) and markets. In the Derwent valley, huge reservoirs have created the effect of another Lake District; and across the moors runs the memorable Snake Pass drive to Glossop. Canals, nature trails, gorges, rivers, birdwatching: there is plenty here for a very varied holiday. For more information about the area, see page 331–2.

Readers' comments: Quite delightful; beautifully furnished; friendly and obliging; very impressed – made most welcome, very caring of our comfort. Friendly welcome, most enjoyable.

The following facts have been supplied by the owners:

Bedrooms There are 6 rooms, which include single, double and family rooms. Bed-and-breakfast costs from £12 (per person), including VAT. There are reductions for stays of 7 nights or more.

    The rooms have the following amenities: electric heaters; electric blankets; washbasin, shaver-point; armchairs; views of moors, farmland, garden; choice of duvets or blankets; tea/coffee-making facilities; door keys. Breakfast in bed is available.

Public rooms There is a sitting-room with open fire, colour TV, local guides and leaflets and indoor games (such as Scrabble, solitaire etc.).

Surroundings The grounds consist of a garden and 900 acres of farmland. These are available in the neighbourhood: riding, pony trekking, swimming-pool, golf, bowls, trout fishing.

Cars The nearest main road is the A625 from Sheffield to Castleton and Manchester.

Closed to visitors The farm is closed to visitors in winter.

Hillands, Russ Hill, Charlwood, north of Gatwick Airport, Surrey, RH6 0EL   *Tel: 0293 862079*   **C D S X ⌗ 1**

Beneath the flight-path of the intercontinental jets lies this one-time farmhouse, at least five centuries old, a lovely black-and-white timbered building surrounded by garden and woods, with a vast barn and other outbuildings. Down the lane is a donkey farm.

Here Maggie Scott-Dale gives visitors an unaffectedly warm welcome to her home, furnished with antiques to which she is constantly adding.

Her visitors' breakfast/sitting-room has a great inglenook with the original jack (she lights a log fire on cold nights), low beams, rugs on the board floor and lattice windows which (like all in the house) are soundproofed by double-glazing: air-conditioners bring fresh air to each room.

Each bedroom has attractive colours (the single one has a particularly pretty bed, with iron curlicues at head and foot); and in the children's room of the family suite are a rocking horse, rocking chair and soft toys. Windows are tiny; carpets thick.

If, like many, you use Hillands as a stopover before flying out of Gatwick, you can save a lot of money by leaving your car here: a taxi will take you to the airport in 7 minutes.

Only breakfast (continental, unless you pay more) is served, but you can dine in Charlwood village at Limes Bistro, at nearby inns, or at a big hotel only a minute's walk away – it has an indoor swimming-pool and other sports facilities usable for a fee.

This might be a good place to bring children who would enjoy the grounds, the viewing platform at the airport, the Gatwick aviary and zoo-park and, not far away, the Bluebell Line steam railway. It's ideal for plane-spotters because the aircraft are low enough to identify and numerous in summer (those who value quiet will prefer other seasons).

The following facts have been supplied by the owners:

Bedrooms There are 4 rooms, which include single, double and family rooms. Bed-and-breakfast costs from £12.50 (per person in a double room) including service and VAT; prices go up in high season. There are reductions for stays of 7 nights or more.

    Some if not all of the rooms have the following amenities: central heating or electric heaters; electric blankets, washbasin, shaver-point; views of countryside; tea/coffee-making facilities. Breakfast in bed is available.

Public rooms There is a sitting-room with central heating, open fire, TV (colour), books, magazines, local guides and leaflets, indoor games, record-player and records.

Surroundings The grounds consist of 4½ acres of woods and garden. These are available in the neighbourhood: swimming-pool, tennis.

Cars The nearest main road is the A23 from London to Brighton.

Holdfast Cottage Hotel, Welland, south of Malvern,
Worcestershire, WR13 6NA   *Tel: 0684 310288*   **C D PT S X✡3**

At the end of a winding drive flanked by flowering shrubs is a
building which, from the approach side, looks like an early
Victorian house: shuttered sash windows and a glass-roofed
verandah wreathed in wisteria. But indoors it becomes apparent
that the heart of the house is far older – 17th century, in fact.
Ceilings here are low and beamed, and the doors are made of
wooden boards.

When Dennis Beetlestone and his wife Diana took over the
house some years ago, it was run-down and many of its best
features were concealed. In restoring it, they have given a lot of
attention to detail – even down to small things like putting solid
brass fastenings on doors. Dennis has kept and refurbished a
pretty little kitchen-range, its tiny oven and fretted trivets gleaming black. He has not pursued an 'olde worlde' style, however, but
added many individual touches that reflect his own interests –
especially natural history. In the bay-windowed sitting-room
(furnished with comfortable old 'club' armchairs, leather-upholstered) are some exceptional portrait-drawings of Gladys
Cooper, Constance Cummings and other celebrated actresses of
the 'twenties.

All the bedrooms have very good, out-of-the-ordinary colour
schemes and patterns, deep carpets and individual character.
From many there are views of the hills or of the old-fashioned
garden where an ancient mulberry tree provides fruit for some of
the puddings served at meals.

Diana likes cooking elaborate dishes such as pork fillet with an orange-and-sultana stuffing and apricot sauce, or a meringue, apple and rum pudding, but there are always more conventional dishes to choose from, too – and servings are generous.

Welland lies close by the lovely Malvern hills, and the spa town of Malvern has an Elgar festival (every May), concerts, theatre and good shops. The cathedrals of Hereford, Gloucester and Worcester are within reach (the porcelain factory at Worcester is open to visitors, and 'seconds' are sold there at bargain prices). Other historic places well worth exploring include Ledbury, Tewkesbury (with its great abbey) and many picturesque villages, as well as the Wye Valley, with the famous beauty-spot Symonds Yat; and the Forest of Dean. In June there is the great Three Counties Agricultural Show, in August the Three Choirs Festival, and in autumn the book fair at Cheltenham and cider-making in various places.

Readers' comments: Everything we could have wanted – food excellent. Delightful rooms, immaculate. Carefully cooked and enterprising food.

The following facts have been supplied by the owners:

Bedrooms There are 9 rooms, which include single, double and family rooms. Bed-and-breakfast costs £18 (per person) including VAT, but there are reductions for stays of 3 nights or more; and 'bargain breaks' as well.

   Some if not all of the rooms have the following amenities: central heating; washbasin, shower, own bathroom and wc, shaver-point; armchairs; views of countryside, farmland, garden; door keys; tea/coffee-making facilities; electric blankets; bed-board available.

Meals The dinner menu is fixed price (£9) or à la carte. There is a choice of dishes on the fixed menu, which consists of 4 courses. Dinner is served from 7.30–9 pm. Special diets can be prepared. Lunches or packed lunches can be provided; and snacks at other hours. Morning, afternoon or bedtime drinks (coffee, tea etc.) can be ordered for a charge. Wine and other alcoholic drinks can be ordered. Vegetarian dishes available.

Public rooms There is a sitting-room with central heating, open fire, colour TV, books, magazines, local guides and leaflets, indoor games (such as Monopoly and chess); also a bar, and a glass sunroom.

Surroundings The grounds consist of a 2½ acre garden, with croquet. These are available in the neighbourhood: riding, golf and fishing.

Cars The nearest main road is the A4104 from Welland to Little Malvern.

Holmhead, Hadrian's Wall, Greenhead, west of Haltwhistle, Northumberland, CA6 7HY   *Tel: 0697 2402*   **C PT S ⌗15**

When Pauline and Brian Staff stopped one day for tea at Greenhead, not far from Carlisle, they fell in love with this former farmhouse and bought it. It stands beside a salmon river, just where the walkers' Pennine Way crosses the Roman Wall. This is a remote spot, surrounded by farmland and with the ruins of Thirlwall Castle looming overhead (Edward I once stayed there). Just outside are the remains of a Roman turret, somewhere under the lawn or sunken garden, awaiting excavation; and some Roman stones were re-used when the house was built. All this, with the distant moors, is within view through the windows of the guests' large and comfortable sitting-room upstairs – copiously equipped with games, toys, facilities to make unlimited hot drinks, books and maps. Pauline used to be a tour guide, and so is immensely helpful with advice on sightseeing. She occasionally gives visitors talks with slides, or may even show them around. Pre-Christmas party weekends are run; and discounts on tickets to local museums are available to guests.

There are all kinds of unexpected 'extras' in this out-of-the-way house: a solarium; foot-massager for weary walkers; pure spring water; table tennis; snooker; snacks at any hour; and the freedom of the kitchen – shared with Rex, a Hungarian visla hound. Pauline likes to cook local dishes and has even experimented with Roman recipes cooked in the area around AD 300 (one favourite is honey-roast ham in pastry). She makes all the preserves, chutneys, cakes and scones. A typical dinner menu: melon with kiwi fruit;

227

trout with Hollandaise sauce; almond meringue with wild raspberries in whipped cream. The trout will probably have come from the adjacent river and all ingredients are 'wholefood'. Local cheeses and sausages are a speciality.

Breakfast choices include haggis, black pudding, kedgeree, muffins, crumpets and occasionally a Scandinavian buffet.

The house is full of family treasures, their own paintings, and finds from travels all over the world. Occasionally, Pauline's uncle (Tom Finch) runs painting weekends here. Winter bargain breaks include talks with slides, an escorted visit and loan of maps etc.

This is a splendid area for walks (with or without a National Trust guide). The Northumbria National Park starts here; there are associations with Walter Scott and Catherine Cookson. You can look at working shire horses, Roman or prehistoric remains (including rock carvings), four castles, Hexham Abbey, Lanercost Priory, Beamish and Hunday open-air museums, stately homes. Even Scotland, the spectacular Northumbrian coast and the Lake District are within reach, as well as the wild and beautiful moorland heights of the north Pennines.

The following facts have been supplied by the owners:

Bedrooms There are 4 rooms, which include double and family rooms. Bed-and-breakfast costs from £9.50 (per person in a double room) including service and VAT; prices go up in high season. There are reductions for stays of 3 nights or more; and winter 'bargain breaks' as well (20% discount). Sampler breaks (see page 14).

Some if not all of the rooms have the following amenities: central heating; washbasin, shaver-point; armchairs; views of river, countryside, farmland, garden; choice of duvets or blankets; tea/coffee-making facilities; door keys; hair drier; laundering facilities. No smoking.

Meals The dinner menu is fixed price (£6). There is no choice of dishes on the menu, which consists of 3 courses and coffee. Dinner is served at 7.30 pm. Special diets can be prepared. Lunches and packed lunches can be provided; and snacks at other hours. No smoking. Morning, afternoon or bedtime drinks (coffee, tea etc.) can be made in the lounge, free. Non-residents are not admitted to the dining-room. Wine and other alcoholic drinks can be ordered.

Public rooms There is a sitting-room with central heating, TV (colour), tape recorder, books, magazines, local guides and leaflets, indoor games (such as chess, cards, Scrabble, Yhatzy, ¼ snooker table, table tennis), piano, record-player and records. Maps on loan.

Surroundings The grounds consist of an acre of garden and a patio; with badminton, cricket, swingball, and a swing. Golf, riding and heated swimming-pool are available locally. Helicopter flights over the Roman Wall start from the garden.

Cars The nearest main road is the A69 from Newcastle to Carlisle.
Languages spoken Norwegian.
Credit cards accepted Access, Visa, Amex.

Holwell Farm, Bampton, north of Tiverton, Devon, EX16 9AD
Tel: 0398 31452　　　**PT S ♯ 4**

This is a real 'find': a mediaeval longhouse, very well furnished indeed, and with truly exceptional food – all at a very modest price.

The 'holy well' which gave the farm its name (and which still exists below one of the floors) lies in a very pretty valley, well placed for visiting many interesting tourist sights all around it (see below). The house was built about 1470, and much of it is still unchanged. You can see the curving 'cruck' timbers that support the roof, the old beams and inglenook fireplace down below, the immensely thick walls of cobb.

Long, creaking passageways lead to spacious bedrooms, pleasantly furnished. There are two big sitting-rooms, one with an open fire, creamy Chinese carpet and slow-ticking grandfather clock; the other with an ornate 'dragon' stove to supplement the central heating (this is a very warm house: it has 22 radiators in all).

At the heart of it is the great kitchen where Pauline and Bob Fleming join their guests for meals at a long refectory table made of pine – like the dresser, the doors and the kitchen units. In one corner, armchairs and an old settle are drawn up around a log-burning stove.

The Flemings came here when their large Berkshire farm was carved up by a motorway, and they speak with enthusiasm about the area, and the friendliness of north Devon people. They have named their ducks and geese after some of these (and after some of their visitors). They also keep cows, sheep, chickens and guinea-fowl which supply the table; they have an organic vegetable garden and asparagus bed; and in winter Bob shoots game.

Pauline is an inspired natural cook. I recall with pleasure a dinner of creamy carrot soup served with herb bread; fish with mushroom stuffing en croûte and imaginative vegetables; then plum ice cream accompanied by sablé biscuits made with ground walnuts. The meal was accompanied by cider made from their own apples. At breakfast, there was a choice of hen, duck or goose eggs; home-made croissants, bread and preserves.

Outside the iron-studded, oak front door is a courtyard with ancient half-ruined walls covered in ivy. Gates of lacy ironwork lead to a south-facing garden with valley views, and at one side is an 18th-century barn with unusual circular pillars.

Bampton itself is a pretty village which has won awards for its floral decorations, and beyond it lies the best of Devonshire awaiting discovery. Plenty of National Trust houses, horse-drawn barge trips, an outstanding country museum, crafts centres, a man-made lake, and other pleasures are around.

Some of Devonshire's more unusual 'sights' include Morwellham Quay (an old port reconstructed), Bickleigh Mill farm, the maritime museum at Exeter, a living bee and honey exhibition, steam railways, watermills, potteries, the vintage motor and motorcycle collections, Dartington glassworks, bird gardens, a brass-rubbing centre, a 'combat vehicles' museum, a lace-making school, and innumerable mansions or castles.

The following facts have been supplied by the owners:

Bedrooms There are 4 rooms, which include singles and doubles. Bed-and-breakfast costs from £9 (per person in a double room) including service and VAT. There are reductions for stays of 7 nights.
   Some if not all of the rooms have the following amenities: central heating; washbasin, own bathroom and wc, shaver-point; armchairs; views of countryside/farmland/garden. Hair drier, curlers, and laundering facilities available.

Meals The dinner menu is fixed price (£6) or à la carte. There is no choice of dishes on the fixed menu, which consists of 3 courses and coffee. Dinner is served at 7–7.30 pm. Special diets can be prepared. Non-residents are not admitted to the dining-room. Wine and other alcoholic drinks can be brought in. Free tea on arrival.

Public rooms There are 2 sitting-rooms etc. The following are available in one or both of them: central heating, open fire, TV (colour), books, magazines, local guides and leaflets, indoor games (such as darts, exercycle, board games).

Surroundings The grounds consist of 25 acres of farmland and gardens. These are available in the neighbourhood: riding, golf, swimming, tennis and fishing. Maps and gumboots on loan.

Cars The nearest main road is the A361 from Barnstaple to Taunton.

Languages spoken Some French.

Horncastle Farm, Kirkwhelpington, north-west of Newcastle-upon-Tyne, Northumberland, NE19 2RA
Tel: 0830 40247   **D PT S ♯10**

The same family has farmed here for five generations, and many pieces of the furniture are heirlooms, including the wood cradle in which so many of their babies have been rocked. The house itself dates back to the 17th century, a solid building with deep-set sash windows, their shutters and the doors elegantly panelled.

A spacious sitting-room has armchairs of ample size, plenty of books and records. Bedrooms are large and light, with country-style fabrics and wallpapers, flowers and towels changed daily. Visitors love the atmosphere, comfort and peacefulness of all the rooms.

Janet White cooks local produce – beef, lamb, pork and salmon. Blackcurrants and raspberries go into her pies and pavlovas. She takes one evening off every week, recommending local restaurants for dinner. Everyone on arrival gets tea and cakes (free).

On a guided walk round the farm you will see Limousin and Sussex breeds of cattle, lambing (if you are there in spring) or sheep-dipping (in summer), the free-range chickens, and the farm's own protected nature reserve. Rivers form two of the farm's boundaries. All around is superb scenery – hills and valleys, forests and crags.

On warm evenings meals are often served in the sloping garden, where there are two immense copper-beeches and a weeping ash, rhododendrons in early summer, and marigolds and wallflowers later.

As to sightseeing, there is an abundance of castles and historic houses in the vicinity, some beautiful gardens, and (within driving distance) the historic cities of Newcastle, Carlisle and Edinburgh. It is an area too often hurried through en route to Scotland, but anyone who pauses finds that even a week is not enough to explore it thoroughly.

The following facts have been supplied by the owners:

Bedrooms There are 3 rooms, which include single, double and family rooms. Bed-and-breakfast costs from £12 (per person in a double room) including service and VAT; prices go up in high season. There are reductions for stays of 3 nights or more. Sunday night accommodation free to over-60s staying 3 days.

Some if not all of the rooms have the following amenities: central heating or electric heaters; electric blankets, washbasin, shaver-point; armchairs; views of countryside, farmland, garden; choice of duvets or blankets; tea/coffee-making facilities. Laundry facilities available. No smoking upstairs.

Meals There is no choice of dishes on the fixed menu (£6), which consists of 3 courses and coffee. Dinner is served at 6.30 pm. Special diets can be prepared. Lunches and packed lunches can be provided; and snacks at other hours.

Morning, afternoon or bedtime drinks (coffee, tea etc.) can be ordered. Non-residents are not admitted to the dining-room. Wine and other alcoholic drinks can be brought in.

Public rooms There are 2 sitting-rooms etc. The following are available in one or both of them: central heating, open fire, TV (colour), books, magazines, local guides and leaflets, indoor games (such as Scrabble, cards and computer games), piano, video films. Maps on loan.

Surroundings The grounds consist of 300 acres of farmland and garden, with fishing, snooker and table tennis. In the neighbourhood are pony trekking, fishing, tennis and swimming.

Cars The nearest main road is the A696 from Newcastle to Edinburgh.

Closed to visitors We are not open from October to March.

Howe Villa, Whitcliffe Mill, Richmond, North Yorkshire
Tel: 0748 2559   **C**(5) **PT S S-C ♯ 9**

Once past an unpromising approach, all you are aware of from the house is the large and beautiful garden and the River Swale rushing by it. (The river once powered the paper mill which went with Howe Villa.) The house is late Georgian, with large, light, rather grand rooms where house plants abound.

The bedrooms are spacious, each provided with fresh fruit, chocolates and flowers. All are on the ground floor – an advantage for those who do not like stairs.

The upstairs dining- and sitting-rooms have views across the river to a National Trust landscape. The plasterwork of the sitting-room ceiling is shown to advantage by an antique crystal chandelier, its drops reflecting the firelight.

Anita Berry is an enthusiastic cook who does a refresher cordon bleu course each winter. There is always a choice of first courses and of sweets, served by candlelight on tables spread with dark blue cloths, lace covered. Dinner is preceded by an aperitif (free): as one of my readers put it, 'you are made to feel more like a house guest than a paying guest'. Breakfasts have a varied choice.

The house is within walking distance of the centre of Richmond, which is sufficiently unchanged for an 18th-century map to be used as the basis for a 'town trail' leaflet. Best known for its Norman castle and hardly altered Georgian theatre (and for the 'Sweet Lass of Richmond Hill'), it is a town of many attractions and a good base for outings into the Yorkshire Dales.

Readers' comments: Lovingly renovated, relaxing, welcoming. Food delicious and plentiful. Very comfortable; cooking excellent.

The following facts have been supplied by the owners:

Bedrooms There are 4 rooms, which include single, double and family rooms. Dinner, bed-and-breakfast costs from £25 (per person in a double room) including service and VAT. There are reductions for stays of 4 nights or more; and 'bargain breaks' as well.

    Some if not all of the rooms have the following amenities: central heating; own bathroom and wc, shaver-point; radio, TV (colour), armchairs; views of garden; door keys.

Meals There is a choice of dishes on the fixed menu, which consists of 4 courses and coffee. Dinner is served at 7.30 pm. Special diets can be prepared. Packed lunches can be provided; and snacks at other hours. Morning, afternoon or bedtime drinks (coffee, tea etc.) can be ordered free. Non-residents are not admitted to the dining-room. Wine and other alcoholic drinks can be ordered or brought in.

Public rooms There is one sitting-room with central heating, open fire, books, magazines, local guides and leaflets, indoor games (such as jigsaws, Monopoly etc.).

Surroundings The grounds consist of ¾ acre of riverside garden. These are available in the neighbourhood: tennis, golf, riding.

Cars The nearest main road is the A6108 from Richmond to Reeth.

Closed to visitors We are not open from December to February.

Hurdon Farm, south of Launceston, Cornwall, PL15 9LS
Tel: 0566 2955   C D H S ⌗ 4

This 18th-century stone house is in a picturesque area, not far from Dartmoor and Bodmin Moor (both the north and south coasts are within reach, too). It has large sash windows with the original panelled shutters and built-in dressers in the dining-room – Margaret Smith's daughter made the quilted, leaf-shaped place mats which decorate the tables. The sitting-room has large and comfortable chairs and a great log stove. The most interesting room is, however, the big kitchen-scullery where an old slate sink and pump stand alongside the modern washing machine, and in the granite fireplace is an array of old jacks, trivets, and a built-in Dutch oven.

    Upstairs, all is spick-and-span with fresh paintwork and light, bright colour schemes in the bedrooms. There is also a family suite (made pretty by an old-fashioned rosebud wallpaper) on the ground floor, where the dairy used to be.

Margaret's meals are above average 'farmhouse fare', with imaginative starters, in particular. Her soups are accompanied by home-made rolls; lamb or coq au vin by such vegetables as courgettes au gratin, cabbage cooked with onion and bacon, potatoes Lyonnaise (with milk and cheese) or creamed turnips; her puddings include raspberry pavlovas, chocolate rouleau and home-made ice creams – always followed by cheeses. She uses the farm's own produce and clotted cream.

From Launceston you can visit the majestic and romantic north Cornish coast, described elsewhere in this book, or head inland to wild Bodmin Moor to discover hidden, unspoilt villages. The coast has stark cliffs, waterfalls and wide sands; the moor, high tors that can be reached only on foot or horseback. Don't miss the elaborately carved church (St Mary's) in Launceston itself, an old-world market town. The area is full of Arthurian legends; and Daphne du Maurier's Jamaica Inn is on the moor.

The following facts have been supplied by the owners:

Bedrooms There are 5 rooms, which include single, double and family rooms. Bed-and-breakfast costs from £8.50 (per person in a double room) including service and VAT; prices go up in high season. There are reductions for stays of 2 nights or more.

    Some if not all of the rooms have the following amenities: washbasin, shaver-point; armchairs; views of countryside/farmland/garden; door keys.

Meals The dinner menu is fixed price (£4.50). There is no choice of dishes on the fixed menu, which consists of 4 courses and coffee. Dinner is served at 6.30 pm. Special diets can be prepared, Thermoses for picnics, and snacks. Morning or bedtime drinks (coffee, tea etc.) can be ordered. Non-residents are not admitted to the dining-room. Wine and other drinks can be brought in. Free tea on arrival.

Public rooms There is a sitting-room with open fire, TV (colour), books, magazines, local guides and leaflets, indoor games (such as Trivial Pursuit).

Surroundings The grounds consist of ½ acre garden and 400 acres of farmland with livestock and a pony for children. These are available in the neighbourhood: heated swimming-pool, squash, golf, fishing, tennis, riding.

Cars The nearest main road is the A30 from Launceston to Bodmin.

Closed to visitors We are not open from October to April.

Innsacre Farmhouse Hotel, Shipton Gorge, east of Bridport, Dorset, DT6 4LJ   *Tel: 0308 56137*   **C D PT S X ⌗3**

This is an excellent example of a new type of hotel increasingly to be found in the countryside. Pig-farming having ceased to be profitable, Jim and Helen Smith decided to change course – and converted their substantial stone farm buildings into delightful accommodation for guests and a sophisticated restaurant.

Innsacre nestles in a steep-sided and sun-trapping valley, the 17th-century buildings surrounded by lawns, orchard and patio for guests. What was once a great barn now has attractive bedrooms upstairs (modern striped duvets contrasting with turn-of-the-century furniture) and a sitting-room with cherry buttoned chairs and cottage flowers on the curtains. Downstairs there is a bar with log stove in a stone fireplace, salvaged pews and comfortable armchairs. Only a pink pleated curtain separates this from the

dining-room – good silver and glass, pink-and-white bone china, pink damask napkins and velvet-upholstered ladderback chairs (but still with the rugged stone walls and pine joists of the barn exposed to view).

There are about five choices at each course. You might start with crab pilaff or pears in a Roquefort dressing, for example; then perhaps duck breast in a cassis sauce with figs, or sirloin chasseur; and a pudding such as pineapple Romanoff or crême caramel made with Tia Maria.

After dinner, coffee can be enjoyed at tables by the fish-pool outside, where clematis climbs up the old stone walls and you can watch ducks and chickens running free, Tamworth pigs and sheep in pens.

(The attractions of west Dorset are described on page 97).

The following facts have been supplied by the owners:

Bedrooms There are 7 rooms, which include single, double and family rooms. Bed-and-breakfast costs from £16 (per person) including service and VAT; prices go up in high season. There are reductions for stays of 4 nights or more; and 'bargain breaks' as well.

Some if not all of the rooms have the following amenities: central heating or electric heaters; electric blankets, washbasin, shower, own bathroom and wc, shaver-point; armchairs; views of countryside and garden; choice of duvets or blankets; orthopaedic mattress or bed-board; door keys. Breakfast in bed is available.

Meals The dinner menu is fixed price (£12.25) or à la carte. There is a choice of dishes on the fixed menu, which consists of 3 courses and coffee. Dinner is served at 7 pm. Vegetarian or special diets can be prepared. Lunches and packed lunches can be provided; and snacks at other hours. Morning, afternoon or bedtime drinks (coffee, tea etc.) can be ordered for a charge. Wine and other alcoholic drinks can be ordered.

Public rooms There are 3 sitting-rooms etc. The following are available in one or more of them: central heating, open fire, TV (colour), books, magazines, local guides and leaflets, indoor games (such as cards, Monopoly, Trivial Pursuit), record-player and records.

Surroundings The grounds consist of 10 acres of pasture and gardens. These are available in the neighbourhood: golf, horse riding.

Cars The nearest main road is the A35 from Dorchester to Bridport.

Credit cards accepted Yes.

Please check prices before booking, and whether there has been any change of ownership (or cook!)

Ivy House Hotel, Marlborough, Wiltshire, SN8 1HJ
Tel: 0672 53188   **C**(8) **PT X⌗7**

I have included in this book a few hotels which, although not 'off the beaten track', are nevertheless peaceful, and in many cases with an attractive garden or rural view at the back. Ivy House, in the main street of Marlborough, is just such a place.

Since David Ball took it over, the bedrooms – reached via winding corridors – have been improved, many with Laura Ashley papers, pine bedheads and private bathrooms. Those at the back have views of the garden and of the higgledy-piggledy, mossy rooftops of the old town; one, with king-size bed, has a view of an old well and immense copper-beech. A ground-floor suite has its own patio.

In the formal, big-windowed restaurant at the back, which projects into the garden, the menu has many choices at each course. (Terry Law is the chef.) One might, for instance, choose a crêpe filled with smoked haddock, followed by kidneys sautéed with mushrooms and then pears poached in red wine. Even breakfasts are memorable: kedgeree and smoked haddock are among the choices. There is also an excellent vegetarian menu. Occasionally, meals are served in one of the flagstoned courtyards, around the well; while in winter there are Saturday dinner-dances.

The big, chintzy sitting-room has windows overlooking a tiny court with tubs of petunias and lobelias.

There is quite a lot of history to Ivy House. In the 18th century it was a coaching inn (hence the courtyards behind it). Marlborough College – whose handsome buildings now dominate the end of the town – was preceded by a boys' school here. And it was once the home of the Sutton family (of Suttons' Seeds fame) who used its walled garden as a test ground for seeds of flowering shrubs. This is why the garden is, to this day, especially well stocked with unusual species in its herbaceous borders. (It is illuminated at night.) The huge copper-beech spreads welcome shade on hot days; and a vegetable and herb garden supplies the kitchen.

The hotel is much used by walkers (the Ridgeway path is near) and cyclists. For sightseers, the area's attractions are shown on videos which (along with feature films) can be played on the bedroom television sets. Stonehenge is close and (to my mind, far more interesting) Avebury Ring, the Marlborough Downs, Savernake Forest, and innumerable stately homes, thatched villages and peaceful country lanes.

Reader's comments: Everything excellent. Food superb – the best hotel cooking we've had.

The following facts have been supplied by the owners:

Bedrooms There are 15 rooms, which include doubles and suites. Bed-and-breakfast costs from £15 (per person in a double room) including service and VAT. There are 2-day 'bargain breaks' all through the year. Sampler breaks (see page 14). Free Sunday accommodation for over-60s staying 3 days.
  Some if not all of the rooms have the following amenities: central heating; washbasin, shower, own bathroom and wc, shaver-point; alarm radio, TV (colour), phone, armchairs; views of garden or town; tea/coffee-making facilities; drinks-fridge; door keys. Breakfast in bed is available. Hair drier, video films, laundry service and shoe-cleaning machine are available.

Meals The dinner menu is fixed price (£8.50) or à la carte. There is a choice of dishes on the fixed menu, which consists of 3 courses and coffee. Dinner is served from 7 pm. Special diets can be prepared. Lunches and packed lunches can be provided; and snacks at other hours. Morning, afternoon or bedtime drinks (coffee, tea etc.) can be ordered for a charge. Wine and other alcoholic drinks can be ordered.

Public rooms There are 2 sitting-rooms etc. The following are available in one or both of them: central heating, books, magazines, local guides and leaflets, bars.

Surroundings The grounds consist of ½ acre garden.

Cars The nearest main road is the A4 from Bath and Bristol to London.

Languages spoken German, French, Italian.

Credit cards accepted Access, Visa.

**Karslake House, Winsford, south of Minehead, Somerset,
TA24 7JE**   *Tel: 064 385 242*   **C D S X ⌗ 3**

For generations the Jenkins family have run this one-time malt
house as a restaurant and small hotel. Parts of it date from the 15th
century. Spring is an ideal time to visit, when it is surrounded by
daffodils and azaleas in bloom.

Beyond the large, light dining-room is a small bar; and, for
residents, two sitting-rooms – one crowded with cretonne armchairs around a fire; the other, which has TV, still retaining an
ancient bread-oven and cauldrons suspended on ratchets. Narrow,
scarlet-carpeted passages twist and turn. Upstairs are pleasant
bedrooms – two of the nicest have views of the garden lawn and
herbaceous borders (no. 12, primrose-coloured, with stable roof-
beams overhead; no. 7, a spacious cherry-coloured room with
window-seat built under the big sash window). The bathrooms are
attractive.

Both Richard and Heather Jenkins are qualified cooks. There
are always choices on the four-course menu, which features simple
English dishes like vegetable soup, roast beef, rhubarb crumble,
and a choice of cheeses.

Winsford, an ancient village (and birthplace of Ernest Bevin),
has eight bridges over the several streams which converge here,
thatched cottages, a crafts centre in an 18th-century chapel, and
the Royal Oak inn (12th century) which provided material for
Blackmore's book *Lorna Doone*. It is a good centre from which to
explore Exmoor: quite near are the Caractacus Stone, a 5th-
century memorial to a nephew of Caradoc, one of the most valiant

defenders of Britain against the Romans; prehistoric burial mounds; and Tarr Steps, a prehistoric bridge. Other features of Exmoor are described on pages 111 and 417–18.

The following facts have been supplied by the owners:

Bedrooms There are 11 rooms, which include single, double and family rooms. Bed-and-breakfast costs from £13.50 (per person) including VAT; prices go up in high season. There are reductions for stays of 2 nights or more; and 'bargain breaks' as well, out of season.

    Some if not all of the rooms have the following amenities: electric heaters; electric blankets, washbasin, shower, shaver-point; armchairs; views of countryside or garden; orthopaedic mattress; door keys. Breakfast in bed is available.

Meals The dinner menu is fixed price (£7.25) or à la carte. There is a choice of dishes on the fixed menu, which consists of 4 courses and coffee. Dinner is served at 7.30–8.30 pm. Vegetarian or special diets can be prepared. Lunches and packed lunches can be provided; and snacks at other hours. Morning, afternoon or bedtime drinks (coffee, tea etc.) can be ordered for a charge. Wine and other alcoholic drinks can be ordered.

Public rooms There are 2 sitting-rooms etc. The following are available in one or both of them: open fire, TV (colour), books, magazines, local guides and leaflets.

Surroundings The grounds consist of ⅔ acre of garden. These are available in the neighbourhood: riding, fishing and guided walks.

Cars The nearest main road is the A396 from Minehead to Exeter.

Kimberley Home Farm, Wymondham, south-west of Norwich, Norfolk *Tel: 0953 603137* C(2) S♯7

This is a beautifully furnished farmhouse with stables at the front and a large garden at the back, onto which the glass doors of the large sitting-room open. From time to time, guinea-fowl parade across the lawn and there is a pond with ducks. Apart from the hundreds of acres of crops, the main activity at Kimberley is training and racing horses.

The bedrooms are particularly pretty, and the dining-room has a long Regency table. Jenny Bloom is not only an excellent cook but a generous one, leaving pheasants, guinea-fowl or joints of meat on a hot-tray from which guests may help themselves, and apt to whisk away a half-demolished chicken merely in order to replace it with a fresh one. Starters are imaginative (avocado mousse, for instance), and puddings delicious.

241

You can have the exclusive use of rooms if you wish, or get more involved with the family and the activities of the farm. Jenny is a charming hostess, and unflappable too. On our first of several stays, Michael Bloom fell while racing and was rushed into hospital with a broken pelvis, yet dinner was no more than a few minutes late.

Norwich is one of the most beautiful of mediaeval cities, complete with castle and cathedral, full of craft and antique shops in cobbled byways. The county has a great many stately homes and even statelier churches, wonderful landscapes and seascapes, and, of course, the Broads. The Sainsbury Art Centre outside Norwich is exceptional. The Norfolk coast, King's Lynn and Cambridge are all about one hour away.

The following facts have been supplied by the owners:

Bedrooms There are 3 rooms, which include single, double and family rooms. Dinner, bed-and-breakfast costs from £25 (per person) including service and VAT.

Some if not all of the rooms have the following amenities: central heating or electric heaters; electric blankets; armchairs; views of countryside, farmland, garden; ironing facilities; double glazing. Hair drier, bed-board and laundering facilities available.

Meals There is no choice of dishes on the menu, which consists of 3 courses and coffee. Dinner is served from 7–9 pm. Special dishes can be arranged in advance. Morning or bedtime drinks (coffee, tea etc.) can be ordered for a charge.

Public rooms There is a sitting-room with central heating, open fire, colour TV, books, magazines, local guides and leaflets, playing cards, etc. Maps on loan.

Surroundings The grounds consist of a large garden with tennis, and meadows beyond. Golf is available nearby.

Cars The nearest main road is the A11 from Norwich to London.

King's Lodge, Long Marston, south of Stratford-upon-Avon, Warwickshire, CV37 8RL
Tel: 0789 720705   **C D PT S S-C**(incl. **H**) ♯4

With his father beheaded and Cromwell ruling England, young Charles II (only twenty-one) made a desperate attempt in 1651 to regain the throne. Badly defeated at Worcester, however, he became a fugitive on the run – for weeks eluding escape by means of disguises and hiding-places, as he made his way to the coast to cross to France.

To get through Stratford-upon-Avon, swarming with Cromwellian troops, he dressed himself as the manservant of Miss Jane Lane (sister of one of his colonels), and together they rode to Long Marston and the house of her kinsman, John Tomes. This was on 10 September; and I stayed there on almost the same date, dining in the hall with great inglenook fireplace where he had a narrow escape. For, on being asked by the cook to wind up the jack that operated the roasting-spit, his ignorance of this homely task nearly gave the game away. Although other parts of the Tudor house have changed, this room is much as it was when he stayed here – and outside, too, the scene has altered very little. Probably, the willow-fringed duck pond and the trees laden with mulberries and pears are very like what he saw.

When the house came up for sale a dozen years ago, George and Angela Jenkins (who lived locally) could not resist buying it, even though it was very neglected and rather too large for their family. To pay for its restoration and upkeep, they decided to take paying guests.

After dinner (plain home cooking, often with produce from the garden) at a big refectory table, visitors can sit in small armchairs around the famous fireplace, or out in the large garden. Two of the bedrooms are small, but one has a four-poster made from elms felled in the grounds and a fine stone fireplace on which the Tomes children inscribed their initials over three centuries ago. The house is full of old pictures and trifles which the Jenkins have collected, many relating to Charles II or the Tomes family who sheltered him.

The house is ideally placed for visiting the beauty-spots and historic sights of three counties – Warwickshire, Gloucestershire (the Cotswolds), and Oxfordshire.

The following facts have been supplied by the owners:

Bedrooms There are 4 rooms, which include singles and doubles. Bed-and-breakfast costs from £10 (per person in a double room) including service and VAT; prices go up in high season. There are reductions for stays of 7 nights or more. Sampler breaks (see page 14).

All rooms have the following amenities: central heating; washbasin, shaver-point; views of countryside, farmland, garden; door keys. Some have bathrooms. Breakfast in bed is available, and hair drier.

Meals The dinner menu is fixed price (£6). There is a choice of dishes on the fixed menu, which consists of 3 courses and coffee. Dinner is served at 7 pm. Special diets can be prepared. Packed lunches can be provided; and snacks at other hours. Morning, afternoon or bedtime drinks (coffee, tea etc.) can be ordered for a charge. Non-residents are not admitted to the dining-room. Wine and other alcoholic drinks can be brought in.

Public rooms There is a sitting-room with central heating, open fire, TV (colour), books, magazines, local guides and leaflets, indoor games (such as Monopoly and Scrabble).

Surroundings The grounds consist of 5 acres of garden and parkland, with croquet. These are available in the neighbourhood: fishing, riding, squash, golf, tennis and swimming-pool.

Cars The nearest main road is the A46 from Stratford-upon-Avon to Cheltenham.

Lamb Inn, Great Rissington, north-west of Burford (Oxfordshire), Gloucestershire, GL54 2LJ *Tel: 0451 20388* **D PT ⌂5**

This is exactly what one asks of a typical old Cotswold inn – the interior a place of little windows, zigzag corridors, quaint oak doors and thick stone walls; outside, magnificent views of the countryside, looking across to some of the highest points in Gloucestershire. Kate Cleverly has furnished the bedrooms with care – restful colours, everything neat, a pretty tulip wallpaper in one room, and in the dining-room pine chairs at lace-covered tables with candle-lamps lit at night. The menu is à la carte, with good simple food such as home-made pâtés, local trout, lamb steaks and individual steak-and-kidney pies. Outside is a landscaped garden from which to enjoy the summer view with a glass of local 'real ale' in hand; a covered swimming-pool (heated) and a summerhouse-cum-aviary. In cold weather, there is a log fire in the bar, and in the attractive residents' sitting-room.

Richard is an imaginative as well as skilled craftsman: the carving of a lamb over the sitting-room fire is his, and so are the conversions of old doors, pews and even school desks to new uses. When I last visited the Lamb, he was making a four-poster with carved decorations.

The Lamb is midway between two famous Cotswold villages (Bourton-on-the-Water and Burford, described elsewhere in this book). Most people come here simply for the scenery, but also in the vicinity are the Cotswold Wildlife Park, a rare breeds farm, and – only a little further – Oxford, Stratford-upon-Avon, Warwick and Woodstock (with Blenheim Palace).

The following facts have been supplied by the owners:

Bedrooms There are 7 rooms, which include singles and doubles. Bed-and-breakfast costs from £12 (per person in a double room) including VAT. Sunday night accommodation free to over-60s staying 3 days.

Some if not all of the rooms have the following amenities: central heating; washbasin, shaver-point; armchairs; views of countryside, garden; door keys. Breakfast in bed is available; also hair drier and iron.

245

Meals The dinner menu is à la carte. Dinner is served at 7 pm. Lunches and packed lunches can be provided. Morning, afternoon and bedtime drinks (coffee, tea etc.) can be ordered for a charge. Wine and other alcoholic drinks can be ordered.

Public rooms There is a sitting-room with fire, colour TV and indoor games (such as chess and Trivial Pursuit). Also bars with malt whiskies, ports and real ales in considerable variety.

Surroundings The grounds consist of 1½ acres of garden and swimming-pool. These are available in the neighbourhood: golf, fishing, riding.

Cars The nearest main road is the A40 from London to Wales.

Credit cards accepted Visa, Access.

Lansdowne House, Clarendon Street, Leamington Spa, Warwickshire, CV32 40F   *Tel: 0926 21313*   C(5) **PT X ▦4**

A pretty creeper-covered house built in the 18th century, this small hotel cannot be described as truly 'off the beaten track' for it stands at a crossroads not far from the centre of Leamington. But bedroom windows are double-glazed to reduce any sound from traffic – and the hotel is of such excellence that I wanted to include it despite its position!

David and Gillian Allen took it over only a few years ago and have furnished it to a very high standard and in keeping with its architecture. There is a particularly pretty sitting-room with sea-green and strawberry Victorian sofas, for example; in the small dining-room, meals are served on fluted Rosenthal china and wine in elegant glasses; the bar has cherry buttoned seats; and every bedroom is attractively decorated in soft colours with well-chosen fabrics, stripped-pine furniture and thick, moss-green carpet. (No. 2 is the quietest, with roof-light not windows.)

The same care goes into the food. David, who trained as a chef in Switzerland, is a perfectionist. He sends to Scotland for his steaks, to the Cotswolds for his trout, has coffee specially blended to his taste, and damson and other sorbets made for him on a fruit farm nearby. Connoisseurs will appreciate some little-known wines among his very good selection, and the range of malt whiskies.

There are always several choices of good English dishes at dinner. Starters include particularly imaginative soups (such as celery-and-walnut or cream of parsnip), while main courses are likely to be such things as roast pork with freshly chopped rosemary or liver-and-bacon with fresh sage. Pudding might include walnut and chocolate fudge pudding or fruit cobbler.

Royal Leamington Spa is a health resort with a saline spring. It has fine Georgian terraces and lovely riverside gardens. A good base from which to visit not only Warwick and Kenilworth, described elsewhere, but also Coventry (modern cathedral, some historic buildings), Southam (old market town), Stoneleigh (mediaeval village and the great National Agricultural Centre) and fine countryside towards Stratford-upon-Avon.

The following facts have been supplied by the owners:

Bedrooms There are 10 rooms, which include single, double and family rooms. Bed-and-breakfast costs from £15 (per person in a double room) including service and VAT; prices go up in high season. There are reductions for stays of 2 nights or more; and 'bargain breaks' as well. **If included in a 3-night stay, Sunday's accommodation is free to readers of this book.**

    Some if not all of the rooms have the following amenities: central heating or electric heaters; washbasin, shower, own bathroom and wc, shaver-point; radio, TV (colour), armchairs; tea/coffee-making facilities; door keys. Breakfast in bed is available and hair driers.

Meals The dinner menu is fixed price (£9.65) or à la carte. There is a choice of dishes on the fixed menu, which consists of 3 courses and coffee with home-made petits fours. Dinner is served from 6.30 pm. Special diets can be prepared. Lunches and packed lunches can be provided; and snacks at other hours. Morning, afternoon or bedtime drinks (coffee, tea etc.) can be ordered for a charge. Wine and other alcoholic drinks can be ordered.

Public rooms There are 2 sitting-rooms and a bar. The following are available in one or all of them: central heating, TV (colour), books, magazines, local guides and leaflets, indoor games (such as executive games, cards, etc.).

Surroundings These are available in the neighbourhood: golf, fishing, bowls, swimming. For residents there are discounts at Warwick Castle and other 'sights'.

Cars The nearest main road is the A425 from Warwick to Banbury.

Languages spoken French, German.

Credit cards accepted Access.

Laskill House Farm, north of Helmsley, North Yorkshire
Booking service: 0498 81563   **C D S S-C ♯15**

This stone farmhouse lies in a hilly, wooded area of great scenic splendour ('Herriot country'), and close to famous Rievaulx Abbey. Its courtyard is made pretty with stone troughs, flowers and rocks; and around lie 600 acres with cattle and sheep or wheat. There are white iron chairs for guests in the garden. Children are welcome to help feed the calves and to hold the lambs in spring.

In the sitting/dining-room is oak furniture hand-carved by local craftsmen, each of whom 'signs' his work with his own particular symbol – an acorn, a beaver or a stag's head. Here Sue serves home-made soup or pâté before a main course which is likely to comprise meat and vegetables from the farm, followed by (for instance) lemon meringue pie or a fruit fool, and then an interesting selection of cheeses. Later she joins her guests for a cup of tea and tells them what is on in the neighbourhood and which places are most interesting to visit. Often there is a chance to see James Herriot himself, as he sometimes opens fêtes or gives talks about his books and his experience as a vet.

The bedrooms vary in style: I particularly liked 'the blue room' with its sprigged wallpaper, thick carpet and cretonne fabrics. Sue aims eventually to make a patchwork quilt for every bed.

The North York Moors are one of England's finest national parks: whether you walk or drive, the views are spectacular, particularly when the heather is in bloom (late summer to autumn). Steep lanes dive down into innumerable valleys where grey stone villages shelter. The area is dotted with prehistoric remains and there are Norman castles and churches, Cistercian abbeys, cosy wayside inns, small market towns, gliders on the heights and a fine folk museum at Hutton-le-Hole. The equally scenic coast is easily reached to the east, the dales to the west, and to the south the lush Vale of Pickering and York.

Readers' comments: Comfortable, welcoming, and good food. Excellent meals, complete relaxation. Charming and considerate hostess.

The following facts have been supplied by the owners:

Bedrooms There are 4 rooms, which include single, double and family rooms. Bed-and-breakfast costs from £9.25 (per person in a double room), or £16.50 with dinner, including service and VAT; prices go up in high season.
   Some if not all of the rooms have the following amenities: central heating or electric heaters; electric blankets, washbasin, shaver-point; armchairs; views of countryside, farmland, garden; choice of duvets or blankets; door keys. Breakfast in bed is available, and an orthopaedic mattress.

Meals There is no choice of dishes on the fixed menu, which consists of 4 courses and coffee. Dinner is served at 6.30 pm. Lunches and packed lunches can be provided; and snacks at other hours. Morning, afternoon or bedtime drinks (coffee, tea etc.) can be ordered for a charge. Non-residents are not admitted to the dining-room. Wine and other alcoholic drinks can be brought in. Free tea on arrival.

Public rooms There is a sitting-room with central heating, open fire, TV (colour), books, magazines, local guides and leaflets, indoor games (such as Monopoly, dominoes and jigsaws).

Surroundings The grounds consist of garden and farmland. Fishing and pony trekking are available in the neighbourhood; also golf and a swimming-pool.

Cars The nearest main road is the B1257 from Stockesley to Helmsley.

Closed to visitors We are not open from November to March.

A little further south is **Newton Grange Farm** (booking service: 0498 81563), where Sue Ward's immaculate rooms have exception-ally fine views. Bed-and-breakfast only — but excellent pub meals at nearby Ampleforth.

Leigh Court, Leigh, west of Worcester, WR6 5LB
Tel: 0886 32275　　　**C D S S-C ⌗4**

Passers-by often pause here, just to look – not only at the 16th-century manor house of mellow brick, with gables in both Dutch and Flemish style, but also at the 14th-century cruck barn, the biggest of its kind in the world, now undergoing restoration by English Heritage.

Sally Stewart's ancestors were bailiffs here when, before Henry VIII dissolved the monasteries, the abbots of Pershore were lords of the manor. She can tell intriguing stories of their doings, and why one was reputed to haunt the house until exorcised in 1901 – which is perhaps why she has never seen him.

She and her civil engineer husband modernized the comforts of the house when they inherited it in 1960, but have carefully preserved all the fine architectural detail. The entrance hall is particularly striking, a tiled floor and traditional acanthus-patterned wallpaper (blue-and-white) setting off the white staircase, handsome sash windows and fanlight over the door. The sitting-room has a pretty fireplace, all curlicues and swags, round which velvet or cretonne chairs are drawn up, while portraits of ancestral aunts adorn the walls. In the dining-room (in fact, in all rooms) there are family antiques; sprigged blue cloths cover the tables; and from the bay window there is a fine view of a weeping ash, the nearby 13th-century church and a huge copper-beech. Throughout the house, there are good wallpapers, old-fashioned furniture and (from room 3 in particular) fine views of river, woods and fields.

This is a good place for anyone who enjoys dogs and other animals for Sally breeds pedigree pugs, King Charles spaniels and golden retrievers. (If you want to bring your own dog, a current vaccination certificate must be produced.) In the grounds, where hens range free, you will find a variety of rare farm breeds: a Tamworth pig, silver Dorkings (a poultry breed introduced to England by the Romans), Brecon Buff geese, and Silver Apple-yard ducks. There are two nature reserves nearby.

Sally trained in Switzerland in the Ecole Hotelière of Lausanne, and had a career in some of London's top hotels before applying these standards to guests in the totally different setting of Leigh Court. Using produce from the grounds and from her son's adjoining farm (which includes pork, lamb, poultry, eggs, game, vegetables and fish from the River Teme), Sally serves such dishes as prawn vol-au-vents, chicken breasts in wine-and-mushroom sauce or pot-roast pheasant, peppermint ice-pudding or treacle tart (except on Wednesdays, her night off).

In the grounds, a riverside walk appeals to many visitors (there is another good, level walk along the track where once a railway ran). In October, you can see the farm's cider mill in action, and taste the results. People touring by car use Leigh Court as a base to visit Malvern, Worcester, Upton-on-Severn, Ledbury, Stourport-on-Severn, Evesham, Bewdley, Tewkesbury and Hereford: none more than 20 miles away.

The following facts have been supplied by the owners:

Bedrooms There are 3 rooms, which include twin, double and family rooms. Bed-and-breakfast costs from £10 (per person) including service and VAT; prices go up in high season. There are reductions for stays of 7 nights or more.

Some if not all of the rooms have the following amenities: central heating and electric heaters; electric blankets, washbasin, shaver-point; radio, armchairs; views of countryside and garden; choice of duvets or blankets; backboard; tea/coffee-making facilities; door keys.

Meals The dinner menu is fixed price (£6.50). There is no choice of dishes on the menu, which consists of 4 courses and coffee. Dinner is served at 7 pm. Vegetarian or special diets can be prepared if ordered in advance. Packed lunches can be provided. Non-residents are not admitted to the dining-room. Wine and other alcoholic drinks can be brought in.

Public rooms There are 2 sitting-rooms etc. The following are available in one or both of them: central heating, open fire, TV (colour), books, magazines, local guides and leaflets; indoor games (such as snooker, darts, dominoes, shove-halfpenny, cards, board games, jigsaws). Bridge can be arranged.

Surroundings The grounds consist of 270 acres of garden and farmland; fishing in river is available. These are available in the neighbourhood: riding, tennis, squash, golf, swimming.

Cars The nearest main road is the A4103 from Worcester to Hereford.

Languages spoken French.

Closed to visitors We are not open in November and December.

Leworthy Farm, Holsworthy, east of Bude (Cornwall), Devon, EX22 6SS *Tel: 0409 253488* **C H PT S S-C X ⊞ 4**

Genial Eric Cornish deservedly won the AA's Farmhouse of the Year award in 1981. His guests are greatly appreciated by him, and he goes to considerable lengths to give them a good time – young children in particular. Dozens of their drawings and letters to him are pinned up around the bar.

He has added to the rooms in the farmhouse to provide more accommodation in a bungalow close by, and sometimes has as many as forty people staying – laying on for this huge house-party all kinds of evening entertainments (games, dancing, conjuror, film) for which there is no extra charge. This is obviously appreciated by families tired of the spend-spend-spend involved in keeping the youngsters entertained in most resorts. Eric also takes visitors on tractor-drawn hay-rides (dogs following) to see his crops, sheep, beef-cattle, lake, river and woods, while explaining to them what work is going on. It's a place where parents can leave their older children to go their own way – they find plenty to do, like organizing table tennis or badminton competitions. There are deer, herons and even otters to be spotted; abundant wild flowers; and lots of good picnic spots within the farm estate. Eric has produced a nature trail, with quiz. In low season, crafts including patchwork and farm activity courses are run; the latter include wine-making, clay pigeon shooting, fishing and pub skittle matches. And there is a wheelchair for handicapped visitors.

Something new is always afoot, so Eric and Marion keep in touch with past guests by means of a circular letter with news of what has been happening to the stock, the pets and the family. Cormorants steal the trout, son Paul moves to Australia, 'Just Country' gets booked for next season – it's all reported in these letters. Many guests become lifelong friends, and most get involved in Leworthy Farm in one way or another (the gumboot rack was made by a group of dads one rainy afternoon).

The bedrooms, like all the other rooms, are comfortable and unfussy: the best ones are in the converted farm building called Leeside. Marion produces typical farmhouse meals such as soup, roast beef, fruit pie and cream, cheese, coffee.

There is so much going on that many people hardly stir from the Leworthy lands. However, within a short drive are the beaches of

Bude (where the Cornishes have a beach hut) and superb clifftop views, Hartland's dramatic reefs and lighthouse, quaint little Clovelly with its steep cobbled street going down to the sea, Tamar lake, north Dartmoor, the sands and surf of Westward Ho!, old Bideford and Appledore. You can get to Tintagel and the ruined castle that is reputedly King Arthur's, Widemouth Bay for surfing, and Launceston – a hilly market town, part mediaeval. Holsworthy, too, has its markets.

Readers' comments: Very much enjoyed the Cornishes' company; they make you feel welcome. A delightful couple who spared nothing to see that everyone had a good time.

The following facts have been supplied by the owners:

Bedrooms There are 12 rooms, which include single, double and family rooms. Dinner, bed-and-breakfast costs from £16.50 (per person in a double room) including service and VAT; prices go up in high season. There are reductions for stays of 6 nights or more; and off-season 'bargain breaks' as well. Sunday accommodation free to over-60s who stay 3 days.

    Some if not all of the rooms have the following amenities: central heating or electric heaters; electric blankets, washbasin, shower, wc, shaver-point; armchairs; views of countryside, farmland, garden; choice of duvets or blankets; tea/coffee-making facilities; door keys. Breakfast in bed is available; also bed-boards, hair drier and clothes washing.

Meals There is a choice of dishes on the menu, which consists of 4 courses and coffee. Dinner is served at 7 pm. Special diets can be prepared. Lunches and/or packed lunches can be provided; and snacks at other hours. Morning tea is free; afternoon or bedtime drinks (coffee, tea etc.) can be ordered for a charge. Wine and other alcoholic drinks can be ordered.

Public rooms There are 3 sitting-rooms and a bar. The following are available in one or more of them: central heating, open fire, colour TV, books, magazines, local guides and leaflets, indoor games (such as table skittles, snooker, table tennis, cards, darts, badminton), piano, record-player and records. Video films.

Surroundings The grounds consist of lawns, farmlands and lake. The following games or sports are available in the grounds: clay pigeon shooting, croquet, tennis, trout fishing, archery and pony riding. These are available in the neighbourhood: hunting, golf, bowls, swimming, and cycle or fishing rod hire.

Cars The nearest main road is the A388 from Bideford to Plymouth.

Languages spoken German and French.

NOTE For the cost of postage you can borrow a video about Leworthy.

Little Byres, Battle Road, Dallington, east of Heathfield, East Sussex, TN2 19LE *Tel: 042482 230* C D(see below) H PT ♯3

A barn, cowsheds and stables have become an outstanding restaurant, with attractive bedrooms (at ground-floor level, in an outbuilding, and ideal for anyone who finds stairs difficult); but there is no sitting-room – young Tim Westlake, who took over recently, plans to build one overlooking the pond.

A typical dinner (cooked by Chris Davies, who used to work at Woods of Bath, well known to gourmets) might comprise a seafood bouchée with creamy vermouth sauce; chicken breast stuffed with mushrooms and orange; a cointreau parfait surrounded by mango sauce. There are plenty of choices on the menu, and on the good, classic wine list.

The vast barn is a spectacular setting for the dining-room, its huge oak timbers soaring overhead and an immense log stove warming the place well in winter. Thick carpet, exposed brickwork, whitewash and tapestry-covered ladderback chairs are all in keeping with this setting. Board doors have wrought-iron hinges specially made by a local blacksmith; the main doors came from a demolished church.

In the bedrooms, armchairs and bedheads are of cane; sprigged Mary Quant curtains match the duvets, with soft greens and browns predominating; old beams have been stripped clean. To these rooms continental breakfasts (with hot croissants, fruit etc.) are brought.

Dogs can be accommodated at the adjoining farm.

Little Byres, standing in the Sussex High Weald, has magnificent views – on clear days all the way to the sea. Immediately outside it is a lawn with tables, and a paddock with chickens.

Within a few miles are Battle (see page 256), Batemans (Kipling's Tudor house), south coast resorts, Herstmonceux (see page 109), Great Dixter (mansion and gardens), lovely Bodiam Castle and Bedgebury Pinetum. There are forest walks nearby and 'Fuller's Follies' – curious monuments erected by a local squire on the boundaries of his estate.

Readers' comments: Very smart, comfortable, with excellent food.

The following facts have been supplied by the owners:

Bedrooms There are 5 double rooms. Bed-and-breakfast costs from £13 (per person in a double room) including VAT; prices go up in high season. There are reductions for stays of 7 nights or more; and 'bargain breaks' as well.

All rooms have the following amenities: central heating; washbasin, shower, wc, shaver-point; TV (b&w), armchairs; views of countryside, farmland, garden; choice of duvets or blankets; tea/coffee-making facilities; door keys. Breakfast in bed is provided.

Meals The dinner menu is fixed price (£13.50). There is a choice of dishes on the fixed menu, which consists of 3 courses and coffee. Dinner is served at 7–10 pm. Special diets can be prepared. Packed lunches can be provided. Wine and other alcoholic drinks can be ordered.

Surroundings The grounds consist of 2 acres of garden and meadow. Riding, golf and swimming (sea and pool) are available in the neighbourhood.

Cars The nearest main road is the B2096 from Battle to Heathfield.

Credit cards accepted Access, Visa.

Languages spoken French and some German.

Closed to visitors We are not open in January.

Little Hemingfold, Telham, south of Battle, East Sussex
Tel: 04246 2910　　　　C(12) **PT S X ♯3**

Down a long woodland track one finds a group of buildings that have grown up over three centuries, in a very lovely setting with a stream that has been dammed to make a large trout lake. There's a pretty garden and vine-covered pergola, and woods full of birds. Indoors are a parrot, dog and cats.

The beamy interior has been most attractively furnished by Don and Ann Benton, daughter of sculptor William Reid Dick, with interesting pictures and objects everywhere, delightful fabrics and antique furniture. Guests are free to use the piano and the large collection of books (many about art), and may wander around the 26 acres, where there are pigs, Jacob's sheep, glasshouses for strawberries, melons and courgettes and all the rest. Three Jersey cows supply milk and cream for the house. Bread is home-baked.

Ann is a superb cook. Guests are seated round three large candlelit tables and help themselves from dishes abundantly filled, and from carafes of wine that are included in the price. There's a wide choice of dishes for breakfast. What makes this place so very pleasant is the caring, warm yet fuss-free concern shown for visitors – a casual, natural and friendly atmosphere to be in. You can buy glasshouse produce, trout and eggs to take home.

The historic town of Battle, with its abbey on the site where William the Conqueror defeated Harold, is near and so is the seaside resort of Hastings. The Cinque Ports of Rye and Romney are within reach; they have bird reserves and so does Dungeness. (These towns are described under other entries.)

Readers' comments: Wholly delightful. Excellent food, accommodation and company. A perfect week – nothing was too much trouble, food wonderful, setting perfect.

The following facts have been supplied by the owners:

Bedrooms There are 10 rooms, which include singles and doubles. Bed-and-breakfast with dinner costs from £25 (per person in a double room) including service and VAT. There are reductions for stays of 5 nights or more; and 'bargain breaks' as well.
  All of the rooms have the following amenities: central heating or electric heaters (some bedrooms have log stoves); electric blankets, own bathroom and wc, shaver-point; radio, TV (colour), phone, armchairs; views of countryside, farmland, lake, garden; balcony; choice of duvets or blankets; tea/coffee-making facilities. Breakfast in bed is available, also orthopaedic mattress and hair drier. One four-poster.

Meals There is some choice of dishes on the menu, which consists of 4 courses, wine and coffee. Dinner is served at 7.15 pm. Special diets can be prepared. Lunches and/or packed lunches can be provided; and snacks at other hours. Morning, afternoon or bedtime drinks (coffee, tea etc.) can be ordered for a charge. Non-residents are not admitted to the dining-room. Wine and other alcoholic drinks can be ordered.

Public rooms There are 3 sitting-rooms etc. The following are available in one or more of them: central heating, open fire, colour TV, books, magazines, local guides and leaflets, indoor games (such as cards and chess), piano, record-player and records, and a bar. No smoking in certain rooms.

Surroundings The grounds consist of 26 acres of woods, fields and a lake. The following games or sports are available in the grounds: swing ball, croquet, badminton, boules, trout fishing, grass tennis, archery, dinghy and swimming in the lake. These are available in the neighbourhood: golf, sea bathing, tennis, bowls, riding. (There is a sports centre at Hastings.)

Cars The nearest main road is the A2100 from Hastings to Battle.

Little Orchard, West Street, Rye, East Sussex, TN31 7ES
Tel: 0797 223831   **PT X ⌗5**

A narrow passageway leads to a big surprise: a quite large garden hidden behind the tight-crammed houses of mediaeval Rye. It belongs to an exceptionally elegant and immaculate house, built in the 18th century by Thomas Procter who combined being Mayor with a lucrative trade as a smuggler. The tower in the garden was erected by his son as a lookout post: when the Excise men approached, contraband goods (brandy, tea, lace, or gloves from France) were hurriedly carried away down tunnels.

My cream-and-caramel bedroom, papered with Victorian cabbage-roses, had glimpses of old roofs and chimneypots, honeysuckle and apple trees, a distant hill with sheep. One room has a four-poster. Corridors have striking wallpapers, with exotic birds, and local views sketched by Graham Clark.

rear view

In the sitting-room a vast bouquet of dried roses and lavender fills the fireplace when no logs are burning there. There is a throne of an armchair in strawberry velvet, a green sofa and garden views: paved paths, espaliered pears, urns of plants, nooks with seats, tall clipped yew contrasting with wayward clematis.

The newly built breakfast-room, too, looks onto all this through large arched windows. The floor is of herringbone tiles; the craftsman-made pine table has bentwood chairs around it; and at the end is the open-to-view kitchen where Geraldine and Robert Bromley prepare breakfast while talking to their guests. (For dinner, there are numerous restaurants in Rye.)

Rye has a celebrated church at the heart of its narrow mediaeval streets, lined with antique and craft shops. There is a weekly sheep market and a general market. Romney Marsh (famous for its autumn sunsets and its spring lambs) attracts painters and bird-watchers. Rye itself was the setting for E.F. Benson's 'Mapp and Lucia' stories. Benson lived in Georgian Lamb House, formerly the home of Henry James (now a National Trust property).

The following facts have been supplied by the owners:

Bedrooms There are 3 double rooms. Bed-and-breakfast costs from £17 (per person in a double room) **less 5% discount to readers of this book,** including service; prices go up in high season. There are reductions for stays of 3 nights or more (November to March).

The rooms have the following amenities: central heating or electric heaters; own bathroom and wc, shaver-point; TV (colour), armchairs; tea/coffee-making facilities; door keys.

Meals Packed lunches can be provided.

Public rooms There is a sitting-room with central heating, open fire, books, magazines, local guides and leaflets, indoor games (such as Monopoly, playing cards, chess, backgammon).

Surroundings The grounds consist of ½ acre of garden. These are available in the neighbourhood: tennis, squash, golf, riding, fishing.

Cars The nearest main road is the A21/268 from London to Rye.

Another recommended hotel in Rye (near the church): Ernest Thompson's **Old Vicarage** for attractive rooms, bed-and-breakfast only, tel: 0797 222119.

Longdon Manor, Darlingscott, west of Shipston-on-Stour, Warwickshire, CV36 4PW   *Tel: 0608 82235*   **C S ⌗5**

This great building of tawny Cotswold stone is found at the end of a long, stony track – truly secluded. In the courtyard are beds of old-fashioned white roses, stone troughs of geraniums and, facing the house, big granaries. The small windows have stone mullions (some date from the 13th century), the door is studded with wood pegs, and moss softens the outline of the roof. Five hundred acres of sheep and corn surround the house; there are chickens, and an organic vegetable garden.

The sitting-room is a great stone-flagged hall with paintings, a Steinway and a square piano, oak settles and cretonne-covered armchairs. Here, once a month, Jane Brabyn organizes concerts of chamber music (a former singer, she is grand-daughter of Sir Thomas Beecham). Built-in heating is supplemented by logs which burn in a vast stone fireplace. Dried flowers, seedheads and berries stand in the deep, shuttered window embrasures.

Up a handsome oak staircase are bedrooms full of character, with good rugs on each landing: paintings, books and ornaments everywhere. I particularly enjoyed Elijah taking flight (in wax);

259

and pirouetting Great-Aunt Dolly who, as a girl, ran away to Italy to be a dancer during the last years of Victoria's reign. One bedroom is French Empire in style, one has a huge circular bath adjoining, another is an attic room with rush matting, exposed roof-beams and distant views through its lattice windows. (Not for those who feel the cold, however, as there is no heating upstairs.)

Dinner is served at a fine inlaid table or, at the monthly concert, visitors join the artistes for a buffet supper. Jane is an imaginative cook, and might serve (for example) chilled courgette soup or aubergine pâté, pheasant or hare (or the farm's own beef or lamb), puddings such as gooseberry fool or blackcurrant tart (her pastry is beautifully crisp and light), then cheese. Vegetables are unsprayed and meat is free from hormones.

For details of Shipston and its environs, see page 460.

The following facts have been supplied by the owners:

Bedrooms There are 3 rooms, which include single, double and family rooms. Bed-and-breakfast costs from £15.50 (per person) including service and VAT.

Some if not all of the rooms have the following amenities: central heating or electric heaters; own bathroom and wc, shaver-point; armchairs; views of countryside, farmland, garden; choice of duvets or blankets. Extra-firm mattress, hair drier and washing machine available.

Meals The dinner menu is fixed price (£7–£12) or à la carte. There is no choice of dishes on the fixed menu, which consists of 4 courses and coffee. Dinner is served from 8 pm. Special diets can be prepared. Lunches and packed lunches can be provided; and snacks at other hours. Morning, afternoon or bedtime drinks (coffee, tea etc.) can be ordered free. Wine and other alcoholic drinks can be brought in.

Public rooms There are 2 sitting-rooms etc. The following are available in one or both of them: central heating, open fire, TV, books, magazines, local guides and leaflets, piano, record-player and records. Maps and gumboots on loan.

Surroundings The grounds consist of 500 acres of farmland. Cycle hire, riding and swimming are available in the neighbourhood.

Cars The nearest main road is the A34 from Oxford to Stratford-upon-Avon.

Languages spoken French and a little Italian.

Closed to visitors We are not open from December to late March, except for house-parties of friends.

Low Murrah, west of Penrith, Cumbria

(Illustrated on front cover) Booking service: 0498 81563   **C D S ⌗6**

There is a large herd of elephants on the piano at Low Murrah – model ones, which Pam collects. She also accumulates books – almost every wall is lined with them – and tribal art, which she and her architect husband acquired during years working in Africa. Many of the paintings on the walls are their own work.

Some years ago, they fulfilled a long ambition to settle in the Lake District and bought this Victorian house, which they have furnished in a well-judged combination of Habitat and antiques. There is a large garden rich in bird life, from which the views are such that one recent visitor spent a week's holiday just painting them.

Mrs Kidd is a keen cook and, like many 'incomers', shows more interest in local dishes than many a native. So you can expect to be given some Cumbrian specialities. Breakfasts are varied too: black pudding or good kippers are likely to appear. Free tea on arrival.

The north of the Lake District is less of a draw than the centre, but it is none the worse for that, being less crowded during holidays. This is John Peel's hunting ground (Caldbeck, where he was born and is buried, is not far away) and very good walking country. Within easy reach are several mansions open to the public – Hutton-in-the-Forest and Mirehouse, for example – and a country park. The market towns of Keswick and Penrith are about equidistant, with – among other attractions – a pencil museum and a steam museum respectively. Though Low Murrah is very secluded, the recently improved Penrith-Keswick road makes it very easy to reach.

Reader's comments: Warm and friendly. Excellent food, well prepared and presented.

The following facts have been supplied by the owners:

Bedrooms There are 3 rooms, which include double and family rooms. Bed-and-breakfast costs from £9.25 (per person in a double room) including service and VAT. There are reductions for stays of 7 nights or more.

   Some if not all of the rooms have the following amenities: central heating or electric heaters; washbasin, shaver-point; armchairs; views of countryside, farmland, garden. Breakfast in bed is available, and hair drier.

Meals The dinner menu is fixed price (£5.25). There is no choice of dishes on the fixed menu, which consists of 4 courses and coffee. Dinner is served at 7.30 pm. Special diets can be prepared. Packed lunches can be provided. Morning, afternoon or bedtime drinks (coffee, tea etc.) can be ordered for a charge. Non-residents are not admitted to the dining-room. Wine and other alcoholic drinks can be brought in.

Public rooms There are 2 sitting-rooms etc. The following are available in one or both of them: central heating, open fire, TV (colour), books, magazines, local guides and leaflets, indoor games (such as cards, Scrabble, etc.), piano. Maps on loan.

Surroundings The grounds consist of 4 acres of garden and field.

Cars The nearest main road is the A66 from Penrith to Keswick.

Languages spoken Some French.

Closed to visitors We are not open between November and February.

Loxley Farm House, Loxley, south of Stratford-upon-Avon, Warwickshire, CV35 9JN   *Tel: 0789 840265*   **C D PT ⚇ 4**

Loxley is a hilltop village with diminutive church. From a seat on its sloping green, where crab-apple trees are bright in autumn, there are far views across woodland and fields of red earth. Just downhill from here Loxley Farm is tucked away: a picture-postcard house of half-timbering and thatch, parts dating back to the 13th century. Perhaps Robin Hood ('Robin of Loxley') knew the house; there's a worn stone in the churchyard on which, tradition has it, he and his companions used to sharpen their arrow-tips. And certainly Charles I stayed here after the nearby Battle of Edgehill.

Inside, everything is in keeping with the style of the ancient house: low ceilings with pewter pots hanging from the beams, flagged floors, small-paned windows, log fires, oak doors. You can see the cruck construction of the house – at its heart, the unhewn trunks of two trees support the roof timbers. There is not a single straight wall or floor.

The Hortons, who keep a few sheep, have furnished the rooms in appropriate style. In the dining-room, leather chairs surround a refectory table; in the sitting-room is a Knoll settee, grandfather clock and wing armchairs, with Staffordshire figures and old silver on the shelves, lavender and dried flowers.

The bedrooms differ in size and style, the largest having a shaggy carpet, antiques and even a sofa; the smallest, flowery frilled bed linen.

Mrs Horton cooks evening meals on request, which may include their own lamb, or venison from the Charlcote estate, with local vegetables or field mushrooms. There is always a choice of starters, and of puddings. At breakfast home-made buns and muesli are included.

It is very easy to visit Stratford-upon-Avon from here, and the rest of Warwickshire, the Cotswolds, and Oxford, all described elsewhere in this book.

Reader's comments: Idyllic surroundings. Much care and attention. Generous, flavoursome fare.

The following facts have been supplied by the owners:

Bedrooms There are 3 rooms, which include single, double and family rooms. Bed-and-breakfast costs from £10 (per person in a double room) including service and VAT; prices go up in high season. There are reductions for stays of 7 nights or more. Sampler breaks (see page 14).

Some if not all of the rooms have the following amenities: central heating; washbasin; armchairs; choice of duvets or blankets; tea/coffee-making facilities.

Meals The dinner menu is fixed price (£7). There is no choice of main dishes on the menu, which consists of 3 courses and coffee. Dinner time is by arrangement. Special diets and packed lunches can be prepared. Wine and other alcoholic drinks can be brought in, and other drinks ordered.

Public rooms There is a sitting-room with central heating, open fire, TV, books, magazines, local guides and leaflets.

Surroundings The grounds consist of garden and 4 acres of paddock, with table tennis. These are available in the neighbourhood: riding, squash, swimming, tennis, golf, angling, cycle hire.

Cars The nearest main road is the A422 from Stratford-upon-Avon to Banbury.

Mains Hall, Little Singleton, east of Blackpool, Lancashire, FY6 7LE   *Tel: 0253 885130*   **C D PT**

A long drive through fields brings one to a vista of this historic house, white with leaded windows, at the end of its shrub-lined drive. Built in the time of Henry VII or VIII, it remained a manor house until the turn of the century.

Robert Owen knew and loved it as a boy. When the opportunity came he bought it; and his wife Beryl, who used to have a catering service, runs it as a country hotel. (He is a lecturer in mechanical engineering.) Its outstanding feature is the exuberant wood-carving: Jacobean garlands and nymphs abound, in the panelling of the hall and up the staircase.

It has a history of romance and plots, with secret hiding-places used by Cardinal Allen and Jesuit priests who were attempting the overthrow of Elizabeth I. The old barn, which carries the date 1686 in its brickwork, housed an illicit chapel. Jacobite rebels stayed here in 1745, and later the Prince Regent – wooing Catholic Mrs Fitzherbert, a connection of the family. All around are other ancient remains – an octagonal brick dovecote (from the time when pigeons were 'farmed' for their meat), a well, pool and fountain.

At the back is the River Wyre, and the grounds are full of wildlife – kestrels, woodpeckers, tawny and barn owls. There are two old walnut trees, and Beryl uses the nuts in the meals she cooks. A typical menu is Stilton soup, lamb in honey and orange, syllabub. (No dinner on Sundays.) Popular breakfast options include stuffed croissants and creamed mushrooms.

My bedroom was spacious and comfortable, with a view right along the drive.

The house stands in an attractive area of countryside, and is within easy reach of plenty of other interesting places to visit (see page 390).

The following facts have been supplied by the owners:

Bedrooms There are 7 rooms, which include single, double and family rooms. Bed-and-breakfast costs from £12.50 (per person in a double room), including service and VAT. There are reductions for stays of 7 nights or more.

All the rooms have the following amenities: central heating; electric blankets, washbasin, shower, own bathroom and wc, shaver-point; radio, armchairs; views of river, countryside, farmland, garden; tea/coffee-making facilities; trouser press; door keys. Breakfast in bed is available. One room has a four-poster bed. Extra-firm mattresses available, and TV.

Meals The dinner menu is fixed price (£9). There is no choice of dishes on the menu, which consists of 3 courses and coffee. Dinner is served at 7 pm. Special diets can be prepared. Packed lunches can be provided; and snacks at other hours. Morning, afternoon or bedtime drinks (coffee, tea etc.) can be ordered for a charge. Wine and other alcoholic drinks can be ordered.

Public rooms There are 2 sitting-rooms and a garden room. The following are available in one or both of them: central heating, open fire, colour TV, books, magazines, local guides and leaflets, indoor games (such as table tennis and Monopoly), and a bar.

Surroundings The grounds consist of an acre of garden, 3 acres of meadow and trees and a summer house; with a riverside walk, croquet and birdwatching. These are available in the neighbourhood: swimming, riding, golf, boating, a sports centre.

Cars The nearest main road is the A585 to Fleetwood.

Credit cards accepted Access.

Malting Farm, Blo Norton Road, South Lopham, east of Thetford, Norfolk, IP22 2HT *Tel: 037 988 201* **C(2) X ✠6**

When her daughters went off to university, Cynthia Huggins began to feel rather lonely. Her solution was to take paying guests in what (though the exterior gives no hint of it) is her very historic farmhouse. Over the years, she and her husband have transformed this – removing modern accretions to reveal the old timbers and a great brick fireplace, where a log stove now stands. Tapestry armchairs, a Berber carpet and folk-weave curtains make a very attractive, big sitting/dining-room. In a smaller sitting-room, there are crimson damask chairs and glass doors opening onto a terrace with fields beyond, where the Huggins' cows graze.

Some of the excellent bedrooms are in a modern extension at the back (which also has a bathroom with huge oval bath); but one – in the old part – had to have the legs of the pine half-tester bed adjusted to the slope of the ancient floor.

Cynthia is a keen craftswoman (active in local societies of

quilters, embroiderers, spinners and weavers); around the house are wall-hangings, bedspreads quilted with Laura Ashley fabrics, and draperies made by her. She has a large caravan outside as a studio where she teaches such crafts every Wednesday.

She uses traditional Norfolk recipes and much of her own produce (including ducks, chickens and pork) in preparing country-style meals; on cold days, her steamed puddings are particularly popular.

The farm is roughly half way between the two historic towns of Bury St Edmunds and Norwich (described elsewhere in this book), in one of the more scenic areas of Norfolk. Nearby Diss has old houses around a mere, and twisting narrow streets. Bressingham is famous for the Hall gardens. It is an area of colourful cottages, flint walls, elaborate and colourful village signs and the lovely River Waveney. The Norfolk Wildlife Park (with otters) is well worth visiting; and there are lovely rides, with picnic spots, in Thetford Forest. Head for the Norfolk Broads to the north; or Beccles and the coast around Lowestoft further south.

The following facts have been supplied by the owners:

Bedrooms There are 3 rooms, which include double and family rooms. Bed-and-breakfast costs from £10 (per person in a double room) including service and VAT. There are reductions for stays of 2 nights or more; and 'bargain breaks' as well.

Some if not all of the rooms have the following amenities: central heating or electric heaters; washbasin, shower, own bathroom and wc, shaver-point; armchairs; views of farmland or garden; choice of duvets or blankets; orthopaedic mattress; tea/coffee-making facilities; door keys.

Meals The dinner menu is fixed price (£5.50). There is a choice of dishes on the menu, which consists of 3 courses and coffee. Dinner is served at 6.30 pm. Diabetic diets can be prepared. Lunches and packed lunches can be provided; and snacks at other hours. Morning, afternoon or bedtime drinks (coffee, tea etc.) can be ordered free. Wine and other alcoholic drinks can be brought in.

Public rooms There are 2 sitting-rooms. The following are available in one or more of them: central heating, open fire, TV (colour), books, magazines, local guides and leaflets; indoor games (such as cards, needlecrafts, snooker).

Surroundings The grounds consist of 70 acres of farmland. These are available in the neighbourhood: golf, riding, gliding, sports centres.

Cars The nearest main road is the A1066 from Thetford to Diss.

Languages spoken A little French.

Manor Farm Barn, Taynton, north-west of Burford, Oxfordshire, OX8 4UH   *Tel: 099382 2069*   C(8) **PT ♯ 5**

The approach to this unusual house is very lovely, past old cottages and their colourful gardens, a thatched byre and a courtyard with old copper and stone tubs brimming with flowers.

Breakfast is taken at a huge mahogany table in a room, full of antiques, where once the loaded farm-wagons pulled out (one, now a museum-piece, still stands outside). Now, through huge glass doors, there is a view of lawn, walled garden, clematis and wallflowers in raised beds, and the distant hills. At the side is a terrace from which to enjoy the sunset, over coffee, unless you prefer the huge sitting-room with its many chairs and big windows opening onto the garden. Twice a week, a gifted local girl comes in to renew the beautiful flower arrangements in every room.

The conversion of this great 17th-century barn was done with flair. One impressive feature is the double staircase of oak, up to

the exceptionally attractive bedrooms – many with rugged stone walls and beams, all most attractively decorated and well carpeted. For instance, one has clematis wallpaper even in its bathroom too, and a Kate Greenaway print on its armchairs. Everything is of the very best: luxurious bathrooms; hair driers provided; good water-colours on the wall. Children adore the big attic suite which is perfect for families: virtually, a flat to themselves but costing no more per head than other rooms.

Janet Florey provides only breakfast (Burford has many choices for other meals: I enjoyed the Sunday evening buffet at the Lamb), but these, too, are exceptional. You may start by helping yourself from apricots, melon, raspberries, yogurt, 18(!) kinds of cereal and other starters. Then, in addition to all the usual items of a cooked breakfast, haddock or kippers will be among the choices. Eggs are from Janet's hens, and jams are home-made.

Floreys have farmed around here for five centuries. Although the Manor Barn acreage is now small, you are still likely to recapture the sights of the old days for there are often cattle, horses, orphan lambs and even wild geese on the wing to be seen. For details of the area see page 245.

The following facts have been supplied by the owner:

Bedrooms There are 3 rooms, which include double and family rooms. Bed-and-breakfast costs from £15 (per person in a double room) including service and VAT. There are reductions for stays of 2 nights or more.
   All rooms have the following amenities: central heating and electric heaters; washbasin, shower or own bathroom and wc, shaver-point; TV (colour), armchairs; views of countryside, farmland, garden; fruit; tea/coffee-making facilities; door keys. Hair driers and washing machine available.

Public rooms There are 2 sitting-rooms etc. The following are available in one or both of them: central heating, open fire, TV (colour), books, magazines, local guides and leaflets, board games, record-player and records.

Surroundings The grounds consist of 12 acres of gardens and farmland. Golf, tennis, bowls, fishing, windsurfing and racing are available in the neighbourhood.

Cars The nearest main road is the A40 from London to Wales.

Manor Hotel, West Bexington, south-east of Bridport, Dorset, DT2 9DF   *Tel: 0308 897785*   **C PT S ♯3**

Richard Childs, once a chef at London's prestigious Carlton Towers Hotel, now owns this elegant stone house close to the sea,

Lyme Bay and Chesil Bank. Built in the 16th century, it is surrounded by a mature garden with palm trees, and a patio where guests often take their coffee at sunset. One area is set aside for children's play.

Through the stone-flagged hall with carved woodwork one comes to a long sitting-room with Knoll sofas in grey velvet, from which to enjoy the garden view beyond the bay window. Stairs lead down to a cellar-bar, hung with harness and other tack, some of its seats made from oak casks, gingham cloths on the tables and logs crackling in the hearth if the weather turns chilly. Here bar snacks are available.

Another big inglenook fireplace, crowded with copper kettles and pans, warms the stone-flagged dining-room where good silver, candle-lamps and nosegays are on every apricot-clothed table; horse-racing prints and mementos decorate the walls. This is where you will be offered a very wide menu from which to choose: mainly sophisticated dishes such as crab-and-asparagus pancakes in a mornay sauce or mushrooms à la crême (for a starter), and veal Madeira or guinea-fowl Normande as a main course, for instance.

Bedrooms are spacious – with curtains chosen to match the quilted bedspreads. Many have sea views.

The coastal road here is one of the most scenic in England. It leads to such attractive old towns as Weymouth, Charmouth and Lyme Regis; to harbours of small fishing boats; and to stretches of carefully conserved coastal path for unspoilt walks. Sightseeing possibilities include Abbotsbury (see pages 39–40) and such stately homes as Parnham, Mapperton, Cricket St Thomas, Clapton Court (for its gardens) and Athelhampton – as well as Thomas Hardy's cottage: all within a half-hour drive.

Reader's comments: Excellent food, friendly service, comfortable rooms.

The following facts have been supplied by the owners:

Bedrooms There are 10 rooms, which include single, double and family rooms. Dinner, bed-and-breakfast costs from £25 (per person) including service and VAT; prices go up in high season. There are reductions for stays of 2 nights or more; and 'bargain breaks' as well.

Some if not all of the rooms have the following amenities: central heating or electric heaters; electric blankets, washbasin, shower, own bathroom and wc, shaver-point; radio, TV, armchairs; views of sea, countryside or garden; bed-board; tea/coffee-making facilities; door keys. Breakfast in bed is available.

Meals There is a choice of dishes on the fixed menu, which consists of 3 courses and coffee. Dinner is served at 7–9.30 pm. Vegetarian or special diets can be prepared. Lunches and packed lunches can be provided; and snacks at other hours. Morning, afternoon or bedtime drinks (coffee, tea etc.) can be ordered for a charge. Wine and other alcoholic drinks can be ordered.

Public rooms There is a sitting-room with open fire, TV, books, magazines, local guides and leaflets; indoor games (such as Trivial Pursuit, Monopoly, Ludo, etc.); and a bar.

Surroundings The grounds consist of 3½ acres of gardens with children's play area. These are available in the neighbourhood: tennis, swimming, golf, riding, sailing.

Cars The nearest main road is the A35 from Bridport to Dorchester.

Credit cards accepted Access, Amex, Visa.

Marina Hotel, The Esplanade, Fowey, Cornwall, PL23 1HY
Tel: 072683 3315   **C D PT S ⌗3**

Built in 1830 as a seaside retreat for the Bishop of Truro, this fine house has been furnished with the elegance it deserves. The handsome mouldings, arches and panelling of the hall and octagonal landing are now decorated in brown and cream; and each bedroom is different – a pale colour scheme in one; sprigged covers and pine in another (its rounded window overlooking the sea); four with covered verandahs of lacy ironwork facing the tiny walled garden and waterfront beyond it. The dining-room has

Indian Tree china on peach tablecloths, with spectacular views from the big picture-window; the bar, rosy armchairs and a thick pale carpet.

David Johns gives equal attention to the standard of the food. Dinner is priced according to your choice of main dish, from a selection that includes (for instance) boned chicken in a sauce of port-and-cream, escallopes of veal with mushrooms and apple flamed in calvados, steak in Madeira sauce, and local fish cooked (by Stephen Vincent) in a variety of ways. In spring, painting holidays are run.

Fowey (pronounced Foy) is on that mild stretch of the coast known as the Cornish Riviera. It is an old and picturesque harbour of steep, narrow byways (parking is difficult), its waters busy with yachts and fishing boats. Some people arrive by car ferry. It is easy to find secluded coves and beaches nearby, or scenic walks along clifftops. The little town is full of antique, book and craft shops; historic buildings; restaurants and good food shops.

rear view

The following facts have been supplied by the owners:

Bedrooms There are 12 rooms, which include single, double and family rooms.
  Bed-and-breakfast costs from £17 (per person in a double room) including VAT; prices go up in high season. There are reductions for stays of 2 nights or more.
   Some if not all of the rooms have the following amenities: central heating; electric blankets, washbasin, shower, own bathroom and wc, shaver-point;

272

TV (colour), armchairs; views of sea/garden; balcony; door keys. Breakfast in bed is available.

Meals The dinner menu is fixed price (about £9.50) or à la carte. There is a choice of dishes on the fixed menu, which consists of 4 courses and coffee. Dinner is served at 7–8 pm. Special diets can be prepared. Lunches and packed lunches can be provided; and snacks at other hours. Morning, afternoon or bedtime drinks (coffee, tea etc.) can be ordered for a charge. Wine and other alcoholic drinks can be ordered.

Public rooms There are 3 sitting-rooms etc. The following are available in one or more of them: central heating, TV (colour), books, magazines, local guides and leaflets, board games and cards, piano, record-player and records, bar. Bridge can be arranged.

Surroundings The grounds consist of a lawn. The following sports are available from the grounds: sailing, fishing, windsurfing etc. These are available in the neighbourhood: golf, riding, indoor swimming, badminton, squash.

Cars The nearest main road is the A390 from St Austell to Liskeard.

Credit cards accepted Visa, Amex, Access, Diners Club.

Closed to visitors We are not open from November to March.

Marquis of Lorne, Nettlecombe, north-east of Bridport, Dorset, DT6 3SY   *Tel: 030885 236*   **C S ♯3**

Bob Bone himself shoots most of the game – from quail to venison – which is a speciality at his inn. But there are plenty of other choices on the menu: chicken-and-rabbit vol-au-vent, for example; large local plaice; seafood pancakes; pigeon braised in cider; steaks with chasseur, pepper or beer-and-cheese sauces; and much else, including vegetarian dishes. From the dining-room there is a view of hills, rose-garden and fish-pool (with underwater lighting at night); and after dinner guests can relax there or in big, deep armchairs around the fire in a snug, stone-walled sitting-room – or in the bar, its plank walls thronged with rosettes won at shows by his father's pedigree cattle.

Bedrooms are pleasantly furnished – one, for instance, in a navy-and-white colour scheme; another with rose-garland wallpaper complementing the pink-and-white quilted bedspread.

During winter, anyone dining at the inn midweek is offered bed-and-breakfast afterwards for a trifling £5.

Outside the inn is a pleasant beer-garden with cherry trees, an area of children's play equipment, and a prospect of Egerton Hill with the remains of a Roman fort on top. (The Bridport area of Dorset is described on page 97.)

The following facts have been supplied by the owners:

Bedrooms There are 8 rooms, which include single, double and family rooms. Bed-and-breakfast costs from £13 (per person) including VAT, or from £17.50 with dinner; prices go up in high season. There are reductions for stays of 5 nights or more; and 'bargain breaks' as well.

Some if not all of the rooms have the following amenities: electric heaters; washbasin, shower and wc, shaver-point; armchairs; views of countryside and garden; bed-board; tea/coffee-making facilities; door keys. Breakfast in bed is available.

Meals The dinner menu is à la carte. Dinner is served from 7–9.30 pm. Vegetarian or special diets can be prepared. Lunches and packed lunches can be provided; and snacks at other hours. Morning, afternoon or bedtime drinks (coffee, tea etc.) can be ordered. Wine and other alcoholic drinks can be ordered.

Public rooms There is one sitting-room with open fire, TV, books, magazines, local guides and leaflets, indoor games (such as cards, Scrabble, Trivial Pursuit); and a bar.

Surroundings The grounds consist of 2½ acres with swings, slides, climbing frames etc. These are available in the neighbourhood: fishing (trout), golf.

Cars The nearest main road is the A35 from Weymouth to Honiton.

Languages spoken French.

Credit cards accepted Access.

Menagwins Cottage, Gorran, south of Mevagissey, Cornwall, PL26 6HP   *Tel: 0726 843507*   C(5) **D PT S ♯ 3**

Artist John Grahn and his wife Joan live in a pretty stone cottage, built in the 18th century, which they have furnished most attractively. In the low-beamed dining-room are an old pine dresser, John's paintings and pretty dining-chairs (cane-backed and with pink velvet seats) around a table over which hangs a lampshade of latticework china. Around the sitting-room are grouped chairs covered in a faded poppy pattern, and from this room rises the staircase to the bedrooms.

The bedrooms are pretty, with matching curtains and duvets – even the towels match the colour schemes. Stripped-pine furniture and fresh flowers are in keeping with the cottage.

As to meals, everything is home-cooked from fresh produce. A typical menu might comprise salmon mousse, lamb cutlets en croûte, trifle with raspberries and Cornish cream.

Of course, scenery is Cornwall's main attraction. But around here there are also at least 40 'sights' to visit: unusual museums and collections, steam rail, fishing villages, gardens, seal sanctuary, tin mines, tropical bird gardens, waterfall, shire horse centre, watermills, river trips, craft centres, a trout farm and much else.

Reader's comment: Superb cooking; extremely high standard of comfort.

The following facts have been supplied by the owners:

Bedrooms There are 4 rooms, which include single, double and children's rooms. Bed-and-breakfast costs from £8 (per person) including service and VAT.
Some if not all of the rooms have the following amenities: electric heaters; electric blankets, washbasin, shaver-point; radio, armchairs; views of garden.

Meals The dinner menu is fixed price (£6). There is no choice of dishes on the fixed menu, which consists of 3 courses and coffee. Dinner is served at 7.30 pm. Special diets can be prepared. Morning or afternoon tea can be ordered free. Non-residents are not admitted to the dining-room. Wine and other alcoholic drinks can be brought in.

Public rooms There is a sitting-room with central heating, open fire, TV (colour), books, magazines, local guides and leaflets, indoor games (such as Scrabble, jigsaws, quiz games), record-player and records.

Surroundings The grounds consist of a garden.

Cars The nearest main road is the A390 from Plymouth to St Austell.

Mill Hay House, Snowshill Road, Broadway, Worcestershire, WR12 7JS   *Tel: 0386 852498*   **C PT X ⊞ 4**

Picturesque Broadway, now world-famous, can get unpleasantly crowded with tourists – but Mill Hay House lies well away from all that, a very lovely house of Cotswold stone with a mossy roof and leaded windows. At the front is a formal garden of rosebeds and clipped yews; at the back, terraced lawns are surrounded by flowering shrubs, more roses and yew hedges, and a rock garden through which a tiny rivulet trickles down to where an old watermill still stands, its great wheel spotlit at night. From some of the yews a bower has been created, sheltering a seat on which to sit and enjoy this romantic view.

One bedroom (with king-size bed) has a view of the mill and garden. Others (one with four-poster and balcony) overlook the rose garden and pond. There is also a separate family suite with two rooms and its own bathroom.

Dinner is served at a large circular table in a room with a stone fireplace, after which guests can relax in big leather or velvet sofas by the fireside in the panelled sitting-room, its floor covered with handsome oriental rugs.

Cooking is done by Mary Loggie (who manages the house for Mr and Mrs Hanswill). Dinners are served only during winter – at other seasons, visitors have a wide selection of eating-places in the village – and comprise such choices as leek soup or stuffed

276

mushrooms; carbonnade of beef or chicken in a cream sauce; peach mousse or cheesecake.

The family also own nearby Broadway Tower and its surrounding country park. From the top of this 18th-century folly there are fine views and inside is a museum, including displays about William Morris who once lived in the Tower. In the park (famous for spring wild flowers and autumn colours) are a barbecue, with meat on sale, wildlife trails, and animals for the children as well as an imaginative play centre. It's worth a whole day for the family.

Not only is there the whole of the Cotswold area to explore, but three of England's most popular tourist cities or towns are equidistant – Stratford-upon-Avon, Oxford and Cheltenham, their environs all described elsewhere in this book.

The following facts have been supplied by the owners:

Bedrooms There are 6 rooms, which include single, double and family rooms. Bed-and-breakfast costs from £15 (per person) including service and VAT. There are reductions for stays of 3 nights or more; and 'bargain breaks' as well.

    Some if not all of the rooms have the following amenities: central heating or electric heaters; electric blankets, washbasin, shower, own bathroom and wc, shaver-point; armchairs; views of countryside or garden; balcony; orthopaedic mattress or bed-board; tea/coffee-making facilities; door keys.

Meals Dinner is à la carte, served at 7 pm. Vegetarian or special diets can be prepared. Morning, afternoon or bedtime drinks (coffee, tea etc.) can be ordered free. Non-residents are not admitted to the dining-room. Wine and other alcoholic drinks can be brought in.

Public rooms There is a sitting-room with central heating, open fire, TV (colour), books, magazines, local guides and leaflets.

Surroundings The grounds consist of a 1½ acre garden. These are available in the neighbourhood: tennis, golf.

Cars The nearest main road is the A46 from Stratford-upon-Avon to Cheltenham.

Closed to visitors We are not open in January and February.

Milton Farm, East Knoyle, north of Shaftesbury (Dorset), Wiltshire, SP3 6BG   *Tel: 074783 247*   **C S ♯8**

This is a truly picturebook farmhouse – a stone-flagged floor in the entrance hall, glimpse of a kitchen with pine table and a gun-case beside the gleaming Aga, narrow oak staircase. In the sitting-room, which has a boarded ceiling, logs hiss gently on the stone hearth. There are old oak furniture, deep chairs, silver and flowers everywhere (including the bedrooms, each of which has its own bathroom).

The Hydes removed a lot of later accretions to reveal the original beams in this mainly Queen Anne house, and then added comfortable furniture and elegant fabrics (such as Sanderson's 'Country Trail'). Janice Hyde serves candlelit dinners – she is a superb cook – which consist of interesting dishes using local produce. One example: onion quiche, followed by a huge trout from the River Nadder (stuffed with almonds, mushrooms, lemon and I-know-not-what) and then the lightest of mousses. Clotted cream, milk and butter are from the farm's cows; pheasant, hare and rabbits are local. Her breakfasts are equally excellent.

Outside is a paved area with chairs facing a view of the hills, and total silence – except for the call of a distant cuckoo. The farm itself is partly arable and partly beef-cattle.

East Knoyle is a tiny old village with just one claim to fame: Christopher Wren was born there (his father was rector). So was Edward Strong, who became Wren's master mason and worked on St Paul's. In 1674, Strong built the cottage opposite, and possibly parts of Milton Farm too. Janice Hyde can sometimes show visitors a fascinating scrapbook of village history compiled by the local Women's Institute, including the memories of the local blacksmith and of the postman who used to deliver the letters on horseback. Every summer, there is a music festival in two local castles. Just wandering around here is a pleasure in itself, enjoying willows or magnolias or buttercups, and details like the old stone troughs or a well, and looking for the Victorian 'bun' penny set in the wall of Penny Cottage or the fire-bell on Bell Cottage. There are views over the Blackmoor Vale, a windmill, bluebell and rhododendron woods, and the old Seymour Arms where Jane Seymour once lived.

Salisbury (see page 319) lies in one direction and in the other the ancient, cobbled, hilltop town of Shaftesbury, followed by Sherborne – one of England's jewels, and much underrated. It has two castles, a golden abbey, a quaint museum, and a nearby butterfly and silkworm centre in a historic house. The Palladian mansion of Stourhead is within easy motoring distance: it has art treasures, superb woodwork and furniture, landscaped gardens and lake. This is a region of hills and woodland, tiny villages and sparkling rivers: all very rural and tranquil.

The following facts have been supplied by the owners:

Bedrooms There are 4 rooms, which include single, double and family rooms. Bed-and-breakfast costs £13 (per person in a double room) including service and VAT. There are 'bargain breaks'.
   Some if not all of the rooms have the following amenities: central heating; washbasin, shower, own bathroom and wc, shaver-point; TV (colour or b&w), armchairs; views of countryside, farmland, garden; tea/coffee-making facilities.

Meals The dinner menu is fixed price (£9) and consists of 3 courses and coffee. Dinner is served at 7 pm. Bedtime drinks (coffee, tea etc.) can be ordered free. Wine can be ordered. Vegetarian dishes on request.

Public rooms There is a sitting-room with central heating, open fire, books, magazines, local guides and leaflets.

Surroundings The grounds consist of ½ acre of garden with heated (80°) swimming-pool. These are available in the neighbourhood: golf, riding.

Cars The nearest main road is the A350 from Shaftesbury to Warminster.

Closed to visitors We are closed to visitors in winter.

Moatenden Priory, Headcorn, south-east of Maidstone, Kent, TN27 9PT *Tel: 0622 890413* **C D PT ⌗9**

This is among the most ancient of the houses described in this book. It comprises the moated remains of a monastery founded in 1224, when Henry III was king: one of the monks' activities was the raising of money to ransom crusaders held prisoner by the infidels. The walls are of thick stone, the oak doors fit into arched doorways, pointed windows are deep-set.

After Henry VIII dissolved the monasteries, the Priory was owned by a succession of famous people – among them, Thomas Cromwell (Henry's chancellor) and the court poet Sedley, whose daughter became James II's mistress. Then for many years the building was used as a farmhouse.

It is not just the house (hidden at the end of a little lane) that is so outstanding, but the furnishings, too, which Jessie Barclay-Deane has kept entirely in character. Guests eat at the big table in her huge dining-kitchen, under a ceiling of great oak timbers. The floor is of quarry tiles and wood, the seating consists of old wood benches and chairs. The big sink is the original stone one, which she retrieved from the garden. Even her Aga is something of an antique: its covers are not cream enamel but polished copper. The walls are whitewashed brick, the windows diamond-paned.

Here Mrs Barclay-Deane serves weekend meals made largely with her own produce (vegetables, fruit, little bantams' eggs). A typical dinner might consist of egg mayonnaise, casseroled chicken, and a blackberry crème brulée. Everything she prepares is fresh and simple, and she enjoys cooking for vegetarians. (On weekdays, visitors dine at local inns.)

The sitting-room has comfortable tapestry chairs and a Persian carpet; its walls are painted a soft terracotta and its paintwork white. The only sound is likely to be the slow ticking of the clock or the crackle of logs on the great hearth.

Bedrooms are equally attractive and peaceful: beamed ceilings, antique furniture, warm colour schemes, pretty cast-iron fireplaces, and interesting furnishings (a fur spread from India and a woven wall-hanging from Peru, for instance).

Some visitors come for the peace, some for the many sightseeing possibilities in Kent, and many to visit Vita Sackville-West's famous garden at Sissinghurst (before she bought Sissinghurst she nearly decided to take Moatenden Priory, but it did not have enough land for her needs). The Priory's own pretty garden, surrounded by high beech hedges, has two ancient pillars over which honeysuckle clambers and an old orchard where mallards, moorhens and sometimes partridges wander.

Within easy reach are many of Kent's spectacular mansions and castles (Knole, Leeds and Hever, for example), and historic cities (such as Canterbury and Maidstone). The country lanes are particularly beautiful in apple-blossom time (usually May) or even earlier, when the cherry trees are in flower. In September, the hops are gathered and taken to the oast houses for drying – a few allow visitors.

Reader's comment: A delightful place.

The following facts have been supplied by the owner:

Bedrooms There are 4 rooms, which include single, double and family rooms. Bed-and-breakfast costs from £12.50 (per person in a double room) including service and VAT. There are off-season 'bargain breaks'.

    Some if not all of the rooms have the following amenities: central heating; electric blankets, shaver-point; armchairs; views of countryside, farmland, garden; choice of duvets or blankets; door keys; bed-boards. No smoking.

Meals The dinner menu is fixed price (£10). There is no choice of dishes on the menu, which consists of 3 courses, wine and coffee. Dinner is served at 7.30 pm. Special diets can be prepared. Morning, afternoon or bedtime drinks (coffee, tea etc.) can be ordered. Wine and other alcoholic drinks can be brought in.

Public rooms There are 2 sitting-rooms. The following are available in one or both of them: central heating, open fire, colour TV, books, magazines, local guides and leaflets.

Surroundings The grounds consist of 2¼ acres of garden.

Cars The nearest main road is the A274 from Maidstone to Tenterden.

Mon Bijou Hotel, Manor Road, Bournemouth, Dorset, BH1 3EU
Tel: 0202 21389   C(8) **PT X ♯6**

Once an early-Victorian coach-house, this low white-shuttered building has more character than most of Bournemouth's innumerable small hotels. Beyond lies a pretty little garden. Bedrooms are very well furnished, and there is a family suite (two bedrooms sharing one bathroom). It was recently taken over by Mel Baggott, a former Cunard head-waiter who worked on the *Queen Mary*, and his wife Yvonne who does the cooking.

Dinners comprise a fixed menu with several choices at the four courses, conventional fare such as prawn cocktail, roast beef, apple pie with cream, and cheese. Occasionally, there is dancing to a band.

The hotel stands in the select East Cliff area of Bournemouth, where roads are wide and tree-lined (including many of the fragrant pines for which this end of Bournemouth has always been famous); but it takes only a few minutes to get to the busy centre with its shops (famous department stores or speciality boutiques in the arcades), theatres, concert halls (the city has its own celebrated symphony orchestra), pier and museums. The sea and miles of golden sands are five minutes' walk away.

Although Bournemouth attracts a great number of older visitors, who like the absence of the razzmatazz which spoils some other resorts, it has an immense amount to keep children happy, too. The swimming is safe, and there are many entertainments for them, as well as outings which adults, too, enjoy. Here are just a few of the sights within easy reach: New Forest (ponies, wagon-rides, cycling paths), ancient Christchurch (historic priory, boat-hire on the river), Beaulieu (vintage motor museum in a delightful setting), Bucklers Hard waterfront (maritime museum), Lymington (sailing centre, trips to Isle of Wight), Salisbury and Winchester cathedrals, Poole harbour (trips to Brownsea Island, aquarium, maritime museum), Marwell Wildlife Sanctuary and Longleat Safari Park, the tank museum at Bovington, the gardens of Compton Acres, innumerable stately homes, and the breath-takingly beautiful coastline of Dorset at Lulworth Cove, Studland and Shell Bay with equally lovely hill and valley scenery inland from here (Corfe Castle, picturesque thatched villages).

The following facts have been supplied by the owners:

Bedrooms There are 8 rooms, which include single, double and family rooms. Bed-and-breakfast costs from £13.50 (per person in a double room) including service and VAT. There are 'bargain breaks', and sampler weekends (see page 14).

Some if not all of the rooms have the following amenities: central heating; washbasin, shower, own bathroom and wc, shaver-point; armchairs; views of garden; door keys.

Meals The dinner menu is fixed price (from £10) or à la carte. There is a choice of dishes on the fixed menu, which consists of 4 courses and coffee. Dinner is served at 6 pm. Bedtime drinks (coffee, tea etc.) can be ordered for a charge. Wine can be ordered.

Public rooms There is a sitting-room with central heating, TV (colour), books, magazines, local guides and leaflets, indoor games (such as cards, dominoes, etc.). Also a bar.

Cars The nearest main road is the A35 from Dorchester to Lymington.

Languages spoken German.

Morar Farm, Weald Street, Bampton, south of Witney, Oxfordshire, OX8 2HL   *Tel: 0993 850162*   C(5) **PT** ⚫3

This modern stone house, comfortable and trim, stands in an attractive garden; but what makes it a particularly nice place at which to stay is the personality of its owners. Janet and Terry Rouse are a lively couple, numbering among their accomplishments Morris-dancing, bell-ringing, barn-dancing and spinning (their tame ram provides the fleece); and they gladly involve their guests too. One reader described Morar as the best place he had ever stayed at, because of the helpful hospitality and excellent food.

Janet takes quite exceptional care of her visitors, with much attention to detail – for instance, two fresh towels are provided every day; there are unlimited fruit juices at breakfast and a wide range of home-made preserves, as well as help-yourself strawberries and raspberries or figs, stewed fruits, etc.; she does washing free for visitors who stay two weeks; and has plenty of maps on loan, fills vacuum flasks free, and gives refrigerator space to chill drinks visitors bring in.

For dinner Janet may, during winter, serve a menu such as soup made from home-grown vegetables; their own beef with Yorkshire pudding and six vegetables including red cabbage cooked with honey and juniper berries; Bakewell pudding and cream; a wide choice of cheeses and fruit. (In summer most visitors eat at the nearby Poacher's Rest.)

This is a 'no smoking' house.

Bampton, a pretty village, is famous for its spring festival of Morris dancers when the village children all make wild flower garlands. It is well placed to visit Oxford, the Cotswold villages, Cheltenham, Blenheim Palace, Bladon (Churchill's grave), Cirencester (Roman museum), Avebury stone circle, and the Berkshire Downs. There's a wildlife park, rare farm breeds centre, arboretum, trout farm, restored watermill and farm museum all within easy reach. Also, unfortunately, RAF Brize Norton is near too, so be prepared for some aircraft noise.

The following facts have been supplied by the owners:

Bedrooms There are 3 double rooms. Bed-and-breakfast costs from £9.50 (per person in a double room) including service and VAT. **There are reductions to readers of this book** staying 7 nights or more; for winter bookings by over-60s.
   The rooms have central heating; washbasin, shaver-point; views of countryside or garden; bed-board on request; tea/coffee-making facilities; door keys. Breakfast in bed is available.

Meals The dinner menu is fixed price (£8.30). There is no choice of dishes on the menu, which consists of 4 courses and coffee. Dinner is served at 6.30 pm. Vegetarian or special diets can be prepared. Lunches (in low season only) and packed lunches can be provided. Morning, afternoon or bedtime drinks (coffee, tea etc.) can be ordered free. Non-residents are not admitted to the dining-room. Wine and other alcoholic drinks can be brought in.

Public rooms There is a sitting-room with central heating, open fire, TV (colour), books, magazines, local guides and leaflets, indoor games (such as Othello, Scrabble, cards and Mastermind), piano.

Surroundings The grounds consist of 2 acres of gardens and paddock, with climbing frame, sandpit and swing ball. These are available in the neighbourhood: golf, riding, sailing, surfing, swimming, squash.

Cars The nearest main road is the A4095 from Woodstock to Faringdon.

Languages spoken French.

Also in Bampton is larger (and dearer) **University Farm**, built in the 17th century – elegantly furnished, and with a 'carvery' restaurant open to non-residents. (Tel: 0993 850297.)

Mytton Fold Farm Hotel, Langho, Whalley, north of Blackburn, Lancashire, BB6 8AB   *Tel: 0254 48255*   C(6) **PT**

Frank and Lilian Hargreaves started by doing bed-and-breakfast in a couple of rooms in their farmhouse, found it both successful and enjoyable, and converted the old stable block into further accommodation, with a restaurant.

The well-heated bedrooms are painted in pastel shades with matching duvet covers and curtains. Downstairs is a beamed bar with a big French window looking on to a lawn and crazy paving; the bar itself is solidly built of stone and elm. In the restaurant, with lace tablecloths and flowers on every table, they serve à la carte meals cooked by their professional staff. The choice extends to about eight first courses and as many main dishes (the mixed grill is impressive).

Being within easy reach of the big towns of Lancashire, Mytton Fold has proved very popular with travelling businessmen.

Holidaymakers stay for a night or two, or spend a week exploring rural Lancashire – its panoramic views and picturesque villages are a pleasant revelation to many southerners – and the nearby Yorkshire Dales. The Ribble valley is very attractive, and not far away is Pendle Hill, famous for 17th-century witch-hunts, so there is scope for outings even though the farm's immediate surroundings are not particularly appealing.

The professional way in which Mytton Fold is run almost seems to belie the fact that this is still a working farm where sheep and beef-cattle are kept, now run by the genial Hargreaves' son – fourth generation of the family to do so.

The following facts have been supplied by the owners:

Bedrooms There are 12 rooms, which include double and family rooms. Bed-and-breakfast costs from £15 (per person in a double room) including VAT. There are 'bargain breaks'.

All rooms have the following amenities: central heating; own bathroom and wc, shaver-point; radio, TV (colour), phone, armchairs; views of farmland/garden; tea/coffee-making facilities; door keys; trouser press; hair drier.

Meals The dinner menu is à la carte. Dinner is served at 6.30–9.30 pm. Special diets can be prepared. Lunches and packed lunches can be provided; and snacks at other hours. Wine and other alcoholic drinks can be ordered.

Public rooms There are 2 sitting-rooms etc. The following are available in one or both of them: central heating, open fire, books, magazines, local guides and leaflets, organ, bar.

Surroundings The grounds consist of 100 acres of farmland. These are available in the neighbourhood: golf, fishing, riding, swimming, tennis, bowls.

Cars The nearest main road is the A59 from Preston to Skipton.

Credit cards accepted Access, Visa.

**Nankersey Hotel, Flushing, east of Falmouth, Cornwall,
TR11 5TP** *Tel: 0326 74471* **C S** (except July-Aug.) **X ▦3**

When, in the 17th century, Dutch workers were brought to the
tiny harbour of Nankersey to build a quay, a new name was given
to the place: Flushing (after their home port of Flushing).

This elegant little house, which is perched on the steep road
leading down to the waterfront, was built in the 18th century as the
home of a celebrated sailing-ship captain (Sir Edward Pellew):
many of Falmouth's sea captains lived in Flushing. Nelson once
stayed at the house.

From its front bedrooms there are splendid views across the
estuary to the colourful houses of Falmouth, piled up steeply on
the opposite bank. A passenger ferry goes to and fro across the
waters which once were crowded with great sailing-ships. At the
end of the village is a small beach (safe and sheltered) found by
few holidaymakers, for Flushing is not on the usual tourist track: a
bay of sand, rocks and jetty.

In the hotel's sitting-room at the back a huge William Morris
sofa curves round, with a view through a wall of glass doors to a
tiny walled patio. It was here that Sir Edward's horses were once
stabled, and the cobbled floor of the adjoining bar (with a ship's
wheel, lantern and other nautical mementos) was once the stable-
yard.

In an eight-foot thick wall of the panelled dining-room was a secret passage to the next house – a not uncommon feature in coastal villages where smuggling used to be an accepted way of life – now used as a linen cupboard.

Bedroom armchairs are placed in the bay windows to make the most of the sea views. The village, facing south and sheltered by hills, is reputedly the warmest one in England – camellias are often in bloom as early as January. This house, now run by Joan and Michael Blakey, is simply but pleasantly decorated.

Meals, too, are simple but appetizing. Prawn-and-grapefruit cocktail might be followed by lamb, pork or perhaps a really big lemon sole caught only three hours earlier; then might come gooseberry granola (the topping is made from oats, nuts and honey) or an apricot sundae with clotted cream.

Flushing, completely uncommercialized, is at the centre of very pretty countryside and a network of lanes brimming with wild flowers. There are plenty of good beaches near (Michael provides guests with his personal guide to all 300 miles of Cornwall's coastline); and from Falmouth one can take sea and river trips, or watch the many yacht races. All of southern Cornwall can be explored from here – Land's End, Polperro, Newquay, St Mawes (a boat goes there from Falmouth), for instance.

Readers' comments: Very friendly and pleasant; pretty decor. Good home cooking. A charming welcome and delicious food (including packed lunches).

The following facts have been supplied by the owners:

Bedrooms There are 8 rooms, which include double and family rooms. Bed-and-breakfast costs from £11 (per person in a double room) including service and VAT; prices go up in high season. There are reductions for stays of 7 nights or more.

Some if not all of the rooms have the following amenities: central heating or electric heaters; washbasin, shaver-point; armchairs; views of sea/farmland/garden; tea/coffee-making facilities; door keys; orthopaedic mattress.

Meals The dinner menu is fixed price (£8). There is some choice of dishes on the menu, which consists of 4 courses and coffee. Dinner is served at 7 pm (but not on Fridays). Morning, afternoon or bedtime drinks (coffee, tea etc.) can be ordered for a charge. Wine and other alcoholic drinks can be ordered.

Public rooms There is a sitting-room with central heating, TV (colour), books, magazines, local guides and leaflets, indoor games (such as Monopoly, draughts, dominoes, cards, roulette).

**Nansidwell Hotel, Mawnan, near Helford, east of Helston,
Cornwall, TR11 5HU** *Tel: 0326 250340* **C D H S-C X ⚏2**

There can be few places in England where not only camellias but
mimosas bloom in abundance, and early in the year: one of many
delights in the very lovely grounds surrounding this fine country
mansion, designed by architect Leonard Stokes in 1903. It has
been run as a hotel by three generations of the same family, who
from the 1930s onwards have maintained an ideal combination of
comfort and dignity without pretentiousness.

One steps into a large double sitting-room with two log fires,
cushioned seats at the bay windows – granite-mullioned and lead-
paned – and oriental carpets on polished wood. At the foot of the
walnut staircase beyond is a cleverly concealed bar, also walnut-
panelled, with an East Indian goddess perched on top, the gift of a
Dutch admiral who used to stay here.

The dining-room is equally handsome, its yellow-clothed tables
laid with white-and-gold china; it overlooks the terrace and a
beautiful valley beyond. Here David Evans' young chef serves
such traditional five-course dinners as: crab cocktail, Stilton-and-
celery soup, sirloin steak, cherry crumble with clotted cream,
cheeses. Much produce is home-grown or comes from local farms.

All the bedrooms, spacious and well carpeted, have pleasing
views of the gardens, fish-pool and countryside, beyond which lie
secluded cove and clifftop or woodland walks, in a lovely area
preserved by the National Trust.

The Helford area is one of wooded creeks, sandy coves and cliffs
around a scenic estuary (visit Porth Navas if you enjoy oysters).
Nearby is Falmouth, a resort in a lovely setting for bathing or
sailing, cliff walks or boat trips. So mild is the climate that you may
even see bananas growing among subtropical flowers reminiscent
of the Riviera.

The following facts have been supplied by the owners:

Bedrooms There are 18 rooms, which include single, double and family rooms. Dinner, bed-and-breakfast costs from £26 (per person in a double room) including VAT; prices go up in high season. There are reductions for stays of 6 nights or more; and 'bargain breaks' as well.

Some if not all of the rooms have the following amenities: central heating; washbasin, own bathroom and wc, shaver-point; TV (colour), armchairs; views of sea/countryside/farmland/garden; door keys. Tea or breakfast in bed is available.

Meals There is a choice of dishes on the fixed menu, which consists of 5 courses and coffee. Dinner is served at 7–9 pm. Special diets can be prepared. Lunches and packed lunches can be provided; and snacks at other hours. Morning, afternoon or bedtime drinks (coffee, tea etc.) can be ordered for a charge. Wine and other alcoholic drinks can be ordered. No smoking at table.

Public rooms There are 2 sitting-rooms etc. The following are available in one or both of them: central heating, open fire, TV (colour), books, magazines, local guides and leaflets.

Surroundings The grounds consist of 12 acres of garden and fields, with hard tennis court. These are available in the neighbourhood: golf, bowls, fishing, boating, riding.

Cars The nearest main road is the A39 from Truro to Falmouth.

Credit cards accepted Access, Visa, Diners, Amex.

Closed to visitors We are not open in January and February, except for house-parties of friends.

Neals Farm, Wyfold, north of Reading, Berkshire, RG4 9JB
Tel: 0491 680258   C D S ♯2

This is very much a place for animal-lovers because the handsome 18th-century house (flint-and-brick, typical of this area) is at the heart of a large farm with nearly a hundred beef-cattle, as many chickens, a flock of sheep, Jersey cows, six horses (the rosettes they've won at shows stretch the length of one wall in the kitchen), and a tiny black Shetland pony called Syllabub so friendly that she comes indoors to greet visitors. The pond has tench and carp; and there are acres of beechwoods in which children can safely roam.

Visitors are free to use every room as if this were their home – from the pleasant sitting-room (damson carpet, big sash windows, classical marble fireplace, antique furniture) to the useful washing and drying room. Everyone eats in the big wood-panelled, quarry-tiled kitchen. And downstairs is a huge cellar room for children and teenagers, with a walk-in cupboard full of games. Bedrooms are prettily decorated – the bathroom too.

Bridget Silsoe has two enthusiasms – horses and cooking, using meat and produce from the farm (she even makes the butter herself). A typical dinner might consist of baked eggs with smoky bacon, home-produced lamb and vegetables, and her own special kind of apple pie.

Neals Farm is high up in the lovely Chiltern Hills – very near London (and Heathrow Airport) yet truly rural. You could spend a fortnight here and every day do something different, for within easy reach are woodland walks, boat-hire or pleasure trips on the Thames, historic mansions, Oxford (its colleges and museums), riverside towns (Henley in particular), waterfront inns, Reading's museum of rural life, Windsor Castle, historic West Wycombe with its 'hell-fire' caves, Norman churches, hilltop views and bluebell valleys, watercress beds . . . the list is endless.

The following facts have been supplied by the owners:

Bedrooms There are 4 rooms, which include single, double and family rooms. Bed-and-breakfast costs from £9 (per person in a double room) including service and VAT.

291

Some if not all of the rooms have the following amenities: central heating or electric heaters; washbasin; armchairs; views of countryside or garden; choice of duvets or blankets; tea/coffee-making facilities; door keys. Breakfast in bed is available.

Meals The dinner menu is fixed price (£5). There is no choice of dishes on the menu, which consists of 2 or 3 courses and coffee. Dinner is served at times to suit guests. Vegetarian or special diets can be prepared. Lunches and packed lunches can be provided. Morning, afternoon or bedtime drinks (coffee, tea etc.) can be ordered free. Non-residents are not admitted to the dining-room. Wine and other alcoholic drinks can be brought in.

Public rooms There is a sitting-room with central heating, open fire, TV (colour), books, magazines, local guides and leaflets, indoor games (such as Scrabble, shove halfpenny, backgammon); piano, record-player and records.

Surroundings The grounds consist of 100 acres of farmland and beechwoods. Riding is available. Swimming and fishing (coarse). Golf course nearby.

Cars The nearest main road is the A423 from Oxford to Henley-on-Thames.

Languages spoken Some French.

New Bridge Hotel, Lanercost, north of Brampton, Cumbria
Tel: 06977 2224   C(5) **D PT S X ⌗8**

Where two rivers converge to the sound of rushing water, there is an old hump-backed bridge of red sandstone built in the time of James II. The traffic ignores it, hurrying across over a modern bridge further along. From it you can see part-ruined Lanercost Priory, or leave it to walk along riverside paths. Right here, Mr and Mrs Arthur run the New Bridge Hotel, old despite its name which has been changed at least four times – once, when the reforming Countess of Carlisle made it 'dry', it was called the Temperance Hotel.

It's a snug place to stay, particularly when log fires are blazing in the lounges, or after a day's strenuous walking in the Border hills. The bedrooms are simply furnished, and the Arthurs, who took over the hotel recently, have been busy improving them. Their first achievement was the renovation of what was once a black-smith's forge, dating back to the 17th century, where meals (other than breakfast) are served to residents and non-residents. It is a barn-like building with gnarled rafters and white-painted walls. The bar and sitting area downstairs are made cosy by a big iron stove. Up a specially made wrought-iron spiral staircase is a gallery where one eats beneath wrought-iron chandeliers with flickering electric candles.

The food consists of superior bar meals (such as home-made burgers and a quiche of the day, with a help-yourself salad table), plus a chef's dish of the day, such as pork cordon bleu.

Drinks or coffee can be enjoyed sitting under sun-umbrellas on the old bridge itself; or in the garden, frequented by the Arthurs' Great Dane.

As well as scenic walks or drives, and the beautiful priory, there is plenty to do or see in the area: 14th-century Naworth Castle, Hadrian's Wall, the Saxon church at Over Denton, and historic villages like Gilsland and Bewcastle with Roman remains. Bewcastle has a decorated stone cross which is one of Britain's greatest Saxon treasures. In the river at Corby Castle on the way to Carlisle are salmon-traps built by 12th-century monks and still in use today. The road from Brampton to Alston is particularly attractive, running alongside the South Tyne River, with views of the northernmost Pennines.

Reader's comments: A wonderful stay. Very high standard, excellent food, thoroughly to be recommended. Exceptional interest in the well-being of guests; outstanding value for money.

The following facts have been supplied by the owners:

Bedrooms There are 4 rooms, which include single and double rooms. Bed-and-breakfast costs from £14 (per person in a double room) including service and VAT.

Some if not all of the rooms have the following amenities: central heating; washbasin, own bathroom and wc, shaver-point; armchairs; views of countryside or garden; choice of duvets or blankets. Breakfast in bed is available.

Meals The dinner menu is à la carte. Vegetarian or special diets can be prepared. Lunches and packed lunches can be provided; and snacks at other hours. Morning, afternoon or bedtime drinks (coffee, tea etc.) can be ordered for a charge. Wine and other alcoholic drinks can be ordered.

Public rooms There are 3 sitting-rooms etc. The following are available in one or more of them: central heating, open fire, TV (colour), books, magazines, local guides and leaflets, indoor games (such as draughts and dominoes), piano, record-player and records; and a bar.

Surroundings These are available in the neighbourhood: fishing, golf, windsurfing, sailing.

Cars The nearest main road is the A69 from Carlisle to Newcastle.

Languages spoken German.

New Capernwray Farmhouse, Capernwray, Carnforth, north of Lancaster, Lancashire, LA6 1AD   *Tel: 052473 4284*   CDX⌗2

So close to the busy M6 motorway and yet so rural, this is a place of absolute peace. The oak beams and stone walls that are features of most rooms date from the 17th century when the house was built as a farm. Now it is simply the home of Peter and Sally Townend, who are both teachers. They moved north, to this house, when Peter got a deputy headship locally and they say frankly that it was only when the cost of central heating soared that they began, a little doubtfully, to take paying guests – and then found they really enjoyed the experience. Sally encourages people to treat the house as if it were their own home. After serving breakfast, she leaves for her work at the nearby primary school while her domestic help gets busy; she returns at 3.30 to cook an excellent dinner which could consist of avocado with prawns, roast turkey, a choice of two puddings (meringues, chocolate gâteau etc.), cheese, fresh fruit and coffee. Guests help themselves to as much as they want – all served on bone china.

Meals are eaten in what was once the dairy, now furnished with Ercol elm chairs and table. In the sitting-room, deep velvet armchairs and sofa contrast with the rugged stone of fireplace and walls. My bedroom had a shaggy carpet, doors of dark wood with brass knobs, white built-in furniture and attractive colours.

Capernwray not only lies in attractive countryside but is midway between the Lake District and the Yorkshire Dales, neither much more than a half-hour in a car. Scenic walks, pretty villages, market towns and inns abound. Lakeland has its steamer trips, nature trails, theatres, arts and crafts. In the Dales are streams, waterfalls and caves open to the public.

Other areas 'of outstanding natural beauty' are the Lune valley, Arnside and Silverdale, and the Trough of Bowland. Canal cruisers can be hired by the hour or day, there are bird reserves, stately homes, castles and a steam railway museum. Morecambe's beaches are near, so is historic Lancaster and its quaint little port at Glasson Dock with salmon smoke-house. Mediaeval Thurnham Hall has a permanent exhibition about the mysterious Turin Shroud. Capernwray is well placed for a stopover between London and Scotland.

Reader's comments: Every bit as comfortable as you describe it, if not more so!

The following facts have been supplied by the owners:

Bedrooms There are 3 rooms, which include singles and doubles. Bed-and-breakfast costs from £15 (per person in a double room), including service and VAT. There are reductions for stays of 7 nights or more. Sampler breaks (see page 14).

   The rooms have central heating; own bathroom or shower and wc; radio, armchairs; views of countryside, farmland, garden; door keys; tea/coffee/Ovaltine-making facilities; hair drier.

Meals The dinner menu is fixed price (£10). There is no choice of dishes on the menu, which consists of 4 courses and coffee. Dinner is served at 7.30 pm. Morning, afternoon or bedtime drinks (coffee, tea etc.) can be ordered free. Wine and other alcoholic drinks can be brought in.

Public rooms There is a sitting-room with central heating, books, magazines, local guides and leaflets.

Surroundings The grounds consist of 1½ acres of lawns. These are available in the neighbourhoood: riding, fishing, golf, clay pigeon shooting (with tuition).

Cars The nearest main road is the A6 from Lancaster to Kendal.

New Inn, Winchelsea, East Sussex, TN36 4EN
Tel: 0797 226252   **C PT S ⌗5**

Some of the bay-windowed bedrooms in this 18th-century inn enjoy one of my favourite views – of mediaeval Winchelsea, its ancient guildhall and great church. Unlike its neighbour, Rye, it is not particularly famous and I have always found it quiet when Rye was thronged with tourists. It is a delightful, unspoilt little town in which to wander, with beautiful countryside and coast nearby.

Richard Joyce tries, successfully, to keep an informal country inn atmosphere, and so rooms and meals alike are simple. There is a useful family suite of two connecting bedrooms; and a large garden in which meals can be eaten, as an alternative to the dining-room or bars. Food is conventional pub fare: home-made pâtés or soups, grills and local fish – in generous portions. The Sussex coastal area is described on pages 172 and 429.

The following facts have been supplied by the owners:

Bedrooms There are 6 rooms, which include single, double and family rooms. Bed-and-breakfast costs from £12 per person including service and VAT. There are reductions for stays of 3 nights or more.

    Some if not all of the rooms have the following amenities: central heating; washbasin, shower, shaver-point; armchairs; choice of duvets or blankets; tea/coffee-making facilities; door keys.

Meals The dinner menu is fixed price (£6+) or à la carte. Dinner is served from 6.30–9.30 pm. Lunches and snacks can be provided. Wine and other alcoholic drinks can be ordered.

Surroundings The grounds consist of a garden. These are available in the neighbourhood: golf, beach and other fishing, sailing.

Cars The nearest main road is the A259 from Folkestone to Brighton.

Credit cards accepted Access, Visa, Diners Club, Amex.

New Moor House, near Edlingham, south-west of Alnwick, Northumberland, NE66 2BT   *Tel: 066574 638*   **C D H P T S ⌗ 5**

At a moorland crossroads stands this 200-year-old stone house, with a row of pansy-filled yetlings outside. (Yetlings? Those three-legged pots that were once used, standing over peat fires, for baking or boiling food.) It is simple and unassuming.

One steps into a dining-room which Dorothy Hankin has furnished with high-backed pews salvaged from a disused church. The beamed sitting-room, with cretonne armchairs and an open fire, is upstairs. Through its windows you can see a field with the goats that have won the hundred or so rosettes pinned on the sitting-room walls. The 'clippie' rugs, here and in other rooms, were made by Dorothy's mother from hooked strips of Cheviot tweed (it was she who made the patchwork bedspreads, too).

The Hankins are a busy family: Mr Hankin, an electrical engineer, catches the trout which regularly appear on the menus, young Kirstie helps with the hens and ducks (she had eggs hatching in the airing-cupboard when I was there), Dorothy's father – a retired shepherd – gives a hand with the few sheep on the smallholding, and Dorothy herself finds time in between looking after her guests to make jars of marmalade and chutney for sale. Visitors may feed the animals.

Much of the older furniture which gives character to the house has been in the family for three generations. The food is excellent – made with their own vegetables, free-range eggs and goats' milk, or with meat produced locally. A typical meal might be home-made vegetable soup, a roast, strawberry mousse made with double cream, cheese and coffee. The biscuits that come with a bedtime drink are home-made. Dorothy sometimes cooks her great-grandmother's favourites: she will show you an 1860 photograph of her, in goffered bonnet, that has been reproduced in a book of *Old Northern Recipes*.

The house has its own soft, filtered, spring water which makes a very good cup of tea. Dorothy gives herself one evening off a week (Wednesday) but can recommend good restaurants in the area for dinner.

People who pause here for a night on the way to Scotland have sometimes got no further, for the area is so full of interest that one could easily spend a fortnight exploring it all. The best part of the Northumbrian coast is nearby, with its castles (Bamburgh, Dunstanburgh, Warkworth); its islands – the Farnes for seabirds, Lindisfarne for its ancient history, priory ruins and castle; and Craster where the kipper teas are so luscious that they stand comparison with treats like smoked salmon. You can find beaches with firm 'sugar' sands and rock-pools, or go on walks – strenuous or gentle – in, for instance, Coquetdale, the Ingram valley and Langleeford or along clifftops. National Trust properties include Cragside (best at rhododendron time, early summer) and Wallington Hall (tapestries, dolls' houses and a lovely garden). Alnwick Castle, Brinkburn Priory, Chillingham's wild cattle or hanggliders: take your pick!

The following facts have been supplied by the owners:

Bedrooms There are 4 rooms, which include single, double and family rooms. Dinner, bed-and-breakfast costs from £18 (per person), including service and VAT. There are reductions for stays of 7 nights or more. Sampler breaks (see page 14).

    Some if not all of the rooms have the following amenities: gas heaters; electric blankets, washbasin, shaver-point; armchairs; views of countryside, farmland, garden; choice of duvets or blankets; door keys.

Meals There is no choice of dishes on the fixed menu, which consists of 3 courses and coffee. Dinner is served at 7 pm. Special diets can be prepared. Packed lunches can be provided; and snacks at other hours. Morning, afternoon or bedtime drinks (coffee, tea etc.) can be ordered free. Non-residents are not admitted to the dining-room. Wine and other alcoholic drinks can be brought in.

Public rooms There is a sitting-room with open fire, colour TV, books, magazines, local guides and leaflets and indoor games (such as board games, cards and dominoes).

Surroundings The grounds consist of a 6-acre smallholding. These are available in the neighbourhood: riding, fishing, golf and sailing.

Cars The house is on the A697 from Morpeth to Wooler.

The Nodes, Alum Bay, Old Totland, west of Yarmouth, Isle of Wight, PO39 0HZ   *Tel: 0983 752859*   C D H PT S ♯4

At the far west end of the island (with spectacular marine sunsets to enjoy after dinner) is a handsome mid-Victorian mansion standing in its own grounds, and surrounded by farmland. It is now a small hotel with food that is well above the Isle of Wight's average.

Some of the bedrooms are in the original part of the house; while others (more modern and compact; each with its own front-door) line a courtyard at the back. The one in the house that particularly appealed to me was the 'blue room', which has a magnificent sea-captain's bed and a view of the Solent. The spacious sitting-room is furnished in keeping with the period of the house (rosy cretonne or strawberry velvet chairs contrasting with moss-green carpet; Victorian watercolours, clock and other items). The dining-room is more rustic: Italian pine and rush chairs, pink candles on chocolate or pink tablecloths. There are a number of choices at dinner – one might select, for example, salmon mayonnaise before beef carbonnade, and then cream-filled brandy-snaps. There is a long wine list, and Robert Godden enjoys showing visitors his cellar or discussing the choice of wine in the small bar – which is dotted with mementoes of Australia, from koalas to a miniature dunny (the British need to have that explained to them!).

The foothills of Tennyson Downs extend into the grounds (which include lawns, a play-area for children, a golf practice-net and a vegetable garden) and all around are good walks into the hills or around the many bays – as the hotel is only a 10-minute taxi ride from the Yarmouth ferry, you need no car. One barn has been converted into a games room.

This end of the island and its superb coastline are unspoilt (much of it is controlled by the National Trust): an area of pretty little villages, lanes and country inns; with sandy beaches ideal for children.

The following facts have been supplied by the owners:

Bedrooms There are 11 rooms, which include single, double and family rooms. Bed-and-breakfast costs from £12 (per person) including service and VAT; prices go up in high season. There are reductions for stays of 7 nights or more; and 'bargain breaks' as well.

Some if not all of the rooms have the following amenities: central heating; washbasin, shower, own bathroom and wc, shaver-point; radio, TV (colour), armchairs; views of sea, countryside or garden; choice of duvets or blankets; orthopaedic mattress or bed-board; tea/coffee-making facilities; door keys.

Meals The dinner menu is fixed price (£6.50) or à la carte. There is a choice of dishes on the fixed menu, which consists of 5 courses and coffee. Dinner is served at 6.30–7 pm. Vegetarian or special diets can be prepared. Lunches and packed lunches can be provided; and snacks at other hours. Morning, afternoon or bedtime drinks (coffee, tea etc.) can be ordered for a charge. Wine and other alcoholic drinks can be ordered.

Public rooms There are 2 sitting-rooms etc. The following are available in one or both of them: central heating, open fire, TV (colour), books, magazines, local guides and leaflets, indoor games (such as table tennis, darts, cards, Scrabble, etc.), piano; bar.

Surroundings The grounds consist of 2½ acres of lawns and trees, with golf practice, putting-green and badminton. These are available in the neighbourhood: riding, golf, indoor heated swimming-pool, sailing.

Cars The nearest main road runs from Yarmouth to Alum Bay.

Closed to visitors We are not open from November to March.

Also at this end of the island, and within two minutes of sand and sea, is **Rockstone Cottage**, Colwell Bay, which Sheila Reason runs as an immaculate and comfortable guest-house with good home cooking. Tel: 0983 753723.

Oak House, Great Yeldham, west of Colchester, Essex, CO9 4PR
Tel: 0787 237653   C D PT S X ⌗4

It is the remains of a 1000-year-old oak outside which gives this listed building its name. Once, this was part of Epping Forest (long since much reduced in area) and the timber frame of the mediaeval house doubtless came from other forest oaks.

The house was in a bad way when it was taken over by Patrick Whitford, an architectural technician who specializes in the restoration of old houses. He did most of the work himself, exposing the old timbers and big hearth to view again, relaying the brick floors, repairing the leaded panes of the windows and the pink pargetting (plasterwork) outside. He and his wife Lesley have furnished the rooms with antiques and with collections of bygones, including things they have found in the grounds, such as old coins, keys, tiles and bottles. Winding corridors lead to the bedrooms, which vary in standard: the best one, with windows on two sides, has a sofa, two armchairs and a stereo cassette-player.

Breakfasts here are varied – you can even have pancakes with maple syrup – and bread is home-baked. For dinner visitors go to the White Hart or the King's Head.

The garden is surrounded on three sides by a curve of the River

Colne. Ducks and forty other kinds of bird visit the wilder parts of the garden, some nesting here (Patrick showed me blue tit's eggs inside an old pump). There are frogs under the weeping willows and where the water trickles quietly over a small weir. When I visited, Patrick was paving an area beside the water and making ready to build a tea-house for his visitors. Next on his list were a croquet lawn and a play-area for children. Visitors can buy seedlings of some of his more unusual plants. Altogether a place of great individuality.

From Great Yeldham one can readily visit many of East Anglia's beauty-spots. Colchester, Castle Hedingham, Lavenham, Long Melford and even Cambridge are within motoring distance. The Colne Valley steam railway is near, and four vineyards.

Reader's comments: Excellent; very good hosts.

The following facts have been supplied by the owners:

Bedrooms There are 3 rooms, which include single, double and family rooms. Bed-and-breakfast costs from £9.75 (per person in a double room) including service and VAT. There are good reductions for stays of 7 nights or more.

Some if not all of the rooms have the following amenities: central heating or electric heaters; washbasin, shower, own bathroom and wc, shaver-point; radio, phone, armchairs; views of river, countryside, farmland, garden; tea/coffee-making facilities; door keys; bed-boards available.

Public rooms There is a family sitting-room open to guests, with central heating, open fire, TV, books, magazines, local guides and leaflets, indoor games.

Surroundings The grounds consist of an acre of garden with river. Cycle hire available.

Cars The nearest main road is the A604 from Colchester to Hadfield.

Old Bull, Church Street, Sudbury, Suffolk, CO10 6EL
Tel: 0787 79044   **D PT S ⌗4**

To include a town guest-house in a book called *Staying Off the Beaten Track* is stretching things a bit, but the Old Bull (no longer an inn) is away from the centre, and main traffic is one day going to be diverted from the road outside. Ask for a back bedroom. It is a house of great individuality – pink-walled outside; and with archways, pine doors with leaded panes, and other interesting architectural features inside. The sitting-room is especially attractive, with chamfered beams and a brick chimneybreast. It is hard to believe that when Mrs White took it over only a few years ago, the whole place was derelict. Now it is furnished with antiques, rosy curtains, good wallpapers and plenty of pictures. At the back is a patio. Only breakfast is served, except by special arrangement, but one can eat close by at Trivets or the Spread Eagle, for instance.

Sudbury (which has plenty of restaurants and other eating-places) is the market town where Gainsborough was born, and his house is open to the public. There are a great many Georgian and older buildings. The weaving tradition continues (the Princess of Wales' silk wedding-dress was woven here); and mediaeval weavers' cottages still stand. Concerts and exhibitions take place in one of the great churches, and plays in a former granary. There are crooked alleys to explore; and the lovely River Stour runs through, with attractive waterside paths, or boats to row. Sudbury is a lively little town, which has events like regattas or flower festivals all through the summer. Within easy reach of it are

303

festivals all through the summer. Within easy reach of it are Saffron Walden, Bury St Edmunds, Ipswich, Colchester and all the villages in between. Cycles can be hired.

The following facts have been supplied by the owners:

Bedrooms There are 5 rooms, which include single, double and family rooms. Bed-and-breakfast costs from £10 (per person) including service and VAT. There are reductions for stays of 3 nights or more.

Some if not all of the rooms have the following amenities: central heating, double glazing; washbasin, shower, shaver-point; TV (colour), armchairs; tea/coffee-making facilities; door keys.

Public rooms There is a sitting-room with central heating, books, magazines, local guides and leaflets.

Cars The nearest main road is the A134 from Halstead to Sudbury.

REMINDERS

Mention *Staying Off the Beaten Track,* **and check prices, when you book**

Check that there has been no change of owner

Book rooms well ahead, and ask to be sent precise details about how to find the house

Give ample notice of cancellation, otherwise you may be charged

If you write to me and want a reply, please enclose a stamped addressed envelope

It is unwise to use the current edition for more than a year. (To make a request for the next edition see page 19.)

Old Forge, 19 Main Street, Rockingham, north-west of Corby, Northamptonshire, LE16 8TG
Tel: 0536 770559   **C D PT S X ⌗6**

Rockingham is one of those former market towns, now slumbering quietly in forgotten beauty, which often go unmentioned in guidebooks. It is worth seeking out, for it is a lovely place: one long, wide street flanked with houses made of the local limestone (which the iron in the soil has tinted red-gold), their roofs slated with mossy slabs of grey Collyweston stone. In summer, the flowery cottage gardens add to the colourful scene. The wide grass verges to the street are where horses and cattle used to be tethered while awaiting sale.

At the top of this street stood a smithy, which was long ago converted to a cottage home full of character. Mr Steggles (a genial and courtly Mr Pickwick) is a fount of knowledge about the history of the place, and of anecdotes about local affairs, because for more than twenty years he ran the local shop and post office. On retirement, he and his wife Eileen (who makes and sells pressed-flower pictures) started a small guest-house where the blacksmith once lived and worked.

The small bedrooms are modestly furnished but comfortable. One, a little cheaper than the others, is in the walled garden (a small courtyard brimming with nasturtiums and geraniums). It has the advantage that it is quiet but the disadvantage of being distant from the bathroom. Small though the sitting-room is, its armchairs of oak and tapestry are big and comfortable and the broad window-sill is crowded with African violets and fuchsias. An open fire blazes in the snug little dining-room on cold days. Ordinarily Eileen serves only breakfast (there are good eating-places for dinner elsewhere in the village), but by special arrangement she may cook good, homely evening meals for people unable to go out – couples with small children, for instance. Her breakfasts include a choice of omelettes, kidneys or liver with bacon, kippers and smoked haddock.

Many people stop for only a night or two, en route to somewhere else, in which case they miss a great deal, for the area has not merely fine scenery but a lot of other attractions. There is a multitude of stately homes: Rockingham Castle (featured in TV's 'By the Sword Divided'), Boughton House, Belvoir Castle, Belton House, Burghley and many smaller halls. One of England's least spoilt mediaeval towns, Stamford, is close by; so are Oakham (with the museum in an old riding school) and Market Harborough (fine church and market hall). There are old inns, beautiful churches, pretty villages galore, and streams, lakes and reservoirs, too – with every kind of water-sport. There is the spectacular Seaton Viaduct (Mr Steggles will tell you its ghost story), a prehistoric maze, picnic areas, deer in Rockingham Forest, and places with good birdwatching opportunities. Three hunts hold their meets in or near Rockingham. This is 'the county of squires and spires', where point-to-points (or steeple-chasing) first began with racing from one church steeple to another.

The following facts have been supplied by the owners:

Bedrooms There are 3 rooms, which include single, double and family rooms. Bed-and-breakfast costs £9 (per person in a double room) including service and VAT. There are reductions for stays of 7 nights or more.

Some if not all of the rooms have the following amenities: central heating or electric heaters; washbasin, shaver-point; TV (b&w), armchairs, choice of duvets or blankets; tea/coffee-making facilities on request; door keys. Breakfast in bed is available.

Meals Packed lunches can be provided; and snacks. Morning, afternoon or bedtime drinks (coffee, tea etc.) can be ordered for a charge.

Public rooms There is a sitting-room with central heating, open fire, colour TV, books, magazines, local guides and leaflets and indoor games (such as cards and Monopoly).

Surroundings The grounds consist of a small walled garden with chairs. These are available in the neighbourhood: fishing (trout and coarse), riding, golf (3 courses), swimming, cycling and a sports complex.

Cars The nearest main road is the A6003 from Kettering to Oakham.

Closed to visitors We are not open from Christmas to Easter.

Old Granary, The Quay, Wareham, Dorset, BH20 4LP
Tel: 09295 2010 **D PT ⌗6**

Standing right on the quay by the River Frome, this 18th-century brick building was once a warehouse for grain that went by barge to Poole, and it still has much of its old character.

Derek and Rose-Marie Sturton run a restaurant on two floors, with good food served on flowery china in two dining-rooms furnished with cane chairs and attractive colours. A typical meal might comprise haddock mornay, duckling and raspberry mousse. There is a riverside terrace with seats, for cream teas and drinks (the terrace is lit up at night), and a bar with open fire. Upstairs are two floors with pretty, beamed bedrooms, their windows giving a view of the river, swans and the Purbeck hills beyond. The local landscapes on their walls are for sale.

Wareham is a most interesting old town, encircled by great earth banks built by the Saxons to fortify their village against Viking raids. The roads within this were laid out, Roman-style, on a grid. St Martin's church is Saxon and contains, rather oddly, a memorial to Lawrence of Arabia (whose home at Clouds Hill is open to the public). Wareham is a great mixture of history and of architectural styles. One of its noblest buildings, the Priory, is now a particularly lovely hotel – too expensive for this book, alas, but people staying at the Old Granary (or with Mrs Elvins, see below) could at least enjoy its lovely Tudor rooms and waterside garden for the price of a first-rate meal or even tea on the stone terrace, surrounded by roses.

All around this area are marvellous places to visit – the following is merely a selection. Poole Harbour, the second largest and loveliest natural harbour in the world, the Blue Pool, Corfe Castle, Lulworth Cove, the Purbeck hills; Arne – heathland nature reserve; Swanage, old-fashioned resort with sandy bay and architectural curiosities salvaged from London; Durlston Head – cliffs, birds, country park, lighthouse; Studland's beaches with Shell Bay beyond; Wool and Bere Regis (with Thomas Hardy associations); Bindon Abbey; the army Tank Museum at Bovington; and any amount of pretty villages down winding lanes.

Readers' comments: Superb in every respect; a real find; haven't words to describe food, room and attention to detail; absolutely professional but very personal; welcoming and friendly, spotlessly clean, excellent food.

The following facts have been supplied by the owners:

Bedrooms There are 4 double rooms. Bed-and-breakfast costs from £16 (per person in a double room) including service and VAT.
    Some if not all of the rooms have the following amenities: electric heaters; washbasin, own bathroom and wc, shaver-point; radio, TV (b&w or colour), phone, armchairs; views of river, countryside, farmland; tea/coffee-making facilities; door keys. Breakfast in bed is available.

Meals The dinner menu is à la carte. Dinner is served from 6.30–9 pm. Special diets can be prepared. Lunches and/or packed lunches can be provided; and snacks at other hours. Morning, afternoon or bedtime drinks (coffee, tea etc.) can be ordered for a charge. Wine and other alcoholic drinks can be ordered. There is a bar.

Surroundings The grounds consist of a riverside terrace. These are available in the neighbourhood: riding and golf.

Cars The nearest main road is the A351 from Wareham to Swanage.

Adjoining the Old Granary is a private house (**1 The Quay**) where guests are welcomed, for bed-and-breakfast only. Mrs Elvins has furnished each room with antiques – even the bathroom is pretty, with pot-plants and flowery wallpaper. The rooms have views of river, church or a small, paved rose garden; and there is a sitting-room for guests. Self-catering available. (Tel: 09295 3201.)

Old Hall, Denholme, east of Bradford, West Yorkshire,
BD13 4EN *Tel: 0274 833914* **C D PT S X ⌗8**

Over 140 years ago, this stone building with 'Gothick' windows
was erected as a Sunday school. Richard and Susan Balmforth did
much of the conversion themselves and, having been antique
dealers, have filled it with a fascinating collection of Victoriana, in
particular, many unusual clocks – six in the sitting-room and more
elsewhere. Even the bathroom has a Victorian shaving-mirror,
statue and trailing plants. Throughout, thick Berber carpets and
deep, velvet-covered armchairs make for comfort. The best and
largest bedroom faces the garden not the road. Other smaller
ones, tucked under the roof, have skylight windows.

Susan produces traditional Yorkshire meals: home-made soups,
roasts, and pies or filling puddings. At bedtime, she produces tea
and 'sticky bread' made from a family recipe so popular that even
Japanese and Australian visitors have taken copies home to the
other side of the world.

The house stands a little way aside from the main road to
Keighley, Skipton and the Dales. Within easy reach are Harrogate
(see page 41), Bingley and Brontë country. Bradford is well worth
several day-trips for its splendid architecture, the outstanding
National Photographic Museum, bargains at the many woollen
mills and much else. The moors are very close, as is a reservoir for
sailing.

Also in the vicinity is Ilkley, a delightful little town in the valley
of the River Wharfe. It was once a spa and its shops and gardens
are faintly reminiscent of Harrogate. There is plenty for holiday

makers to do. The moors and the dales can both be explored from here, with their great crags, tremendous views, waterfalls and steams. Some people come for the climbing, golf, riding, angling or other sports; many simply for the peace.

Ilkley is particularly pretty in spring when the cherry-blossom is out on the trees that line its shopping streets, and the riverside gardens are coming into flower. It has excellent restaurants, tea-rooms and bakers; a grocer specializing in cheeses and ham on the bone for picnics; plenty of bookshops, antique and craft shops; and historical interest, from ancient Saxon monuments to Tudor and 18th-century buildings. The excellent local guide (free from the Tourist Information Centre in the library) gives maps for walks, short and long; tells you where to watch fell-racing, hang-gliding or international tennis. It lists other places for outings, such as Haworth (the Brontës), Skipton (castle and market), the five-rise locks on the Leeds and Liverpool canal, Bolton Abbey, caverns, ruins, picturesque villages and much else.

The following facts have been supplied by the owners:

Bedrooms There are 7 rooms, which include single, double and family rooms. Bed-and-breakfast costs from £10 (per person) including service and VAT.

　　Some if not all of the rooms have the following amenities: central heating or electric heaters; electric blankets, washbasin, shower, own bathroom and wc, shaver-point; radio, TV (colour), armchairs; views of countryside, farmland, garden; choice of duvets or blankets; tea/coffee-making facilities; door keys. Breakfast in bed is available.

Meals The dinner menu is à la carte, served at whatever time is requested. Special diets can be prepared. Lunches and packed lunches can be provided; and snacks at other hours. Morning, afternoon or bedtime drinks (coffee, tea etc.) can be ordered for a charge. Wine and other alcoholic drinks can be ordered.

Public rooms There are 2 sitting-rooms etc. The following are available in one or both of them: central heating, TV (colour), video recorder, books, magazines, local guides and leaflets, indoor games, piano, record-player and records, bar.

Surroundings The grounds consist of an acre of garden. Boating, fishing, golf and pony trekking are available in the neighbourhood.

Cars The nearest main road is the A629 from Halifax to Keighley.

Old Inn, Black Bourton, west of Oxford, Oxfordshire, OX8 2PF
Tel: 0993 841828　　　　**C(7) D PT ✤3**

No longer an inn, this 17th-century house is now the elegant home of Pat and John Baxter, filled with fine antiques and old prints. It has 'gothick' windows in its thick stone walls, low beams in the sitting/dining-room and outside are views of the village and old houses, with the mediaeval church close by.

The bedrooms are very attractive: one is all-white (a crisp and light effect); another is a beamy room with antiques. They have board doors with old iron latches. Even the bathroom has been furnished with style – soft green carpet and William Morris wallpaper. The breakfast-room has pine chairs, scarlet cloths and a garden view.

Mrs Baxter provides the best of typically English food. Melon with port might be followed by a joint or a steak-and-kidney pie, and then perhaps brandy-chocolate cake – all served on pretty Blue Baltic china with good silver. Afterwards, when guests relax on the flowery blue-and-white sofas and armchairs in front of the log stove, the Baxters may join them for coffee. And only a minute or two away is the very pretty village of Clanfield (a tiny stream runs alongside the road) where, as an alternative, The Plough serves meals of gourmet standard. Non-smokers preferred.

Black Bourton is well placed to explore the Cotswolds, Oxford and Abingdon, the Berkshire Downs, Woodstock and Stratford-upon-Avon; all areas described elsewhere in this book.

The following facts have been supplied by the owners:

Bedrooms There are 2 double rooms. Bed-and-breakfast costs from £12 (per person in a double room) including service and VAT.

One if not both of the rooms have the following amenities: central heating, electric blankets; own bathroom and wc, shaver-point; TV (b & w), armchairs; views of countryside, church, garden; tea/coffee-making facilities; door keys. Breakfast in bed is available.

Meals The dinner menu is fixed price (£7.50). There is no choice of dishes on the fixed menu which consists of 4 courses and coffee. Dinner is served at 7.30 pm. Special diets can be prepared. Packed lunches can be provided; and snacks at other hours. Afternoon or bedtime drinks (coffee, tea etc.) can be ordered free. Non-residents are not admitted to the dining-room. Wine and other alcoholic drinks can be brought in.

Public rooms There is a sitting-room with central heating, open fire, TV (colour), books, magazines, local guides and leaflets. Bridge can be arranged.

Surroundings The grounds consist of garden and patio, with rough croquet.

Cars The nearest main road is the A40 from London to Wales.

Closed to visitors We are not open in March.

Old Jordans, Jordans, east of Beaconsfield, Buckinghamshire, HP9 25W   *Tel: 02407 4586*   **C H X ⌗3**

This is a place of beehives and belfry, granary and lily pool, flagstoned paths bordered by lavender and honeysuckle clambering over old stone walls. It was a farm when Elizabeth I was on the throne, and a deed of purchase, 'signed' by thumbprints and dated 1618, hangs in one of the rooms. A brick-floored kitchen added in 1624 is now a dining-room, with Windsor chairs and elm tables, chintz curtains and a big inglenook with James I fireback and built-in bread oven.

The farm became a meeting-place for Quakers (including Fox and Penn), though many were arrested for gathering here; Penn's grave is at the 17th-century Quaker meeting-house just beyond the orchard. In 1910 the almost derelict farm was bought by the Quakers, repaired and turned into a guest-house, surrounded by gardens.

Its Mayflower barn (built from the timbers of the historic *Mayflower* that carried the Pilgrim Fathers to America) is used for art exhibitions, concerts and so forth. There is something going on throughout the year (except in winter) but none of the events is noisy.

All told, this is a most unusual guest-house, open to all as a 'well from which to draw waters of peace'. Inside the house, winding corridors lead to simple but comfortable bedrooms and prettily decorated bathrooms. Board doors have wrought-iron latches and decorative hinges, each slightly different in design. Old furniture, pictures and other details in the sitting-rooms are all in character. Some carvings are from the *Mayflower*.

Meals are plain and wholesome: home-made soup, a roast or stew, gooseberry flan or pears in wine might be on the menu, followed by good coffee. (Cook, Gill Perryman.)

The neighbourhood is very interesting with beautiful scenery (typical of the chalk Chilterns, with beech woods on the hills, far views, and wooded valleys with tumbling streams). The village of Penn has a Norman church with the tomb of William Penn's grandchildren. Milton's cottage is at Chalfont St Giles, as is the Chiltern Open Air Museum, where ancient buildings (some 500 years old) have been saved from destruction and re-erected to provide a view of life in the Chilterns from past centuries. The area has innumerable antique and craft shops. Windsor is near (and at its Brass Rubbing Centre you can make rubbings of casts from Penn family brasses).

The following facts have been supplied by the owners:

Bedrooms There are 30 rooms, which include single, double and family rooms. Bed-and-breakfast costs from £14.50 (per person in a double room) including VAT. There are reductions for stays of 7 nights or more; and 'bargain breaks' as well.

    All the rooms have the following amenities: central heating and electric heaters; washbasin, shaver-point; armchairs; views of countryside, farmland, garden; door keys.

Meals The dinner menu is fixed price (£6). It consists of 3 courses and coffee. Dinner is served at 7 pm. Special diets can be prepared. Lunches and/or packed lunches can be provided. Morning and afternoon drinks (coffee, tea etc.) can be ordered.

Public rooms There are 4 sitting-rooms. The following are available in one or more of them: central heating, electric fire, colour TV, books, magazines, local guides and leaflets, indoor games (such as chess, draughts, Scrabble) and a piano.

Surroundings The grounds consist of gardens, summer-house, orchards and fields. These are available in the neighbourhood: tennis, bowls, riding, leisure centre and golf.

Cars The nearest main road is the A40 from London to Wales.

Old Malt House, School Lane, West Lulworth, east of Weymouth, Dorset, BH20 5SA   *Tel: 092941 224*   C(12) **PT** ⚘4

This conversion of a 200-year-old thatched cottage has been done to an immaculate standard: every detail is spick-and-span, and, throughout, each room is spotless. In the big white breakfast-room, tapestry chairs surround the table; and a pine staircase rises to the very well furnished bedrooms. Wendy Wilbraham serves only breakfast, but other meals of high standard – even the bar snacks – are available just across the road, at the Castle Inn. (No smoking.)

Ten minutes' walk away is famous Lulworth Cove (seething with visitors in high summer, but delightful at other times). All around is Thomas Hardy countryside. Walkers make for the coastal path; others for some of the best south-coast resorts and sandy beaches – Bournemouth, Weymouth, etc. Some of England's most scenic coastal stretches lie here along the Dorset 'heritage' coast, and inland are Dorchester (historic market town), Moreton (cut-glass windows in the church, T.E. Lawrence's grave outside it), Tolpuddle (home of the Tolpuddle Martyrs), Abbotsbury (described elsewhere in this book), Bovington (tank museum), picturesque Corfe (village and spectacular castle ruins).

The following facts have been supplied by the owners:

Bedrooms There are 3 rooms, which include single, double and family rooms. Bed-and-breakfast costs from £9 (per person in a double room) including service and VAT; prices go up in high season. There are reductions for stays of 7 nights or more.

Some if not all of the rooms have the following amenities: central heating or electric heaters; washbasin, shaver-point; TV (colour), armchairs; views of countryside or garden; choice of duvets or blankets; orthopaedic mattress or bed-board; tea/coffee-making facilities; door keys. Breakfast in bed is available.

Public rooms There is a dining/sitting-room with central heating, open fire, TV (colour), books, magazines, local guides and leaflets.

Cars The nearest main road is the A352 from Wareham to Dorchester.

Languages spoken A little German.

Old Manor Farmhouse, Norton Fitzwarren, north-west of Taunton, Somerset, TA2 6RZ   *Tel: 0823 89801*   C PT ⌗4

This building is neither old nor a manor; and the farm lands passed into other hands long ago. Now it is a small hotel run by a hospitable couple, Eric and Vera Foley. I found a warm, spontaneous welcome there, a comfortable bedroom, well-prepared food, everything very spick-and-span and altogether excellent value for money. Norton Fitzwarren is not in itself an interesting village (although there is a cider factory which can be visited), but it is close to Taunton, a historic town of such interest (once you get away from the hustle of the main streets) that it is an excellent stopover on the way to the far west country.

At breakfast as well as dinner there is much emphasis on wholefood, with a wide range of imaginative vegetarian dishes – such as pear with tarragon cream, cauliflower and almond stir-fry served with wholemeal noodles, and fruit pies; but steaks, lamb and quail are available too. Bread is made from flour ground at Dunster watermill. There is an excellent selection of very good value wines.

The River Tone winds through Taunton and there are attractive riverside paths. The historic heart of the town lies around the castle remains (with excellent county museum inside). There are two notable churches and, after walking along pedestrianized shopping streets, one can wander through a particularly fine park which was where monks once had their fish-ponds.

315

The surrounding countryside is not only beautiful but varied: the Quantock Hills are gently rolling and well wooded, with small villages (Combe Florey, for instance, which is as pretty as its name suggests) and sparkling streams. Red sandstone is used for many buildings here. Eastward are the limestone Mendips – far more gaunt, with gorges and crags. The Vale of Taunton Deane is a fertile land, with apple orchards supplying the cider-makers. The sea is within easy motoring distance, and the little port of Watchet. There is fen country too; and Exmoor is quite close. As well as scenery, there are a number of stately homes in the area; numerous country shows and festivals; and excellent walks, easy or strenuous.

The following facts have been supplied by the owners:

Bedrooms There are 5 rooms, which include single, double and family rooms. Bed-and-breakfast costs from £13 (per person in a double room) including service and VAT; prices go up in high season. There are reductions for stays of 4 nights or more; and 'bargain breaks' as well. Sunday accommodation free to over-60s staying 3 days.

    Some if not all of the rooms have the following amenities: central heating; electric blankets, washbasin, shower, own bathroom and wc, shaver-point; radio, colour TV, armchairs; views of countryside, farmland, garden; choice of duvets or blankets; tea/coffee-making facilities; door keys.

Meals The dinner menu is fixed price (from £6.50). Dinner is served at 7 pm. Special diets can be prepared. Morning, afternoon or bedtime drinks (coffee, tea etc.) can be ordered for a charge. Wine and other alcoholic drinks can be ordered.

Public rooms There is a sitting-room with central heating, colour TV, books, magazines, local guides and leaflets, and a bar.

Surroundings The grounds consist of an acre of kitchen garden and orchard. These are available in the neighbourhood: tennis, golf, swimming, squash, cricket, sailing, angling, riding, skittles, bowls, boating.

Cars The nearest main road is the A361 from Taunton to Barnstaple.

Credit cards accepted Access, Visa, Diners Club.

Old Mill Hotel, Buxton, north of Norwich, Norfolk, NR10 5JF
Tel: 060546 774   C D PT S X ☼7

The great weatherboarded watermill stretches right across the clear waters of the River Bure, an 18th-century building on a site where there has been a mill ever since Saxon times. Part of it is now a restaurant and crafts centre; the rest is run as a hotel by Barry Wootton and his pretty wife Phyllis. To one side of the quarry-tiled hall is a large and pleasant sitting/dining-room, a log fire at one end and glass doors at the side through which to stroll onto the riverside terrace and watch the swans glide by or take the hotel's rowing-boat out. Traditional English meals are served here – home-made soups, roasts or grills, and perhaps trifle to follow (fresh local vegetables are used, and trout from the River Bure).

The bedrooms are immaculate, with thick carpets, hefty black beams and river views: the spacious Blue Room seemed to me the most attractive, after the balconied Mill Suite (which costs more). And – a thoughtful touch – the Woottons' brochure tells you which rooms get morning and which get evening sunshine.

Buxton is an ideal spot from which to explore historic Norwich, the Broads and the superb Norfolk coastline – all described elsewhere.

Readers' comments: Friendly welcome; warm and comfortable; meals excellent and attractively served. A great joy.

The following facts have been supplied by the owners:

Bedrooms There are 5 rooms, which include single, double and family rooms. Bed-and-breakfast costs from £13 (per person in a double room) including service and VAT; prices go up in high season. There are reductions for stays of 7 nights or more; and 'bargain breaks' as well.

Some if not all of the rooms have the following amenities: electric heaters; washbasin, shower, own bathroom and wc, shaver-point; TV (colour), armchairs; views of river and countryside; balcony; choice of duvets or blankets; door keys. Breakfast in bed is available.

Meals The dinner menu is fixed price (£7). There is a choice of dishes on the fixed menu, which consists of 3 courses and coffee. Dinner is served at 7.30 pm. Vegetarian or special diets can be prepared. Lunches and packed lunches can be provided; and snacks at other hours. Morning, afternoon or bedtime drinks (coffee, tea etc.) can be ordered for a charge. Non-residents are not admitted to the dining-room. Wine and other alcoholic drinks can be ordered.

Public rooms There is a sitting-room with electric heating, open fire, books, magazines, local guides and leaflets, indoor games (such as cards and Trivial Pursuit), record-player and records; bar.

Surroundings The grounds consist of ½ acre of water frontage. These are available in the neighbourhood: golf, squash, tennis, sailing, riding.

Cars The nearest main road is the A140 from Norwich to Cromer.

Old Mill Hotel, West Harnham, Salisbury, Wiltshire, SP2 8EJ
Tel: 0722 27517   **C**(5) **PT S X ♯9**

It was by this ancient watermill that John Constable painted his famous view of Salisbury Cathedral seen across the water-meadows, and little has changed since then. The mill dates back to the 12th century, and was used to house the church records while the cathedral was being built. It is now a hotel run by Jerry Such.

The bedrooms are simply furnished but some are pretty, with William Morris wallpaper and river views.

The meals served in the much better-furnished restaurant (in the oldest part) are traditionally English: devilled whitebait, game pie, jugged hare and so forth (cooked by Caroline Kelley and Alison Hayward). This is an unpretentious place to stay, in an idyllic setting and well placed for touring. The hotel can arrange day-permits for trout or coarse fishing.

In addition to Salisbury's ancient streets and cathedral, there are such outstanding places of interest as Wilton House, Stonehenge, Salisbury Plain (wide open spaces, changing skies and mossy villages), Marlborough and its downs, innumerable prehistoric sites, old Amesbury (where Queen Guinevere is said to have been buried), Devizes with its noble market square and Norman church, Shaftesbury (abbey and cobbled lanes) and, of course, the coast with Bournemouth and its sandy beaches.

The following facts have been supplied by the owners:

Bedrooms There are 7 rooms, which include single, double and family rooms. Bed-and-breakfast costs from £14 (per person) including service and VAT. There are reductions for stays of 7 nights or more.

All the rooms have the following amenities: electric heaters; washbasin, shaver-point; views of river and garden; choice of duvets or blankets; door keys; tea/coffee-making facilities. One has a shower.

Meals Dinner menu is à la carte. Dinner is served from 7–10 pm. Lunches, teas and bar snacks are served in summer; special diets and packed lunches to order.

Public rooms There is a bar and a TV room.

Cars The nearest main road is the A3094 from Salisbury to Wilton.

Credit cards accepted Amex, Diners Club, Visa, Access.

Closed to visitors We are not open in winter.

Old Town House, College Street, Stratford-upon-Avon, Warwickshire, CV37 6BN   *Tel: 0789 204789*   **C(14) PT ⊞4**

Once the vicarage to Holy Trinity Church (where Shakespeare is buried), this beautifully furnished house is – despite being within a few minutes' walk of all the popular 'sights' of Stratford, and of the Royal Shakespeare Theatre – as peaceful as you could wish. Across its secluded brick-walled garden, one bedroom has a view of Hall's Croft where Shakespeare's daughter lived, as beautiful a house as the Birthplace but not spoiled by throngs of tourists.

The owner James Monteith, formerly an architect, is now an official guide – so who better to advise you on where to go and what to see? He does one-day tours by car (yours or his), as well.

It is Mary Monteith (she deals in antiques) who is responsible for the outstanding interiors of the house. From the wide hall (it has sofas from which to enjoy the bronzes and Staffordshire spaniels, old mirrors, bowls of pot-pourri and grandfather clock) stairs lead to particularly attractive bedrooms: in one there is dusty-pink brocade, arrangements of dried flowers, windows on two sides and armchairs from which to enjoy the garden view; another, with a charming blue-and-white colour scheme, looks over historic houses and the Memorial Gardens. Mary has sought out some lovely wallpapers – a grey-and-buff paeony pattern in one room, and colourful pheasants in another. Even the toilet is prettily furnished.

Breakfast (with home-made preserves and muesli) is served in a room with pretty Victorian tables and chairs, nosegays filling Victorian jugs on each one. You can take your coffee or tea through the glass doors onto a paved terrace overlooking the winding herbaceous beds and the old yew tree under which a marble nymph shelters.

(This is a no-smoking house.)

The following facts have been supplied by the owners:

Bedrooms There are 2 double rooms. Bed-and-breakfast costs from £14 (per person in a double room) including service and VAT; prices go up in high season. There are reductions for stays of 7 nights or more.

Both rooms have central heating; washbasin, shower, own bathroom and wc, shaver-point; TV (b&w) in one; armchairs; views of garden; tea/coffee-making facilities; door keys.

Public rooms There is a sitting-area with central heating, books, magazines, local guides and leaflets.

Surroundings The grounds consist of a garden. These are available in the neighbourhood: golf, tennis, bowls, river boating.

Cars The nearest main road is the A34 from Birmingham to Oxford.

Languages spoken Some French.

Closed to visitors We are not open between November and Easter.

Old Vicarage, Affpuddle, east of Dorchester, Dorset, DT2 7HH
Tel: 030584 315   S ♯4

Before Anthea and Michael Hipwell moved here, it was an ambassador's country home: a handsome Georgian house with fine doorways, windows and fireplaces – surrounded by smooth lawns and rosebeds within tall hedges of clipped yew, the old church alongside.

Anthea has a flair for interior decoration. Even the corridors are elegant, with portraits and flower-prints on walls of apple-blossom pink which contrast with the cherry carpet. In my bedroom, the curtains were of ivory moiré, the silky bedhead and bedspread patterned with rosebuds.

Breakfast is served in the prettiest dining-room in this book. Taking as the starting-point her collection of aquamarine glass (housed in two alcoves) and a series of modern lithographs in vivid turquoise, Anthea decorated the walls to match, and chose a dramatic turquoise curtain fabric reproduced from a Regency design in Brighton's royal pavilion. Against this all-blue colour scheme, the pale limed oak furniture shows to advantage.

As no evening meal is provided, many visitors go to the New Inn at nearby West Knighton or the Hambro Arms, Milton Abbas.

The Old Vicarage is well placed for a stopover on the long journey (by A35) to the west country; when arriving or departing on the Weymouth-Cherbourg ferry; or while learning to fish for trout at the nearby angling school (tel: 0305 84450).

The Hipwells lend walkers Ordnance Survey maps, and will advise them on sightseeing possibilities (see other Dorset entries in this book), including less obvious ones – such as the huge bric-à-brac market held at Wimborne every Friday, or little-known beaches (one favourite is at Ringstead, surrounded by National Trust land). And, at the end of the day, you are welcome to relax in their garden chairs under sun umbrellas.

The following facts have been supplied by the owners:

Bedrooms There are 3 rooms, which include single and double rooms. Bed-and-breakfast costs from £11 (per person in a double room) including service and VAT. There are 'bargain breaks'.
　　Some if not all of the rooms have the following amenities: central heating and electric heaters; own bathroom and wc, shaver-point; radio, TV on request, armchairs; views of countryside/farmland/garden; tea/coffee-making facilities on request; door keys. Breakfast in bed is available.
Surroundings The grounds consist of a garden, with croquet. These are available in the neighbourhood: fly-fishing, riding, sailing, coarse fishing, tennis lessons.
Cars The nearest main road is the A35/31 from Dorchester to Poole.

Old Vicarage, Higham, north of Colchester (Essex), Suffolk, CO7 6JY　*Tel: 020637 248*　　　**C D PT S S-C X ⊞4**

One of the most elegant houses in this book, the Old Vicarage stands near a tranquil village and is surrounded by superb views, with the old church close by. Everything about it is exceptional, from the Tudor building itself (its walls colourwashed a warm apricot), and the lovely furnishings, to the pretty south-facing garden – which has unheated swimming-pool, tennis and safe river boats (it's surprising that few families with children have discovered it, particularly since the coast is near; Felixstowe and Frinton have sandy beaches).

Colonel and Mrs Parker have lived here for many years, and their taste is evident in every room. Lovely colours, pretty wallpapers and chintzes, antiques, flowers and log fires all combine to create a background of great style. In the breakfast-room, eight bamboo chairs surround a huge circular table (marble-topped), and the walls have a trellis wallpaper the colour of water-melon. Bedrooms are equally pretty: one green-and-white with rush flooring; another has mimosa on walls and ceiling (its tiny windows are lattice-paned); the family room is in lime and tangerine. There are lace bedspreads, Indian watercolours, baskets of begonias – individual touches everywhere.

Lynne, from the village, comes in to help and (herself a lively source of information) is evidently as greatly impressed as the visitors themselves with all that the Parkers do to help people enjoy their stay – from information on sightseeing and eating-places or where to watch local wildlife, to offering a mother the use of their own washing machine. Even Petra, the dog, gives one a friendly welcome.

Higham is very well placed for a great variety of activities and outings. One could easily spend a fortnight doing something totally different each day. There are Roman Colchester, Constable's East Bergholt, the seaside, racing at Newmarket, sailing, music festival at Aldeburgh, the mediaeval villages and great churches of central Suffolk, tide-mill at Woodbridge, market and Gainsborough's house at Sudbury: the list is endless. And everywhere superb scenery, with few people on the roads even in midsummer.

Reader's comments: Lovely house, very calm, beautifully ap-pointed, charming staff.

The following facts have been supplied by the owners:

Bedrooms There are 4 rooms, which include single, double and family rooms. Bed-and-breakfast costs from £15 (per person in a double room) including service and VAT; prices go up in high season. There are reductions for stays of 3 nights or more.

Some if not all of the rooms have the following amenities: central heating or electric heaters; electric blankets, washbasin, shower, own bathroom and wc, shaver-point; radio, TV, phone, armchairs; views of river, countryside, farmland, garden; balcony; choice of duvets or blankets; tea/coffee-making facilities; door keys. Breakfast in bed is available.

Meals Packed lunches can be provided; and snacks at other hours. Morning, afternoon or bedtime drinks (coffee, tea etc.) can be ordered free.

Public rooms There are 2 sitting-rooms etc. The following are available in one or both of them: central heating, open fire, TV (colour), books, magazines, local guides and leaflets, piano, record-player and records.

Surroundings The grounds consist of 12 acres of garden and fields, with tennis, swimming, boating and fishing. In the neighbourhood are golf and riding.

Cars The nearest main road is the A12 from London to Norwich.

Old Vicarage, Muker, west of Richmond, North Yorkshire
Tel: 0748 86498   **C(7) X ✸9**

Once the vicarage of the most extensive parish in England, this century-old house at the head of lovely Swaledale has now been modernized to provide very comfortable accommodation, furnished in character with the age of the house. King-size beds (with duvets), good carpets, fruit and flowers in the bedrooms, and open fires all contribute to its comfort; and from every room there are fine views – for close by is Great Shunner Fell (2400 feet), the famous Buttertubs Pass, and Kisdon Hill – good walking country.

The Old Vicarage and its surroundings were filmed in the TV series 'All Creatures Great and Small'.

Marjorie Bucknall's five-course meals are based on fresh produce; and all the bread (both white and brown) is home-baked. A typical menu might comprise home-made tomato soup, eggs mimosa, chicken casseroled in white wine with yogurt, pears in a ginger syrup, local cheeses, and coffee with mints. If you want a daytime TV programme videoed for evening viewing, the Bucknalls will do it for you.

Muker is the largest of the villages of Swaledale. It houses a shop for woollens hand-knitted by a team of 40 farmers' wives and daughters, mostly from the wool of the breed of sheep to which the dale has given its name. From it, you can also visit the rest of the Yorkshire Dales, the North Yorkshire Moors and the Lake District: each makes an excellent day-trip.

Reader's comments: Warm welcome, excellent value.

The following facts have been supplied by the owners:

Bedrooms There are 4 rooms, which include double and family rooms. Dinner, bed-and-breakfast costs from £24 (per person in a double room) including service and VAT.

    All rooms have central heating; own bathroom and wc, shaver-point; radio, TV (colour), armchairs; views of countryside; orthopaedic mattress; tea/coffee-making facilities; door keys.

Meals There is no choice of dishes on the fixed menu, which consists of 5 courses and coffee. Dinner is served at 7.30 pm. Vegetarian or special diets can be prepared. Lunches and packed lunches can be provided. Non-residents are not admitted to the dining-room. Wine and other alcoholic drinks can be ordered.

Public rooms There is a sitting-room with central heating, open fire, books, magazines, local guides and leaflets, indoor games.

Surroundings The grounds consist of an acre of lawns and trees.

Cars The nearest main road is the A6108 from Ripon to Richmond.

Languages spoken French.

Closed to visitors We are not open between November and February.

Old Vicarage, Parc-an-Creet, St Ives, Cornwall, TR26 2ET
Tel: 0736 796124   **C D PT S ⚹2**

Although part of the once extensive grounds (on the outskirts of this steep little town) were sold off long ago to build modern houses all round, the trees in the remaining garden shut these (and the church) from view.

The house itself, built of silvery granite in the 1850s, is entered via a small conservatory and a great iron-hinged door of ecclesiastical shape, which opens into a hall with red-and-black tiled floor. Mr and Mrs Sykes have done their best to preserve this period ambience, furnishing the bar with crimson-and-gold flock wallpaper and all kinds of Victoriana. There's a piano here, which occasionally inspires visitors to join in singing some of the old songs of that period. In addition there is a sitting-room, and blue-and-white dining-room. Big windows (some with floor-length velvet curtains on poles) and handsome fireplaces feature throughout; and the Sykeses have put in excellent carpets, along with good, solid furniture – a 'thirties walnut suite in one bedroom, for instance, and velvet-upholstered bedheads. There is a refurbished Victorian loo, carefully preserved in all its glory of blue lilies and rushes.

Jack Sykes, formerly an engineer, did all the modernization himself, even the plumbing; while Irene, who used to be a confectioner and later took a hotel management course, is responsible for the meals. At every course she provides three choices which include such dishes as Stilton-and-walnut mousse, haddock Wellington, and pineapple in kirsch with Cornish cream; then cheeses and coffee.

There are chairs and sun umbrellas in the garden; and a path leads down (in 10 minutes) to the sandy beach where there are beach chalets for visitors' use. A bus will bring you uphill again –

while another will take you out to the moors and rugged cliffs that lie between St Ives and Land's End.

The colourful, one-time fishing village of St Ives, famous for its artists' colony, is now a crowded tourist centre in summer. Beyond it lies (on the north coast) some splendid scenery, outstanding prehistoric remains, tin mines and lighthouses. The sheltered south coast has sandy coves, the cliffside Minack theatre, wild flowers in abundance and historic fishing-harbours (Mousehole and Newlyn in particular). The byways and curio shops of Penzance, as well as its subtropical gardens, are well worth exploring on foot and from here there are day-trips to the lovely Isles of Scilly (described on pages 54, 90–91 and 119–20) and to the castle on the little islet of St Michael's Mount. Much of the land around here belongs to the National Trust.

Readers' comments: Beautifully restored; excellent in all aspects.

The following facts have been supplied by the owners:

Bedrooms There are 10 rooms, which include single, double and family rooms. Bed-and-breakfast costs from £11.50 (per person in a double room) including service and VAT; prices go up in high season. There are reductions for stays of 3 nights or more.
   Some if not all of the rooms have the following amenities: central heating; washbasin, shower, own bathroom and wc, shaver-point; TV (colour or b&w), armchairs; views of countryside and garden; choice of duvets or blankets; tea/coffee-making facilities; door keys.

Meals The dinner menu is fixed price (£7). There is a choice of dishes on the fixed menu, which consists of 4 courses and coffee. Dinner is served at 6.45 pm. Vegetarian or special diets can be prepared. Packed lunches can be provided; and snacks at other hours. Bedtime drinks (coffee, tea etc.) can be ordered free. Non-residents are not admitted to the dining-room. Wine and other alcoholic drinks can be ordered.

Public rooms There are 2 sitting-rooms etc. The following are available in one or both of them: central heating, open fire, TV (colour), books, magazines, local guides and leaflets, indoor games (such as chess, bar skittles, backgammon, snooker, dominoes etc.), piano, record-player and records; bar.

Surroundings The grounds consist of a garden with swing, putting, badminton and swing ball. These are available in the neighbourhood: riding, golf, tennis, squash, surf-riding (boards available at hotel).

Cars The nearest main road is the A30 from London to Penzance.

Languages spoken French.

Credit cards accepted Visa, Access.

Olde Farm, Asthall Leigh, Minster Lovell, north-west of Witney, Oxfordshire, OX8 5PX   *Tel: 0993 87608*   C(10) S-C ⚫3

After a delectable woodland-and-stream drive, one parks in a courtyard surrounded by stone buildings, three centuries old, hung with baskets of flowers. The sitting-room, once a barn, has stone walls, a moss-green carpet, William Morris curtains and, in one corner, a pretty spiral staircase to one of the bedrooms (all of which have garden views). This one is a beamed room decorated in powder-blue; others have their own colour schemes, pretty wallpapers matching their bedspreads. Doorways are low, passages have steps up and down: it's a house of great character. Although only breakfast is served by Elizabeth Woodin, visitors are welcome to use croquet lawn and swimming-pool sheltering behind beech hedges, and to look round the small farm – 15 acres of hay and sheep.

When and if the local Cotswold sights (which include the beautiful ruins of Minster Lovell Hall) are exhausted, it is easy to reach Bath, Stratford, Stonehenge, Warwick Castle, Cheltenham and even London from here.

Readers' comments: Warm welcome, comfortable rooms; most peaceful.

The following facts have been supplied by the owners:

Bedrooms There are 3 rooms, which include double and family rooms. Bed-and-breakfast costs from £10 (per person in a double room) including service and VAT. There are reductions for stays of 2 nights or more.

328

Some if not all of the rooms have the following amenities: central heating or electric heaters; washbasin, shower, own bathroom and wc, shaver-point; armchairs; views of countryside/farmland/garden; tea/coffee-making facilities; hair drier; washing machine for overseas visitors.

Public rooms There is a sitting-room with central heating, TV (colour), books, magazines, local guides and leaflets, indoor games (such as Scrabble, cards, and Chinese chequers), piano. Maps on loan.

Surroundings The grounds consist of 15 acres of garden and farmland, with croquet and unheated swimming-pool. In the neighbourhood are golf, fishing and a sports complex.

Cars The nearest main road is the A40 from London to Wales.

Oldfields, 102 Wells Road, Bath, Avon, BA2 3AL
Tel: 0225 317984   **PT ♯5**

Although this late Victorian house (or, rather, two) of honey-coloured stone stands just off the steep main road out of Bath to Exeter, I spent a quiet night; and in a particularly attractive and spacious bedroom (pine-louvred doors to cupboards, a terracotta-and-cream colour scheme, sprigged Laura Ashley wallpaper, attractive modern pictures and lots of pot-plants). The big sitting-room is decorated in soft browns and mossy greens, with a marble fireplace (crackling fire in winter) and lace curtains from ceiling to

floor at the high windows with their fine views of the city. But what I liked best about Oldfields were the owners, Anthony O'Flaherty and his wife Nicole, who are great fun. Breakfasts are generous (with herbal teas, if you like). For their winter breaks, they collaborate with two excellent Bath restaurants which provide dinner as part of the 'package'.

Apart from Bath itself (which deserves at least a week-long stay: see pages 341–2), you can visit the cathedral city of Wells, the Cheddar Gorge and the lovely Mendip Hills, the sea at Weston-super-Mare, old market towns like Warminster and Chippenham, historic Bristol (a lively city now, with plenty to interest tourists, theatre-goers etc.) and, of course, the beauties of Devon, the south Wales coast and hills, and the Cotswolds are not far away with delectable villages like Laycock, Bradford-on-Avon, Biddestone and Castle Combe.

The following facts have been supplied by the owners:

Bedrooms There are 14 rooms, which include single, double and family rooms. Bed-and-breakfast costs from £15 (per person in a double room) including service and VAT; prices go up in high season. There are reductions for stays of 4 nights or more; and 'bargain breaks' as well.

Some if not all of the rooms have the following amenities: central heating; washbasin, shower, own bathroom and wc, shaver-point; TV (b&w), phone, armchairs; views of town/hills/garden; one has a balcony; choice of duvets or blankets; tea/coffee-making facilities; door keys; orthopaedic mattresses; hair driers.

Public rooms There is a sitting-room and a separate breakfast-room. The following are available in one or both of them: central heating, open fire, books, magazines, local guides and leaflets, indoor games (such as Scrabble, chess, cards, backgammon, etc.). Maps on loan.

Surroundings The grounds consist of ½ acre of terraced garden. These are available in the neighbourhood: golf, tennis, rowing, swimming, squash, badminton, weight training (at the Bath Sports and Leisure Centre).

Cars The nearest main road is the A367 from Bath to Exeter.

Languages spoken French.

Credit cards accepted Visa, Access.

Closed to vistors We are not open from mid December to mid January.

Nearby is **Charnwood House** (tel: 0225 334937) with equally attractive rooms; also sauna and Jacuzzi whirlpool bath (free). Linda Cooney's breakfast options include a platter of about nine fresh fruits and little pots of three fruit yogurts so decoratively displayed that visitors have been known to photograph it before eating!

Onecote Old Hall, Onecote, east of Leek, Staffordshire, ST13 7SD
Tel: 05388 357   **C D S ♯5**

Although no longer a farm, this 1640 farmhouse on the edge of Staffordshire's little-known moorland is surrounded by farmland, and Mary Sotheran has a prize collection of goats and many ducks and chickens, which provide truly fresh milk and eggs. The house is old and cosy. The bedrooms with their exposed beams have been charmingly, though simply, decorated to preserve their character. The comfortable sitting-room leads to an attractive dining-room that has old pine tables. There was a posy of sweet williams on each of these; a tray of pickles; a bowl of lettuce, radishes, cucumber, tomatoes, spring onions and green peppers; a dish of marinaded mushrooms; and a basket of freshly made rolls to go with chicken salad after a real home-made vegetable soup. An enormous gooseberry pie which came to the table whole was followed by cheeses, including her goats'. The emphasis is on wholefood. (No smoking.)

Mary, like her husband, used to work for ICI until her daughter was born. She will give all the help you need in discovering this little known part of the southern Peak District, and where to buy bargains from famous china factories. Nearby Ashbourne is one of England's least spoilt market towns, with many of its 16th- to 18th-century buildings intact and a great church of quite exceptional interest. If you are in luck, you may be shown round by plumber George Shaw – the most erudite and enthusiastic verger I have ever encountered, and an absorbing guide to the church's many splendours. All round lie beauty-spots: famous Dovedale, the Manifold valley for birds and wild flowers, nine stately homes of

331

exceptional grandeur, ancient villages (stone to the north, brick-built to the south), craft centres and lovely gardens. Several disused railway routes are now level 'trails' for walkers and cyclists (cycles can be hired at Ashbourne). The Peak District (see pages 222–3) is accessible; and there is a great variety of other diversions which include visiting the Bass brewery and the Elvaston working estate (where you can see a blacksmith, saddler, joiner and many other rural craftsmen at work). Ashbourne lies near the Matlocks – a group of towns and villages in the Derwent valley. Matlock Bath (once a spa) is picturesque, with nearby cliffs for splendid views, boating, and the strange petrifying wells, where any object left for a while is in effect turned to stone by the lime in the water. There are still thermal swimming baths. The Heights of Abraham has terraces and caverns. This is a particularly good area in which to bus about – in particular, using the summer 'Pathfinder', devised for bus-and-walk or bus-and-bike days in local beauty-spots.

Readers' comments: Exceptionally good; relaxed family atmosphere. Very well looked after.

The following facts have been supplied by the owners:

Bedrooms There are 3 rooms, which include single, double and family rooms. Bed-and-breakfast costs from £9 (per person) including service and VAT. There are reductions for stays of 7 nights.
  Some if not all of the rooms have the following amenities: central heating; electric blankets, shower, shaver-point; armchairs; views of countryside/farmland/ garden.

Meals The dinner menu is fixed price (£6). There is no choice of dishes on the fixed menu, which consists of 4 courses and coffee. Dinner is served at 7–7.30 pm. Special diets can be prepared. Packed lunches can be provided. Morning, afternoon or bedtime drinks (coffee, tea etc.) can be ordered free. Wine and other alcoholic drinks can be brought in.

Public rooms There is a sitting-room with central heating, open fire, TV (colour), books, magazines, local guides and leaflets, indoor games (such as Scrabble, cards, Go, jigsaws), piano, record-player and records.

Surroundings The grounds consist of a garden. These are available in the neighbourhood: cycle hire, riding.

Cars The nearest main road is the A523 from Leek to Ashbourne.

Closed to visitors We are not open from December to February.

Near here is the very prettily furnished **White House** at Grindon (tel: 05388 250); Mrs Bunce is an exceedingly good cook.

The Orchard, Bathford, near Bath, Avon, BA1 7TG
Tel: 0225 858765   C(11) **PT ⊞5**

All the pleasures of Bath are within about ten minutes by car (or bus), yet this little village perched on a hillside seems deep in the countryside. There are stunning views over the River Avon to the far countryside.

The Orchard is a luxurious Georgian house standing in its own grounds. The bedrooms are amongst the most elegant in this book, with private bathrooms and big windows overlooking the garden; and the other rooms are equally handsome with attractive colour schemes and antique furniture. Olga London is an excellent cook and hostess. A typical menu might be tomato and orange soup, grilled trout and chocolate mousse. Breakfasts include home-made muesli, free-range eggs and locally baked wholemeal bread.

Mr and Mrs London own a health club in Bath normally open only to members, but their own house-guests can (for one-third the usual fee) make use of it during their stay at The Orchard. It offers saunas, steam bath, cold plunge, Jacuzzi whirlpool, solarium, exercise room and health bar.

The Bath area is described on page 330.

Readers' comments: House and appointments are a delight. Complete peace, beautiful surroundings, everything done perfectly. Went out of their way to make us feel welcome; the vegetarian meals we requested were a gourmet's delight. Rooms fabulous.

The following facts have been supplied by the owners:

Bedrooms There are 4 double rooms. Bed-and-breakfast costs from £16.50 (per person in a double room) including service and VAT. There are reductions for stays of 7 nights or more.

All of the rooms have the following amenities: central heating and electric heaters; own bathroom and wc, shaver-point; armchairs; views of countryside or garden; orthopaedic mattress, hair drier and TV are available.

Meals The dinner menu is fixed price (£8.50). There is no choice of dishes on the menu, which consists of 3 courses and coffee. Dinner is served at 7.15 pm. Morning, afternoon or bedtime drinks (coffee, tea etc.) can be ordered for a charge. Non-residents are not admitted to the dining-room. Wine and other alcoholic drinks can be brought in.

Public rooms There is a sitting-room with central heating, open fire, books, magazines, local guides and leaflets, indoor games (such as cards, chess, draughts).

Surroundings The grounds consist of 1½ acres of garden, with croquet.

Cars The nearest main road is the A4 from London to Wales.

Languages spoken Dutch, German, French.

Closed to visitors We are closed to visitors in winter (except for house-parties of friends).

Orchard House, High Street, Rothbury, Northumberland, NE65 7TL *Tel: 0669 20684* **C #10**

Rothbury, a pleasant little market town with some interesting shops, stands in the very centre of Northumberland; so many of the pleasures of that large and underestimated county are within an easy drive: the Roman wall to the south, Holy Island to the north, and in between countryside which can change from open moorland to woods and arable fields within a few miles, with picturesque villages and historic monuments for punctuation. Only the castles and peel towers (fortified farmhouses) remind one that it is here that the Scots and the English raided each other for centuries.

The Orchard is a Georgian house which stands above Rothbury's bustling main street. Jeff and Sheila Jefferson took it over several years ago when Jeff left the RAF after years as an engineer (some of them spent in Malaysia) and have turned it into a comfortable and unpretentious place to stay. Like many people who provide good accommodation in relatively unknown spots, they have found that guests who stayed a night or two while passing through have returned for a longer holiday later.

Sheila's three-course menus are out of the ordinary and varied, the only fixture being roast beef every Sunday. Otherwise you might get (for instance) French onion soup, pork scallopine with two vegetables (at least one of which is always fresh), and strawberry meringue. There is no choice except when fish is on the menu. Coffee is included, and free tea on arrival. In the lounge is a cabinet well stocked with miniatures of drinks for you to help yourself and enter in a book.

The 'sight' closest to Rothbury is Cragside, the mansion which Norman Shaw (best known, perhaps, for his government buildings in London) designed for Lord Armstrong, the armaments king. It is one of the most complete late-Victorian houses there are and was opened to the public by the National Trust only a few years ago. Among the oddities it contains are a Turkish bath and a hydraulic lift, but its main distinction is that it was the first house in the world to be lit by electricity. The elaborately landscaped grounds are also notable.

Readers' comments: Very impressed. A delightful couple, friendly and helpful. Outstanding food; rooms sparkling clean and spacious. Spotless, comfortable, excellent food – first-rate value.

The following facts have been supplied by the owners:

Bedrooms There are 6 rooms, which include double and family rooms. Bed-and-breakfast costs from £11 (per person in a double room) including service and VAT. There are reductions for stays of 7 nights or more.

The rooms have central heating and electric heaters; electric blankets, washbasin, shaver-point; TV (colour); tea/coffee-making facilities; views of countryside, garden; choice of duvets or blankets; door keys. Some have own shower and toilet.

Meals The dinner menu is fixed price (£7). There is no choice of dishes on the fixed menu, which consists of 3 courses and coffee. Dinner is served at 7 pm. Special diets can be prepared. Packed lunches can be provided. Morning, or bedtime drinks (coffee, tea etc.) are available free. Non-residents are not admitted to the dining-room. Wine and other alcoholic drinks can be ordered.

Public rooms There is a lounge which has central heating, books, magazines, local guides and leaflets, indoor games (such as cards, dominoes, Scrabble, chess); bar.

Surroundings There is a garden. Available in the neighbourhood: golf, fishing, riding.

Cars The nearest main road is the A697 from Morpeth to Coldstream.

Osborne House, Lower Chapel Street, Looe, Cornwall, PL13 1AT   *Tel: 05036 2970*   **C D PT ☆3**

Local gourmets beat a path to this little Jacobean inn, hidden away in the web of narrow, cobbled lanes near the waterfront of the old fishing village that is Looe. It is squeezed in amongst other cottages but distinguished from them by a colourful ship's figure-head that projects from the upper storey.

The ground floor is packed with scarlet-clothed dining-tables, and a small snug bar is tucked away at the back. The walls are of rugged stone (even in some of the bedrooms), with oak timbers. Old farm implements and brass pans decorate every surface; and in the bar, with its barrel chairs, dozens of coronation mugs hang from the beams.

This is a building of nooks and crannies – short of space but full of character. The little bedrooms, many with sloping ceilings, have fresh and pretty colour schemes. People who come to stay at Osborne House do so because of its quaintness, its gregarious character (no one could remain aloof in that little bar) and in particular its food.

Even the table d'hôte menu (which offers plenty of choice) has dishes such as devilled sole as a starter and coq au vin as one of the main courses; and the à la carte choice is very extensive, too. Seafood is a speciality – sole, scallops, crab and mackerel are prepared in a variety of ways. Mr Greenhouse has also made Osborne House famous for pancakes (a dozen different kinds).

Although the house is close to the quays, it is reasonably quiet because cars are not allowed to clog the small lanes.

Looe is a centre for water-sports, shark-fishing and safe swimming from nearby sandy coves that trap the sun. There are countryside and clifftop walks, a unique monkey sanctuary (not a zoo), historic buildings, fishing-boats and ferries. The train journey to the market town of Liskeard is particularly pretty. Prehistoric remains, picturesque hamlets, a watermill with a museum of old pianos and organs, potteries, a miniature steam railway, museums and a great deal more make for a varied holiday.

Readers' comments: Food excellent. Delicious.

The following facts have been supplied by the owners:

Bedrooms There are 6 rooms, which include single, double and family rooms. Bed-and-breakfast costs from £13 (per person) including service and VAT; prices go up in high season. There are reductions for stays of 7 nights or more; and 'bargain breaks' and special family rates as well.

Some if not all of the rooms have the following amenities: central heating or electric heaters; washbasin, shower, own bathroom and wc, shaver-point; radio, TV, armchairs; tea/coffee-making facilities; door keys. Breakfast in bed is available.

Meals The dinner menu is fixed price (£8) or à la carte. There is a choice of dishes on the fixed menu, which consists of 3 courses and coffee. Dinner is served at 6.30 pm. Special diets can be prepared. Lunches or packed lunches can be

337

provided; and snacks at other hours. Morning, afternoon or bedtime drinks (coffee, tea etc.) can be ordered. Wine and other alcoholic drinks can be ordered.

Public rooms There is a bar with open fire, TV, books, magazines, local guides and leaflets.

Surroundings These are available in the neighbourhood: golf, riding, squash, sea sports.

Overcombe Hotel, Horrabridge, south of Yelverton, Devon, PL20 7RN *Tel: 0822 853501*   C D H PT S S-C X ♯6

Conveniently placed for one to explore Dartmoor and the coast, the Overcombe Hotel consists of two houses now joined in one to make a very comfortable small hotel. You can relax in any of three sitting-rooms, according to what you want – a bar in one, TV in another, log fires, pleasant views. From the bay window of the dining-room, one looks across to the moors. The walls are hung with local paintings, some of which are for sale.

Richard Kitchin used to be in the Army, stationed overseas. To raise the air fares to visit him, his wife Pam started with some hesitation to take visitors for bed-and-breakfast. Finding the experience enjoyable, the Kitchins expanded this modest enterprise until it gradually grew into today's hotel, open all the year round.

There is always a selection of dishes on the menu (my choice was: avocado with prawns, carbonnade of beef, grape pavlova and cheese). In the morning, I was pleasantly surprised to find that not only was the marmalade home-made (and on sale to guests), but the orange juice freshly squeezed.

Visitors come here for a variety of reasons (the least of which is that it's a good staging-post if you are on that long slog to furthest Cornwall). The Dartmoor National Park attracts people touring by car, anglers, riders, golfers and – above all – walkers (for them, Richard organizes special two- to seven-day bargain breaks, with experienced guides accompanying visitors on walks of eight miles or more, and illustrated after-dinner talks about the moors). Plymouth is near; and among visitors' favourite outings are Cotehele (National Trust) and Morwellham and the shire horse centre.

Further east lie the delectable South Hams: flowery valleys, sands, mildest of climates. To the west is the Cornish coast:

dramatic cliffs, sandy coves and some harbours so picturesque (Polperro, Looe, etc.) that popularity threatens to ruin them. But go inland, and you will still find undisturbed villages and market towns – and any number of stately homes.

Plymouth was heavily bombed, which means that its shopping centre is very modern. But the old quarter, the Barbican, which Drake and the Pilgrim Fathers knew so well, survived, and it is to this that visitors throng. Here are the old warehouses and the harbours full of small boats, the narrow alleys with beguiling little shops and restaurants, the mediaeval houses now turned into museums, the fish market and, high above, the 17th-century citadel. Plymouth has an outstanding aquarium, Drake's Island out in the Sound (to be visited by boat), the naval dockyard and the famous clifftop – the Hoe – with its unique seascape, memorials and flowers. The Looe area is described on page 337.

Reader's comments: Excellent. Friendly and comfortable. Wonderful home cooking.

The following facts have been supplied by the owners:

Bedrooms There are 11 rooms, which include single, double and family rooms. Bed-and-breakfast costs from £13.80 (per person) including service and VAT; prices go up in high season. There are reductions for stays of 2 nights or more (except in high season) or for 7 nights or more (at any period); and 'bargain breaks' as well.

Some if not all of the rooms have the following amenities: central heating; washbasin, shower, own bathroom and wc, shaver-point; armchairs; views of countryside, farmland, garden; choice of duvets or blankets; door keys; TV; tea/coffee-making facilities.

Meals The dinner menu is fixed price (£8). There is a choice of dishes on the menu, which consists of 4 courses and coffee. Dinner is served at 7.30 pm. Special diets can be prepared. Lunches and packed lunches can be provided; and snacks at other hours. Morning, afternoon or bedtime drinks (coffee, tea etc.) can be ordered for a charge. Wine and other alcoholic drinks can be ordered.

Public rooms There are 2 sitting-rooms and a bar. The following are available in one or all of them: central heating, open fire, colour TV, books, magazines, local guides and leaflets, indoor games (such as Scrabble, backgammon, chess, Mastermind).

Surroundings The grounds consist of an acre of garden. Swing ball is available. These are available in the neighbourhood: golf, trout and salmon fishing, riding.

Cars The nearest main road is the A386 from Plymouth to Tavistock.

Paradise House, 88 Holloway, Bath, Avon, BA2 4PX
Tel: 0225 317723   **C PT ♯5**

It stands half way up a steep, curving road which was once indeed a 'hollow way': a lane worn low between high banks by centuries of weary feet or hooves entering Bath from the south: the last lap of the Romans' Fosse Way. It is now a quiet cul-de-sac in the lee of Beechen Cliff, with panoramic views over the city, the centre of which is only 7 minutes' walk away – downhill. As to uphill – take a taxi! (Or else a bus to the Bear Flat stop.)

The house itself was built about 1720, with all the elegance which that implies: a classical pediment above the front door and well-proportioned sash windows with rounded tops in a façade of honey-coloured Bath stone. But it had been sadly neglected in later times.

David and Janet Cutting took it over only a few years ago and have restored it impeccably throughout, stripping off polystyrene to reveal pretty plasterwork ceilings, for instance, and gaudy tiles to expose a lovely marble fireplace in which logs now blaze. They stripped dingy paint off the panelled pine doors and put on handles of brass or china. They have furnished to a very high standard indeed, with both antique and modern furniture, elegant fabrics (many with matching wallpapers) and well-chosen colours, predominantly soft greens and browns. The breakfast-room is especially pretty, with Liberty fabrics and wisteria wallpaper, pictures in maple frames and a collection of Coalport cottages. The bedrooms have been given as much care as the rest.

At the back, beyond a verandah with ivy-leaf ironwork, is quite a large walled garden (a sun-trap in the afternoon), with lawns, fish-pool, a rose-covered pergola and marvellous views of the city and hills all around. This secluded setting extends behind the mediaeval Magdalen Chapel next door, which was once a hostel for lepers banned from the city. In 1982 David and Janet acquired the adjoining Georgian house, which has now also been completely restored. It provides two lovely suites comprising sitting-room, bedroom and private bathroom, furnished and decorated to the same elegant standards as the main house.

As to Bath itself – which attracts more visitors than any other place in England except London – the attractions are so varied that they can hardly be compressed into one paragraph. Just wandering among the Georgian perfections of its streets and squares, which spread from the historic centre right up the sides of the surrounding hills, is a pleasure in itself, and it would take many days to explore them all (the best method is to take a bus to each hilltop in turn and walk back downhill, with far views succeeded by discoveries of lovely houses, streets, alleys or gardens all the way). Roman Bath is famous worldwide, and as the Temple excavations proceed there is always something new on show. Now more is being discovered about the city's Celtic origins too. Bath has about 80 restaurants, bistros or wine bars from which to choose; and no one has counted all the shops (and markets) which specialize in things of quality and elegance. Antiques, crafts, books, art: all are there in abundance. Bath has over a dozen museums, some highly specialized (bookbinding, for instance, and postal history). There are riverside and canalside walks, boat trips, a constant programme of musical and other events. Bath regularly wins awards for the flowers in its many public parks. It has a new sports and leisure centre. Its great festival of music takes place in early summer, followed by the Royal Bath & West Show, then county cricket, and much else all the year round: I prefer it out-of-season when it is less crowded. If the sophisticated pleasures of the city do pall, there's a lot to enjoy in the country around too.

Readers' comments: Top-class! Truly excellent. Ideal, with excellent facilities.

The following facts have been supplied by the owners:

Bedrooms There are 8 rooms, which include single, double and family rooms. Bed-and-breakfast costs from £14.50 (per person in a double room) including service and VAT; prices go up in high season. There are reductions for stays of 5 nights or more.
    Some if not all of the rooms have the following amenities; central heating; washbasin, shower, own bathroom and wc, shaver-point; colour TV, armchairs; views of city, countryside, garden; tea/coffee-making facilities; door keys.

Public rooms There is a sitting-room with central heating, books, magazines, local guides and leaflets and indoor games.

Surroundings The grounds consist of ½ acre of garden. The following games or sports are available in the grounds: croquet and swing ball. These are available in the neighbourhood: golf, sports centre (within 10 minutes' walk), canal and river fishing.

Cars The nearest main road is the A367 from Bath to Exeter.

Parkfield House, Hogben's Hill, Selling, west of Canterbury, Kent, ME13 94X *Tel: 022 785 898*   **C S X ⌗15**

There were Hogbens on this hill in 1086 (they are named in Domesday Book)... and there still are!

It is Mr and Mrs Hogben who own Parkfield, a largely modern house with a pretty garden, as well as the small joinery alongside – John Hogben's principal activity. It is worth staying at Parkfield House simply to listen to him talk about Kentish ways and history (especially his stories of past Hogbens, who were blacksmiths, farmers, wheelwrights and smugglers). Next door there used to be an inn, called Ye Olde Century in memory of a Hogben who lived there until he was 101.

The house, built in 1820, had become run-down until twenty-five years ago when Mr Hogben renovated and extended it. Now it is immaculate and very comfortable. Although only bed-and-breakfast guests are taken (they can dine, very well indeed, at the old village inn – the White Lion), there are two sitting-rooms for their use in the evening, one with television and both with big, velvet armchairs in which to relax. One has a log fire. And if you want something special for breakfast, (fish, fresh fruit, ham, cheese) Mrs Hogben will get it. (No smoking at table.)

Selling is in a very beautiful and tranquil part of Kent, well situated for touring, walking and sightseeing. It is, of course, the cathedral which brings most visitors to nearby Canterbury: one of Britain's finest and most colourful, with many historical associations, it is the site of Becket's martyrdom (commemorated in some of the finest stained glass in the world), the splendid tomb of the Black Prince, and much more.

The ancient walled city still has many surviving mediaeval and Tudor buildings, the beautiful River Stour, old churches and inns, Roman remains, a very good theatre, and lovely shops in its small lanes. It is in the middle of some of Kent's finest countryside, with a coast of great variety quite near (cliffs, sands or shingle; resorts, fishing harbours or historic ports) and ten golf courses. It would be very easy to spend a fortnight here without discovering all there is to see in one of England's most beautiful and most historic counties.

343

Reader's comments: Excellent in all respects, exceptional hospitality.

The following facts have been supplied by the owners:

Bedrooms There are 6 rooms, which include single, double and family rooms.
   Bed-and-breakfast costs from £11 (per person in a double room) including service and VAT. There are reductions for stays of 2 nights or more.
   Some if not all of the rooms have the following amenities: central heating or electric heaters; washbasin, shaver-point; armchairs; views of countryside, farmland, garden. Bedtime drinks (coffee, tea etc.) can be ordered free.
Public rooms There are 2 sitting-rooms etc. The following are available in one or both of them: central heating, open fire, TV (colour), books, magazines, local guides and leaflets.
Surroundings The grounds consist of ½ acre of garden.
Cars The nearest main road is the A251 from Faversham to Ashford.

Peacock Inn, Chelsworth, west of Ipswich, Suffolk
Tel: 0449 740758   C(10) **PT S ♯3**

Of Suffolk's many, little-known villages that have hardly changed since the Middle Ages, Chelsworth is one of the prettiest. It is not now on a road to anywhere in particular (even though it is in the centre of an excellent area for sightseeing), so it remains undisturbed: a small village of thatched, half-timbered and colour-washed cottages and a fine church beside the sparkling River Brett with its flotilla of ducks.

Facing the twin humped-backed bridges stands its only inn, the Peacock, an ancient, pink-walled building with great hexagonal brick chimneys looming above the mossy tiles of a roof bowed with age. Behind the mediaeval front, later additions have gradually extended the inn, which started life as a hospice for pilgrims travelling to St Edmund's once-famous shrine at Bury.

When Tony Marsh, an engineer, took over the inn a few years ago, passing visitors often asked him where to find accommodation in the village. There was none – so Tony and his wife Lorna set about providing it. There are now several pretty bedrooms above the bars – pink-and-white, with flowery bedspreads and cherry velvet bedheads, in low-beamed rooms with simple board doors.

The Marshes have built up the inn's reputation for good food – particularly in winter. This is when the spit over the huge log fire in one of the bars is set turning every Saturday night, to start the slow roasting of a colossal joint of beef for Sunday lunch. They use local game in hand-raised game pies, the local baker makes crusty granary loaves to their own recipe, soups (such as fish chowder) and sweets are home-made and hams are honey-roasted in traditional style. Meals are eaten in a small dining-room, in the bars, or, in summer, on teak tables in the garden.

The bars are all you might expect of a mediaeval inn: flagged floors, beams with horse-brasses, tapestry-cushioned benches and inglenook fireplace.

From Chelsworth it is easy to visit such famous beauty-spots as Lavenham and Long Melford, Sudbury on the River Stour (Gainsborough's house), Norman Castle Hedingham, Roman Colchester and many charming villages such as Kersey, Clare and Cavendish. All these grew wealthy on wool, and many of their superb houses or richly decorated churches have survived the centuries – alongside old inns, antique shops and country craft centres. Bury St Edmunds is famous for its abbey ruins among gardens, Adam buildings, several museums and a Regency theatre now in the care of the National Trust. The countryside undulates, with streams threading their way through it. You can find working mills (wind or water), country parks, forests, priories and abbeys, pargetting galore (that is, decorative plasterwork peculiar to Suffolk), racing at Newmarket – the list of things to do and see in this peaceful part of England is endless. At the end of June, two dozen Chelsworth houses (from mansions to cottages) open their gardens to the public in aid of charity. For more about this part of Suffolk, see pages 167 and 353.

Readers' comments: Loved it! Marvellous hospitality.

The following facts have been supplied by the owners:

Bedrooms There are 5 rooms, which include a single and doubles. Bed-and-breakfast costs from £14.50 (per person) including service and VAT.

Some if not all of the rooms have the following amenities: central heating; shaver-point; radio; views of countryside/farmland/garden; tea/coffee-making facilities; door keys. Breakfast in bed is available.

Meals The dinner menu is à la carte. Vegetarian diets can be prepared. Lunches and packed lunches can be provided; and snacks at other hours. Morning, afternoon or bedtime drinks (coffee, tea etc.) can be ordered; wine and other alcoholic drinks too.

Cars The nearest main road is the A12 from London to Ipswich.

Peat Gate Head, Low Row, west of Richmond, North Yorkshire, DL11 6PP   *Tel: 0748 86388*   **C H S X ♯9**

It sometimes seems that anywhere north of Leeds now calls itself Herriot country, what with almost countless books, films, and television series. Though the author actually practises to the east of the county, much filming of his books was done in the Yorkshire Dales, and Peat Gate Head is just along the moor road (with watersplash) where the opening sequence of every television episode was recorded.

Alan Earl had long loved Peat Gate Head, a 300-year-old Swaledale farmhouse built of the local limestone, and when his job as a history lecturer ended with the closure of the training college where he worked he decided to buy it and to turn his enthusiasm for cooking to good use by opening it as a guest-house. From several choices at each course one might select, for instance, salmon mousse, chicken breasts in an orange-and-tarragon sauce, and 'queen of puddings'.

The beamed house is simply furnished. There is a vast stone chimneypiece in the dining-room, and in the sitting-room a wood-burning stove pleasantly scents the air.

Outside the door, a summerhouse on the lawn looks across a sweep of Swaledale, a textbook illustration of a valley, from the river running along the flat bottom, through stone-walled fields, to open moorland. From the bedrooms on the opposite side of the house, you are at eye level with peewits and curlews.

The following facts have been supplied by the owners:

Bedrooms There are 5 rooms, which include single, double and family rooms. Bed-and-breakfast costs from £11.50 (per person in a double room) including service and VAT.

    Some if not all of the rooms have the following amenities: central heating; electric blankets, washbasin, shower, own bathroom and wc, shaver-point; armchairs; views of countryside/farmland/garden; choice of duvets or blankets; tea/coffee-making facilities; door keys. Breakfast in bed is available.

Meals The dinner menu is fixed price (£9.50). There is no choice of dishes on the fixed menu, which consists of 3 courses and coffee. Dinner is served at 7 pm. Special diets can be prepared. Morning, afternoon or bedtime drinks (coffee, tea etc.) can be ordered for a charge. Wine and other alcoholic drinks can be ordered.

Public rooms There is a sitting-room with central heating, open fire, TV (colour), books, magazines, local guides and leaflets, indoor games (such as draughts, chess and cards), bar.

Surroundings The grounds consist of 2 acres of meadow and garden. These are available in the neighbourhood: riding, climbing, fishing, golf.

Cars The nearest main road is the A6108 from Richmond to Leyburn.

Penscot Farmhouse Hotel, Shipham, north of Cheddar, Somerset, BS25 12W *Tel: 093 484 2659*   **C D H PT S X ⌗5**

Built in the 15th century as farm cottages, Penscot became an inn on the village green, and still retains much of that character. It is a long low building, white-walled and with low beams and log fires inside. The atmosphere is informal and comfortable. Bedrooms are simple, the sitting-room well provided with plenty of deep armchairs and doors straight out into the garden where one can sit in the sun. There is a small conservatory with a flourishing vine; hanging baskets of flowers; a sunken rose garden and a swimming-pool. Cream teas are a speciality – and 80 malt whiskies.

There are two dining-rooms. The one reserved for residents has pine alcoves and Scandinavian-style chairs. Here a set meal is served (such as home-made soup, chicken casserole with local vegetables, and cheesecake), while in a converted barn there is an à la carte menu, too: mainly conventional food such as trout, duck, steaks etc. Wine is poured into pottery goblets made locally. The chef is Malcolm Harwood.

The Tildens are lucky to have an enthusiastic young staff who clearly enjoy Penscot and want to share their pleasure in it with visitors.

Most of the bedrooms are quite simple but two (on the ground floor) have special features. One very attractive room has a four-poster, plus an extra bed; and the other would be ideal for a family as there is a children's room adjoining the parents'.

From peaceful Shipham there are far views to Bridgewater Bay and the Welsh hills. It lies on the edge of the beautiful Mendip Hills (and half way along the walkers' Mendip Way which winds from the coast to Wells). In the neighbourhood are facilities for riding, golf, caving and painting. Plenty of sightseeing, too: castles, stately homes, gorges, woods, viewpoints, museums, wildlife, gardens, old villages, the coast, entertainments and centres for shopping. Shipham itself is full of quaint lanes. Within an hour are Exmoor and the Quantock Hills, the cathedral cities of

Wells and Glastonbury, Bath, Bristol (and its zoo) and innumerable churches of architectural interest.

Readers' comments: Delightful. Tasty home cooking. Every comfort, good service, happy atmosphere. Good food and welcoming atmosphere. Nice to see everyone smiling.

The following facts have been supplied by the owners:

Bedrooms There are 18 rooms, which include single, double and family rooms. Bed-and-breakfast costs from £12.50 (per person) including service and VAT. There are reductions for stays of 2 nights or more; and 'bargain breaks' as well. Discounts to people who make a second visit; free Sunday accommodation for over-60s staying 3 days; and sampler breaks (see page 14).
   Some if not all of the rooms have the following amenities: central heating or electric heaters; washbasin, shower and wc, shaver-point; radio, armchairs; views of countryside/farmland/garden; tea/coffee-making facilities; door keys; bed-boards. Breakfast in bed is available. TV for hire.

Meals The dinner menu is fixed price (£6) or à la carte. There is no choice of dishes on the fixed menu, which consists of 3 courses and coffee. Dinner is served at 7 pm. Special diets can be prepared. Lunches and packed lunches can be provided; and snacks at other hours. Morning, afternoon or bedtime drinks (coffee, tea etc.) can be ordered for a charge. Non-residents are not admitted to the dining-room (but there is a restaurant too). Wine and other alcoholic drinks can be ordered.

Public rooms There are 2 sitting-rooms etc. The following are available in one or both of them: central heating, open fire, TV (colour), books, magazines, local guides and leaflets, indoor games (such as Scrabble, Monopoly and cards); bar. Bridge can be arranged.

Surroundings The grounds consist of 1½ acres of gardens with unheated swimming-pool. These are available in the neighbourhood: riding, sports centre and guided walks (or use the Tildens' own booklet of walks).

Cars The nearest main road is the A38 from Bristol to Taunton.

Languages spoken French.

Credit cards accepted Visa, Access, Diners Club, Amex.

Closed to visitors We are not open in December and January except for Christmas.

Pepperday Cottage, Church Lane, Barrowden, east of Uppingham, Leicestershire, LE15 8ED   *Tel: 057 287 874*   C(12) S ♯6

Barrowden is a delightful village with two greens, an old inn, even older church and just a few houses – of which this cottage (early Tudor) is one of the oldest.

It has been beautifully furnished by Beryl Maxwell. There are two sitting-rooms, one with a Chinese carpet, grey-and-white fabrics, pots of gloxinias and tapestry cushions stitched by Beryl;

the other has wing chairs around a wood-stove in an inglenook, soft colours, white walls and board ceiling – there is a stone-arched doorway and an open-tread stair leading up to the bedrooms. The dining-room (also with an inglenook fireplace, with old salt-cupboard built into it) has tapestry chairs around the refectory table (laid with Japanese porcelain and good silver), Staffordshire china on the oak dresser. Bedrooms are equally distinctive – in one, the window is made from a big cartwheel set in the stone wall; the blue room has a patchwork bedspread which took Beryl years to make. The bathrooms are luxurious. The rooms have views of the garden and its pond, lawns terraced with rock plants, and an unusual pantile-topped wall.

Beryl is a cookery teacher, so dinners are of a high order. A typical meal might include watercress soup, chicken breasts in sherry and cream, hazelnut meringue with raspberries, and cheese. Vegetables are home-grown, bread home-baked, bacon farm-cured. Varied breakfast choices include even devilled mushrooms.

This is a no-smoking house.

Barrowden is in a superb part of England, the scenery and architecture standing comparison with the Cotswolds. There are a great many stately homes and castles (Belvoir and Rockingham, for instance), innumerable antique shops, the vast expanse of Rutland Water (for water-sports, wildfowl etc.), Oundle, cathedrals at Ely and Peterborough, ancient villages, concerts and first-class theatre at Corby, Wildfowl Trust at Peakirk, and at Little Gidding a charming early 18th-century church associated with the influential religious community founded there by Nicholas Ferrar over three centuries ago. (There is more about this area on pages 150–51.)

Readers' comments: Full of atmosphere, food excellent, a place we go back to often.

The following facts have been supplied by the owners:

Bedrooms There are 3 rooms, which include single and double rooms. Bed-and-breakfast costs £15 (per person in a double room) including service and VAT. There are reductions for stays of 5 nights or more.
   Some if not all of the rooms have the following amenities: central heating or electric heaters; electric blankets, washbasin, shower, own bathroom and wc, shaver-point; armchairs; views of river, countryside, farmland, garden.

Meals The dinner menu is fixed price (£10). There is no choice of dishes on the fixed menu, which consists of 4 courses and coffee. Dinner is served at 7.30 pm. Special diets can be prepared; and snacks at other hours. Morning, afternoon or bedtime drinks (coffee, tea etc.) can be ordered for a charge. Non-residents are not admitted to the dining-room. Wine and other alcoholic drinks can be ordered or brought in.

Public rooms There are 2 sitting-rooms etc. The following are available in one or both of them: central heating, open fire, TV (colour), books, magazines, local guides and leaflets, indoor games (such as cards, draughts, chess, etc.).

Surroundings The grounds consist of a garden. These are available in the neighbourhood: fishing, sailing, golf, riding, swimming.

Cars The nearest main road is the A47 from Leicester to Peterborough.

Pipps Ford, Needham Market, north of Ipswich, Suffolk, IP6 8LJ
Tel: 044979 208   **C H PT S ⌗3**

On a stretch of the River Gipping that has been designated an 'area of outstanding natural beauty' stands a large Tudor farm-house, its black-and-white half-timbered walls an ideal background to old-fashioned roses: everyone's idea of a rural idyll. (It is hard to find: ask for directions.)

When Anthony Hackett-Jones, a lawyer, bought the old farm-house and eight acres of land, it was in poor shape; it is now not only comfortable but beautifully furnished with antiques, interesting painting, good china, silver and pretty fabrics. Mrs Hackett-Jones has made patchwork quilts or cushion-covers for every room and searched out attractive fabrics (Laura Ashley, French ones and so on) for curtains or upholstery. She puts flowers in each bedroom. Many of the beds are collectors' pieces: a four-poster, a French provincial one and several ornamental brass beds. Oriental rugs cover floors of wood or stone. Even the bathrooms attached to each bedroom are attractive, with carpet and William Morris wallpapers. One is spectacular, with a huge oval bath. Some bedrooms are in newly converted stables, with sitting-room.

This is a house of inglenook fireplaces, sloping floors, low beams and historic associations, for it once belonged to the Tudor explorer Richard Hakluyt, and later to the wife of Sir William Harvey, discoverer of blood circulation. Visitors who use the sitting-room, with its deep armchairs and log fire, can enjoy the family's huge collection of classical records. Meals are served in a conservatory with tropical plants.

Breakfasts are exceptional. From an enormous choice, you could select exotic juices; home-made sausages or black pudding; home-made yogurt, croissants, jams, honey; eggs cooked in nine ways (coddled, baked etc. – from duck, goose or hen); French or cinnamon toast; waffles, crumpets, muffins; kidneys, mackerel, sardines, fishcakes, kedgeree; five kinds of tea . . .

Raewyn Hackett-Jones, a New Zealander, is an excellent cook. A typical dinner might comprise, for guests of conventional tastes: home-made soup or pâté; a pie such as chicken and asparagus, or a roast; raspberries and redcurrants with cream, a gâteau or a hot pudding; cheese; coffee. She also enjoys cooking game and adventurous dishes for guests who like these. Fruit, vegetables, eggs and other produce, including chicken, veal and pork, are organically home-grown (in season) and bread is home-made.

The Hackett-Joneses keep a fluctuating population of calves, chickens, bees and pigs; and visitors, especially children, are welcome to get involved with collecting eggs or feeding pigs, for example. The milk and cream are provided by Annabel, their Jersey cow. Occasionally there are courses on upholstery, art and other subjects.

Beyond the garden, there is coarse fishing in the river, where cricket-bat willows grow, and a Roman site. Interesting places to visit by car are Sandringham, Constable country, Lavenham, Aldeburgh, Southwold, Norwich, Ipswich and Bury St Edmunds. The area is full of pretty villages, ancient churches, antique shops, stately homes and a museum of East Anglian life at Stowmarket.

Readers' comments: Most impressed; made very welcome; food absolutely super; most hospitable place; relaxed and informal, thoroughly happy and comfortable; delightful house beautifully furnished; food and service outstanding; one of the best holidays ever; food superb; friendly good humour.

The following facts have been supplied by the owners:

Bedrooms There are 6 rooms, which include singles, doubles and a family wing. Bed-and-breakfast costs from £11.50 (per person in a double room). Winter discounts. Sampler breaks (see page 14).

Some if not all of the rooms have the following amenities: central heating or electric heaters; electric blankets, washbasin, shower, own bathroom and wc, hair drier, shaver-point; armchairs; views of countryside, farmland, garden; tea/coffee-making facilities; radio-alarms; colour TV on request and iron.

Meals The dinner menu is fixed price (£9.50 or £10). There is a choice of dishes on the menu, which consists of 3 or 4 courses and coffee. Dinner is served at 7.15 pm. Wine can be ordered and other alcoholic drinks. Salmon, venison, etc. are extra. Vegetarian meals by arrangement. Occasional curry weekends. Afternoon teas with cakes etc.

Public rooms There is a sitting-room with central heating, open fire, books, magazines, local guides and leaflets, record-player and records, indoor games (such as Monopoly, chess, Scrabble, jigsaws, Trivial Pursuit). Also a TV room.

Surroundings The grounds consist of garden, unheated swimming-pool, children's play equipment, croquet lawn, river, meadow and woodland, with coarse fishing and a new tennis court. These are available in the neighbourhood: riding, canoeing, tennis, golf, birdwatching, windsurfing. Cycles for hire.

Cars The nearest main roads are the A45 from Ipswich to Bury St Edmunds and the A140 from Ipswich to Norwich.

Polraen, Sandplace, north-west of Looe, Cornwall, PL13 1PJ
Tel: 05036 3956   **C D PT S ⌗3**

In the 18th century this stone building was a coaching-inn, but for a long time it has been a country house hotel, now run by Peter and Joyce Allcroft. They were still in the throes of making improvements when I visited it, creating a large bar (using local slate blocks for the fireplace and the bar itself) and decorating the bedrooms in soft colours. The brown-and-white sitting-room opens onto an attractive south-facing garden with old apple trees, huge cedars and woodland rising up behind. At night, the fountain is lit up; and by day guests can sit at tables under sun umbrellas. Round the corner is the Allcrofts' vegetable garden.

The dining-room has a cottagey look, with the old cooking-range still in position and Windsor chairs around the tables. Here plain English meals are served – such as home-made soup, topside of beef with Yorkshire pudding and baked parsnips, and apple amber – or, if you're in luck, chocolate and whisky gâteau. Bread is locally baked.

The house is in a very lovely river valley with woodland walks, in an area fully described on page 337.

The following facts have been supplied by the owners:

Bedrooms   There are 5 rooms, which include single, double and family rooms. Bed-and-breakfast costs from £12.50 (per person) including service and VAT; prices go up in high season. There are reductions for stays of 7 nights or more; and 'bargain breaks' as well.

Some if not all of the rooms have the following amenities: central heating; own bathroom and wc, shaver-point; armchairs; views of countryside and garden; tea/coffee-making facilities; door keys; hair driers.

Meals The dinner menu is fixed price (£8) or à la carte. There is no choice of dishes on the fixed menu, which consists of 5 courses and coffee. Dinner is served at 7 pm. Special diets can be prepared. Lunches and packed lunches can be provided; and snacks at other hours. Morning, afternoon or bedtime drinks (coffee, tea etc.) can be ordered for a charge. Wine and other alcoholic drinks can be ordered.

Public rooms There is a sitting-room with central heating, open fire, TV (colour), books, magazines, local guides and leaflets. Also a bar.

Surroundings The grounds consist of 2½ acres of garden. These are available in the neighbourhood: golf, fishing, tennis, riding.

Cars The nearest main road is the A38 from Plymouth to Liskeard.

Credit cards accepted Access, Visa.

Pond Cottage, The Green, Warmington, north-west of Banbury (Oxfordshire), Warwickshire, OX17 1BU

Tel: 029589 682 (evenings best)   S ⌗5

This village is so well tucked away that, beauty-spot though it is, few tourists find it. Around a sloping village green with duck-pond and waterlilies, dominated at one end by a Tudor manor house, are ranged rows of charming cottages built from warm Cotswold stone, roses and clematis climbing up their walls. Mrs Viljoen's home is one of these.

She has furnished its small rooms with great elegance. Gleaming antique furniture and silver contrast with the rugged stones of the sitting-room walls and hearth. She has chosen browns and buffs to

harmonize with the colour of the stone. One pretty bedroom is all-blue – from the silk spread and the cover of the armchair to the flowery Victorian wallpaper.

At the back is a tiny garden with a seat among roses and nasturtiums climbing up the walls.

Vi asks visitors to say what kind of food they like. A typical menu might include home-made soup, chicken in almond sauce or creole pork, and a tart of her own fruit, or home-made ice cream.

Vi Viljoen, once a teacher, is now a Tourist Board guide – so is well qualified to advise visitors on sightseeing (she will even, for a fee, drive them around herself).

Pond Cottage has appeared on the cover of *Forever Ambridge* by Norman Painting (who plays Phil Archer in the radio series), a resident in the village. Within a few miles of it are the castles of Broughton, Warwick and Kenilworth; Ragley Hall; Stratford-upon-Avon; Sulgrave Manor (home of George Washington's ancestors); and six stately homes belonging to the National Trust. The Cotswolds, Worcester, Althorp and Oxford are not much further.

This is an excellent area for winter breaks because such a large number of 'sights' remain open all through the year.

Readers' comments: A delightful stay. A pleasure to see so many lovely things in the house. Welcomed us like friends, and made our wedding anniversary dinner a feast.

The following facts have been supplied by the owner:

Bedrooms There are 2 rooms (a single and a double). Bed-and-breakfast costs from £10 (per person) including service and VAT. **10% reductions for readers of this book if they stay a week.**

Some if not all of the rooms have the following amenities: central heating or electric heaters, double-glazing; electric blankets, washbasin, shower and wc, shaver-point; armchairs; views of village green and duck-pond, garden; hair drier and iron available.

Meals The dinner menu is fixed price (£7.25). There is no choice of dishes on the fixed menu, which consists of 3 courses and coffee. Dinner is served at 7.30 pm, or by arrangement. Bedtime drinks (coffee, tea) can be ordered free. Non-residents are not admitted to the dining-room. Wine and other alcoholic drinks can be ordered or brought in.

Public rooms There is a sitting-room with central heating, open fire, TV (b & w), books, magazines, local guides and leaflets.

Surroundings In the neighbourhood are flying, gliding, shooting, trout and coarse fishing, riding, swimming, squash, tennis, golf, racing.

Cars The nearest main road is the A41 from London to Chester (via Birmingham).
Languages spoken French and some German.
Closed to visitors The house is not open between November and March.

**Pool House Hotel, Hanley Road, Upton-on-Severn, south of
Worcester, WR8 0PA**   *Tel: 06846 2151*   **C ☼4**

I have included this hotel for its superb river-bank setting, with
gardens that make the most of this. Herbaceous borders wander
among lawns with fruit trees, sloping down to the waterside. The
18th-century house is simply furnished: I thought the bedrooms
more attractive than the dining-room, particularly room 2 – which
has a rose-and-white colour scheme and a good view of the river.
Meals are traditional: home-made soup or a prawn cocktail might
be followed by roast beef (with fresh local vegetables) and a
rhubarb-and-raisin crumble, for instance.

From the house one enjoys views of the Malvern Hills. Not far
off is the River Avon, the Cotswolds, 'Shakespeare country' and
the lovely Wye valley. Other sightseeing possibilities include
Tewkesbury Abbey, Cheltenham Spa, Worcester Cathedral (and
the Royal Porcelain factory), Hereford and Gloucester (two more
cathedrals). Upton itself is a delightful old market town.

The following facts have been supplied by the owners:

Bedrooms There are 9 rooms, which include single, double and family rooms. Bed-and-breakfast costs from £14 (per person in a double room) including service and VAT. There are reductions for stays of 7 nights or more; and 'bargain breaks' as well.

   Some if not all of the rooms have the following amenities: central heating or electric heaters; washbasin, shower, own bathroom and wc, shaver-point; armchairs; views of countryside or garden; choice of duvets or blankets; door keys. Breakfast in bed is available.

Meals The dinner menu is fixed price (£6). There is a choice of dishes on the fixed menu, which consists of 3 courses and coffee. Dinner is served at 6.30 pm. Vegetarian or special diets can be prepared. Packed lunches can be provided; and snacks at other hours. Morning, afternoon or bedtime drinks (coffee, tea etc.) can be ordered for a charge. Wine and other alcoholic drinks can be ordered.

Public rooms There is a sitting-room with central heating, open fire, TV (colour), books, magazines, local guides and leaflets, board games, piano, bar.

Surroundings The grounds consist of 3 acres of gardens, with fishing and croquet. Riding and fishing are available in the neighbourhood.

Cars The nearest main road is the A38 from Worcester to Tewkesbury.

Credit cards accepted Amex, Access.

Portwell House, Market Place, Faringdon, Oxfordshire, SN7 7H11   *Tel: 0367 20197*   **C D H PT ⌗5**

Margo Manning runs two enterprises in this pink Jacobean house. There is a tea-room where home-made cakes, scones and éclairs are served from a pine counter. Upstairs, she runs a small and friendly guest-house. The bedrooms are neat and fresh, each with its own bathroom, and the sitting/dining-room has hanging baskets of plants and an aquarium.

Margo used to be a hairdresser but enjoys this complete change of activity. She does a lot of the baking herself, and cooks such meals as: prawn cocktail or egg mayonnaise, followed by a roast or steak, with gâteau or cheese and coffee to follow. She enjoys doing special diets. David used to be a fruiterer, so there is often a good choice of fresh fruit and vegetables.

Faringdon is a pretty town – a place of mossy roofs, old inn signs, swinging lamps and clocks on brackets, with a colonnaded buttermarket. Brickwork, stone and colourful stucco give the streets variety, and there is an ancient church half-hidden behind great yews (one of many in this area). A good centre for public transport and for many sports, it is at the heart of an area full of interest with plenty to explore. In the spring, the grounds of nearby Faringdon House produce a wonderful display of flowers. This was the home of Lord Berners (the model for Lord Merlin in *The Pursuit of Love*), who also built the Folly Tower on the nearby hill. In his will, he asked to be stuffed and placed on top of it, but his executors thought otherwise.

In the surrounding Vale of the White Horse there are plenty of good canalside walks (with revitalizing little inns along the way); Uffington church, which has memories of Tom Brown (of *Tom Brown's Schooldays*); the prehistoric white horse itself, cut out of the turf on the chalk downs; and adjacent earthworks with far views. The old Ridgeway Path runs here, with Wayland's Smithy close by. Great Coxwell has a superb tithe barn; Coleshill and Buscot Park are two National Trust properties, and Ashdown and Littlecote are not much further. Then there are the wilder reaches of the Thames – Lechlade, the source, and Kelmscott (William Morris's lovely house). The theatres of Oxford, Swindon and Newbury are accessible.

Readers' comments: Kindness, attention and hospitality. Pleasant and comfortable; meals delicious; the best bargain for a long time. Excellent standards, friendliness, very happy atmosphere.

The following facts have been supplied by the owners:

Bedrooms There are 7 rooms, which include single, double and family rooms. Bed-and-breakfast costs £14 (per person in a double room) including service and VAT. There are reductions for stays of 4 nights or more; and 'bargain breaks' as well.

   The rooms have the following amenities: central heating or electric heaters; washbasin, own bathroom and wc, shaver-point; colour TV, armchairs; choice of duvets or blankets; tea/coffee-making facilities; door keys. Hair drier and laundering facilities available.

Meals The dinner menu is fixed price (£4–£7) or à la carte. There is a choice of dishes on the fixed menu, which consists of 3 courses. Dinner is served from 6.30–8 pm. Special diets can be prepared. Lunches or packed lunches can be provided; and snacks at other hours. Non-residents are not admitted to the dining-room. Wine and other alcoholic drinks can be ordered.

Public rooms There is a sitting area with central heating, books, magazines, local guides and leaflets.

Cars The nearest main road is the A420 from Oxford to Swindon.

Preston Farm, Harberton, south of Totnes, Devon, TQ9 7SW
Tel: 0803 862235   C(2) S ♯4

It's unusual to find a working farm with its house right in a village (a very quiet one), but there used to be several such clustered together in Harberton. The Steers' land is elsewhere – 250 acres, with dairy cows. The house itself, built in 1680, has been in the same family for generations. All the rooms are comfortable, and there is good home cooking at dinner-time, with meals that may start with melon or soup, to be followed by trout, chops or, three times a week, a roast, and then home-made mousse, trifle or gâteau. The ingredients are mostly home-grown or local. One bedroom is in 'Country Diary' fabrics; another has a matching pink-and-cream bathroom. Breakfast comes on 'help-yourself' platters – conventional bacon and eggs or less usual things like hog's pudding or smoked haddock.

Harberton is a picturesque cluster of old cottages with colourful gardens, set in a valley. Its 13th-century church has a magnificent painted screen and stained glass windows. The local inn is of equal antiquity. Preston Farmhouse was once a manor house, which is why rooms are spacious.

Unusually for a farm, a bus stops close by to take people to historic Totnes and its castle, or to Dartmouth and Salcombe, for example, via country lanes. Dartmoor lies to the north, the coast to the south, and neither is far off. Modbury is one of many picturesque towns near here, its Georgian or slate-hung houses clinging to a steep hill. Buckfastleigh (with abbey built in 1938; notable stained glass) is where the Dart Valley steam trains go, along a lovely route. Dartmeet, one of the most famous of beauty-spots, is where two rivers join – there is a pretty 'clapper' bridge of stone slabs nearby. A little further is Widecombe-in-the-Moor with its huge old church, its September fair and 'Uncle Tom Cobleigh an' all'. Exeter, Plymouth and Torbay are easily accessible by car.

Readers' comments: Far more than we had hoped for; made most welcome; meals were excellent, good variety and generous help-ings. Warm welcome, excellent accommodation, superb cooking. Absolutely marvellous. Everything perfect – especially the fish pie! Very comfortable; delicious meals; perfect company.

The following facts have been supplied by the owners:

Bedrooms There are 3 rooms, which include double and family rooms. Bed-and-breakfast costs £10 (per person), including service and VAT. There are big reductions for stays of 7 nights or more.

Some if not all of the rooms have the following amenities: central heating or electric heaters; electric blankets, washbasin, shaver-point; armchairs; views of countryside, farmland, garden; tea/coffee-making facilities; door keys. Breakfast in bed is available, and videos. Hair drier and washing machine available.

Meals The dinner menu is fixed price (£4.50). There is no choice of dishes on the menu, which consists of 4 courses and coffee. Dinner is served at 6.45 pm. Snacks can be ordered at other hours. Morning, afternoon or bedtime drinks (coffee, tea etc.) are free. Non-residents are not admitted to the dining-room. Wine and other alcoholic drinks can be brought in.

Public rooms There is a sitting-room with central heating, open fire, colour TV, books, magazines, local guides and leaflets, record-player and records.

Surroundings The grounds consist of gardens and fields. These are available in the neighbourhood: riding, fishing, swimming-pool, golf.

Cars The nearest main road is the A381 from Totnes to Kingsbridge.

Closed to visitors The farm is closed to visitors in winter.

Prospect Hill Hotel, Kirkoswald, north of Penrith, Cumbria, CA10 1ER *Tel: 076883 500*　　　C D PT S X ⊞6

A group of 18th-century farm buildings close to a village that feels remote (though the M6 is only 9 miles away) has been turned into a hotel with great individuality by Isa and John Henderson (he was formerly a television designer). His style is visible in every detail: even the drawings in the brochure are his.

The one-time farm is in the beautiful Eden valley. It was virtually derelict when Isa and John started, in 1974, on the long process of conversion – at the same time building up his collection of old farm implements and domestic bygones. These are displayed on the sandstone walls in the bar (once a byre, with low beamed ceiling and flagged floor) which has a wide choice of malt whiskies and vintage port.

During 1984 they reconstructed a fairly rare 19th-century farm building known as a gin case. This is a half-round room, dominated by a central pine beam 32 feet by over 1 foot square, within which yoked mules or ponies walked round and round powering wheels and belts to grind the grain. ('Gin' is northern slang for engine, and 'ginny' is an Irish word for mule.)

Every bedroom is individually decorated, and traditional materials have been used in many new features – even radiator shelves and curtain poles are of solid oak with brass screws, and old beams have been re-used as lintels. Though modern improvements are provided where they matter (bathroom fitments, for instance), many rooms still have walls of rugged stone, and a number have brass bedsteads with patchwork quilts. Home-spun curtains, thick carpets and country colours like peat or moss are all in keeping with the character of the place. Even the corridors have well-chosen touches such as woven hangings with a Celtic look, and the spiral staircase is of cast iron. The former granary has been turned into an annexe that is ideal for a family.

There is a glassed-in porch with cane furniture and a terrace. The view, beyond a group of old ploughshares, is of fields, trees and hills, and of an old tractor which John has renovated for guests to drive around the fields.

In the beamed dining-room with wood-block floor, guests sit at Victorian tables. A typical dinner: leek-and-mushroom soup, turkey in asparagus sauce, strawberry shortcake and good, plentiful coffee. There is a vegetarian menu; and the good wine list includes plenty of half-bottles. For breakfast there is a huge choice including even such things as green figs and smoked haddock, followed by locally produced honey, marmalade and bread.

John and Isa do a great deal to help visitors enjoy the neighbourhood. They have lots of guidebooks, and John produced his own leaflets of walks from evening strolls to half-day hikes with notes about where deer can be seen, a spectacular waterfall in a gorge, riverside paths, a forest nature reserve with hide for watching badgers and hares or wildfowl, caves, old quarries and castle ruins. The neighbourhood is full of ancient villages; there's a working watermill, the prehistoric stones of 'Long Meg' and a traditional pottery still using a Victorian steam engine. Outings in an estate car are arranged. Less prone to snow, Kirkoswald is a good choice for a winter break.

One nice touch: a wrought iron screen dated 1974–80, which incorporates the initials of everybody who had a hand in the conversion. And another: John produces for 'regulars' a news-sheet of Prospect Hill happenings – weddings, the installation of solar heating, tree-planting, staff doings and local conservation endeavours.

Within easy motoring distance along scenic roads are the interesting old towns of Penrith and Alston, the city of Carlisle, the Lake District and Hadrian's Wall.

Readers' comments: Comfortable and well organized; good cuisine; excellent amenities; nothing was too much trouble; very good in all respects; well decorated rooms; good and thoughtful service; value for money.

The following facts have been supplied by the owners:

Bedrooms There are 10 rooms, which include single, double and family rooms. Bed-and-breakfast costs from £15 (per person) including VAT. There are reductions for stays of 3 nights or more. Special breaks include honeymoons (with champagne), autumn and spring breaks and Christmas and New Year (with dinner-dance). Over-60s and newly-weds can have Sunday accommodation free if they stay 3 days.

Some if not all of the rooms have the following amenities: central heating; washbasin, shower, own bathroom and wc, bidet, shaver-point; armchairs; views of countryside and farmland; choice of duvets or blankets; tea/coffee-making facilities; door keys. Breakfast in bed and portable colour TV are available. There are clothes-washing and ironing facilities.

Meals The dinner menu is à la carte. Orders for dinner are taken from 7.15–8.30 pm. Special diets and half portions can be prepared. Bar lunches and/or packed lunches can be provided. Morning, afternoon or bedtime drinks (coffee, tea etc.) can be ordered for a charge. Wine and other alcoholic drinks can be ordered.

Public rooms There are 2 sitting-rooms and a bar. The following are available in one or more of them: central heating, open fire, colour TV, books, magazines, local guides and leaflets and indoor games (such as cards, dominoes, chess).

Surroundings The grounds consist of lawns, shrubs and fields. A patio overlooks ponds. These are available in the neighbourhood: swimming, squash, bowling, golf, fishing and pony trekking. Maps, gumboots and cycles for hire.

Cars The nearest main road is the A6 from Penrith to Carlisle. To find the hotel, ask for directions when you book.

Red House, Sidmouth Road, Lyme Regis, Dorset, DT7 3ES
Tel: 02974 2055   C(6) **PT ⚏3**

Delightful old Lyme has many claims to fame – the profusion of fossils (including dinosaur bones) found along its beaches; the landing of the rebel Monmouth in 1685 to start his abortive rebellion; Jane Austen's *Persuasion*; and most recently *The French Lieutenant's Woman*, the author of which, John Fowles, is honorary curator of the local museum.

When Geoffrey Griffin retired, he and his wife Elizabeth, a journalist, decided to move here and (inspired by reading previous editions of *Staying Off the Beaten Track*) run a bed-and-breakfast house. It wasn't any olde worlde cottage that they fell in love with but this handsome 'twenties house that had been built for Aldis (inventor of the famous signal-lamps which bear his name) on a superb site with a 40-mile sea view south-east as far as Portland Bill. It is a house with handsome features – iron-studded oak doors, leaded casements and window-seats, for example. On sunny mornings (occasionally even in late autumn), you can take breakfast on the wide verandah and enjoy sea breezes while you eat – at your feet, sloping lawns with colourful flowering shrubs such as rhododendrons, camellias, fuchsias and wisteria. On chilly mornings, breakfast is served in an attractive room with crackling fire.

The bedrooms are excellent. Mine was 20 feet long, very comfortably furnished in period with the house, with a thick carpet. By contrast, the even larger family room in scarlet-and-white has Habitat furniture. Each bedroom is equipped with armchairs, TV, a refrigerator, flowers and books – the aim being to provide individual bed-sitters for guests, as there is no communal sitting-room, only a large landing which has seats and a supply of local leaflets, maps and the menus of nearby eating-places (though Elizabeth is prepared to cook evening meals by pre-arrangement – mainly traditional English dishes).

This is a perfect base from which to explore the locality. Sandy beaches with their shrimp-pools are ideal for children. There are excellent walks (in Marshwood Vale or along the coast) including nature trails; drives along lanes of primroses, bluebells and subtropical wild flowers in the downs; Hardy villages; National Trust houses and gardens. You can watch or take part in sea sports, cider-making, pony-trekking and fossil-hunting. Sight-seeing options include a butterfly farm, a vineyard, the Fleet Air Arm Museum, an old tramway and miniature steam railway at Seaton, and Dorset County Museum. The mansion of Cricket St Thomas is where 'To the Manor Born' was filmed.

The following facts have been supplied by the owners:

Bedrooms There are 3 rooms, which include double and family rooms. Bed-and-breakfast costs from £10 (per person in a double room) including service and VAT. There are reductions for stays of 2 nights or more.

All rooms have central heating; washbasin, own bathroom and wc, shaver-point; TV (colour), armchairs; drinks refrigerators; views of sea or garden; tea/coffee-making facilities; door keys.

Surroundings The grounds consist of ⅔ acre of shrubs and lawns. These are available in the neighbourhood: deep sea fishing, riding, canoeing, bowls, golf, safe bathing.

Cars The nearest main road is the A3052 from Lyme Regis to Exeter.

Closed to visitors We are not open from December to February.

Please check prices before booking, and whether there has been any change of ownership (or cook!)

Red Lion, Lacock, south of Chippenham, Wiltshire
Tel: 024973 456   **C(10) D PT ⌗7**

The National Trust owns this historic stone building run by the Levis family. In the 17th century it was a major coaching inn. Its big bars have been kept unspoilt and are full of character. Against terracotta walls hang old farming gear and birdcages; tapestry benches or carved oak settles on Turkey rugs face the stone fireplaces.

Upstairs is a huge dining-room with leather chairs, as well as attractive bedrooms – one has an old half-tester bed. Here, stuffed owls and modern paintings contrast; and on some walls a local artist has painted flowery murals – it was she who chose the good colour schemes of the bedrooms.

rear view

Local produce and home-baked bread contribute to the Red Lion's reputation for good food. Some of the house specialities are duck-liver and damson pâté, pork stuffed with almonds and apricots (served with cider sauce), and ginger snaffles – a confection of shortbread, honey, ice cream, cream and ginger.

Lacock is a showpiece village (not one of its stone or half-timbered buildings is later than the 18th century). Its winding streets lead to Lacock Abbey (National Trust) which dates from the 13th century but was turned into a mansion in Tudor times. The village is within an area of great beauty, its rural peace unspoilt still. In days of wealth (from wool) fine houses and churches were built in creamy Bath stone, still to be found among the wooded dells or fields. Within a short distance are such beauty-spots as Bradford-on-Avon, Castle Combe, Biddestone, Holt and Corsham. The market town of Calne has some fine buildings.

The following facts have been supplied by the owners:

Bedrooms There are 3 rooms, which include single, double and family rooms. Bed-and-breakfast costs from £16 (per person in a double room) including service and VAT; prices go up in high season.

    Some if not all of the rooms have the following amenities: central heating or electric heaters; washbasin, shower, own bathroom and wc, shaver-point; radio, armchairs; views of countryside or garden; orthopaedic mattress or bed-board; tea/coffee-making facilities; door keys. Breakfast in bed is available.

Meals The dinner menu is fixed price (£7.50) or à la carte. There is a choice of dishes on the fixed menu, which consists of 3 courses and coffee. Dinner is served at 7–9 pm. Lunches and packed lunches can be provided; and snacks at other hours. Morning, afternoon or bedtime drinks (coffee, tea etc.) can be ordered for a charge. Wine and other alcoholic drinks can be ordered.

Public rooms There is a sitting-room with central heating, open fire, books, magazines, local guides and leaflets, piano.

Surroundings These are available in the neighbourhood: riding, fishing, golf, clay pigeon shooting, gym.

Cars The nearest main road is the A350 from Chippenham to Warminster.

Redford Cottage, Redford, north-west of Midhurst, West Sussex, GU29 02F   *Tel: 042876 242*   C(6) **D PT S ⌗5**

So tucked away is the little hamlet of Redford that one elderly villager has never been further afield than the nearest small town – and that only once. There was no electricity until some 15 years ago. You might suppose it to be in some remote part of Britain: not so – it's only 1½ hours from London.

In this secluded spot, Caroline and David Angela have made a delightful home from what is basically a Tudor farm cottage with later enlargements that make its rooms zigzag this way and that, and some doors are so low that you must 'duck or grouse'. The big L-shaped sitting/dining-room has a stone hearth with iron fireback dated 1626, a baby grand piano and, in one arm of the L, green velvet chairs around the circular table where meals are served. Numerous paintings and cretonne armchairs furnish the rest of the beamed room.

Glass doors lead to a paved terrace with tubs of hydrangeas where sometimes David (an RAF officer) barbecues steaks by lamplight for visitors relaxing in cushioned cedar chairs, helped by little Charlotte.

There is a second, snug little sitting-room (with log fire) exclusively for visitors using the adjoining ground-floor bedroom. It is almost like having your own suite. The bedroom is delightful: leaded windows on each side (with hydrangea curtains), tufted white spread, and its own celadon-tiled shower-room. There is another attractive bedroom upstairs, overlooking the plum and apple trees with occasional glimpses of deer which stray in from the woods.

Caroline is a gifted cook, using much garden or local produce. On the night when I stayed, she served a prawn-and-haddock savoury followed by pork in a creamy oregano sauce and then rhubarb-and-blackcurrant compôte topped with meringue.

This very attractive area around Haslemere, Petersfield and Petworth is fully described under other entries.

The following facts have been supplied by the owners:

Bedrooms There are 3 rooms, which include single, double and family rooms. Bed-and-breakfast costs from £12 (per person) including service and VAT.

All rooms have central heating or electric heaters; electric blankets, washbasin, own shower or bathroom and wc, shaver-point; radio, TV (colour), armchairs; views of countryside or garden; choice of duvets or blankets; tea/coffee-making facilities; door keys. Breakfast in bed is available.

Meals The dinner menu is fixed price (£6.50). There is no choice of dishes on the menu, which consists of 3 courses. Dinner is served at 7.30 pm. Vegetarian or special diets can be prepared. Morning, afternoon or bedtime drinks (coffee, tea etc.) can be ordered free. Non-residents are not admitted to the dining-room. Wine and other alcoholic drinks can be brought in.

Public rooms There is a sitting-room with central heating, open fire, TV (colour), books, magazines, local guides and leaflets, piano and radio.

Surroundings The grounds consist of 2 acres of garden and paddock. These are available in the neighbourhood: riding, tennis, swimming.

Cars The nearest main road is the A3 from Hindhead to Petersfield.

Languages spoken French, German.

Regency House, Neatishead, north-east of Norwich, Norfolk, NR12 8AD *Tel: 0692 630233* **C D PT X ♯7**

Former Manchester bank-manager Alan Wrigley was so touched by the friendliness of Neatishead people towards a newcomer that, after a few years here, he began planting wayside trees as a 'thank you': the total had reached 1000 when I visited. He and his wife Sue, previously a *Daily Express* reporter, run not only this 18th-century guest-house to an immaculate standard but also the village stores adjoining it.

The breakfasts are outstanding: standard issue is 2 sausages, 4 rashers of bacon, 6 mushrooms, 2 whole tomatoes, 2 slices of fried bread and as many eggs as you request! But if you prefer it, she will produce a vegetarian breakfast instead. This is served in a fresh, white room with stoneware crockery on tables that were specially made by a local craftsman. On the walls are photographs of bygone Neatishead. Bedrooms have Laura Ashley fabrics (the bed in no.6 is king-size) and, in some cases, garden views. (As to dinner, there are two good places in the village to choose from, and others at popular Horning – such as The Swan.)

Pretty little Neatishead, at the centre of the Norfolk Broads, fortunately does not attract the crowds which sometimes ruin Horning, Wroxham and other villages. There is a staithe (mooring) here for fifteen boats – the Wrigleys have a 14-foot dinghy which visitors can use for fishing – and pleasant picnic-spots by the waterside at, for instance, Burton Turf. Some families choose to divide themselves between cabin cruisers (for the younger generation) and Regency House (for older members, who prefer to sleep on shore and boat with their family only by day). There is good cycling around here, too; wildlife and birdwatching; and plenty of sightseeing in mediaeval Norwich and elsewhere. The sandy beaches are easily accessible, too.

The following facts have been supplied by the owners:

Bedrooms There are 5 rooms, which include double and family rooms. Bed-and-breakfast costs from £10 (per person in a double room) including service and VAT; prices go up in high season. There are reductions for stays of 3 nights or more; and 'bargain breaks' as well.

Some if not all of the rooms have the following amenities: electric heaters; washbasin, shaver-point; radio, TV (colour), armchairs; views of countryside or garden; bed-board available; tea/coffee-making facilities; door keys. Breakfast in bed is available.

Meals Lunches and packed lunches can be provided; and snacks at other hours. Morning, afternoon or bedtime drinks (coffee, tea etc.) can be ordered for a charge.

Surroundings The grounds consist of a garden. These are available in the neighbourhood: boating, sailing, fishing.

Cars The nearest main road is the A1151 from Norwich to Yarmouth.

River Park Farm, Lodsworth, west of Petworth, West Sussex, GU23 9DS   *Tel: 07985 362*   C S ⌗5

This farm with 340 acres of corn, bullocks, sheep and poultry is in a secluded position among woods where, if you are up early enough, you may encounter deer. There is a 4½ acre lake with plentiful carp and ducks, and in front a pretty garden. The house itself, built in 1600, is old and beamy with comfortable bedrooms along twisting passageways, and outside are golden roses and wisteria clambering around the door. Altogether it is a pretty and tranquil spot, full of nooks and crannies.

Pat Moss does not do full-scale dinners (available elsewhere locally) but has a list of homely dishes like shepherd's pie or macaroni cheese, and for puddings like banana split she uses rich Jersey cream from the farm's own cow. Bread is home-baked and eggs free-range. There are flowers in every room.

People come for the local walks and birdwatching (Pat has pinned up bird-identification charts and gives visitors field notes on the crops and wildlife in each season, with map, and her own daily nature notes); or to visit the many outstanding 'sights' in this neighbourhood – beginning with one of England's greatest houses at Petworth; or the polo or point-to-points at Cowdray; or to see the local game of stoolball played at Midhurst. There are many small country towns around here, streams running down into the River Rother, woodlands and picturesque villages with greens and duckponds, old inns and ancient churches, Arundel Castle, wildfowl reserve, Goodwood House and Roman remains. Turner knew and loved this area, staying at Petworth House where many of his paintings can be seen. It's a good area for antique shops, too.

Reader's comments: Warm hospitality, generous home cooking.

The following facts have been supplied by the owners:

Bedrooms There are 5 rooms, which include single, double and family rooms. Bed-and-breakfast costs from £8 (per person) including service and VAT. There are reductions for stays of 3 nights or more.

Some if not all of the rooms have the following amenities: central heating or electric heaters; electric blankets, washbasin, shaver-point; armchairs; views of countryside, farmland, garden.

Meals There is a choice of dishes on the fixed menu, which consists of 2 courses and coffee (about £4.50). Dinner is served at 7–8 pm. Packed lunches can be provided. Morning or afternoon drinks (coffee, tea etc.) can be ordered for a charge. Non-residents are not admitted to the dining-room. Wine can be brought in.

Public rooms There is a sitting-room with central heating, open fire, colour TV, books, magazines, local guides and leaflets.

Surroundings The grounds consist of ¾ acre of garden (mainly lawn) and farmland. The following games or sports are available in the grounds: coarse fishing, table tennis. These are available in the neighbourhood: riding, golf, polo, racing, cricket, wildfowl reserve and theatre.

Cars The nearest main road is the A272 from Petworth to Midhurst.

Closed to visitors in winter.

Rhydspence Inn, west of Whitney-on-Wye, Herefordshire
Tel: 04973 262   C ⌗1

This spectacular black-and-white building, typical of so many fine old Herefordshire houses, is perched slightly uphill with splendid views of the lovely Wye Valley and the hills beyond – even so far as Brecon Beacons and the Black Mountains (sometimes snow-capped, sometimes hidden in cloud). There is no other building for miles. A one-time ford ('rhyd') in the River Wye brought the inn into being in the 14th century (though most of the present building is Tudor), at the spot where the Welsh drovers took their sheep and cattle across for sale in English markets. The border between England and Wales runs through the inn's grounds, and the Radnor hills shoot up steeply beside it.

The ground floor is everything you might expect of an ancient inn. Its snug bars have low beams, small windows, stuffed fish in glass cases, and handpumps drawing real ale or draught cider from the cellars below. There's draught barley-wine in winter. Here locals – farmworkers (who drop in after milking the cows) and local doctors or businessmen – meet to chat and play darts or dominoes. Through little windows are views of the valley and hills, and the stone terrace where Peter and Pam Glover put out tables and sunshades in summer.

The building is full of crooked twists and turns, with some walls at a tipsy angle. The bedrooms have been furnished with an elegance and comfort rare in country inns. Flowers are put on the dressing-table, a jar of biscuits on the tea tray. If you want complete quiet, ask for a room not over the bar.

The food is equally exceptional, whether you choose a four-course dinner or just a bar snack (such as game pie). Even the breakfasts are outstanding, with choices that include kidneys and breaded whiting, cooked to perfection (orange juice is freshly squeezed, marmalade and bread are locally made). Some of chef Ray Grosvenor's beautifully cooked specialities for dinner are Wye salmon, guineafowl, beef stroganoff, smoked eel, asparagus with Hollandaise sauce, lemon meringue pie and strawberry pavlova. There are always vegetarian dishes available. Not, I fancy, the kind of fare provided when Kilvert wrote about the inn in his diary: 'ablaze with light and noisy with the songs of revellers' (May Day, 1872). But he may well have seen in use the old cider-mill (horse-operated) which stands outside, or heard the Cwmrafwr brook rushing down its pebbly bed through the dell adjoining the inn.

Herefordshire is a superb county for a holiday. Not only is the scenery exceptional, but it has what other, more famous areas of natural beauty lack: tranquillity, and the feeling of stepping back half a century. There is no difficulty in avoiding busy roads or industrial areas because there are virtually none. Nor is this an area overridden by tourists, though there are plenty of 'sights' to visit.

Within easy reach are the Brecon Beacons National Park, Llanthony Priory, Offa's Dyke (and a long-distance footpath), stately homes and gardens such as Hergest (the azaleas are at their best in May or June), prehistoric sites (go to King Arthur's Stone on Merbach ridge-top for spectacular views – or to Hay Bluff), reservoirs for birdwatching (there are even cormorants on the river, roosting in the trees!), any number of winding lanes and streams and picturesque black-and-white villages like Weobley (cream teas), Pembridge and Eardisland. Hay-on-Wye (full of bookshops) is near; and the Usk valley with canal.

Readers' comments: Very nice rooms and good food. Extremely comfortable and food excellent.

The following facts have been supplied by the owners:

Bedrooms There are 6 bedrooms, which include single and double rooms. Bed-and-breakfast costs £18 (per person in a double room) including VAT. There are 'bargain breaks'.
   All of the rooms have the following amenities: central heating; washbasin, shower or own bathroom and wc, shaver-point; TV (colour and b&w), armchairs; views of countryside, farmland, garden; tea/coffee-making facilities; door keys.

Meals The dinner menu is à la carte. Dinner is served from 7 pm. Special diets can be prepared. Lunches and/or packed lunches can be provided. Wine and other alcoholic drinks can be ordered. Bar snacks are available.

Public rooms There are two bars. The following are available in one or both of them: central heating, open fire, books, magazines, local guides and leaflets, indoor games (such as dominoes, darts, backgammon and chess).

Surroundings The grounds consist of lawns and a stream. These are available in the neighbourhood: theatre, canoeing, pony trekking, salmon and trout fishing, free coarse fishing and golf.

Cars The nearest main road is the A438 from Hereford to Brecon.

Rose-in-Vale Hotel, Mithian, east of St Agnes, Cornwall, TR5 0QD   *Tel: 087255 2202*   C D H S S-C X ⚑5

This handsome 18th-century mansion was originally the home of a local mine captain. A regular visitor to the Nankivel family here was the portrait painter, John Opie, who grew up nearby and painted Joyce Nankivel, 'the belle of Mithian'.

The Arthurs, who honeymooned here only a few years ago, had just taken over the hotel and were still making improvements –

and discoveries – when I was there. In what is now the bar at the back, they have uncovered an unusual stone fireplace with a fringle (bread oven) built into what had been an inglenook fireplace in an old cottage adjoining the 18th-century house. They have added fire-baskets welded by Tony himself: he says his past experience as an engineer has come in handy! He installed central heating himself, too.

There are two large sitting-rooms, now being refurbished to a higher standard, with fine details preserved, such as sash windows with folding shutters. The curving staircase has a decorative window. In a modern extension at the back is a third sitting-room and a very long dining-room with huge windows giving a view of the lawns and rosebeds, with a primrose-banked stream behind. There is a small, sheltered swimming-pool heated by solar panels which, in a good summer, keep the water temperature at 78°. Some ground-floor bedrooms open onto this, but for one with outstanding views from its four windows choose no.1 upstairs. There is also a family suite.

The Arthurs have a good chef – Philip Sims was once at the Imperial Hotel, Torquay, and now lectures part-time at Camborne Catering College. He enjoys preparing such specialities as a hot fish mousse in crab sauce to start with; game or local fish as a main course – or perhaps duck in a sauce of Grand Marnier served with little pancakes containing orange segments and zest; and delicious puddings like an iced soufflé of peaches, surrounded by a purée of raspberries and cream. Take your mother here for the mid-March weekend when he does a special Mother's Day luncheon.

Beyond the sheltered valley and quaint village of Mithian are the well-known surfing beaches of St Agnes and Perranporth (a quieter one is at Trevellas).

The following facts have been supplied by the owners:

Bedrooms There are 15 rooms, which include single, double and family rooms. Dinner, bed-and-breakfast costs from £15.75 (per person in a double room) including service and VAT; prices go up in high season. There are reductions for stays of 2 nights or more; and 'bargain breaks' as well. Sunday accommodation free to over-60s staying 3 days. Sampler breaks (see page 14).
   Some if not all of the rooms have the following amenities: central heating or electric heaters; washbasin, shower, own bathroom and wc, shaver-point; armchairs; views of countryside/farmland/garden; balcony; tea/coffee-making facilities; door keys. Bed-boards on request; hair drier, iron, shoe-cleaning gear.

Meals There is some choice of dishes on the menu, which consists of 3 courses and coffee. Dinner is served at 7 pm. Special diets can be prepared. Lunches and packed lunches can be provided; and snacks at other hours. Morning, afternoon or bedtime drinks (coffee, tea etc.) can be ordered for a charge. Wine and other alcoholic drinks can be ordered.

Public rooms There are 3 sitting-rooms etc. The following are available in one or more of them: central heating, open fire, TV (colour), books, magazines, local guides and leaflets, indoor games (such as cards, darts, table tennis, bar billiards, board games – in separate games room); bar. Bridge can be arranged.

Surroundings The grounds consist of a garden with croquet and swimming-pool. These are available in the neighbourhood: riding, fishing, golf (special terms), gliding, swimming (sea), sailing, surfing, tennis, water skiing, wind surfing.

Cars The nearest main road is the A30 from London to Penzance.

Languages spoken French, German.

Credit cards accepted Access, Visa.

Roundham House Hotel, West Bay Road, Bridport, Dorset, DT6 4BD   *Tel: 0308 22753*   **C D PT S X ⬚3**

Imagine my surprise when I learnt that it was a Gundry (minus my 'e') who built this house in 1903, on the most imposing site between historic Bridport and the quaint harbour at West Bay. He was one of three brothers who founded the ropeworks which is still one of this market town's principal industries – making tennis nets for Wimbledon and helicopter nets used in the Falklands war. From its windows, or from chairs on the terrace, there are superb views across its landscaped and terraced grounds towards sea and countryside.

The Ackermans' choice of Turkey carpet and scarlet hessian on the walls give the big entrance hall (with bar) a warmly welcoming effect. Bedrooms have plenty of space, and I particularly liked room 2, in Wedgwood blue, because from the window-seat in its bay window there are such excellent views.

In the dining-room, where yellow cloths complement brown velvet chairs, one has a choice of freshly cooked dishes that is extraordinarily wide for such a small hotel. After, perhaps, chicken-and-mushroom vol-au-vent or cockles in cheese sauce, you might select venison cooked in port, or plaice with scallop mousse inside puff pastry (served with saffron sauce), and then sherry trifle or apricot flan with whipped cream. Most vegetables come from the garden.

Virtually the whole of west Dorset ('Hardy country') has been designated an area of outstanding natural beauty, and protected as such. Along the coast, cliffs and sands alternate (a good fossil-hunting area). Inland are picturesque thatched villages with mediaeval churches to explore, many stately homes, heaths, woods and well waymarked footpaths. You can go on wagon-rides as a change from motoring or walking.

Reader's comments: Very comfortable; good food and large helpings.

The following facts have been supplied by the owners:

Bedrooms There are 9 rooms, which include single, double and family rooms. Bed-and-breakfast costs from £15 (per person in a double room) including service and VAT; prices go up in high season. There are reductions for stays of 7 nights or more; and 'bargain breaks' as well. Sampler breaks (see page 14).

Some if not all the rooms have the following amenities: central heating or electric heaters; washbasin, shower, own bathroom and wc, shaver-point;

radio, TV (colour), armchairs; views of sea, countryside or garden; choice of duvets or blankets; tea/coffee-making facilities. Breakfast in bed is available.

Meals The dinner menu is fixed price (£7.35) or à la carte. There is a choice of dishes on the fixed menu, which consists of 4 courses and coffee. Dinner is served from 7.30 pm. Vegetarian or special diets can be prepared. Lunches and packed lunches can be provided; and snacks at other hours. Morning, afternoon or bedtime drinks (coffee, tea etc.) can be ordered for a charge. Wine and other alcoholic drinks can be ordered.

Public rooms There are 4 sitting-rooms etc. The following are available in one or more of them: central heating, open fire, TV (colour), books, magazines, local guides and leaflets, indoor games (such as cards, cribbage, dominoes, etc.), organ.

Surroundings The grounds consist of an acre of garden. These are available in the neighbourhood: golf, tennis, squash, bowling (indoor and outdoor), fishing (freshwater and sea), riding, swimming, boating.

Cars The nearest main road is the A35 from Bournemouth to Exeter.

Languages spoken French.

Credit cards accepted Access.

The Russell, Warrior Square, St Leonards-on-Sea, west of Hastings, East Sussex, TN37 6BG
Tel: 0424 431990   C D PT S X ♯3

I have great difficulty in finding houses of real character in the south coast's seaside resorts: a deadly uniformity prevails. The Russell stands out as a glorious exception.

Warrior Square is a stately enclave along the seafront. Its houses were built in the 1860s as holiday retreats for the royal household, which is why a statue of Queen Victoria presides over its wide lawns. It was one of her doctors who owned this particular house: a handsome building on six floors, with decorative ironwork around its bay windows and, indoors, finely carved marble fireplaces with pretty plasterwork decorating the ceilings. The house was named after the doctor.

Only a few years ago, the artistic Streames family moved in and redecorated each room in distinctive colours, using pretty wallpapers, festoon blinds at the vast sash windows, and, on every wall, their own paintings. Most of the soft furnishings were designed and sewn by daughter Laurie, who is also the cook. She made many of the patchwork cushions on the generous sofas that are grouped around gas log fires in the upstairs sitting-room, which is well furnished with antiques, books and interesting objects.

Occasionally, music evenings are held in the house; and beyond the little garden (a courtyard bright with roses in summer) is son Fraser's studio and art gallery which guests are welcome to visit.

The bedrooms vary, but even (unusually) the single rooms are pretty. Those at the front have sea views. The cheapest rooms are on the top floor; but for anyone who finds stairs difficult, a ground-floor bedroom is available.

The kind of meals you may be served in the attractive dining-room (coral walls and chairs contrasting with pale pine furniture) vary, for Laurie will, if given notice, cook whatever guests prefer. But she particularly enjoys producing such French classics as oeufs Florentine or cassoulet de moules for starters and porc Dijonnaise or steak au poivre as main courses.

The half-board tariff, per week, is very good value. St Leonards is a handsome resort which was laid out when doctors started to advocate sea air for health. It has a three-mile seafront parade with all the usual entertainments, stretching to far less sedate Hastings (see page 172). Inland lie the lovely Sussex Downs, where far views contrast with picturesque valley villages. Westward lie Pevensey (Roman and Norman remains) and spectacular Beachy Head. One of the most popular 'sights' in the area, particularly for children, is Drusilla's (outside mediaeval Alfriston): zoo, butterfly farm, rural museum, rides on miniature railway, and adventure playground mainly for the children; winery, pottery, bakery, restaurant for the adults.

Eastbourne is arguably the best of the south coast resorts, neither big nor brash, but with plenty to do and see (pier, boat trips, lifeboat museum, all kinds of entertainments and shops). Its esplanade flowerbeds are outstanding. And here's a tip you'll not find in the guidebooks: at the Grand Hotel (and some others) non-residents who take meals (including tea) are welcome to use the sheltered garden swimming-pool, and to enjoy all its other 5-star amenities too.

The following facts have been supplied by the owners:

Bedrooms There are 13 rooms, which include single, double and family rooms. Bed-and-breakfast costs from £16 (per person in a double room) including service and VAT; prices go up in high season. There are reductions for stays of 7 nights or more; and 'bargain breaks' as well.

Some if not all of the rooms have the following amenities: electric heaters; washbasin, shower, own bathroom and wc, shaver-point; TV (colour), phone, armchairs; views of sea or small garden; tea/coffee-making facilities; door keys.

Meals The dinner menu is fixed price (£7.95) or à la carte. There is a choice of dishes on the fixed menu, which consists of 3 courses and coffee. Dinner is served from 6.30 pm. Vegetarian or special diets can be prepared. Lunches and packed lunches can be provided; and snacks at other hours. Morning and afternoon drinks (coffee, tea etc.) can be ordered for a charge. Wine and other alcoholic drinks can be ordered.

Public rooms There are 2 sitting-rooms etc. The following are available in one or both of them: open fire; books, magazines, local guides and leaflets, piano, record-player and records; bar.

Surroundings The grounds consist of a small walled garden. These are available in the neighbourhood: sports centre, golf, riding.

Cars The nearest main road is the A21 from London to Hastings.

Languages spoken A little French and German.

Credit cards accepted Access, Visa, Diners Club, Amex.

St Christopher's, Boscastle, south of Bude, Cornwall, PL35 0BD
Tel: 08405 412   **C(6) D PT S ⊞4**

This 18th-century house in an unspoilt harbour village (a conservation area) was bought a few years ago by Pierre Bowman who, on being made redundant as a maintenance engineer in Sussex, took a course in catering in order to embark on a new career. He and his wife now run it with their daughter and son-in-law.

One enters the house through a slate-floored hall with roughcast walls. There is a large sitting-room, well furnished with damask wallpaper and a big velvet sofa. It is heated by an open fire, while a log stove warms the cottage-style dining-room that adjoins it. Bedrooms have well-chosen colour schemes: no. 2, for instance, which is L-shaped, is decorated in celadon green-and-white, with cane chairs; the family suite is in tangerine, chocolate and white with pretty cushions and pictures. Right at the top – with high views – is another suite, equipped with velvet sofa, a refrigerator for drinks, and old fiddle-back chairs.

A typical dinner might comprise tuna or vegetable pâté; carbonnade of beef; pavlova; cheeses. (There are choices of starters and puddings.) The wine list is long.

Boscastle lies on one of the most scenic parts of the rugged north Cornwall coast, with Tintagel and its King Arthur associations nearby. This is an area of great contrasts. Castles, sandy beaches, traditional crafts, moorland or coastal footpaths, National Trust houses or gardens and quaint inns all abound.

Reader's comments: Bedrooms, home cooking and atmosphere very good.

The following facts have been supplied by the owners:

Bedrooms There are 8 rooms, which include single, double and family rooms. Bed-and-breakfast costs from £10.50 (per person) including service and VAT; prices go up in high season. There are reductions for stays of 7 nights or more; and 'bargain breaks' as well.

Some if not all of the rooms have the following amenities: central heating; washbasin, shower, own bathroom and wc, shaver-point; TV (colour), armchairs; views of sea/countryside/farmland/garden; door keys.

Meals The dinner menu is fixed price (£7). There is a choice of starters and sweets on the fixed menu, which consists of 4 courses and coffee. Dinner is served at 7 pm. Special diets can be prepared. Packed lunches can be provided. Morning, afternoon or bedtime drinks (coffee, tea etc.) can be ordered for a charge. Wine and other alcoholic drinks can be ordered.

Public rooms There is a sitting-room with central heating, open fire, TV (colour), books, magazines, local guides and leaflets, indoor games (such as cards, Scrabble, cribbage, Monopoly etc.).

Cars The nearest main road is the A39 from Bude to Truro.

Closed to visitors We are not open from mid-November to March.

Scole Inn, Scole, east of Diss, Norfolk, IP22 3HH
Tel: 0379 740481   **C D H X   8**

One of the most remarkable buildings in this book, the inn started life as a grandiose mansion built by a wealthy wool merchant in the 17th century who told his carpenter he wanted the richness of its details to impress 'all the first families in these counties'. One of his visitors was Charles II. Many of these fine architectural features still survive (even in the ladies' loo there is a historic fireplace).

The inn, now managed by Bob Nylk, was originally called The White Hart; and a hart is represented in sculpture over the stables (now bedrooms) which used to service some 40 stage coaches a day – for the inn is near a crossroads where the routes from Ipswich,

383

Norwich, Bury St Edmunds, Thetford and Great Yarmouth converge. (For which reason, avoid travelling here on Saturday mornings in summer – when cars struggle bumper-to-bumper to reach Yarmouth, the Blackpool of the east coast.)

This big building of outstanding historic interest has much carved woodwork as well as a huge and famous staircase – up which young horsemen used to ride for wagers until an irate landlord installed the gate at the top to prevent this.

If you want to sleep in a room haunted by a murdered lady, you can – or spend a quieter night in the sundial room (there's a dial painted on the wall, where the sun strikes it). Modern comforts are in all the bedrooms, though these vary in style. The most striking ones are on the first floor – for instance, one has a half-tester bed, fireplace with coat-of-arms and pretty blue-sprigged fabrics; and two have four-posters. (The residents' large sitting-room is on this floor.) The more modestly furnished rooms (costing less) are at attic level. Those in the stable block are uncompromisingly modern: blue velvet and polished pine fitments contrast with the brick walls.

Locals use the public bar, still with board floor and a spit in the crested fireplace (good bar food is served here). There's another with old settles, and a vast oak fireplace which has the biggest iron grate and fireback I've seen. (Cutting wood and tending all these fires is, in winter, the full-time job of one man.)

The handsome dining-room (with white hart above one of its fireplaces) has tall brass barleysugar candlesticks to light tables laid with brown and gold linen. Here your dinner may, in summer, comprise (for example) melon-and-raspberry cocktail followed by duck with cherries or local crab, then a wide choice of home-made puddings.

This is an excellent spot from which to explore in all directions. Bressingham Hall has fine gardens and steam engines. Beyond Diss (market on Fridays) are the very colourful villages of Burston and Shelfanger. East Dereham has an unusual town sign (two legendary does), an interesting church, an archaeological museum in cottages with decorative plasterwork. Go to the Norfolk Wildlife Park to see bears and others, to Harleston for spring blossom or summer roses and the River Waveney, and Norwich itself is only a few miles away (described elsewhere) with the Broads beyond.

On the Suffolk side, there are historic Bungay and Earlsoham, riverside Debenham, Framlingham's castle, Heveningham Hall and a museum of rural life at Stowmarket. Yoxford village is famous for its cottage gardens. Farming is done on a prairie-size scale, but villages with their little greens, and occasional wind-mills, are a pretty sight.

The following facts have been supplied by the owners:

Bedrooms There are 23 rooms, which include single, double and family rooms. Bed-and-breakfast costs from £22 (per person in a double room) including service and VAT. There are reductions for stays of 2 nights or more; and very good value 'bargain breaks'.

All the rooms have central heating; shower or own bathroom and wc, hair drier, shaver-point, trouser-press; radio, TV (colour), phone, armchairs; views of farmland; orthopaedic mattress or bed-board on request; tea/coffee-making facilities; door keys. Breakfast in bed is available.

Meals The dinner menu is fixed price (£7.50) or à la carte. There is a choice of dishes on the fixed menu, which consists of 3 courses and coffee. Dinner is served from 7 pm. Vegetarian or special diets can be prepared. Lunches and packed lunches can be provided; and snacks at other hours. Morning, afternoon or bedtime drinks (coffee, tea etc.) can be ordered for a charge. Wine and other alcoholic drinks can be ordered.

Public rooms There is a sitting-room with central heating, TV (colour), books, magazines, local guides and leaflets. Also bars.

Surroundings The grounds consist of a beer garden. These are available in the neighbourhood: golf, swimming, riding, fishing, boating.

Cars The nearest main road is the A140 from Ipswich to Norwich.

Credit cards accepted Access, Visa, Amex, Diners Club.

Ship Stores, Callis Street, Clare, east of Haverhill, Suffolk, CO10 8PX *Tel: 0787 277834* **C D PT S X ▦4**

Miles from the sea, this one-time inn was originally called the Sheep not the Ship. Now it is a small shop run by former teacher Norman Kies, with a few simply furnished bedrooms and an upstairs sitting-room for guests. Norman is still uncovering secrets in this building, 400 years old; fireplaces long boarded up, and the original brick floor downstairs, for instance. It is a place of low beams, creaking floors, undulating roof and pink-plastered front: full of character, but very modest (as are its prices). In the breakfast-room there is solid elm furniture locally made; and anyone who wants an out-of-the-ordinary breakfast (pâté? sardines? beans?) is welcome to select from the stock in the grocery.

Clare is a place to explore on foot, to enjoy all the details of its ancient houses – plasterwork decoration, exuberant inn signs, the old Priory. It is close to Cavendish, Sudbury and other attractive parts of Suffolk described elsewhere in this book.

The following facts have been supplied by the owners:

Bedrooms There are 3 rooms, which include single, double and family rooms. Bed-and-breakfast costs from £8 (per person in a double room) including service and VAT. There are reductions for stays of 3 nights or more.

Some if not all of the rooms have the following amenities: central heating or electric heaters; washbasin, shaver-point; TV (b&w), armchairs; view of garden; door keys. Breakfast in bed is available.

Meals Lunches and packed lunches can be provided; and snacks at other hours. Morning, afternoon or bedtime drinks (coffee, tea etc.) can be ordered for a charge.

Public rooms There is a sitting-room with central heating, TV (b & w), books, magazines, local guides and leaflets.

Cars The nearest main road is the A1092 from Long Melford to Haverhill.

Shottle Hall Farm, Shottle, west of Belper, Derbyshire, DG5 2EB
Tel: 077 389 276   **C D H PT S S-C ⌗4**

The house is over a century old and has all the solid Victorian quality of that period: big rooms, fine ceilings and doors, dignity in every detail. Not only the bedrooms but even the bathrooms are large and close-carpeted, with paintwork and everything else in pristine condition. As well as a sizeable sitting-room, there are two dining-rooms – one is used for breakfasts because it gets the morning sun. From both, the huge windows have views of hills and of the fertile valley stretching below the house – much of it is the Matthews' land, on which 120 cows graze (and they also grow cereals). There are a rose garden and lawns – and not another house in sight.

Philip is a former county chairman of the National Farmers Union, a governor of the county agricultural college and an extremely interesting person with whom to discuss agricultural politics, Common Market affairs and so forth. Occasionally, vintage cars rally here. All her guests enjoy Phyllis's straightforward home cooking. A typical dinner menu might include: salmon mousse, chicken in apricot sauce, meringue with raspberries, English cheeses, and coffee with cream. Phyllis collects antique cheese dishes; and has other antiques for sale.

Shottle is in the middle of a rural area of fine landscapes. Close by are the Derbyshire Dales with the Peak District beyond (see pages 222–3). The Matlocks are a hilly area with pretty villages to be found. The old spa of Matlock Bath has interesting places to visit (stately gardens, wildlife park, model village, a museum of mining, and the tower, terraces and caverns of Abraham's Heights). Cromford is both attractive and historic, with Arkwright's first mill, old waterside buildings, a good bookshop, etc. At Crich is a tramway museum. There are six stately homes, a museum of childhood and innumerable good walks in the Peak District, the famous Alton Towers gardens and leisure park, and a cable-car up the Heights of Abraham.

The following facts have been supplied by the owners:

Bedrooms There are 9 rooms, which include single, double and family rooms. Bed-and-breakfast costs from £13 (per person) including service and VAT. There is a discount for over-60s.

   Some if not all of the rooms have the following amenities: central heating; electric blankets, washbasin, shaver-point; armchairs; views of countryside, farmland, garden; door keys. Breakfast in bed is available, as are tea and coffee-making facilities.

Meals The dinner menu is fixed price (£7.50). There is a limited choice of dishes on the menu, which consists of 4 courses and coffee. Dinner is served at 7 pm. Special diets can be prepared. Packed lunches can be provided; and snacks at other hours. Morning, afternoon or bedtime drinks (coffee, tea etc.) can be made by the guests, free. Wine and other alcoholic drinks can be ordered.

Public rooms There is a sitting-room with central heating, magazines, local guides and leaflets and indoor games (such as Scrabble and cards). Also a games room with snooker and TV.

Surroundings The grounds consist of a garden with swing etc., and 340 acres of farmland. These are available in the neighbourhood: riding, golf courses, squash, swimming-pools, cycle hire and trail, and fishing.

Cars The nearest main road is the A517 from Ashbourne to Belper.

Silverdale Hotel, Shore Road, Silverdale, Lancashire, LA5 0TP
Tel: 0524 701206   **C D ⊞2**

Too many motorists on the M6 whiz by this 'area of outstanding natural beauty' with its woods, hills, bird reserve (Leighton Moss) and superb sea views across the sands of Morecambe Bay. This attractive countryside is threaded with footpaths.

The hotel is (outside high summer, when the area is full of caravanners) a centre for birdwatchers, and for those who seek out the rare butterflies at Leighton Moss. It is a comfortable, unassuming inn where one can enjoy real ale while watching, in the garden or from a little sun parlour, the sun setting over the fells and bay; or warm one's toes at the log fire in the oak-panelled Copper Room adjoining the bar.

Saturday-night dances, and other gatherings, can make the hotel a bit noisy at times; but the rear bedrooms (which have the best views) are not disturbed by this.

In the dining-room, there is much emphasis on local fish, especially Morecambe shrimps, of course; and sometimes plaice-like flukes which visitors catch with their hands, after treading them out of the sands where they lie hidden at low tide. Among

Nichola Moat's specialities are trout stuffed with celery and almonds, and pork schnitzel.

She and her husband Geoff are a young couple who in 1984 gave up other careers to run the hotel in partnership with their friends Shirley and Graham Hamlett.

This house provides an ideal stopover for a few days on the way to or from Scotland; or as a base from which to explore the wonderful scenery of the Forest of Bowland (moors contrasting with craggy valleys and streams), the southern half of the Lake District, the coast and its estuaries – don't miss quaint little Glasson Dock as well as vast Morecambe Bay, and the Yorkshire Dales. You can take canal boat trips, visit stately homes and museums, or go on a day-trip to the Isle of Man.

(Other attractions in the nearby Carnforth and Lancaster areas are described on page 295.)

The following facts have been supplied by the owners:

Bedrooms There are 9 rooms, which include single, double and family rooms. Bed-and-breakfast costs from £12.50 (per person in a double room) including service and VAT.

   Some if not all of the rooms have the following amenities: electric heaters; washbasin, shower, own bathroom and wc, shaver-point; radio, armchairs; views of sea/countryside/farmland/garden; door keys.

Meals Dinner is served from 7 pm. Special diets can be prepared. Lunches and packed lunches can be provided; and snacks at other hours. Morning, afternoon or bedtime drinks (coffee, tea etc.) can be ordered for a charge. Wine and other alcoholic drinks can be ordered.

Public rooms There is a sitting-room with central heating, open fire, TV, books, magazines, local guides and leaflets, piano, bar.

Surroundings The grounds consist of a garden.

Cars The nearest main road is the A6 from Manchester to the Lake District.

Credit cards accepted Access.

Singleton Lodge Farm, Singleton, east of Blackpool, Lancashire, FY6 8LT   *Tel: 0253 883854*   **C D PT X**

This 18th-century house was in turn a vicarage, a boarding school, and a home for admirals from Fleetwood, but the Smiths have been farming here for several generations. A long drive approaches the house. There is a handsome panelled door in the mellow brick front.

Inside, the rooms upstairs and down are furnished comfortably but without any pretensions to elegance. Mrs Smith, who loves cooking, produces good homely meals with home-made soup, roasts (their own meat) and fruit pies.

It's a tranquil place, yet Blackpool is easily accessible for its sands and entertainments, or the quieter resort of Lytham St Anne's. There are plenty of stately homes to visit, the port of Fleetwood, Lancaster's historic streets, the great sandy bay of Morecambe, and the magnificent, wild Trough of Bowland. The Lake District is within easy motoring distance.

In the immediate neighbourhood are plenty of good walks. Nearby Poulton-le-Fylde has an ancient church, stocks and fish stones.

The following facts have been supplied by the owners:

Bedrooms There are 7 rooms, which include single, double and family rooms. Bed-and-breakfast costs from £10 (per person) including service and VAT. There are reductions for stays of 7 nights or more. Sunday accommodation free to over-60s staying 3 days.

    Most rooms have the following amenities: central heating or electric heaters; electric blankets, washbasin, shower, own bathroom and wc, shaver-point; views of countryside, farmland, garden; tea/coffee-making facilities; colour TV; door keys. Ironing facilities are available.

Meals The dinner menu is fixed price (£6.25). There is a choice of dishes on the menu, which consists of 3 courses and coffee. Dinner is served at 6 pm. Special diets can be prepared. Snacks can be ordered. Afternoon or bedtime drinks (coffee, tea etc.) are free. Wine and other alcoholic drinks can be brought in.

Public rooms There is a sitting-room with central heating, open fire, colour TV, books, magazines, local guides and leaflets and indoor games (such as cards).

Surroundings The grounds consist of a large garden with croquet and swing, and pasture land. Available in the neighbourhood: riding, golf, boating, swimming-pools and a sports centre.

Cars The nearest main road is the A585 from Preston to Fleetwood.

Snowford Hall Farm, Hunningham, north of Southam, Warwickshire, CU33 9ES   *Tel: 0926 632297*   C S ⌗6

A very long drive through fields leads to this spacious 18th-century house at the heart of a 300-acre farm (cattle and crops) with fine views around it. One enters through an interesting hall with old china on a big dresser and polished wood floor. The huge sitting-room is very attractively furnished. Here and there around the house are many things made by Rudi Hancock herself, a skilled craftswoman – samplers, for example, and corn dollies; and furniture which she has restored.

Dutch-born, she was previously a cookery teacher and so (except at harvests, when she has no time to cook evening meals) you can expect a good dinner, if booked in advance. She uses many home-grown vegetables and fruit, and makes her own jam.

The most interesting of the bedrooms has a very unusual and decorative Dutch bed of solid mahogany, handsomely carved.

Snowford Hall is near Leamington Spa and its environs, described on page 247.

The following facts have been supplied by the owners:

Bedrooms There are 3 rooms, which include single, double and family rooms. Bed-and-breakfast costs from £10 (per person) including service and VAT. There are reductions for stays of 2 nights or more.

  Some if not all of the rooms have the following amenities: central heating or electric heaters; washbasin, shower, shaver-point; armchairs; views of countryside, farmland, garden; choice of duvets or blankets. Hair drier available. No smoking.

Meals The dinner menu is fixed price (£7.50). There is no choice of dishes on the fixed menu, which consists of 4 courses and coffee. Dinner is served at 6.30 pm. Afternoon or bedtime drinks (coffee, tea etc.) can be ordered free. Non-residents are not admitted to the dining-room. Wine and other alcoholic drinks can be brought in.

Public rooms There is a sitting-room with central heating, open fire, TV (colour), books, magazines, local guides and leaflets, piano. Maps on loan.

Surroundings The grounds consist of garden and farmland.

Cars The nearest main road is the A423 from Coventry to Banbury.

Somerset House, 35 Bathwick Hill, Bath, Avon, BA2 6LD
Tel: 0225 66451   C(9) **D H PT S X ▒5**

What makes this so special is not just the architecture, nor even the imaginative cooking, nor the 'activity' weekends (of which more later), but the exceptional atmosphere which Malcolm and Jean Seymour unobtrusively create. No one could possibly feel unwelcome or lonely here. Those who come back regularly soon make friends with one another as well as with the Seymours.

The Seymours moved to this handsome Georgian mansion from a smaller house down the steep hill. Above the Doric-columned portico is a decorative iron verandah; wisteria and roses climb up the walls of honey-coloured stone.

The entrance hall (marble-tiled and with a Greek key border round the ceiling) leads to a sitting-room, with conservatory opening onto lawn, grand piano, fire and abundant books and records. There is one bedroom on the ground floor. The dining-room is downstairs (it, too, has an open fire), furnished with pine dresser, etc.; plants are visible through the windows.

On the first floor is another sitting-room with a particularly pretty plasterwork ceiling and very old Venetian glass chandelier. The original panelled shutters flank the huge sash windows; outside is the long verandah, from which there are fine city views beyond the other elegant houses on the hill.

Bedrooms are large and pleasantly furnished, many with antique fireplaces (one has an antique loo) and attractive views. Some have Laura Ashley fabrics and wallpapers. Each is named for one of the children of George III. (This is a no smoking house.)

Malcolm (once director of a regional tourist board and now a part-time adviser on historic churches and their interpretation to visitors) is a mine of information on what to see in the neighbourhood. Throughout the year he arranges weekends with special themes: Georgian Bath, exploring the Mendip and Cotswold hills, Brunel, or opera whenever the Welsh National Opera Company visits nearby Bristol. Jean, formerly a teacher, enjoys finding recipes appropriate to each of these occasions (even Czech ones on the night when a Janáček opera was being performed), and she gladly shares her knowledge with visitors.

At breakfast, few people opt for the full cooked version because there is such an array of home-baked breads (nutty, spicy or fruity), preserves, muesli, freshly squeezed fruit juice and so forth; often haddock, kidneys, Cumberland sausage or muffins are offered. As to dinner, when nothing more exotic is afoot, Jean may produce something like (for example) game soup, her own 'rolypoly, gammon and spinach' recipe with home-grown vegetables, and apples in cider served with home-made ice cream. Vegetarians are welcome.

Jean has found many Somerset recipes to cook; searches out suppliers of good local produce (even the flour is stone-ground at a local mill); makes yogurt and cheeses from her own goats' milk.

Perhaps the greatest glory is the garden. Every tree flowers at a different season, and the centrepiece is a great 300-year-old Judas tree – at its purple best in May. All around, between beds of paeonies and columbines, is a 7¼"-gauge rail track installed by a former owner. Adjoining is a herb and fruit garden, for one corner of which a barbecue area is planned.

From Bathwick Hill it is only a 10-minute walk down to the city centre with its abbey, gardens, shopping arcades, pump-room, Roman temple and baths, award-winning gardens and much else. A bus will bring you uphill again, stopping almost outside the door. Within minutes of Somerset House is a spanking new leisure centre with every kind of indoor sport; refreshing canalside walks and cruises, and the outstanding museum of American arts and historic crafts occupying a beautiful Georgian house and its grounds. There is more about the area on pages 330 and 341–2.

The following facts have been supplied by the owners:

Bedrooms There are 9 rooms, which include single, double and family rooms. **To readers of this book only**, dinner, bed-and-breakfast costs from £25.50 (per person in a double room) including service and VAT. There are reductions for stays of 5 nights or more; and midweek 'bargain breaks' as well. Sampler breaks (see page 14).

   The rooms have the following amenities: central heating; electric blankets, own bathroom, shaver-point; armchairs; views of city or garden; choice of duvets or blankets; phone, tea-making facilities, door keys; orthopaedic mattresses.

Meals There is a choice of dishes on the fixed menu, which consists of 4 courses and coffee. Dinner is served at 7–8 pm. Special diets can be prepared if ordered in advance. Lunches available on Wednesdays, Fridays and Sundays. Wine and other alcoholic drinks can be ordered.

Public rooms There is a sitting-room with central heating, open fire, TV (colour), books, magazines, local guides and leaflets, indoor games (such as Monopoly and backgammon), piano.

Surroundings The grounds consist of a large garden. These are available in the neighbourhood: golf, fishing and a sports centre.

Cars The nearest main road is the A36 from Bath to Southampton.

Languages spoken French, German.

Credit cards accepted Visa, Access.

Spiders Barn, Pickwick, north of Corsham, Wiltshire, SN13 0DT
Tel: 0249 712012   C(4) **D PT S** ⌗7

The Pickwick Papers got its name from this hamlet, for it was here – at the Cross Keys Inn – that Dickens reputedly stayed while writing his book. The old coaching stables adjoining the Cross Keys (which provides good bar meals) are now the very well converted home of Anne Norris who takes guests for bed-and-breakfast.

In the stone-walled sitting-room with parquet floor are a huge chesterfield and pieces of antique furniture. Every bedroom is attractive, with the emphasis on well-chosen fabrics, stripped pine for the latched doors and the staircase, good carpets, cane chairs and pleasant colour schemes such as coffee and cream.

Wiltshire is, I feel, an undervalued county for in addition to its rolling countryside there is so much to see – outstandingly, its 4500 prehistoric sites (of which Stonehenge may be the most famous but is not the most impressive), which make it pre-eminent in England and possibly Europe. And it has nearly a dozen National Trust or comparable stately homes – full of treasures. South of Spiders Barn are, for instance, Wilton, Stourhead, Mompesson House (within the precincts of Salisbury Cathedral); even nearer Bowood, Lacock Abbey and Longleat. In fact, the county has more listed buildings than any other, and many of its villages are little beauties.

Reader's comments: Very comfortable. Made most welcome.

The following facts have been supplied by the owners:

Bedrooms There are 4 rooms, which include single, double and family rooms. Bed-and-breakfast costs from £10 (per person in a double room) including service and VAT.

Some if not all of the rooms have the following amenities: central heating; washbasin, shaver-point; radio, armchairs; views of countryside/farmland/garden; tea/coffee-making facilities; door keys. Breakfast in bed is available.

Public rooms There is a sitting-room with central heating, open fire, TV (colour), books, magazines, local guides and leaflets, indoor games (such as Monopoly, Cluedo, Yahtzee, cards, chess, dominoes).

Surroundings The grounds consist of a garden. These are available in the neighbourhood: swimming, golf, tennis, squash, riding, cycling.

Cars The nearest main road is the A4 from Chippenham to Bath.

Languages spoken French, German.

Sportsman's Arms, Wath-in-Nidderdale, Pateley Bridge, west of Harrogate, North Yorkshire, HG3 5PP
Tel: 0423 711306   C D PT X ⌗12

This 17th-century inn was very run down when the Carters took it over a few years ago. Now it is a delightful place, in an equally delightful setting. The area is described on pages 200–201; Wath is a hamlet tucked away beside the River Nidd.

A pine-panelled bar leads to the dining-room (and, beyond this, two sitting-rooms) which has palms, pale pink wallpaper and bentwood chairs, reflected by the light of cut-crystal candle-lamps in the big mirror of a carved Victorian sideboard. Jane Carter has chosen pink/green and pink/beige colour schemes for bedrooms in which wallpapers, curtains and bedspreads match. Huge Victorian baths have been retained. Ray, who used to be a catering lecturer, cooks all the meals, assisted by a team of enthusiastic young people. A typical summer dinner: mango with a sauce of cucumber, cream cheese and herbs; salmon Hollandaise; and summer pudding. The cooking is outstanding, and most produce is local. Vegetarians are welcome. Wines are outstanding and reasonably priced.

Lovely Nidderdale, being outside the National Park area, is less frequented than some other dales. It has some very old reservoirs created by damming the River Nidd, now well naturalized and full of ducks, geese, herons and other birds (200 species have been recorded, including some rare migrants). The effect is reminiscent of the Lake District. How Stean is a romantic gorge with a stream cascading into a rocky cleft 70 feet deep (good home-made cakes at the modest café nearby). From the churchyard at Middlemoor, high up at the head of the dale, there are spectacular views down the length of it. It's marvellous motoring or walking country, with plenty of other places of interest to visit not far away.

From here one can easily motor to York, Ripon spa (with cathedral), and a great array of spectacular abbeys – Fountains, Bolton, Jervaulx, Rievaulx and Byland. Also Harewood Hall, Newby Hall and half a dozen castles; as well as the strange natural formations of Brimham Rocks and Stump Cross caves.

Readers' comments: Food fabulous, staff well trained and friendly. Food very good, and staff appeared to be one largish happy family.

The following facts have been supplied by the owners:

Bedrooms There are 7 rooms, which include single, double and family rooms. Bed-and-breakfast costs from £17 (per person in a double room) including service and VAT. 20% off in winter (until Easter).

Some if not all of the rooms have the following amenities: central heating or electric heaters; electric blankets; firm mattresses or bed-boards; washbasin, shower, shaver-point; armchairs; views of river, countryside, farmland, garden; tea/coffee-making facilities; door keys. Breakfast in bed is available. No smoking.

Meals The dinner menu is à la carte with a set menu option for residents. Dinner is served at 7.30–9.45 pm. Special diets can be prepared. Lunches and packed lunches can be provided; and snacks at other hours. Morning, afternoon or bedtime drinks (coffee, tea etc.) can be ordered for a charge. Wine and other alcoholic drinks can be ordered.

Public rooms There are 3 sitting-rooms etc. The following are available in one or more of them: open fire, TV (colour), books, magazines, local guides and leaflets, indoor games (such as dominoes, cards, etc.), bar.

Surroundings The grounds consist of ½ acre of garden, with badminton. These are available in the neighbourhood: riding, golf, fishing (hotel has private fly fishing).

Languages spoken French.

Credit cards accepted Diners Club, Access, Visa, Amex.

Spring End, Low Row, west of Richmond, North Yorkshire, DL11 6NL   *Tel: 0748 86341*   **C D S X ⌗9**

Swaledale is a place for active holidays: the roads are too narrow, steep and twisting for relaxed motoring, and there are few contrived 'attractions' for the passive holiday-maker. So the Thompsons have organized their guest-house with walkers in mind.

After a day on the fells, you can have a drink at the bar, eat a meal of generous and fairly simple food (such as leek soup, chicken casserole and chocolate gâteau), and then collapse in a comfortable sitting-room, where there are shelves of books – guides, local history, and fiction – but no television to kill conversation. On sale is a huge selection of books of local interest as well as some well-chosen souvenirs. Vegetarians catered for.

Spring End is a long and rambling house, with additional bedrooms in the adjoining farmhouse and in a modern annexe (a good choice for a large family, who would have it to themselves). The house is furnished for comfort rather than effect, and Marion and David Thompson radiate unpretentious hospitality.

Spring End takes a little finding – it is perched on the fell side with spectacular views, with a village far below – but, once there, visitors tend to abandon the car until it is time to go home again.

There is information about Swaledale on pages 207 and 347.

The following facts have been supplied by the owners:

Bedrooms There are 11 rooms, which include single, double and family rooms. Dinner, bed-and-breakfast costs from £18 (per person) including VAT. There are reductions for stays of 7 nights or more; and 'bargain breaks' as well.

   Some if not all of the rooms have the following amenities: central heating or electric heaters; electric blankets, washbasin, shower, own bathroom and wc, shaver-point; TV (b&w), armchairs; views of countryside; choice of duvets or blankets; tea/coffee-making facilities; door keys.

Meals There is a choice of dishes on the fixed menu, which consists of 4 courses and coffee. Dinner is served at 6.30 pm. Packed lunches can be provided; and snacks at other hours. Morning, or bedtime drinks (coffee, tea etc.) can be ordered free. Wine and other alcoholic drinks can be ordered.

Public rooms There are 3 sitting-rooms etc. The following are available in one or more of them: central heating, open fire, books, magazines, local guides and leaflets, indoor games (such as dominoes, cards and chess), bar. Bridge can be arranged.

Surroundings The grounds consist of a small garden. Pony-trekking and fishing are available in the neighbourhood.

Cars The nearest main roads are the A1 and M6.

Closed to visitors We are not open in January and February.

The Stables, Bootle village, near Millom, Cumbria
Booking service: 0498 81563   **C PT S ⌗2**

Where four horse-drawn coaches were once parked is now a huge sitting-room, with picture windows on three sides. This was the carriage-room of stables which used to serve the great house of a family that grew rich from the manufacture of candles (their tallow was made from sheep fat). The original beams and doors have been kept and the fireplace is simply an opening in the old brick wall, so the room retains something of the character of the original building. Similarly, when the tack-room was converted into a dining-room the hooks on which harness used to hang were kept.

This transformation, completed in only two years, was the work of just two people: Pete and Mary, who now run the old stables as a guest-house. They used to come to this part of Cumbria for their holidays, and fell in love with it – though Pete Walker continues working as one of the BBC's outside broadcast supervisors in London.

The deep-carpeted bedrooms are attractive. One, decorated in a coffee-and-cream colour scheme, has a huge circular window opposite the bed. There are always flowers in the bedrooms (and on the candle-lit dining-tables too). All have private bathrooms.

The same menu is never repeated within a fortnight and, as far as possible, Mary cooks whatever dishes her guests like best. A typical menu might be: eggs with home-made mayonnaise; a joint or chicken which guests carve themselves, or perhaps local trout with almonds; lemon meringue pie, cheese and coffee. As an alternative to traditional breakfasts, Mary offers kedgeree, smoked mackerel or haddock and other choices.

The two are a particularly warm, genial couple who make their guests feel at home – for instance, encouraging them to wander off with a tray of tea to where, at the end of the little bluebell copse, their bubbling stream joins the River Annas. They grow vegetables and fruit, have planted daffodils and forget-me-nots, and laid a terrace of great slabs from St Bees, the red sandstone headland along the coast. There are marvellous views over lawn and fields to the hills, and you can smell the sea in the air. In spring, the grounds have a spectacular display of wild daffodils.

There are sea views from peaks, stone bridges over the river, valley walks and many historic little towns to explore. Black

Combe mountain is nearly 2000 feet high and from its summit can be seen Ireland and the Isle of Man. Not far from the village of Bootle are Muncaster Castle, the fishing village and bird reserve of Ravenglass (remains of a Roman fort, too), an old steam railway up into the hills, and the wildest of all the lakes, Wastwater. A little further are clifftop walks, and the small Georgian port of Whitehaven where you can wander on the quays to watch cargo ships loading or visit some of the old coal-mine workings (there's also a well displayed local museum).

Readers' comments: Memorable holiday. Warm and friendly welcome, excellent accommodation, beautiful situation, superb meals – a jewel of a place.

The following facts have been supplied by the owners:

Bedrooms There are 2 rooms, usable as single, double or family rooms. Bed-and-breakfast costs £11.75 (per person) including service and VAT. Sampler breaks (see page 14).
   Both rooms have the following amenities: central heating; electric blankets, own bathroom and wc, shaver-point; radio, armchairs; views of countryside, farmland, garden; choice of duvets or blankets; bed-boards.

Meals The dinner menu is fixed price (£7.25). There is no choice of dishes on the menu, which consists of 4 courses and coffee. Dinner is served by arrangement. Special diets can be prepared. Packed lunches can be provided. Morning, afternoon or bedtime drinks (coffee, tea etc.) can be ordered. Wine and other alcoholic drinks can be brought in. Free tea on arrival.

Public rooms There are 2 sitting-rooms. The following are available in one or both of them: central heating, open fire, colour TV, books, magazines, local guides and leaflets and indoor games (such as cards, dominoes and table games).

Surroundings The grounds consist of an acre of garden, lawns, river and stream. These are available in the neighbourhood: swimming-pool, horse riding, fishing, walking, hill-trekking and climbing.

Cars The nearest main road is the A595 from Barrow to Whitehaven.

The Steppes, Ullingswick, north-east of Hereford, HR1 3JG
Tel: 0432 820424   C(12) **D H X ♯3**

This is one of the prettiest old houses in this book – typical of the whitewashed stone farm houses in Herefordshire, and now very attractively furnished by its owners Henry and Tricia Howland – added to which is the extra appeal of particularly good food.

   Part of the house is mediaeval, most of it 17th century. Originally, the ground floor was one great hall, with a cross-passage at the end: these now form the dining-room and entrance-hall (the old flagstoned floor is still intact).

The dining-room has a great inglenook fireplace with its original log-irons, and there is a bread oven adjoining its chimney. In the thick walls are original built-in cupboards, and between some rooms 'borrowed lights' (that is, internal windows) with their original glass. The red-and-black tiles of the dining-room are also old. The Howlands have unearthed all sorts of historical curiosities from the house: a stone slab for pig-salting, a Victorian cream separator, a Georgian gambling token (contrasting with the parlour's later use for hymn-singing gatherings round the harmonium) and rare sideways-sliding sash windows.

The beamed dining-room, with a patterned rug on its old tiled floor and dried hop-bines draped across the fireplace, has great character. There are corn-dollies on the white walls, flowers on each table, interesting prints, and a melodiously chiming clock – in total contrast to what the Howlands refer to as the 'little modern box' where they lived until Henry gave up his London practice as a solicitor to move to this remote spot. The Howlands have haunted local auctions to find the unusual bits and pieces which add so much to The Steppes' charm. Virtually all the work of conversion was done by Henry, who had some thirty years of neglect to tackle. He exposed beams and stripped doors, carefully retaining the handsome old iron hinges.

There is a small bar which includes half a dozen kinds of local cider, from clear-and-sparkling to rough-and-heavy. In the sitting-room, flowery chairs and pale velvet curtains contrast with the rugged stone fireplace. Quaint pastry dolls hang on some walls – made by Tricia (a few for sale).

Each bedroom has a different and colourful style – raspberry-pink wall and rosebud fabrics in one, crisp blue-and-white in another; built-in pine storage fitments, pretty lace curtains or deep-pile carpets contribute to the individual character of each one. Each has its own shower. Views are of rounded hills, sheep or cows, hop kilns and the old garden where collared doves perch in cherry trees or lilac spreads its fragrance in early summer. The old pump still draws water to fill a stone trough.

Tricia cooks a wide range of very imaginative dishes and ensures that not one is repeated during a guest's stay. One local speciality which she serves is cheese-and-cider soup (chilled and creamy); another unusual starter is grapefruit with mint ice. The main course might be boned duck with a stuffing of beef, onions, bacon and herbs, or turkey saté (served with peanut sauce and cucumber relish – a Thai recipe). A pudding such as zabaglione, fresh blackberry flan or a raspberry meringue gâteau may follow – and then cheeses. Gourmet food is complemented by cutlery from Harrods, Renaissance music and good-value classic wines.

Breakfast choices include muffins, mackerel, Arbroath smokies and Loch Fyne kippers.

The house is in a tiny hamlet in the Wye valley, near many of the same Herefordshire attractions as are described on pages 406–7. Wales is close, too.

Reader's comment: Thoroughly enjoyed it.

The following facts have been supplied by the owners:

Bedrooms There are 3 rooms, which include double and family rooms. Bed-and-breakfast costs from £14 (per person in a double room), including service and VAT; prices go up in high season. There are reductions for stays of 3 nights or more; and 'bargain breaks' as well.

The rooms have the following amenities: central heating; washbasin, shower and wc, shaver-point; clock-radio, colour TV, armchairs; views of countryside, farmland, garden; door keys. Continental breakfast in bed is available, as are tea and coffee-making facilities. Orthopaedic mattress on request. Laundry room available (for a charge).

Meals There is no choice of dishes on the fixed menu (£10), which consists of 4 courses and coffee, unless other dishes are ordered in advance. Vegetarian and special diets cost more. Dinner is served at 7 pm or later on request. Lunches and/or packed lunches can be provided; and snacks at other hours. Morning, afternoon or bedtime drinks (coffee, tea etc.) can be ordered for a charge. Non-residents are not admitted to the dining-room. Wine and other alcoholic drinks can be ordered. No smoking.

Public rooms There is a sitting-room with central heating, log stove, TV, books, magazines, local guides and leaflets, indoor games (such as Scrabble and Monopoly). Bridge can be arranged.

Surroundings The grounds consist of 1½ acres of garden. These are available in the neighbourhood: riding, fishing. Golf breaks arranged.

Cars The nearest main road is the A417 from Gloucester to Leominster.

Stoke Farm, Broad Chalke, west of Salisbury, Wiltshire, SP5 5EF
Tel: 0722 780209   C PT S S-C ♯9

This is a gracious house at the heart of a 1000-acre farm overlooking the Ebble valley. It is very typical of many other such farms set among the rolling downs of Wiltshire: a mixture of arable fields and of pastures for beef-cattle and dairy-cows (some 600 of them).

One approaches the house past mossy rickstones, old cattle-troughs now filled with flowers, and tree-stumps overgrown by periwinkles. A lovely magnolia covers the front wall. Inside, the early Victorian features have been retained – panelled doors, arches and window shutters. My bedroom had windows on three sides with pretty 'cottage garden' curtains and views across fields of cows to the hills. Late in the year, the pens immediately below are full of calves. Throughout the house, soft colours predominate, with carefully arranged flowers, baskets of trailing plants and interesting paintings well lighted (one is by Cecil Beaton, who used to live in the village). There are good carpets and attractive wallpapers everywhere, even in the bathroom. In the big sitting-room, deep armchairs are grouped around a log fire, a record-player and well stocked bookshelves. Last but far from least, Mrs Pickford is an excellent cook. Meals are served in a dining-room that still has the old built-in bread oven, with local trout and pheasant often on the menu.

Many guests go walking. The Pickfords have produced their own map of local footpaths, all well waymarked in this region, which lead down to watercress beds in the valley or up to the Ridgeway which was once a drove road for oxen being taken to market.

I stayed here in order to visit nearby Salisbury (see page 319). In addition there is plenty to see in the area – Elizabethan Breamore House, attractive villages (like Downton, Fordingbridge or Tilshead), the Celtic fort on top of Figsbury hill, Old Sarum with the ruins of its Norman castle on another hilltop, the Roman villa at Rockbourne and Wilton's historic carpet factory, for example.

The following facts have been supplied by the owners:

Bedrooms There are 3 rooms, which include single, double and family rooms. Bed-and-breakfast costs from £13 (per person) including service and VAT. There are reductions for stays of 7 nights or more; and 'bargain breaks' as well.

Some if not all of the rooms have the following amenities: central heating or electric heaters; hot water bottles, washbasin, own shower or bathroom and wc, shaver-point; radio, TV, phone; armchairs; views of farmland, garden; choice of duvets or blankets; tea/coffee-making facilities. Breakfast in bed is available.

Meals There is no choice of dishes on the fixed menu (£8), which consists of 3 courses and coffee. Dinner is served at 7 pm. Special diets can be prepared. Morning, afternoon or bedtime drinks (coffee, tea etc.) can be ordered. Non-residents are not admitted to the dining-room. Wine and other alcoholic drinks can be ordered or brought in.

Public rooms There is a sitting-room with central heating, open fire, colour TV, books, magazines, local guides and leaflets, indoor games (such as Scrabble, billiards, darts and cards), piano, record-player and records.

Surroundings The grounds consists of ¾ acre of garden with tennis and croquet. These are available in the neighbourhood: golf, riding, squash, swimming-pool, motor racing, coarse fishing, tennis, theatre.

Cars The nearest main road is the A354 from Salisbury to Blandford.

Closed to visitors The farm is closed to visitors in February and for the first week in July.

405

Stone House Farm, Tillington, north-west of Hereford, HR4 8LP
Tel: 0432 760631   **C D PT X ♯3**

This is a good, solid stone farmhouse typical of many in the rich agricultural lands of Herefordshire. Well away from any town or road, it is completely peaceful, and with fine views at both front (distant Aconbury Hill beyond a small orchard) and back (field of grazing horses and then woodlands). At the front, a small garden (with a seat on the stone terrace) still has the old pump which, only a generation ago, was the sole source of water for the house.

In the sitting-room, big velvet armchairs surround the fireplace, but in winter guests use a cosy 'den' with wood stove. The dining-room, too, has an open fire, and a large oak table laid with Royal Worcester bone china. Straightforward dinners are cooked by Judy Seaborne: typically, soup followed by a stew or roast (the farm's own beef, lamb or pork), and then perhaps a pavlova or fruit pie. Milk, butter and cream are usually from Stone House cows, and Mrs Seaborne makes all the cakes, pickles and marmalade and will cook fish for breakfast if you prefer it.

Bedrooms are comfortable; the carpeted bathroom is huge. And Judy's daughter, a qualified beauty therapist, can provide treatments during your stay.

Children particularly enjoy this small farm in spring when lambs, calves and foals are to be seen. Graham Seaborne, whose family has farmed here for generations, will tell visitors where to go to watch the big cattle and horse auctions every week in Hereford, or to see cider being made and ploughing matches in the autumn.

From Tillington, there are plenty of sightseeing options. The picturesque black-and-white village of Eardisland is close, as is Weobley. There are a dozen bookshops (most belonging to Richard Booth) in Hay-on-Wye, now nicknamed 'Book City'. Brecon, Offa's Dyke and numerous stately homes provide other destinations for a day out; and, as this is an area of orchards and nursery gardens, many people return home laden with pot-plants and 'pick-your-own' soft fruits. The Malvern Hills and the Black Mountains are within sight, and several market towns are nearby. Hereford Cathedral is within view. Add to these the Brecon Beacons, Radnor Forest, Welsh and Shropshire market towns, a motor museum and a lovely drive along Wenlock Edge, Iron-bridge Industrial Museum, the Wye Valley, and Hereford's cider museum, and you can see why a fortnight is too short a stay. (There is more about this area on pages 374–5.)

Readers' comments: Very comfortable; well fed and received with great friendliness; no book could describe the warmth and friendliness and the trouble to ensure our stay was enjoyable; accommodation and food of very high quality ... ample. Mrs Seaborne is most welcoming. The best farmhouse we've found in 25 years.

The following facts have been supplied by the owners:

Bedrooms There are 3 rooms, which include single, double and family rooms. Bed-and-breakfast costs £11.50 (per person in a double room) including service and VAT. There are reductions for stays of 7 nights or more, and 'bargain breaks' as well. Sampler breaks (see page 14). Sunday accommodation free to over-60s staying 3 days.
    Some if not all of the rooms have the following amenities: central heating or electric heaters; electric blankets, washbasin, shaver-point; armchairs; views of countryside and farmland; choice of duvets or blankets; tea/coffee-making facilities on request; door keys. Breakfast in bed is available; also hair drier and laundry facilities.

Meals There may be a choice of dishes on the menu (£6), which consists of 4 courses and coffee. Dinner is served at any time. Special diets can be prepared. Lunches or packed lunches can be provided; and snacks at other hours. Morning, afternoon or bedtime drinks (coffee, tea etc.) can be ordered for a charge. Wine and other alcoholic drinks can be ordered. Free tea on arrival.

Public rooms There is a sitting-room with central heating, open fire, colour TV, books, magazines, local guides and leaflets, piano, record-player and records. Maps on loan. No smoking.

Surroundings The grounds consist of farmland. These are available in the neighbourhood: golf, fishing, riding, theatre, swimming-pool, races.

Cars The nearest main road is the A49 from Hereford to Ludlow.

Stubbs House, Stubbs Green, Loddon, south-east of Norwich, Norfolk, NR14 6EA   *Tel: 0508 20231*   C(9) S ⚑7

The Rackhams had farmed here for generations before developing the house itself, built in the 18th century, into a small hotel, still surrounded by their 160 acres of arable fields: a very peaceful setting.

The bedrooms are large and light – particularly no. 5 which has windows on both sides overlooking the green. In the dining-room, tables are laid with good silver and Wedgwood's 'Insignia' bone china on coffee-coloured cloths; and here Jenny serves mainly traditional food on a generous scale. While her husband sees to the roasts, she does the starters (such as scallops in cheese sauce or an hors d'oeuvre that includes smoked salmon among about six kinds of fish) and the puddings, followed by cheeses. Her repertoire of puddings – up to five choices every night – is staggering: parfaits (loganberry, chestnut, etc.), raspberry and cream cheese charlotte, chocolate meringues with brandy cream, marmalade or caramel steamed puddings, chocolate and orange soufflé. Sacher torte, treacle tart, caramelized oranges, coffee and whisky pots, iced lemon or chocolate ripple or rum cheesecake, bread-and-butter pudding . . . the list goes on and on.

Norfolk has a tremendous amount to see, and Loddon is in the middle of it all. There are at least 8 famous mansions, 5 wildlife parks and 3 steam railways or museums. There's a museum of rural life, the famous shrines at Walsingham, windmills and watermills, boat trips, lavender fields and above all the scenery of countryside and unspoilt coast.

The following facts have been supplied by the owners:

Bedrooms There are 9 rooms, which include single, double and family rooms. Bed-and-breakfast costs from £14 (per person in a double room) including service and VAT; prices go up in high season. There are reductions for stays of 2 nights or more; and 'bargain breaks' as well.

    Some if not all of the rooms have the following amenities: central heating; washbasin, shower, own bathroom and wc, shaver-point; armchairs; views of countryside or garden; choice of duvets or blankets.

Meals The dinner menu is fixed price (£7). There is no choice of dishes on the menu, which consists of 4 courses and coffee. Dinner is served at 6.30 pm. Vegetarian diets can be prepared. Morning, afternoon or bedtime drinks (coffee, tea etc.) can be ordered for a charge. Non-residents are not admitted to the dining-room. Wine and other alcoholic drinks can be ordered.

Public rooms There are 2 sitting-rooms etc. The following are available in one or both of them: central heating, open fire, TV (colour), books, magazines, local guides and leaflets, indoor games (such as cards, Scrabble, etc.); bar.

Surroundings The grounds consist of a natural garden with putting green. These are available in the neighbourhood: riding, golf, sailing.

Cars The nearest main road is the A146 from Norwich to Lowestoft.

Closed to visitors We are not open in December and January.

Not far away is **Chedgrave Cottage** (tel: 0508 28444) where Mrs Cornwall provides bed-and-breakfast in this partly Tudor cottage, attractively furnished in simple country style.

Sugarswell Farm, Shenington, south of Stratford-upon-Avon, Warwickshire, OX15 6HW   *Tel: 029 588 512*   C(2) X ♯ 4

Rosemary Nunnely is a cook of cordon bleu calibre – her greatest delight is preparing meals. Visitors who stay with her are likely to get something very different from ordinary 'farmhouse fare': on the day when I arrived, she was preparing seafood gratin to be followed by fillet steak (home-produced) in a sauce of port, cream and garlic, with home-made lemon sorbet to finish. She uses wine and cream in many of her dishes, rum in such specialities as Jamaican torte.

The house is modern but made from old stones taken from a demolished cottage. It has big picture-windows, and a striking staircase with 18th-century portraits. Sofas are grouped round a huge stone fireplace in the sitting-room which, like the dining-room, has lime green walls. Guests sit on Chippendale chairs to dine; there is good silver on the table, and one side of the dining-room consists of a see-through glass wall filled with Rosemary's collection of Crown Derby.

Upstairs are elegant bedrooms, one with a sofa from which to enjoy woodland views beyond the fields where cows graze, and a very large bathroom decorated in bright mulberry.

Included in the price is the gift of a touring map of the region, showing how to get to (for instance) Warwick, Stratford, the Cotswold towns, Woodstock (Blenheim Palace), Oxford, Silverstone (car races) and Sulgrave (the Washington ancestral home).

As to the curious name Sugarswell, Rosemary explained its origin: shuggers (mediaeval slang for robbers) made a settlement here, which their more respectable neighbours destroyed. Vestiges can still be seen from the air.

Readers' comments: Lovely home, superb cooking. A marvellous place. Time-capsule of the good life! *And from the former manager of a 5-star hotel:* We have been back seven times.

The following facts have been supplied by the owners:

Bedrooms There are 3 rooms, which include single, double and family rooms.
Bed-and-breakfast costs from £12 (per person in a double room) including service and VAT; prices go up in high season. There are reductions for stays of 7 nights or more; and 'bargain breaks' as well. Sampler breaks (see page 14).

Some if not all of the rooms have the following amenities: central heating or electric heaters; electric blankets, washbasin, shower, own bathroom and wc, shaver-point; radio, TV, armchairs; views of countryside, farmland, garden; choice of duvets or blankets; tea/coffee-making facilities; door keys.
Breakfast in bed is available.

Meals The dinner menu is fixed price (£10) or à la carte. There is no choice of dishes on the fixed menu, which consists of 3 courses and coffee. Dinner is served at 7 pm. Special diets can be prepared. Lunches and packed lunches can be provided; and snacks at other hours. Morning, afternoon or bedtime drinks (coffee, tea etc.) can be ordered for a charge. Wine and other alcoholic drinks can be brought in.

Public rooms There are 2 sitting-rooms etc. The following are available in one or more of them: central heating, open fire, TV (colour), video recorder, books, magazines, local guides and leaflets.

Surroundings The grounds consist of 300 acres of farm and woodland. These are available in the neighbourhood: golf, riding, shooting.

Cars The nearest main road is the A442 from Stratford-upon-Avon to Banbury.

Swalcliffe Manor, Swalcliffe, north of Banbury, Oxfordshire, OX15 5EH   *Tel: 029578 348*   C(8) **D S ♯5**

Certainly the most striking entrance of any in this book is here: one passes through a 13th-century undercroft, the vaulted stone ceiling supported on massive circular pillars. Beyond is the former great hall of the house with a vast fireplace. Judith and Francis Hitching have furnished this with antiques and oriental rugs, a grand piano, and a carved mediaeval chest which contrasts well with pink walls. Traces of ancient wall-paintings can be seen, Tudor roses much in evidence.

The drawing-room is completely different, for in the 18th century an extension was added in Georgian style. This classical room, decorated in pale green, has Corinthian pilasters and a very pretty fireplace of green marble in a pine surround carved with acanthus leaves. Through high sash windows, set in deep panelled embrasures, is a view of the croquet lawn and a former studio now used as a games room for children. This is part of a large garden which includes a sun-trapping stone terrace, a Saxon font planted with daisies, swimming-pool (unheated) and a sunken garden with a parterre of flowers grown in Tudor times: Judith put much research as well as hard effort into re-creating this. The big arrangements of dried flowers throughout the house are hers: the huge, decorative kitchen is hung with bunches drying out.

She is a gifted cook (and was once nominated 'Gourmet of the Year' by a London newspaper), with much experience of catering for private parties and for banquets. She will cook whatever her visitors prefer, or devise the menu herself – in which case you

411

might be served scallops cooked with ginger and leeks; very good roast meat or game, in which this area excels (accompanied by vegetables from the garden, and herby sauces); then her own Swalcliffe Pudding – a sponge with gooseberries, sultanas and honey. Dinner is served on flowery Portmeirion pottery at a great refectory table in a Tudor room warmed by a handsome stove originally designed by Benjamin Franklin (separate tables can be provided if visitors are not of a sociable turn of mind).

Upstairs, bedrooms open off a broad gallery, full of pictures and antique toys (the dolls' house and gipsy caravan enthrall young visitors). The one Georgian bedroom (apple green, large and light) overlooks thatched roofs in the pretty village; while older ones have small stone-mullioned windows with church views. Pointed stone arches of the 13th-century frame baths or bathroom entrances – ancient and modern complementing one another curiously well. There is a four-poster, with pink cabbage roses (much favoured by honeymooners).

Swalcliffe is well-sited for touring Stratford-upon-Avon and Oxford, the Cotswolds, Warwick Castle and other of England's most popular tourist centres.

The following facts have been supplied by the owners:

Bedrooms There are 4 rooms, which include single and double rooms. Bed-and-breakfast costs from £12.50 (per person) including service and VAT.

Some if not all of the rooms have the following amenities: central heating or electric heaters; washbasin, shower, own bathroom and wc, shaver-point; TV (colour), armchairs; views of countryside and garden; tea/coffee-making facilities; door keys. Breakfast in bed is available.

Meals The dinner menu is fixed price (from £8.50). There is no choice of dishes on the menu, which consists of 3 courses and coffee. Dinner is served at 8 pm. Vegetarian or special diets can be prepared. Lunches and packed lunches can be provided. Non-residents are not admitted to the dining-room. Wine and other alcoholic drinks can be brought in.

Public rooms There are 2 sitting-rooms etc. The following are available in one or both of them: central heating, open fire, TV (colour), books, magazines, local guides and leaflets, indoor games (such as backgammon, Scrabble and jigsaws), piano, record-player and records.

Surroundings The grounds consist of 4 acres of gardens, orchards and fields. The following games or sports are available in the grounds: swimming in unheated pool; table tennis in games room. These are available in the neighbourhood: golf, riding.

Cars The nearest main road is the A423 from Oxford to Banbury.

Closed to visitors We are not open from mid December to March.

Languages spoken Some French.

At the next village, Lower Brailes, is another good choice for gourmets, **Feldon House** where the excellent food of professional chef Allan Witherick is complemented by attractively furnished Victorian rooms (tel: 060885 580).

Talbot Inn, Knightwick, west of Worcester, WR6 5PH
Tel: 0886 21235   **C D ⌗4**

This inn, run by the Clift family, on the banks of the lovely River Teme has a reputation for very good food. Even snacks in its large and homely bar (all cream-and-crimson, with dark oak and a double-sided fireplace in the middle) are exceptional. The wide choice often includes monkfish in a wine sauce or lamb-and-apricot casserole, for instance, and sweets that range from orange-and-cardamom ice cream to treacle pudding.

The building itself grew up in stages from the 14th century to the 19th, when a bathroom was added (with modern bedrooms built over this later). The older rooms are more picturesque: for instance, the one called Ankerdine (for the wooded hill of which it has a view), has antiques, a satin bedhead and spread, and an olive-green Berber carpet.

There is a residents' sitting-room with cretonne chairs around a log fire; and a very pretty dining-room (pink cloths, panelled walls) where gourmets can enjoy such unusual dishes as pike with saffron, sweetbreads en crôute, venison or seafood in a spiced yogurt sauce. The Talbot has its own livestock, and twice a week Billingsgate is visited to find unusual fish – a speciality of the house.

Like many places in the area, the inn is fully booked during the Three Choirs Festival (which moves between Worcester, Gloucester and Hereford cathedrals – all near) but at other periods this is a very 'away from it all' place for a peaceful holiday, sought out even by such a distinguished visitor as the Australian ambassador to Moscow recently. For a description of this area, one of the most beautiful parts of the county (with good walks), see pages 181–2.

The following facts have been supplied by the owners:

Bedrooms There are 10 rooms, which include single, double and family rooms. Bed-and-breakfast costs from £11.25 (per person in a double room) including service and VAT; prices go up in high season. There are reductions for stays of 4 nights or more; and 'bargain breaks' as well.

Some if not all of the rooms have the following amenities: central heating or electric heaters; washbasin, shower, own bathroom and wc, shaver-point; radio, armchairs; views of countryside; tea/coffee-making facilities; door keys. Breakfast in bed is available.

Meals The dinner menu is fixed price (£9.75 or £11.25) or à la carte. There is a choice of dishes on the fixed menu, which consists of 2 or 3 courses and coffee. Dinner is served at 7.30–9.30 pm. Vegetarian or special diets can be prepared. Lunches and packed lunches can be provided; and snacks at other hours. Morning, afternoon or bedtime drinks (coffee, tea etc.) can be ordered for a charge. Wine and other alcoholic drinks can be ordered.

Public rooms There is a sitting-room with central heating, open fire, TV (colour), books, magazines, local guides and leaflets.

Surroundings The grounds consist of ½ acre of riverside with 2 squash courts. These are available in the neighbourhood: golf, riding.

Cars The nearest main road is the A44 from Worcester to Leominster.

Languages spoken French, Italian.

Credit cards accepted Visa, Access.

Teesdale Hotel, Middleton-in-Teesdale, County Durham,
DL12 0QG   *Tel: 0833 40264*   **C D S X ⌗13**

Visitors to this quiet town always comment on the genuinely
unspoiled nature of the surrounding countryside, for rural County
Durham seems like a well-kept secret. Backed by the bleak moors
of the Pennines, the small fields with their hedges and stone walls
have not been taken over by prairie farming, and the county, for
all its attractions, is not one of the tourist honeypots.

It is surprising to find in Middleton's wide main street a hotel
owned by someone with years of experience as a West End chef,
but the Streits family have been here for eight years now, having
previously owned a smaller hotel nearby. The Streits' West End
experience shows in the menus: the table d'hôte might include
calamari or smoked venison as well as more usual first courses,
followed by a choice of three meat dishes and one fish, and with
passion-fruit sorbet or Bavarian raspberry torte among the sweets.
They are very insistent that only fresh ingredients are used.
Snacks, too, are out of the ordinary – goulash or poached salmon,
for example; served in a bar that is popular with locals.

The large dining-room has deep armchairs at one end, and there
is also a small television lounge. In the bedrooms, many with
private bath, wallpapers and fabrics match. A wine-bar is being
created from the stables which overlook the yard where coaches
once stood. On the walls are paintings by a local artist which one
can buy.

Many people have used this hotel as an overnight stopping place on their way to or from Scotland, and then come back to make it their base for a longer stay. Within a few miles are High Force, England's highest waterfall, and the Bowes Museum, a big mansion in the style of a French château which was built by a forebear of the Queen Mother. It now houses a remarkable collection of French furniture and old master paintings, as well as such oddities as a two-headed calf and a mechanical swan. Within a short drive are Raby Castle, Beamish Open-Air Museum, and Barnard Castle, which gives its name to the school on which Dickens is said to have based Dotheboys Hall. The Lake District, Hadrian's Wall, Durham with its grand cathedral and castle, and the Northumbrian coast are within a day's outing, for Middleton stands about 25 miles from both east and west coasts.

The following facts have been supplied by the owners:

Bedrooms There are 14 rooms, which include single, double and family rooms. Bed-and-breakfast costs from £17.75 (per person in a double room) including VAT; prices go up in high season. There are reductions in winter. Over-60s staying 3 nights have Sunday night free.
  Some if not all of the rooms have the following amenities: central heating; washbasin, own bathroom and wc, shaver-point; radio, TV; views of countryside; door keys.

Meals The dinner menu is fixed price (£9.25). There is a choice of dishes on the fixed menu, which consists of 3 courses. Dinner is served at 7.30–8.30 pm. Special diets can be prepared. Lunches and packed lunches can be provided; and snacks at other hours. Morning, afternoon or bedtime drinks (coffee, tea etc.) can be ordered for a charge. Wine and other alcoholic drinks can be ordered.

Public rooms There is a sitting-room with central heating, open fire, TV (colour), books, magazines, local guides and leaflets, indoor games (such as chess, dominoes etc.). Also a bar.

Cars The nearest main road is the A66 from Scotch Corner to Penrith.

Languages spoken German, French.

Credit card accepted Visa.

Three Acres, Brushford, south-west of Dulverton, Somerset, TA22 9AR *Tel: 0398 23426*   C(9) **D S⇕3**

In 1922, local landowner Lord Carnarvon (who, with Howard Carter, discovered the tomb of Tutankhamen in Egypt later that year) built this white, hillside house – for his mistress, it's said.

416

I went there on the recommendation of a reader who had returned 14 times to enjoy its peace and immaculate comfort, in the middle of Lorna Doone country where Wordsworth once lived and described how 'Through primrose tufts, in that green bower, the periwinkle trailed its wreaths . . .'. Periwinkles and primroses still flourish in the lanes.

The house now belongs to Donal Weir (former Royal Marines captain) and his wife Carol. She used to teach domestic science and so, in her handsomely equipped kitchen, has no difficulty in producing imaginative meals, with choices at every course. Some of her most popular dishes include melon, cucumber and tomato salad as a starter; pork baked in cream; and plums in liqueur accompanied by home-made ice cream. Meals are served in a dining-room with pine furniture, gingham cloths and good silver. The entrance hall beyond (parquet floor and cane bergère chairs) doubles as a small bar; on the other side of it are two sitting-rooms (one with TV) with green velvet chairs.

Throughout the house are lots of pictures, many associated with Nelson. Each bedroom is named for one of his captains: the 'Nelson' room itself is, of course, the best – cinnamon carpeted, with a pretty spread on the pine bed and splendid views southwards across the rose-bordered terrace to far hills.

Nearby Dulverton is the principal town of Exmoor: an attractive leisurely place of narrow streets and some interesting small shops. Exmoor is one of the smaller – and most beautiful – National Parks, woodland drives leading to vast moorland expanses, the heather at its best in August, wild ponies and deer occasionally to be spotted. Within a short distance are stately homes (such as Knightshayes or Dunster Castle), a scenic steam railway, a honey farm with bee museum, crafts studios, rushing streams (one with a prehistoric crossing, Tarr Steps), Wimbleball Lake and Clatworthy Reservoir. Visit Taunton, beyond the Quantock Hills, for the excellent county museum and castle; Exeter for its cathedral, shops and maritime museum; Honiton for lace. And not far away is the Somerset/Devon coast with such well known villages and resorts as Watchet, Minehead, Porlock, Lynmouth and Barnstaple.

The following facts have been supplied by the owners:

Bedrooms There are 7 rooms, which include single and double rooms. Bed-and-breakfast costs from £18.95 (per person) including VAT. There are reductions for stays of 7 nights or more. **10% reduction to readers of this book (or 15% on a week or more)**.
  Some if not all of the rooms have the following amenities: central heating, electric blankets; washbasin, shower, own bathroom and wc, shaver-point; radio, TV (colour), armchairs; views of countryside or garden; choice of duvets or blankets; orthopaedic mattress; tea/coffee-making facilities; door keys. Breakfast in bed is available.

Meals The dinner menu is fixed price (£11.30) or à la carte. There is a choice of dishes on the fixed menu, which consists of 3 courses and coffee. Dinner is served at 7.30 pm. Vegetarian or special diets can be prepared. Lunches and packed lunches can be provided; and snacks at other hours. Morning, afternoon or bedtime drinks (coffee, tea etc.) can be ordered for a charge. Wine and other alcoholic drinks can be ordered.

Public rooms There are 2 sitting-rooms etc. The following are available in one or both of them: central heating, open fire, TV (colour), books, magazines, local guides and leaflets; indoor games (such as cards and jigsaws); bar.

Surroundings The grounds consist of 3 acres of garden and paddocks. These are available in the neighbourhood: riding, fishing, hunting, shooting, golf, trim trail.

Cars The nearest main road is the A361 from Taunton to Bampton.

Closed to visitors We are not open from November to the end of March (or to Easter, if sooner).

Tighe Farm, Stone-in-Oxney, north of Rye, Kent, TN30 7JU
Tel: 023383 251   **C(8)5**

This 17th-century house is full of works of art and unusual antiques (collected by Jimmy Hodson's father, a sculptor before he took to sheep-farming here) and also oriental pieces (Elise's family lived in India for many years). The blue bedroom, for instance, has not only a carved mediaeval table but geisha-girl prints and Numdah rugs; a Jacobean chest has Indian paintings above it; in the oldest room, with mullioned windows, are carved marquise chairs from Paris and a Kashmir chainstitch rug. The Hodsons have retained a curious feature – a concealed iron winch above the staircase, which they think was used when hiding contraband (Romney Marsh was notorious for smuggling).

One breakfasts at a polished refectory table with rush chairs in a particularly interesting room – hop-bines are strung across the inglenook, with a copy of a statue of the Virgin Mary in Notre-Dame; there's a carved oak sideboard and brass rubbings from the local church. In the beautiful sitting-room are unusual chests and other antiques; the old iron fireback carries the royal coat-of-arms.

The garden is equally attractive, especially the paved patio, brimming with fuchsias and roses.

As dinner is not served, Elise provides visitors with menus gathered from good local inns and restaurants – and with a series of postcards on which she has detailed routes recommended for sightseeing tours. Being midway between Rye and Tenterden (each described elsewhere), Tighe Farm is ideally placed for exploring historic and beautiful parts of both Sussex and Kent.

The following facts have been supplied by the owners:

Bedrooms There are 3 rooms, which include double and family rooms. Bed-and-breakfast costs from £9.50 (per person in a double room) including service and VAT; prices go up in high season. There are reductions for stays of 7 nights or more; and 'bargain breaks' as well.

Some if not all of the rooms have the following amenities: central heating or electric heaters; electric blankets, washbasin, shaver-point; armchairs; views of countryside or garden; choice of duvets or blankets; orthopaedic mattress or bed-board; tea/coffee-making facilities; door keys. Breakfast in bed is available. Morning, afternoon or bedtime drinks (coffee, tea etc.) can be ordered free.

Public rooms There is a sitting-room with central heating, open fire, TV (colour), books, magazines, local guides and leaflets, board games, piano, record-player and records. Bridge can be arranged.

Surroundings The grounds consist of 100 acres of farmland and gardens, with coarse fishing. These are available in the neighbourhood: golf, tennis, fishing, riding.

Cars The nearest main road is the A259 from Hastings to Folkestone.

Languages spoken French.

Closed to visitors We are not open from mid October to mid April.

Also in this area is **Cliff Farm**, at Iden Lock on the River Rother (tel: 07978 331), the pleasantly furnished home of young Pat and Jeff Sullivan. Ingredients for breakfast come from their own smallholding; most visitors dine at the Horse and Cart Inn, Peasmarsh. Sampler breaks (see page 14).

Torhaven Hotel, King Street, Brixham, south of Torquay, Devon, TQ5 9TH   *Tel: 08045 2281*   **C PT X ⌗ 4**

Built about 1800, this small and quiet hotel run by Pat and Stephen Nicholls has been recommended to me by a friend. Both are artists, and their taste is evident in the attractive wallpapers and furniture. Nearly every window has a panoramic view of the harbour, and of distant lights twinkling at night. Everywhere there are pictures of birds or landscapes, and patchwork wall-hangings by Pat (she gives weekly lessons in this craft, and runs some weekend courses too). Some rooms have exposed stone walls; the little bar is actually cut into the rock face.

At dinner, one of Pat's specialities is Brixham plaice; and her puddings are delicious gâteaux, meringues, summer pudding, etc.

There is, alas, a £1 daily charge for tea-making facilities in bedrooms. But video films for rainy days are free.

The hotel is about five minutes' stroll from the town and harbour, or the beach. There are many good coastal walks to the innumerable bays and beauty-spots of the area. To the north is the west country's leading resort, Torquay (which has a slightly continental air, with sophisticated entertainments and shops), at the centre of golden sands and luxuriant gardens, yachts filling its bay with colour. Behind are lush countryside, flower-farms, and the distinctive red soil of Devon. Steep little Brixham is quite different from all this, a still-busy fishing port that has changed little in the last hundred years.

The following facts have been supplied by the owners:

Bedrooms There are 10 rooms, which include single, double and family rooms. Bed-and-breakfast costs from £12.75 (per person) including service and VAT; prices go up in high season. There are reductions for stays of 2 nights or more; and 'bargain breaks' as well.

    Some if not all of the rooms have the following amenities: electric heaters; electric blankets, washbasin, shower, own wc, shaver-point; radio, TV (colour), armchairs; views of sea; tea/coffee-making facilities; door keys. Breakfast in bed is available.

Meals The dinner menu is fixed price (£5.50) or à la carte. There is a choice of dishes on the fixed menu, which consists of 3 courses and coffee. Dinner is served at 6.30 pm. Vegetarian or special diets can be prepared. Lunches and packed lunches can be provided; and snacks at other hours. Morning, afternoon or bedtime drinks (coffee, tea etc.) can be ordered for a charge. Wine and other alcoholic drinks can be ordered.

Public rooms There are 2 sitting-rooms etc. The following are available in one or both of them: TV (colour), books, magazines, local guides and leaflets; indoor games (such as Scrabble, chess, Upwords, backgammon, darts, etc.); bar.

Surroundings These are available in the neighbourhood: golf, sailing, fishing.

Cars The nearest main road is the A3022 from Torquay to Brixham.

Languages Deaf sign language.

Tregony House, Tregony, east of Truro, Cornwall, TR2 5RN
Tel: 087 253 671   C(5) **D PT S** ⌗**5**

Years ago, some owner had the bad idea of coating the façade of this house with rendering – so from the street it looks quite undistinguished (the drawing shows the back). But inside is a very different story. Part dates from the 17th century; later, additions were made – so the dining-room, for instance, is low-beamed and thick-walled while the hall and sitting-room have 18th-century elegance, particularly since Terry and Mary Lock moved in and added well-chosen fabrics, a pomegranate wallpaper in the hall, rounded alcoves crammed with books, and interesting antiques. One green-and-white bedroom has a quilted bedspread and particularly pretty antique chairs; a pink room at the back, with tiny windows, has velvet bedheads and a patchwork table-cover. Always, fresh flowers are put into the rooms. Two double rooms with bathroom between make a good family suite.

rear view

In the dining-room (furnished with oriental rugs, oak tables and Windsor chairs) Mary, who used to teach at the Cordon Bleu Cookery School, serves such imaginative meals as avocado and orange salad, boned and stuffed chicken with mushroom sauce, and pears cooked with brown sugar and lemon (plus cheeses). Herbs, raspberries etc. come from the walled garden at the back, where you can have tea; their glasshouses provide courgettes, aubergines, tomatoes and pimentos.

Because Tregony, although interesting, is not one of Cornwall's show villages, it remains uncrowded even in high summer. From it you can quickly reach the warm south coast of Cornwall, with all its coves, beaches, harbours and scenic drives in the Roseland peninsula, an area of outstanding natural beauty, with numerous stately homes and gardens to visit too.

Readers' comments: Delightfully furnished, superb cooking. They look after their guests marvellously, truly excellent cooking.

The following facts have been supplied by the owners:

Bedrooms There are 6 rooms, which include singles and doubles. Dinner, bed-and-breakfast costs from £17 (per person) including service and VAT. There are reductions for stays of 7 nights or more.

Some if not all of the rooms have the following amenities: electric heaters; washbasin, own bathroom and wc, shaver-point; armchairs; views of garden; choice of duvets or blankets; door keys.

Meals There is a choice of dishes on the fixed menu, which consists of 4 courses and coffee. Dinner is served at 7 pm. Special diets can be prepared. Morning, afternoon or bedtime drinks (coffee, tea etc.) can be ordered for a charge. Wine and other alcoholic drinks can be ordered.

Public rooms There are 2 sitting-rooms etc. The following are available in one or both of them: central heating, open fire, TV (colour), books, magazines, local guides and leaflets, indoor games (such as Scrabble and solitaire), record-player and records; bar.

Surroundings The grounds consist of a garden.

Cars The nearest main road is the A390 from St Austell to Truro.

Languages spoken French, Italian (little).

Closed to visitors We are not open from November to January.

Trent Vale Farmhouse, Hyde, north-west of Wareham, Dorset, BH20 7NX   *Tel: 0929 471642*   C(10) **PT S ⌗6**

A very long, rough-surfaced rhododendron drive leads deep into the heart of Wareham Forest. Suddenly the scene changes: sunny meadows open out, and there springs into view a spacious modern house with wide picture-windows that have views of the distant Purbeck Hills.

This became the home of Ken Durran when he retired from business, and his wife Joan – an experienced ornithologist who runs wildlife weekends from time to time. Even on their own grounds there is much to see – not only birds but also badgers, glow-worms, rare sand-lizards, and deer from the forest. You can visit the Arne nature reserve (heathland and estuary), Radipole lake, the marine reserve at Kimmeridge, Studland for its wildfowl, and rocky headlands where migratory birds can be spotted. Joan takes you around in a Landrover (packed lunches provided); and wardens act as guides. In the evening there are slides, videos and talks. Or you can stay at the house simply for bed-and-breakfast.

rear view

As to the accommodation, the sitting-room is huge, with corduroy sofas and cork floor. There's a pale-carpeted breakfast room of distinction, with lightly patterned hessian walls, concealed lighting, and rosewood sideboard. Beyond is a sun-room with sliding glass doors, an acacia and a vine growing overhead. Bedrooms, too, are attractive (and bathroom luxurious): for instance, one has white carpet, powder-blue colour scheme and rounded bedhead of cane.

You are welcome to wander round the grounds, which include river, lake with swans, paddocks with Ken's horses (show-jumpers, hunting or racing horses and a Shetland pony), swimming-pool, tennis court, birch woods.

And, of course, all the other pleasures of east Dorset are within reach – Poole Harbour and Brownsea Island, Lulworth Cove and Durdle Door, Corfe Castle and old Wareham itself – described elsewhere in this book.

The following facts have been supplied by the owners:

Bedrooms There are 4 rooms, which include single and double rooms. Bed-and-breakfast costs from £9 (per person in a double room) including service and VAT; prices go up in high season. There are reductions for stays of 5 nights or more.

   The rooms have central heating; washbasin, bathroom and wc, shaver-point; radio, armchairs; views of countryside or garden; choice of duvets or blankets; tea/coffee facilities; door keys.

Public rooms There is a sitting-room with central heating, TV (colour), books, magazines, local guides and leaflets.

Surroundings The grounds consist of 28 acres of woodlands, with tennis court and swimming-pool. Golf course nearby.

Cars The nearest main road is the A35 from Bournemouth to Dorchester.

Trevena House Hotel, Alton Road, Farnham, Surrey, GU10 5ER
Tel: 0252 716908   **C PT S ♯4**

Mr Trimmer, a millionaire brewer, bought himself rolling acres of Surrey parkland in the 1890s on which to build an appropriate home. But Trevena House had fallen into a sorry state when Norman Levitt, formerly managing director of a flooring company, later took it over, to restore to its former handsome style. He even found great club-like oak chairs, deep-upholstered in tapestry, to go with the oak panelling of the bar-lounge. This has a window-seat overlooking the lawns and stately trees such as weeping ash, cedar, mulberry and chestnut, with the lovely Surrey hills beyond. On wintry nights, guests gather round the inglenook fireplace. This is a place of thick carpets, hefty beams and solid brass fittings on the doors. In the summer, drinks can be taken out to the swimming-pool which is illuminated after dark by strings of coloured lights. There is a sauna indoors.

The dining-room, too, overlooks the lawn. Here are served, on tables with nosegays and candle-lamps, such dishes as prawns mornay followed by beef Wellington and unusual ice creams.

The bedrooms are comfortable, furnished in conservative taste. Throughout, the accent is on spaciousness and ease. Being so close to London, the hotel tends to be used by executives on weekdays, but is less full at weekends.

Nearby Farnham is a lovely Georgian town, parts of it still very much as Jane Austen knew them (her house, near Alton, can be visited). It is full of antique and craft shops, wine-bars and boutiques. It has a good repertory theatre, a new sports centre, a monthly country market, fortnightly auctions, weekly street-market.

Close by are: Alice Holt woodlands for walks, the great lakes of Frensham Ponds (at one end, there is a sandy beach for swimming), tropical bird gardens, country inns, National Trust woods and heaths. Riding, golf and Britain's largest car auction attract some guests; Winchester Cathedral and the music festivals of picturesque Haslemere (harpsichord centre) bring others. The north Surrey hills make very varied scenery – oaks and holly alternating with pine and birch. Roads go up and down, streams meander. There are bulrushes and water-lilies in summer, coppery bracken and blackberries in autumn.

The following facts have been supplied by the owners:

Bedrooms There are 19 rooms, which include single, double and family rooms. At weekends bed-and-breakfast costs £16.50 (per person in a double room) including service and VAT. There are 2-day breaks all through the week.

All of the rooms have the following amenities: central heating; washbasin, shower, own bathroom and wc, shaver-point; colour TV, phone, armchairs; views of countryside, farmland, garden; balcony; tea/coffee-making facilities; door keys.

Meals The dinner menu is à la carte. Dinner is served from 7 pm. Special diets can be prepared. Lunches or packed lunches can be provided; and snacks at other hours. Morning, afternoon or bedtime drinks (coffee, tea etc.) can be ordered for a charge. Wine and other alcoholic drinks can be ordered.

Public rooms There are 3 sitting-rooms etc. The following are available in one or more of them: central heating, open fire, TV, books, magazines, local guides and leaflets and a bar. Also a sauna.

Surroundings The grounds consist of 5 acres of lawns and orchard. The following games or sports are available in the grounds: tennis and swimming-pool (70°). These are available in the neighbourhood: riding, golf and sports centre.

Cars The nearest main road is the A31 from Farnham to Winchester.

Turville Lodge, Turville Heath, north of Henley-on-Thames, Oxfordshire, RG9 6LB   *Tel: 049163 475*   **C D S ⌗2**

Apricot walls, with japonica and roses between the leaded casement windows, give this 18th-century house a warm and gracious look – which continues throughout the interior.

Margaret Bruce comes from an artistic family, and this is evident in her taste – from interesting antiques and pictures (many painted by her) to the choice of wallpapers and colour schemes. When she retired from her profession (physiotherapy) she had more time for crafts, and guests are welcome to visit her pottery. She also has a studio where she produces silver jewellery, engraved glass and enamels.

Bill is equally creative – but outdoors, where he has made a succession of cypress-walled 'rooms' each enclosing a different small garden, with vistas glimpsed through openings in the hedges. He wages constant war with the tiny muntjac deer which slip in from the woods to nibble his roses. At the far end is a fine view of the valley, grazing sheep, a hillside ice-house, and a cricket green.

Visitors use a sitting/dining-room with occasional log fire. Margaret serves the main course (such as lamb steaks and quince jelly with generous garden vegetables) and then leaves her guests to help themselves from an array of puddings and cheeses. Breakfast is an informal meal at the pine kitchen-table, overlooking the rose-garden. Sometimes meals are served outdoors.

As to the neighbourhood, this is fully described on pages 100–101, 291 and 313.

The following facts have been supplied by the owners:

Bedrooms There are 3 double rooms. Bed-and-breakfast costs £9.50 (per person in a double room) including service and VAT. There are reductions for stays of 7 nights or more.

   Some if not all of the rooms have the following amenities: central heating or electric heaters; own bathroom and wc, shaver-point; armchairs; views of countryside or garden; choice of duvets or blankets; tea/coffee-making facilities; door keys.

Meals The dinner menu is fixed price (£5.25). There is no choice of dishes on the menu, which consists of 3 courses and coffee. Dinner is served at 7.30 pm. Non-residents are not admitted to the dining-room. Wine and other alcoholic drinks can be brought in.

Public rooms There is a sitting-room with TV (colour), books, magazines, local guides and leaflets.

Surroundings The grounds consist of 1½ acres of garden and paddock. These are available in the neighbourhood: riding, golf, boating, tennis, bowls.

Cars The nearest main road is the A423 from Henley to Oxford.

Closed to visitors We are open only from June to September.

Twenty-One, Charlotte Street, Brighton, East Sussex, BN2 1AG
Tel: 0273 686450   C(12) **D PT ♯3**

Simon Ward used to run the Inigo Jones restaurant in London, then worked in Paris before buying this elegant terrace house, built in the 1840s, to convert it into a small but very distinctive hotel with outstanding decor and cuisine. It is in a quiet road just off the sea front.

He and his partner (Stuart Farquharson) give guests a warm, personal welcome.

They have decorated all the rooms in very good modern taste while preserving the early Victorian architectural details. Each bedroom has its individual colour scheme, as well as colour TV with remote control. One room has been furnished to recapture its Victorian elegance with antique furniture and an original four-poster bed draped in silk. Lots of extras are provided, from pot-pourri to biscuits, with beds turned down and towels renewed while you dine. The residents' sitting-room has a restful blend of apricot and green furnishings, subdued lighting and an open fire.

The cooking (French) is of the highest standard. A typical dinner: warm salad of shellfish; soup made from carrots, onions, oranges and basil; pork served with fruits and game sauce; a good choice of cheeses; assorted sorbets with fresh fruit. Vegetarian meals can be provided. The wines are of good quality.

Brighton's attractions include the Prince Regent's Indian-style Pavilion, two piers, the Lanes crowded with boutiques and antique shops, a concert hall, theatre, conference centre, dolphinarium, shopping centre, art gallery, exceptional swimming-pool, cinemas, discos and museums. There is also the marina, engineerium, and all the pleasures of the Sussex downs: scenery, pretty villages and historic buildings open to the public. Brighton's entertainment and sporting events go on all through the year.

Reader's comments: Cuisine and presentation memorable.

The following facts have been supplied by the owners:

Bedrooms There are 6 rooms, which include singles and doubles (one with four-poster bed). Bed-and-breakfast costs from £15 (per person in a double room) including service and VAT; prices go up in high season. There are 'bargain breaks' as well.

    Some if not all of the rooms have the following amenities: central heating; washbasin, shower, wc, shaver-point; radio, remote-control colour TV, armchairs; views of sea; balcony; intercom; door keys; orthopaedic mattresses; phone; hair drier and rollers. Continental breakfast in bed is available.

Meals Dinner is £18 excluding service; 5 courses plus coffee with home-made petits fours. Dinner is served from 7–8 pm. (Dining-room closed on Sundays.) Snacks available at other hours. Morning, afternoon or bedtime drinks (coffee, tea etc.) can be ordered for a charge. Non-residents are not admitted to the dining-room. Wine and other alcoholic drinks can be ordered.

Public rooms There is a sitting-room with central heating, open fire, music, books and magazines. Local guides and leaflets are available.

Local amenities These are available in the neighbourhood: swimming (indoor or sea), sailing, sea fishing, golf, tennis.

Closed to visitors in January.

Credit cards accepted Access, Visa, Amex, Diners Club.

Under Rock, Shore Road, Bonchurch, east of Ventnor, Isle of Wight, PO38 1RF *Tel: 0983 852714* **C10 H PT S**

Garden-lovers will appreciate the grounds of this small hotel, which clings to a cliff-side. It was built about 1790 for a nephew of Sir Robert Peel (founder of the police force), who created a small paradise around it: from every cleft spring flowers such as New Zealand flax or Californian tree poppies; palms, hydrangeas or Japanese anemones.

Fresh flowers are in every room, too, now that the house is run as a small, award-winning hotel by Mollie and Dennis Kelleway. One steps from the garden into a sitting-room where rosy armchairs contrast with a thick, pale carpet. In the dining-room, curtains are of quilted patchwork and place-mats of crochet (over pink cloths): there's a view of the rock garden, 20 feet high, brimming with tobacco-plants and fuchsias. A curving stair leads to the bedrooms – the prettiest has pink moiré paper and a frieze of roses matching the curtain fabric.

430

Mollie's meals often include fresh fruit starters (such as minneola and orange segments) before, perhaps, a traditional roast and then puddings such as meringues with blackcurrants or grapes. All her soups, bread, preserves and fruit juices are freshly made at home.

Bonchurch is probably the prettiest village in the Isle of Wight and, facing south, gets sunshine even in winter. It adjoins Ventnor, a resort with an old-fashioned air, botanical gardens (bananas fruit outdoors there), a smuggling museum well worth visiting, and a scenic undercliff drive among myrtles, palms and cork trees. It is well placed for visiting the innumerable 'sights' in the lively east half of the island; or the wild and peaceful scenery in the west half.

The following facts have been supplied by the owners:

Bedrooms There are 7 rooms, which include single and double rooms. Bed-and-breakfast costs from £15 (per person in a double room) including service and VAT; prices go up in high season. There are reductions for stays of 3 nights or more.
   Some if not all of the rooms have the following amenities: central heating; washbasin, shaver-point; TV (colour), armchairs; views of sea and garden; door keys.

Meals The dinner menu is fixed price (£6). There is a choice of dishes on the menu, which consists of 3 courses and coffee. Dinner is served at 6.30 pm.
   Vegetarian or special diets can be prepared. Packed lunches can be provided; and snacks at other hours. Morning, afternoon or bedtime drinks (coffee, tea etc.) can be ordered for a charge. Wine and other alcoholic drinks can be ordered.

Public rooms There are 2 sitting-rooms etc. The following are available in one or both of them: central heating, open fire, books, magazines, local guides and leaflets; bar.

Surroundings The grounds consist of an acre of garden.

Cars The nearest main road is the A3055 from Shanklin to Ventnor.

Closed to visitors We are not open between November and February.

Unicorn Hotel, Keighley Road, Skipton, West Yorkshire, BD23 22P   *Tel: 0756 4146*   **C PT ⌗4**

This differs greatly from other hotels described in this book, and I have not come across anything quite like it except perhaps the Christopher at Eton.

For a start, you might not know it was there, hidden in a modest row of shops on a nondescript street leading into the town. You enter through a small door and go upstairs to a receptionist who takes you to your room – she may be the only person you meet – and brings you a tray of tea or coffee with biscuits when you arrive. What makes the Unicorn special is the quality and size of the rooms. Ours had an attractive brown-and-cream colour scheme and was more like a sitting-room than a bedroom, with comfortable armchairs and sofa (convertible into a third bed if required) grouped round the large colour TV. There were good paintings by local artists on the walls, prettily arranged flowers on a table, a pile of magazines, a folder of information (about local events, sights and restaurants) and well-placed lights. It was possible to use the room for snack meals of one's own providing, but there is a restaurant next door. The Butler family serve only breakfast – a generous, continental one – brought to the room; and light snacks (wholefood if you prefer). The restaurant next door will bring in other meals.

The emphasis is on quality and comfort in every detail – each room has a heated, carpeted bathroom, for instance. And, although it was July, the receptionist offered to turn on the central heating because the weather was unseasonably cool. The Butlers will organize conducted tours or walks, or lend maps.

Skipton is an old town of great character, its wide main street thronged with market stalls leading up to the castle and church at the end. Down by the bridge are interesting craft and antique shops, and historic riverside buildings. It is a good centre from which to explore Ribblesdale, Wharfedale, Wensleydale and

Airedale and all the famous beauty-spots – the crags, caves, waterfalls, villages and ruined abbeys with which the region abounds. Ilkley Moor is within reach, as are the stylish spa town of Harrogate (for shopping), and an officially designated 'area of outstanding natural beauty', the Forest of Bowland. This is largely moorland (the heather is superb in September), with parts comparable with the crags and valleys of the Lake District. Some of the finest countryside of the north-west is here. In addition there are charming villages like Bolton-by-Bowland, winding rivers, stately homes and abbeys and castles, the Trough of Bowland scenic route to Lancaster and its castle, a Roman museum, inns and markets. 'Narrow boats' can be hired on the canal. There is a swimming-pool, coarse fishing and golf nearby, as well as cinemas, theatres and coach excursions.

Reader's comments: Fine service, will book again.

The following facts have been supplied by the owners:

Bedrooms There are 10 rooms, mostly family rooms. Bed-and-breakfast costs from £16 (per person in a double room), including service and VAT at weekends; but with substantial discounts for 2 or more nights. Sampler breaks (see page 14); winter 'bargain breaks'; and 3 nights for the price of 2 for over-60s.

All or some rooms have the following amenities: central heating, double-glazing; own bathroom or shower and wc, shaver-point; radio, colour TV, armchairs; choice of duvets or blankets; tea/coffee-making facilities; door keys; orthopaedic mattresses. Continental breakfast is served in your bedroom. Laundering available, and hair drier.

Public rooms There is a sitting-room with central heating, double-glazing, colour TV and magazines. Local guides and leaflets are provided.

Cars The nearest main road is the A65 from Kendal to Leeds.

Uploders Place, Uploders, east of Bridport, Dorset
Tel: 030885 228   C(10) **D S** ♯3

Architect Brian Cocks and his wife Glenda have filled this gracious Regency house with beautiful objects – not simply antiques but also very modern paintings, crafts and furniture too. Examples of contemporary English glass and pottery contrast with an old country dresser and rush-seated chairs; fleecy white carpets with polished parquet; pebbles and shells, hand-made rugs and a white tweed sofa with graceful architectural details – a lovely staircase twining its way up, arched windows, alcoves, shutters. There are prolific pot-plants everywhere. Bedrooms have been furnished with, for instance, Laura Ashley papers on walls and cupboards, big sofas and Victorian rocking-chairs, bouquets of dried flowers, unusual tiles (for bedhead and table), diaphanous curtains. Great care – and inspiration – has gone into the decoration of every room.

The big, park-like garden slopes down to the River Asker and a weir, frequented by ducks. From time to time wildlife weekends are organized, with an expert naturalist as guide.

Glenda serves dinners if pre-booked. Some of her favourite dishes are watercress soup, pork and mushrooms in a creamy ginger sauce, and hot applecake with cream. (She uses much home-grown produce.) The Cockses have converted a large conservatory into a tea-room open to the public.

Uploders, at the foot of a hill with iron-age fort, lies between the historic towns of Dorchester and Bridport, in a particularly beautiful part of Dorset (described elsewhere in this book).

rear view

The following facts have been supplied by the owners:

Bedrooms There are 3 rooms, which include single, double and family rooms. Bed-and-breakfast costs from £8.50 (per person in a double room) including service and VAT. There are reductions for stays of 3 nights or more.

All rooms have the following amenities: central heating; electric blankets,

434

washbasin, shower or own bathroom and wc, shaver-point; TV (colour or b&w), armchairs; views of countryside or garden; choice of duvets or blankets; tea/coffee-making facilities; door keys. Breakfast in bed is available.

Meals The dinner menu is fixed price (£6.50). There is no choice of dishes on the fixed menu, which consists of 3 courses and coffee. Dinner is served at 7 pm. Vegetarian or special diets can be prepared. Lunches and packed lunches can be provided; and snacks at other hours. Morning, afternoon or bedtime drinks (coffee, tea etc.) can be ordered for a charge. Wine and other alcoholic drinks can be brought in.

Public rooms There is a sitting-room with central heating, open fire, books, magazines, local guides and leaflets, indoor games (such as Scrabble, jigsaws, Kensington and cards).

Surroundings The grounds consist of 3 acres of garden, mainly lawn, with badminton and croquet. Riding is available in the neighbourhood.

Cars The nearest main road is the A35 from Dorchester to Bridport.

Closed to visitors We are not open in December and January.

Upper Green Farm, Manor Road, Towersey, east of Thame, Oxfordshire, OX9 3QR *Tel: 084421 2496* ⊞3

One of the most picturesque houses in this book, Upper Green Farm is a mediaeval building of whitewash and thatch with a pretty duckpond at the front. Immaculate now, it was a near-ruin when Marjorie and Euan Aitken took it over not long ago. They uncovered 15th-century beams with the original carpenters' identification marks; came across Elizabethan coins; restored the wood shutters which (window-glass having yet to be invented) were all that kept out wintry blasts five centuries ago; found a secret priest-hole where, in the days of religious persecution, a Catholic priest might have to hide for days when the search was on. In one huge chimney, there were still the iron rungs up which small boys were forced to clamber to clear the soot. In what is now the quarry-tiled breakfast-room, an old kitchen-range and adjoining copper boiler have been preserved, together with the rack on which spits for roasting whole sheep were kept, and the special hooks used for drying the farmer's smocks by the fire. In the hall is a pump (still working) which supplied water from a spring 22 feet below. The barns outside date from 1790.

Marjorie, who used to be an antique dealer, has filled every room with fascinating trifles – Victorian jugs and jam-pots on the sprigged brown tablecloth at breakfast, shelves of old bottles (found discarded in the garden), beadwork pincushions and watch-cases, a huge marble washstand in the downstairs cloakroom, naive Staffordshire figures, old brass scales (which she uses) and tin toys discovered in the attic, a boot-shaped footbath now filled with one of her many bouquets of dried flowers, faded photos in *art nouveau* frames. She collects old lace, embroideries and textiles, so every curtain or cushion in each bedroom is a period-piece.

The Aitkens not only tell visitors about well-known sights nearby (see pages 184–5) but introduce them to other sides of local life. For instance, you may go and see the sorting and grading of sheep fleeces, join in bell-ringing, pick up bargains at local markets or auctions, chat up balloonists as they glide by only a few yards above the farm – silently, unlike the wild swans in clattering flight. In mid-winter, you can learn to skate on their pond, or in summer row on it. They will tell you which inn brews its own beer, and where to find a true country butcher from whom you can load up with game, faggots, deep brown eggs and other treats hard to come by in city supermarkets. They have leaflets of local walks between historic villages, and of the many gardens open to the public.

And, of course, their animals – sheep, ducks, chickens and geese – are an entertainment in themselves.

Bed-and-breakfast only; but with plenty of options for dinner in Thame (I had a particularly good meal at the Bay Tree).

Readers' comments: Charming home, warm hospitality: we arrived as guests and left as friends. Much impressed by warm welcome, delightful house and excellent breakfast.

The following facts have been supplied by the owners:

Bedrooms There are 2 double rooms. Bed-and-breakfast costs from £10 (per person in a double room) including service and VAT.

    The rooms have central heating; electric blankets, TV (b&w); views of countryside or garden; orthopaedic mattress; door keys.

Meals Packed lunches can be provided and morning, afternoon or bedtime drinks (coffee, tea etc).

Public rooms There is a sitting-room with central heating, TV (colour), books, magazines, local guides and leaflets, indoor games (such as chess and Trivial Pursuit).

Surroundings The grounds consist of 7 acres of garden, orchard, large pond and farmland. The following games or sports are available in the neighbourhood: squash, golf, tennis, snooker.

Cars The nearest main road is the A4129 from Thame to Princes Risborough.

Upton House, Upton Snodsbury, east of Worcester, WR7 4NR
Tel: 090560 226   **C D S ♯ 4**

Part 14th century, part Tudor and part 18th century, this listed building is full of character. It has been furnished in character, with antiques collected by Hugh and Angela Jefferson over the years. They decided to take guests to help with the cost of educating four young children, then found how much they enjoyed entertaining them.

Their colour schemes are fresh and imaginative. In the dining-room, chairs covered in watermelon satin contrast with primrose walls (this room has a vast fireplace); in the sitting-room, sofas covered in pink or blue brocade are grouped round another log fire. A feature of this room is the pretty little bay window with wide sill, through which one looks across the lawn (surrounded by trees and rosebeds) to half-timbered cottages and the Norman church, the clock of which chimes every quarter-hour.

The pink bedroom, low-beamed, has sweet peas on curtains and duvet (and in its bathroom, which is lavishly supplied with bath essence, talc etc.), a moss-green carpet and violets on the Royal Albert bone china for early-morning tea. The peach and the blue rooms are almost as attractive. Some visitors eat at the Wheelbarrow and Castle Inn (Radford) or award-winning Brown's (Worcester), but menus at Upton House are good – a typical meal might comprise seafood vol-au-vent, stuffed lamb, chocolate truffle cake and cheeses.

It is hoped to get the old cider-mill at the back restored in due course. Meantime, if you want to see cider being made in the traditional way (in October) there is another mill nearby which you can visit. Children enjoy exploring the orchard, and meeting the family pony and the chickens. From Upton House one can readily visit the Malvern Hills (Hereford and the Wye Valley beyond them); such Cotswold beauty-spots as Broadway or Chipping Camden; and, in the other direction, Stratford-upon-Avon in Warwickshire.

The following facts have been supplied by the owners:

Bedrooms There are 3 rooms, which include single and double rooms. Bed-and-breakfast costs from £11.50 (per person in a double room) including service and VAT. Sunday accommodation free to over-60s staying 3 days.

Some if not all of the rooms have the following amenities: central heating and electric heaters; electric blankets; washbasin, own bathroom and wc, shaver-point; radio, armchairs; views of countryside or garden; tea/coffee-making facilities; hair drier available, trouser-press.

Meals The dinner menu is from (£10). There is no choice of dishes on the menu, which consists of 4 courses and coffee. Dinner is served at 7.30–8 pm. Vegetarian or special diets can be prepared. Wine and other alcoholic drinks can be brought in.

Public rooms There is a sitting-room with central heating, open fire, TV (colour), books, magazines, local guides and leaflets, indoor games (such as Monopoly and Trivial Pursuit).

Surroundings The grounds consist of 2 acres of garden and orchard with croquet. These are available in the neighbourhood: riding, tennis.

Cars The nearest main road is the A422 from Stratford to Worcester.

Languages spoken French.

Venn Ottery Barton, Ottery St Mary, north-west of Sidmouth, Devon, EX11 1RZ   *Tel: 040481 2733*   **C D H X ⌗4**

Two sisters (Pauline Cox and Maureen Critchfield) and their husbands run this hotel, once a farmhouse, built in the reign of Henry VIII, which a friend has recommended to me. It lies in a peaceful valley, with views of river and hills – fine walking country. Big fireplaces are a feature of the house, one with a stone lintel weighing three tons and another with a great beam salvaged from the wreck of a ship from the Spanish Armada. In addition to the sitting-room and bar where these are found, there is a games room.

The four-course dinner features straightforward English dishes such as roasts, pork fillet with mushrooms, local sole or plaice, and turkey pie (with bacon and chestnuts in it). There is a good choice of wines.

Venn Ottery is in the middle of east Devon, and therefore a good base from which to visit the old-fashioned resorts (Exmouth, Sidmouth, Budleigh Salterton) and sandy beaches of this stretch of 'heritage coast', carefully conserved because of its beauty. Inland are picturesque villages, country parks, and historic buildings such as Forde Abbey or Powderham Castle; and sights like Cricket wildlife park or the gardens and scenic railway at Bicton. Exeter (with its cathedral, maritime museum and good shops) is soon reached; Dartmoor is a little further. Ottery St Mary is itself an interesting village: it has a jazz festival every July, and on 5 November (Guy Fawkes Day) a carnival with flaming tar-barrel race.

The following facts have been supplied by the owners:

Bedrooms There are 13 rooms, which include single, double and family rooms. Bed-and-breakfast costs from £14 (per person in a double room) including service and VAT; prices go up in high season. There are reductions for stays of 3 nights or more; and 'bargain breaks' as well.

Some if not all of the rooms have the following amenities: central heating; washbasin, shower, own bathroom and wc, shaver-point; armchairs; views of countryside/farmland/garden; choice of duvets or blankets; bed-board; tea/coffee-making facilities; door keys. Continental breakfast in bed is available.

Meals The dinner menu is fixed price (£8). There is a choice of dishes on the fixed menu, which consists of 4 courses and coffee. Dinner is served at 7–7.30 pm. Vegetarian or special diets can be prepared. Lunches and packed lunches can be provided; and snacks at other hours. Morning, afternoon or bedtime drinks (coffee, tea etc.) can be ordered for a charge. Wine and other alcoholic drinks can be ordered.

Public rooms There are two sitting-rooms etc. The following are available in one or both of them: central heating, open fire, TV (colour), books, magazines, local guides and leaflets, indoor games (such as chess, backgammon, etc.), piano; bar.

Surroundings The grounds consist of 2 acres of gardens. The following games or sports are available in a games room in the grounds: table tennis, pool, darts, video games. These are available in the neighbourhood: golf, tennis, riding, fishing.

Cars The nearest main road is the A3052 from Exeter to Lyme Regis.

Credit cards accepted Visa, Access.

Verrall Cottage, High Halden, north of Tenterden, Kent, TN26 3NA *Tel: 023 385 226* **C(10) PT S ♯15**

This was the family home of Anne and Bill Blackiston for many years. Now, with their sons grown up and Bill retired from industry, they run it as a small guest-house. It is a 15th-century cottage set back from the main road in a particularly pretty garden – at the back are service and willow trees, a large lawn (where cream teas may be served), a pool with yellow flags, and an abundant vegetable garden to serve the kitchen.

All the cooking is done by Bill, and every meal is a five-course feast (preceded by a free sherry, and followed by coffee with brandy-truffles). A typical menu (but you are invited to state your preferences in advance): asparagus with Hollandaise sauce; scallops with tomatoes, mushrooms and cream; roast lamb and four vegetables (which might include parsnip purée with roasted pine kernels or turnips with dill, for example); strawberry syllabub; and either a savoury or cheese. Meals are served in a large, low dining/sitting-room with a log fire in winter, cretonne armchairs, grandfather clock and antiques.

The bedrooms (reached via twisting, low passageways) also have character. Most are beamed and decorated with pretty, flowered wallpapers, antiques and ornaments, and have lots of books, too.

Anne is a qualified beauty consultant, and sessions with her can be booked.

For details of the area, see pages 448–9.

The following facts have been supplied by the owners:

Bedrooms There are 4 rooms, which include single and double rooms. Bed-and-breakfast costs from £12 (per person) including service and VAT; prices go up in high season. There are reductions for stays of 3 nights or more; and 'bargain breaks' as well.

Some if not all of the rooms have the following amenities: central heating; electric blankets, own bathroom and wc, shaver-point; armchairs; views of countryside, garden; tea/coffee-making facilities; door keys. Breakfast in bed is available.

Meals The dinner menu is fixed price (£10.50) or à la carte. There is no choice of dishes on the fixed menu, which consists of 5 courses and coffee. Dinner is served at 8 pm. Lunches and packed lunches can be provided; and snacks at other hours. Morning, afternoon or bedtime drinks (coffee, tea etc.) can be ordered for a charge. Wine and other alcoholic drinks can be brought in.

Public rooms There is a sitting-room with central heating, open fire, books, magazines, local guides and leaflets, indoor games (such as Scrabble, Mah Jong and Boggle), record-player and records.

Surroundings The grounds consist of ¾ acre of garden. Available in the neighbourhood are golf, tennis and fishing (coarse – fly – sea).
Cars The nearest main road is the A28 from Ashford to Tenterden.
Credit cards accepted Visa.

Not far away is **Litle Hodgeham,** Bethersden, furnished with exceptional elegance by perfectionist Erica Wallace, and fully described in previous editions. But it costs more. (Tel: 023385 323.)

Village Farm, Sturton-by-Stow, north-west of Lincoln, LN1 24E
Tel: 0427 788309   C(10) ♯4

In the middle of this usually quiet village stands an early Victorian house, now pleasantly furnished by Sheila Bradshaw – at the heart of a 350-acre farm where pedigree cattle and Suffolk sheep are raised. For the sitting-room she chose a pale green carpet, pink velvet curtains held back in tasselled loops, and flowery chintzes; among many Victorian heirlooms are things of her own making – canvaswork or patchwork cushions, for instance. She is a keen Women's Institute member, a handbell-ringer, loves flower arranging and, when I visited, had just completed a big sampler depicting the house itself. Her husband's family farmed in Sturton for many generations back: among his enthusiasms is driving a gig, with a high-stepping Hackney horse bred for the purpose.

Guests have the use of two small dining-rooms. A typical menu: crême de menthe grapefruit, chicken casserole, chocolate mousse. Upstairs are very attractive bedrooms: one, with matching Sanderson wallpaper and fabrics, has a sloping ceiling and odd windows; in the peach-and-cream one is a rocking-chair; one of the prettiest has blue Laura Ashley sprigged linen and a Philippine cane chair.

In the well-kept garden is a vast walnut tree; to one side is an aviary of lovebirds; on the other, pantiled barns. Sheila sells home-made preserves, and crafts.

Lincoln and the rest of the county are described on other pages. The Wolds, the coast and the great Humber Bridge are easily reached. Nearby sights include Doddington Hall, a country park, Gainsborough Old Hall, Tattershall Castle and Stow's cathedral-like church.

The following facts have been supplied by the owners:

Bedrooms There are 4 rooms, which include single, double and family rooms. Bed-and-breakfast costs from £10 (per person in a double room) including service and VAT; prices go up in high season. There are reductions for stays of 2 nights or more; and 'bargain breaks' as well.

All rooms have the following amenities: central heating or electric heaters; electric blankets, washbasin, shaver-point; armchairs; views of garden; choice of duvets or blankets; door keys. Breakfast in bed is available; hair drier and extra-firm mattresses.

Meals Dinner is £5 for 3 courses with coffee. Morning, afternoon or bedtime drinks (coffee, tea etc.) can be ordered free.

Public rooms There is a sitting-room with central heating, open fire, TV (colour), books, magazines, local guides and leaflets, indoor games (such as Scrabble, Monopoly, dominoes), record-player and records. Maps on loan.

Surroundings The grounds consist of 350 acres of farmland and a garden. The following games or sports are available in the grounds: hard tennis court, coarse fishing, rough shooting. These are available in the neighbourhood: golf, riding.

Cars The nearest main road is the A15 from Lincoln to Humber Bridge.

Closed to visitors We are not open from November to January, except for house-parties of 6 people.

Waldon Cottage, The Square, Sheepwash, Beaworthy, north of Okehampton, Devon, EX21 5NE *Tel: 040923 382* **C D S ⌗3**

This pair of pink cottages with clematis on the walls are the prettiest of all the thatched houses surrounding the village square.

Here Josh Behenna (previously an electronics engineer) and his wife Constance have a tea-room and guest-house. Josh is the author of a book on west country shipwrecks, photos of which fill the walls of the low-ceilinged dining-room, while pot-plants cram the deep windowsills; and, on chilly evenings, a fire crackles on the stone hearth. The sitting-room fireplace has a great beam possibly a thousand years old, from a demolished chapel mentioned in Domesday Book, and a bread oven alongside. The green velvet armchairs are particularly comfortable, and there is an up-holstered rocking-chair too. Bedrooms are attractive; many with antiques, rosy fabrics and latched board doors.

Constance cooks traditional meals such as home-made soup with hot wholemeal rolls; roast beef; fresh fruit salad with clotted cream; followed by cheese and freshly ground coffee (or you can eat at the Half Moon Inn, also in the square). You can hire folding bicycles with which to explore the countryside.

Sheepwash, a conservation village, is near both Dartmoor and Exmoor; and the coast, too, is within reach to the north.

Reader's comments: A gem. Exceptionally nice people.

The following facts have been supplied by the owners:

Bedrooms There are 4 rooms, which include single, double and family rooms. Bed-and-breakfast costs from £11 (per person in a double room) including service and VAT. There are reductions for stays of 7 nights or more.

Some if not all of the rooms have the following amenities: electric heaters; washbasin, own bathroom and wc, shaver-point; armchairs; views of countryside. Early morning tea and breakfast in bed are available.

Meals The dinner menu is fixed price (£7). There is no choice of dishes on the fixed menu, which consists of 4 courses and coffee. Dinner is served at 8 pm. Morning, afternoon or bedtime drinks (coffee, tea etc.) can be ordered for a charge. Wine and other alcoholic drinks can be brought in.

Public rooms There is a sitting-room with open fire, TV (colour), books, magazines, local guides and leaflets, indoor games (such as Scrabble, chess, cards, dominoes, Canasta), piano.

Surroundings These are available in the neighbourhood: riding, fishing, golf.

Cars The nearest main road is the A3072 from Hatherleigh to Holsworthy.

Closed to visitors We are not open from November until Easter.

Walnut Cottage, Old Romsey Road, Cadnam, north of Southampton, Hampshire, SO4 2NP
Tel: 0703 812275   **C**(14) **D H PT ⌗11**

Because the road no longer leads anywhere (its days ended when a motorway replaced it), it is now utterly peaceful. The little white cottage, with brimming window-boxes and a red rambler-rose by the door, stands in a pretty garden (with an old well) which traps the sun. One bedroom opens onto this.

All the rooms have been attractively furnished by Charlotte and Eric Osgood, who did much of the work themselves (even the tiling of the showers, and the flowery china door-knobs on each bedroom door). There are two sitting-rooms with pale carpets, cretonne armchairs, flowers on the window-sills and interesting objects on the shelves. One has windows on all three sides. In the dining-room are Regency chairs, cupboard and mirror; a diminutive iron grate, as old as the cottage, has been preserved (though the only fireplace still in use is in the larger sitting-room). Here Mrs Osgood serves breakfast on Royal Doulton vineleaf china, but for other meals, she recommends a thatched and whitewashed inn a few yards down the lane (the 12th-century Sir John Barleycorn), and has a list of ten others to choose from within three miles, some in superb forest settings; and she will provide packed lunches.

The cottage is on the edge of the New Forest (it was originally occupied by foresters). Romsey and Broadlands are very near; Beaulieu, Salisbury, Winchester and Bournemouth only a little further. From Southampton there are trips to the Isle of Wight, and London is only a two-hour journey.

The Osgoods not only lend maps and cycles free, but have photocopied useful hints for a selection of car outings in the area, describing the route to each, listing sights, and also recommending the best inns for lunches, good bookshops, etc.

This is a good choice for an October break, when the forest colours are superb; but book well ahead if you want to go in September when Southampton's boat show and Beaulieu's 'auto jumble' sale are on.

Readers' comments: Beautifully located ... most helpful people. Delightful couple, charming rooms, comfortable; superb breakfasts. Excellent: a charming couple. Very impressed by their care and attention.

The following facts have been supplied by the owners:

Bedrooms There are 3 rooms, which include single and double rooms. Bed-and-breakfast costs from £10.50 (per person in a double room) including service and VAT; prices go up in high season. There are reductions for stays of 7 nights or more; and 'bargain breaks' as well.

Some if not all of the rooms have the following amenities: central heating; washbasin, shower, own bathroom and wc, shaver-point; radio, TV, hair drier, armchairs; views of countryside, garden; tea/coffee-making facilities; door keys.

Public rooms There are 2 sitting-rooms. The following are available in one or both of them: central heating, open fire, TV (colour), video, books, magazines, local guides and leaflets, indoor games (such as Scrabble and Yahtzee).

Surroundings The grounds consist of ⅓ acre of garden. Riding and golf are available in the neighbourhood. Maps and cycles on loan.

Cars The nearest main road is the M27 from London to Bournemouth.

Languages spoken French.

Wellpritton Farm, Holne, Ashburton, west of Newton Abbot, Devon, TQ13 7RX *Tel: 03643 273* **C(5) D S ⌗3**

Tucked away in a fold of the gentle hills south of Dartmoor is this small farm where sheep and pigs are kept; donkeys, goats and rabbits too.

Sue Townsend has furnished the bedrooms very prettily, and she equips them with supplies of fruit-squash and biscuits as well as tea. There is a 'family unit' of two rooms and a shower, and a ground-floor suite. A comfortable sitting-room is available to guests and in the dining-room four-course dinners are served. After a starter such as melon or pâté, the main course will probably be a roast, poultry or steak-and-kidney pudding, perhaps followed by fruit pie or flan, always accompanied by Devonshire cream, then cheese and coffee. Sue tries to cater for every guest individually. There is no charge for washing and ironing facilities, mealtimes are flexible, the welcome warm, and many extra services provided (loan of maps, hair drier, free tea on arrival, etc.).

From the farm, which has a small swimming-pool, there are views of the moors, and within a short drive one can reach Exeter, all the resorts and beaches of Torbay, Plymouth and innumerable beauty-spots in the countryside and along the coast. Dartmoor has a wild beauty all its own – a vast expanse of open country (one of the National Parks) with market towns and villages here and there, streams in the valleys and rocks high on the hills where sometimes mist or rain are dense. Nature trails, prehistoric remains, minibus tours, Buckfast and Buckland Abbeys, museums and historic buildings are among the possibilities for sightseeing.

Readers' comments: We were pampered, the situation is an absolute dream. Loud praises of all aspects, especially the food. The very best: nothing is too much trouble.

The following facts have been supplied by the owners:

Bedrooms There are 4 rooms, which include doubles and family suites. Bed-and-breakfast costs £9 (per person – no VAT payable). There are reductions for stays of 7 nights or more.

    Some if not all of the rooms have the following amenities: central heating or electric heaters; washbasin, shower, shaver-point; radio; views of countryside, farmland or garden; duvets; tea/coffee-making facilities; door keys; hair drier. Breakfast in bed is available, and bed-boards. Laundering facilities available.

Meals Dinner is fixed price (£6). There is a choice of dishes on the menu, which consists of 4 courses and coffee. Dinner is served at any time to suit guests. Special diets can be prepared. Packed lunches can be provided; and snacks at other hours. Morning, afternoon or bedtime drinks (coffee, tea etc.) are available in rooms at all times. Non-residents are not admitted to the dining-room. Wine and other alcoholic drinks can be brought in.

Public rooms There is a sitting-room with central heating, colour TV, books, magazines, local guides and leaflets and indoor games (such as cards, chess and Monopoly). Games room with snooker and table tennis. Maps on loan.

Surroundings The grounds consist of garden and open fields. There is an unheated swimming-pool. These are available in the neighbourhood: riding, fishing, golf, sailing, guided walks, and canoeing.

Cars The nearest main road is the B3357 from Ashburton to Tavistock.

West Cross House, High Street, Tenterden, Kent, TN30 6JL
Tel: 05806 2224   **C PT S ⌗15**

At the quieter end of the street stands this small Georgian hotel furnished with antiques, oriental carpets and well-chosen wall-papers. There are attractive details, such as fanlight, arches and turned banisters – and a pretty garden of paved paths, roses and magnolias. The big sitting-room, which runs right through from front to back, has a huge log grate in a brick inglenook. Each bedroom is different. I particularly liked one with velvet chairs and Paisley wallpaper.

A typical menu cooked by Mrs May might comprise home-made celery soup, a Dover sole or steak pie with fresh vegetables, and home-made ice cream with strawberries.

Tenterden, an interesting old town itself, is in the middle of an area full of things to see and do and is an agreeable place in which to shop. Within easy reach are the castles of Leeds, Chilham and Bodiam; Battle Abbey; and stately homes such as Penshurst. Canterbury is 45 minutes away. All around are the pretty villages, ancient churches and rural views typical of Kent, 'the market-garden of England'. Seaside resorts and many of the historic Cinque Ports are easily reached. Elegant Tunbridge Wells and its shops (antiques, books, crafts, clothes boutiques) lies a few miles in the other direction. This is an area where there is always something interesting afoot – notices along the country roads announce events like ox roasts and country-and-steam fairs or invite you to buy Jersey cream or to pick your own strawberries. My favourite simply read: 'Beware. Ducks crossing'.

Reader's comments: Excellent standards.

The following facts have been supplied by the owners:

Bedrooms There are 7 rooms, which include single, double and family rooms. Bed-and-breakfast costs from £10 (per person in a double room) including service and VAT. There are reductions for stays of 7 nights or more; and 'bargain breaks' as well.

   The rooms have central heating; washbasin, shaver-point; armchairs; tea/coffee-making facilities; door keys.

Meals The dinner menu is fixed price (£6). There is no choice of dishes on the fixed menu, which consists of 3 courses and coffee. Dinner is served at 7 pm. Special diets can be prepared. Wine and other alcoholic drinks can be ordered.

Public rooms There is a sitting-room with central heating, open fire, TV (colour), books, magazines, local guides and leaflets.

Cars The nearest main road is the A28 from Hastings to Canterbury.

Languages spoken French, German.

Closed to visitors We are not open in winter.

West Ditchburn Farm, Eglingham, north of Alnwick, Northumberland, NE66 2UE *Tel: 0665 78337* C(4) **D S ⧣5**

Set within a walled garden where peacocks and golden pheasants roam, this handsome stone house has roses and clematis around the porch and fine architectural details within: arches and a gracious white staircase with turned balusters, for example. It is at the heart of a 1000-acre farm where ewes and Charolais cattle are bred. A main attraction is listening to James Easton talk about these and his sheepdogs. He is Vice-President of the International Sheepdog Society, has appeared on TV's 'One Man and his Dog' programme, and the many silver cups he has won are on display. Collies which he bred and trained have gone to all parts of the world. Although the Romans knew how to use dogs for herding, driving and holding, in some countries the skill is still unknown, and he has sometimes gone abroad to teach it. He has a remarkable collection of crooks and walking-sticks carved by a local craftsman whose products are collectors' pieces.

Avril is an enthusiastic cook of traditional dishes, and welcomes visitors into her kitchen to watch. In winter when guests are few, she enjoys icing beautiful cakes to serve later.

All the rooms are handsomely furnished. The gold threadwork, fringed pelmets and bedspreads were made by Avril herself, in colours to tone with the thick plain carpets of each room.

She told me of one visitor, a retired bank manager, who has been coming back annually for seven years: I wasn't surprised!

For a description of the area, see page 298.

The following facts have been supplied by the owners:

Bedrooms There are 4 rooms, which include double and family rooms. Dinner, bed-and-breakfast costs from £16 (per person in a double room) including service and VAT; prices go up in high season. There are reductions for stays of 7 nights or more.

    Some if not all of the rooms have the following amenities: central heating or electric heaters; electric blankets, washbasin, shower, shaver-point; TV, armchairs; views of countryside; choice of duvets or blankets; tea/coffee-making facilities; door keys; hair drier.

Meals There is no choice of dishes on the fixed menu, which consists of 3 courses and coffee. Dinner is served at 7 pm. Special diets can be prepared. Lunches and packed lunches can be provided; and snacks at other hours. Non-residents are not admitted to the dining-room. Wine and other alcoholic drinks can be brought in.

Public rooms There is a sitting-room with central heating, open fire, TV (colour), books, magazines, local guides and leaflets.

Surroundings The grounds consist of 1,000 acres of farmland. These are available in the neighbourhood: pony trekking, golf, tennis, fishing.

Cars The nearest main road is the A1.

Closed to visitors We are not open between November and March.

West House, 12 West Street, Warminster, Wiltshire, BA12 8JJ
Tel: 0985 213936   **C(6) D PT S ⌗7**

A very graceful sitting-room extends from front to back of the 18th-century stone house: soft pink sofas and armchairs contrast with a celadon carpet, their colours complemented by those of handsome chinoiserie curtains with pheasants. White-shuttered windows are at each end. On the walls of this and other rooms are some of the sporting prints and watercolours which Charles Lane collects (and writes about). A fine staircase leads to charming bedrooms: I particularly liked one with rosebud wallpaper matching the pink slub spread on the cane-headed bed. Flowers and fruit are put in each room.

In the equally attractive dining-room, Celia Lane uses cordon bleu recipes for such meals as salmon mousse, chicken bonne femme, and the best raspberry pavlova I've ever tasted.

At the back are two large walled gardens with old-fashioned herbaceous beds and an immense tulip tree (it flowers late in July).

Charles is, incidentally, a descendant of the celebrated Jane Lane whose story is told elsewhere (see King's Lodge).

The Lanes love to tell their guests of good places to explore – not just the famous sights (Salisbury, Bath, Glastonbury and

451

Wells) but delightful spots such as Shaftesbury, Frome, Devizes or Bruton, for instance. Quite close by are Amesbury and Stonehenge, Longleat and its famous lions, the lovely vale of Pewsey, Wilton House, Stourhead and many beautiful but lesser known gardens.

The following facts have been supplied by the owners:

Bedrooms There are 2 single or double rooms. Bed-and-breakfast costs from £15 (per person). There are reductions for stays of 3 nights or more.
   Some if not all the rooms have the following amenities: central heating or electric heaters; electric blankets, washbasin, shower, own bathroom and wc, shaver-point; armchairs; views of countryside or garden; tea/coffee-making facilities. Breakfast in bed is available.

Meals The dinner menu is fixed price (£10) and consists of 3 courses with wine and coffee. Dinner is served at 8 pm. Vegetarian or special diets can be prepared. Lunches and packed lunches can be provided; and snacks at other hours. Morning, afternoon or bedtime drinks (coffee, tea etc.) can be ordered free.

Public rooms There are 2 sitting-rooms etc. The following are available in one or both of them: central heating, open fire, TV (colour), books, magazines, local guides and leaflets, indoor games (such as cards and board games), piano, record-player and records.

Surroundings The grounds consist of 2 acres of garden. These are available in the neighbourhood: golf, riding, fishing, swimming, tennis.

Cars The nearest main road is the A36 from Salisbury to Bath.

Only yards away is Warminster's oldest home, **Tudor House** (tel: 0985 215054), where young Lark Harrison – who makes silver jewellery – provides bed-and-breakfast at a modest charge. Built in 1480, it is a house of twists, turns, narrow stairs: furnished with character. Dinner if pre-booked.

Western House, Cavendish, north-west of Sudbury, Suffolk, CO10 8AR   *Tel: 0787 280550*   C S X ♯4

Twice made redundant, Peter Marshall decided he had had enough of industry and – his children now being grown up – would instead make a living from his best asset: his attractive 400-year-old house in the historic village of Cavendish.

He and his wife Jean (who teaches singing) are vegetarians, so at one end they started a wholefood shop, full of the good smells of dried fruit and fresh herbs, and refurnished several bedrooms to take bed-and-breakfast guests. Breakfast is served in bedrooms. Options include all kinds of good things (such as their own muesli, eggs, mushrooms, tomatoes and home-made bread) but no bacon. They are prepared to provide meatless evening-meals, or will recommend good restaurants of all kinds in the village, at Long Melford or in Sudbury which is nearby.

Each beamed bedroom, reached via zigzag corridors, is very pretty, and spacious – well equipped with chairs, table etc. One at the front (double-glazed, because it looks onto the main road through the village) has a fresh white-and-green colour scheme extending even to the sheets, and tomato-red blankets. In the pink room are patchwork curtains made by Jean.

One of the nicest features is the large and informal garden

453

where paved paths wander between old-fashioned flowers, elderly fruit trees, and chimneypots or troughs brimming with plants.

Cavendish is one of a string of mediaeval villages. Clare (see page 386) is close, so is Sudbury town (pages 303–4), Bury St Edmunds (page 457) and Long Melford – very long indeed, lined with dignified houses and good shops. Its church and its great mansions (Melford Hall and Kentwell Hall) are well worth seeing.

Readers' comments: Excellent, with very good breakfasts. Much enjoyed it; and the shop is excellent.

The following facts have been supplied by the owners:

Bedrooms There are 4 rooms, which include single, double and family rooms. Bed-and-breakfast costs from £9 (per person) including service and VAT.
    Some if not all of the rooms have the following amenities: central heating or electric heaters; washbasin, shaver-point; views of countryside, garden; choice of duvets or blankets. Breakfast in bed is available.
Surroundings The grounds consist of an acre of garden.
Cars The nearest main road is the A1092 from Clare to Long Melford.

———————————

Western House, Winchelsea Road, Rye, East Sussex
Tel: 0797 223419   **C PT X ♯5**

The mediaeval port of Rye was perched high on a thumb of land (almost an island) projecting into the sea. But centuries ago the sea receded, leaving behind dry land which became ideal pasturage for sheep. It is here, at the foot of Rye town, that tile-hung Western House was built in the 18th century, commanding far views – you can even see Hastings in clear weather – from its cobbled terrace (with working pump) where tea may be taken, or from the huge lawn surrounded by brilliant flowerbeds set against mellow stone walls. On summer evenings, the terrace is lit by old Victorian street-lamps.

Artist Ron Dellar is the present owner of Western House, and his paintings fill the dining-room walls. The big, cluttered sitting-room has his studio in the bay window at one end. Here, up the staircase, and in the bedrooms are all manner of 'finds' he has amassed over the years: African masks, a parrot in a glass dome, an 1820 box of paints ('Constable was alive then', he comments), Rupert Bear books, antique toys. Melanie, his wife, sells Victorian lace, linen, baby-gowns and books which are laid out in the big entrance hall.

This is a house of character, as befits its long history. A boat-builder lived here and, later on, Members of Parliament. Among its visitors (in 1913) was the impressionist artist Pissarro; and Ron has incorporated him in a mural featuring Rye church which he painted for one of the bedrooms. All these rooms are attractively decorated, with interesting wallpapers and fresh flowers, and have good views of the marshes across which you can walk to Winchelsea. There's a moated Martello tower out there, giant marsh-frogs croak throatily, you may see herons or marsh harriers flying overhead. (There is more about Rye and its environs under other entries.)

Dinner is not usually served because Rye has so many good inns and restaurants (choose the Monastery Hotel for its view of romantic ruins; Simmons for exceptionally good cuisine).

The following facts have been supplied by the owners:

Bedrooms There are 3 rooms, which include double and family rooms. Bed-and-breakfast costs from £10 (per person in a double room) including service and VAT; prices go up in high season. There are reductions for stays of 7 nights or more; and 'bargain breaks' as well.

Some if not all of the rooms have the following amenities: central heating or electric heaters; washbasin, shower and wc, shaver-point; armchairs; views of countryside and garden; orthopaedic mattress; tea/coffee-making facilities. Morning, afternoon or bedtime drinks (coffee, tea etc.) can be ordered for a charge.

Surroundings The grounds consist of 1½ acres of garden. These are available in the neighbourhood: riding, golf, tennis, river and sea fishing.

Cars The nearest main road is the A259 from Dover to the west.

Languages spoken German.

Another modestly priced guest-house, in the middle of Rye, is mediaeval **Swan Cottage** where, above her tea-rooms, Sheila Brown has a few pretty, little, low-beamed bedrooms to let. (Tel: 0797 222423.)

Westley Hall, Westley, west of Bury St Edmunds, Suffolk, IP33 3TQ   *Tel: 0284 4699*   **C PT ⬚4**

One of the most attractive features of this largely Georgian, pink-walled house is its romantic garden. Past a big herbaceous border and fine trees is a secluded pool that has been elegantly landscaped with flowering shrubs and a weeping birch at its brink. It is frequented by wild ducks and moorhens. Big stepping-stones cross it, and a small fountain sparkles upwards from a millstone in the middle. On the other side of the house is a glass verandah with swing-seat beneath an abundant grape-vine.

All the bedrooms are very agreeably furnished, and contain interesting pictures, ornaments and flowers. Vicki Saltmarsh sometimes even puts a bowl of strawberries (already hulled!) in each, from her garden. The sitting-room is large, light and elegant, its big windows set in deep, white-shuttered embrasures. She serves only breakfast, but for dinner recommends eating-places nearby or in Bury St Edmunds, where there are several bistros, excellent food at the Angel Hotel, and an outstanding fish restaurant (Mortimers).

456

Westley is very close to the historic abbey town of Bury, place of mediaeval ruins and churches, fine gardens, Georgian byways, and some good shops for antiques or crafts. It has a Regency theatre (belonging to the National Trust) and some unusual museums. Newmarket and its races are near, too. The famous mediaeval wool villages of Suffolk are within a short distance (see descriptions on other pages of Clare, Cavendish, Lavenham etc.), all with half-timbered houses and richly decorated churches. Georgian Ickworth Hall stands in grounds landscaped by Capability Brown. Among the undulating hills are pretty streams, mills, country parks and inns.

The following facts have been supplied by the owners:

Bedrooms There are 2 rooms, a double and a family room. Bed-and-breakfast costs from £10 (per person in a double room) including service and VAT; prices go up in high season.

Some if not all of the rooms have the following amenities: central heating; electric blankets, washbasin, shaver-point; radio, TV (b & w); tea/coffee-making facilities; door keys. Hair drier and laundry facilities available.

Public rooms There is a sitting-room with central heating, open fire, TV (colour), books, magazines, local guides and leaflets, indoor games (such as chess, cards, etc.)

Surroundings The grounds consist of one acre of garden. These are available in the neighbourhood: golf, leisure centre, riding, roller skating.

Cars The nearest main road is the A45 from the Midlands to Felixstowe.

White Barn, Crede Lane, Bosham, west of Chichester, West Sussex, PO18 8NX   *Tel: 0243 573113*   **C H PT S X ♯5**

As interesting architecturally as any house in this book, White Barn is no barn but a very modern house indeed (single storey), designed only a few years ago by architect Frank Guy, and standing in the seclusion of a former orchard.

The dining-room is impressive: its principal features are a roof of exposed boards, a vast glass wall on one side (opening onto a red-tiled terrace and lawn), and a circular brick-edged flowerbed half indoors and half out.

This room is open to the big kitchen with its scarlet Aga cooker, pans hanging from brass hooks, and solid beech work-counter with old brass grocery-scales built in.

Then there is an oddly-shaped sitting-room, built all around the circular brick hearth on which a modern log stove stands. Its huge sofas face a narrow window 20 feet high. Throughout there are white walls, glossy scarlet doors and natural Berber carpets contrasting with one another.

Few visitors prefer a separate table for meals but join all the others at a huge pine refectory table, laid with flowery Portmeirion pottery, where Susan Trotman serves such appetite-whetting meals as curried parsnip soup (or some very original salad or pâté) before, perhaps, pork cooked with ginger (and four vegetables), then a pavlova topped with lemon curd and Jersey cream, or a Bakewell tart, and cheeses.

Bedrooms open onto the garden, or overlook it. One is an imaginatively planned family suite: the room with children's bunk beds is rather like a ship's cabin, leading onward to the parents' room.

rear view

Not far away is the Saxon harbour of Bosham (its church is depicted in the Bayeux tapestry), thronged with little boats. Chichester, described elsewhere, lies in one direction and the historic naval waterfront of Portsmouth in the other – where you can visit HMS *Victory*, the *Mary Rose*, the dockyard museum, old bastions and byways, Southsea Castle, and the ring of high Victorian forts up in the surrounding hills. Plenty of sea trips from here, some to the Isle of Wight; and several excellent museums.

Reader's comments: Very comfortable, food superb. Excellent value, memorable – not to be missed!

The following facts have been supplied by the owners:

Bedrooms There are 6 rooms, which include single, double and family rooms. Bed-and-breakfast costs from £15 (per person in a double room) including service and VAT; prices go up in high season. There are reductions for stays of 7 nights or more; and 'bargain breaks' as well.

  Some if not all of the rooms have the following amenities: central heating or electric heaters; electric blankets, washbasin, shower, own bathroom and wc, shaver-point; armchairs; views of garden; choice of duvets or blankets; tea/coffee-making facilities; door keys. Breakfast in bed is available.

Meals The dinner menu is fixed price (£10). There is a choice of dishes on the fixed menu, which consists of 4 courses and coffee. Dinner is served at 7 pm. Special diets can be prepared, and snacks. Non-residents are not admitted to the dining-room. Wine and other alcoholic drinks can be brought in.

Public rooms There are 2 sitting-rooms etc. The following are available in one or both: central heating, open fire, TV (colour), books, magazines, local guides and leaflets.

Surroundings The grounds consist of a garden. These are available in the neighbourhood: golf, tennis, sailing, swimming, riding.

Cars The nearest main road is the A27 from Chichester to Portsmouth.

Closed to visitors We are not open for the first two weeks in January.

White Bear Inn, Shipston-on-Stour, Warwickshire, CV36 4AJ
Tel: 0608 61558   ⌗5

In the centre of Shipston – a quiet little town on the edge of the Cotswolds – is this typical old inn. Typical except for the food, which Hugh and Suzanne Roberts have made exceptional. Even the snacks served in the beamed bar are well above the ordinary (delicious stuffed mushrooms, for instance, with a topping of melted cheese). At dinner, one chooses from a lengthy à la carte menu that includes such things as mussel chowder or salmon-and-prawn pâté for starters; beef en croûte with madeira sauce or veal provençale (cooked with aubergine, tomato, garlic and wine); then perhaps an apricot soufflé or chocolate sponge sandwiched with maple cream and chocolate mousse.

Upstairs are pine-doored bedrooms with pretty wallpapers and bedspreads, well insulated from any sounds by their thick stone walls. Two are almost small suites. Fresh flowers and good pictures are everywhere. No sitting-room.

Shipston (itself an attractive town, with interesting little shops) lies conveniently between Oxford and Stratford-upon-Avon. Within easy motoring distance are Warwick Castle, the Cotswold towns, Cheltenham Spa, Woodstock (for Blenheim Palace), the famous garden of Hidcote, and the lovely Vale of Evesham from which comes much of the White Bear's fruit and vegetables.

The following facts have been supplied by the owners:

Bedrooms There are 9 rooms, which include single, double and family rooms. Bed-and-breakfast costs from £17 (per person in a double room) including service and VAT. There are reductions for stays of 7 nights or more; and 'bargain breaks' as well.

Some if not all of the rooms have the following amenities: gas heaters; washbasin, shower, own bathroom and wc, shaver-point; armchairs; choice of duvets or blankets; TV (colour); tea/coffee-making facilities; door keys. Breakfast in bed is available.

Meals The dinner menu is à la carte. Dinner is served from 7.30 pm. Special diets can be prepared. Bar meals are available. Lunches and packed lunches can be provided; and snacks at other hours. Wine and other alcoholic drinks can be ordered.

Surroundings These are available in the neighbourhood: golf, fishing, hunting, shooting.

Cars The nearest main road is the A34 from Oxford to Stratford-upon-Avon.

Credit cards accepted Visa, Diners Club, Amex, Access.

When booking, or enquiring, please mention *Staying Off the Beaten Track* as your source of information

White Hart Inn, Ford, west of Chippenham, Wiltshire, SN14 8RP
Tel: 0249 782213   C(3) H X ♯7

Ken Gardner had won four awards as a Fleet Street reporter when he decided to give up his high-powered career and turn to hotel-keeping.

This stone Tudor inn was derelict when he and Lily bought it a few years ago at auction. Once it had been a coaching inn beside a ford in the River Bybrook (later it was bridged), in the clear waters of which you can watch the trout leaping above the mossy stones, while ducks and chickens wander on its banks. It is an idyllic setting, in an area officially designated as being of outstanding natural beauty, for what is now a very fine inn again.

Inside are low beams, log fires, armour, tapestry seats, and china pump-handles to dispense real ales. The date 1553 is carved into one of the stone walls. There was once a watermill here; and in the little sitting-room you hear the sound of the mill-race which still survives and runs underneath it. The beamed dining-room has black wood walls, green velvet curtains and buttoned velvet seats.

Most of the elegant bedrooms (impeccably equipped – even to trouser presses and bidets) are in the former stable block. Much of the original stonework is exposed, and most furniture is of polished pine. One even has its own dressing-room, and several have four-posters. On the terrace outside there is sometimes Morris dancing or (on sunny Sunday mornings) music. To one side is a sheltered swimming-pool.

As to the food, cooked by Andrew Burchell, this too is

outstanding – with the emphasis on old-fashioned recipes: venison in port, jugged hare, creamed herring-roes on toast (as a starter), lamb braised with honey and rosemary, are examples – and hot beef sandwich with gravy as a bar snack. Pies and pasties are cooked to order.

The two-day break prices are particularly good value.

Within a few miles of the White Hart are Castle Combe (which fairly claims to be England's prettiest village), Bath, several stately homes (Bowood, Longleat, Doddington and Sheldon Manor), the Wildfowl Trust at Slimbridge and the Tropical Bird Gardens at Rode, superb gardens at Corsham Court.

The following facts have been supplied by the owners:

Bedrooms There are 11 rooms, which include single, double and family rooms. Bed-and-breakfast costs from £22 (per person in a double room) including service and VAT; prices go up in high season. There are reductions for stays of 2 nights or more; and very good value 'bargain breaks' all the year round.

All rooms have the following amenities: central heating; washbasin, shower or bathroom and wc, shaver-point; radio, TV (colour), armchairs; and some have views of countryside. Tea/coffee-making facilities and door keys are provided.

Meals The dinner menu is fixed price (£11). There is a choice of dishes on the fixed menu, which consists of 4 courses and coffee. Dinner is served at 7.30-9.30 pm. Vegetarian or special diets can be prepared. Lunches and packed lunches can be provided; and snacks at other hours. Bedtime drinks (coffee, tea etc.) can be ordered for a charge. Wine and other alcoholic drinks can be ordered.

Public rooms There is a sitting-room, well heated, with colour TV, books, magazines, local guides and leaflets, board games.

Surroundings The grounds consist of 2 acres on both sides of trout stream, with swimming-pool (80°), shrubbery and terraces. These are available in the neighbourhood: golf, squash, tennis, riding, fishing.

Cars The nearest main road is the A420 from Bristol to Chippenham.

Languages spoken French.

Credit cards accepted Most.

White Hart Inn, Tetford, north-east of Horncastle, Lincolnshire, LN9 6QQ   *Tel: 065883 255*   **C S-C X ♯4**

The beauty of the Lincolnshire Wolds is at last beginning to be appreciated, now that more people are heading this way en route to the huge, relatively new Humber Bridge as an entry to Yorkshire. This is 'Tennyson country': the poet was born at Somersby and his lines 'Come into the garden, Maud' referred to the garden of nearby Harrington Hall.

The White Hart (built in 1520) is a traditional inn, once visited by Dr Johnson as well as Tennyson. In the bar at the back wainy-edge tables crowd the red-tiled floor, there are bacon hooks in the beams with pewter mugs hanging, and a huge curved oak settle is drawn up by the fireplace, a rag rug in front of it. Everywhere are low doors, and steps up or down. Another lounge bar was added some years ago and this, by contrast, has big windows all around.

Upstairs, every bedroom has not only a bedspread but curtains made of Welsh wool tapestry; and there is a good sitting-room for residents (something often skimped in pubs), with long sofas. Wednesday, incidentally, is the night when the inn has live music.

Colin and Carol Lloyd have built up a reputation for food – mainly conventional steaks and classics like boeuf stroganoff or coq au vin – available on any evening except Mondays; and for real ale. They are now planning fishing holidays.

As to the area, Tetford village is celebrated for having in its greenstone church (adorned with huge gargoyles) the helmet and breastplate of the Sovereign's Champion – last carried at the coronation of George II. The Champion is always a Dymoke, local landowners here – although now nothing more combative than a standard is carried by them at each coronation. It's an attractive, tranquil village of which an 18th-century poet wrote (with a good deal of poetic licence!):

> Far to the North, where Lindsey props the skies,
> Embosomed in her mountains Tetford lies;

Whose rustic bowers present secure retreats
From winter's rigours and from summer heats.

When you have finished touring the Wolds themselves, officially designated an 'area of outstanding natural beauty' (and crossed the bridge to visit Hull's historic waterfront and excellent maritime museum – also Wilberforce's house, I suggest) there is always Lincoln, the coast, Tattershall Castle, the nature reserve at Gibraltar Point, delightful little Louth, and the ancient byways and Pilgrim Fathers' cells in Boston to explore. For walkers, there is the Viking Way footpath which runs through the Wolds, to Woodhall Spa and on to Lincoln etc.; or the shorter Spa Trail. Skegness has a farm museum.

The following facts have been supplied by the owners:

Bedrooms There are 6 rooms, which include singles and doubles. Bed-and-breakfast costs from £12 (per person in a double room) including service and VAT. There are reductions for stays of 3 nights or more; and 'bargain breaks' as well.

All rooms have the following amenities: central heating; washbasin, shaver-point; armchairs; views of countryside/farmland/garden; tea/coffee-making facilities; door keys.

Meals The dinner menu is à la carte. Dinner is served at 7.30–9 pm. Special diets can be prepared, such as vegetarian or hyper-active children's. Lunches and packed lunches can be provided. Wine and other alcoholic drinks can be ordered.

Public rooms There is a sitting-room with central heating, TV (colour), books, magazines, local guides and leaflets. Also bars.

Surroundings The grounds consist of a garden.

Cars The nearest main road is the A152 from Lincoln to Skegness.

Languages spoken French and German.

Credit cards accepted Access, Visa.

The White House, south-east of Penrith, Cumbria, CA10 2EL
Booking service: 0498 81563   **C PT S ⌗6**

There is more to Cumbria than the Lake District, as visitors to the White House have found: intending to make it their base for a holiday among the well-known beauty-spots, they in fact spent all their time getting to know the lesser-known attractions of the county – the picturesque villages of the Eden valley and the grandeur of the north Pennines. While Ullswater is only five miles away, in other directions lie Lowther Park, with plenty of amusements for children; Appleby with its Norman castle and collection of waterfowl and rare breeds of livestock, such as friendly Vietnamese pigs; and an ancient pottery, still working.

The Fowlers started this guest-house quite recently. After years of running a big hotel, their aim is to apply their professional standards of quality while giving a more personal service than the problems of a large establishment usually allow. The rooms in the 18th-century onetime farmhouse are spacious and light, decorated in pale colours and with plain carpets and sprigged wallpaper. One of the two sitting-rooms has a bar. Views from the rooms are of a trim garden, backed by rolling green hills. On one side of the house are riding stables, on the other one of the sandstone villages of the Eden valley.

The village lies on the A6 a couple of miles from Penrith with its mainline station, so it is very easily reached by both rail travellers and motorists using the M6 (which has taken away much of the through traffic from the village). Though a useful overnight stopping place, the White House merits a longer stay.

A typical meal cooked by Jean might consist of salmon and cucumber mousse, a roast or steak-and-mushroom pie, and peach melba with home-made ice cream. She uses nothing but fresh ingredients (she was once thrown out of a restaurant for complaining at being served packet soup!), some of which will have come from the garden.

The following facts have been supplied by the owners:

Bedrooms There are 6 rooms, which include single, double and family rooms. Bed-and-breakfast costs from £10.25 (per person) including service and VAT.

Some if not all of the rooms have the following amenities: central heating; washbasin, own bathroom and wc, shaver-point; armchairs; views of countryside or garden; tea/coffee-making facilities; door keys.

Meals The dinner menu is fixed price (£6). There is a choice of dishes on the fixed menu, which consists of 3 courses and coffee. Dinner is served at 6.45 pm. Vegetarian or special diets can be prepared. Packed lunches can be provided. Wine and other alcoholic drinks can be ordered.

Public rooms There are 2 sitting-rooms etc. The following are available in one or both of them: central heating, open fire, TV (colour), books, magazines, local guides and leaflets, indoor games (such as Scrabble, chess, draughts, cards and Trivial Pursuit), organ, record-player and records; bar.

Surroundings The grounds consist of a garden. These are available in the neighbourhood: pony trekking, swimming-pool, golf.

Cars The nearest main road is the A6 from Kendal to Carlisle.

Languages spoken French.

White Lodge, Grosvenor Road, Swanage, Dorset, BH19 2DD
Tel: 0929 422696   **C(4) PT S ⌗6**

In one of those steep, quiet streets which encircle Swanage and its bay stands a good, solid home of seventy years ago built, I would guess, by some architect influenced a little by Lutyens. In its white walls are stone-mullioned windows of generous size, with leaded panes. The staircase is solid oak, with a striking stained-glass window rising up two floors. Some of the bedrooms have magnificent views over the rooftops to the sea with its boats and water-skiers, while the big bay window of the sitting-room looks on to a flowery little garden.

Fred and Sheila Pope, who now run White Lodge as a small hotel, were both brought up in Wiltshire farming communities, so they know what good, fresh food should be like. Fred grows most of the fruit and vegetables, and there is considerable emphasis on natural ingredients like wholemeal flour for bread and pastry. Local trout and plaice regularly appear on the menu, and there is a particularly good selection of cheeses. Fred is something of an expert on German wines – and, if you are lucky, you may be offered a glass of his own sloe gin. Before Sheila started cooking for guests here, and while they were looking for a small hotel to buy, she did a professional cookery course but has not lost the 'home-made' touch. Each table may have its own steak-and-kidney pie, and she will try to cook your favourite dishes – from light meringues to filling steamed puddings.

The safe, sandy beach and the shops are just down the hill, and within a short distance are all the other beauty-spots and sights of the Purbeck area (see page 188). The Dorset coastal path appeals to walkers, but there are plenty of other scenic walks elsewhere too.

Readers' comments: Excellent cooking and personal attention. The most charming, warm and honest couple, delightful sense of humour; the best holiday we have ever had.

The following facts have been supplied by the owners:

Bedrooms There are 11 rooms, which include single, double and family rooms. Bed-and-breakfast costs from £11.50 (per person), including VAT; prices go up in high season. There are reductions for stays of 6 nights or more; and slight savings on low-season 'bargain breaks' as well.

Some if not all of the rooms have the following amenities: central heating or electric heaters; electric blankets, washbasin, shower and wc, shaver-point; armchairs; views of sea, countryside, garden; choice of duvets or blankets; tea/coffee facilities; door keys. Bed-boards available.

Meals The dinner menu is fixed price (£5.50). There is a choice of dishes on the menu, which consists of 4 courses and coffee. Dinner is served at 6.30 pm. Special diets can be prepared. Packed lunches can be provided. Morning, afternoon or bedtime drinks (coffee, tea etc.) can be ordered for a charge. Non-residents are not admitted to the dining-room. Wine and other alcoholic drinks can be ordered.

Public rooms There are 2 sitting-rooms. The following are available in one or both of them: central heating, colour TV, books, magazines, local guides and leaflets, indoor games (such as chess, draughts, cards, Scrabble), piano and a bar.

Surroundings The grounds consist of ⅓ acre of garden. These are available in the neighbourhood: sailing, sub-aqua diving, wind-surfing, rock climbing, golf, riding, bird watching, tennis, bowls, angling, badminton, squash, cycle hire and a nature reserve.

Cars The nearest main road is the A35 from Poole to Dorchester.

Closed to visitors We are not open in winter.

Whyke House, 13 Whyke Lane, Chichester, West Sussex, PO19 2JR *Tel: 0243 788767* **C PT S X ⌗5**

In an ordinary suburban cul-de-sac, very close to the historic centre of Chichester (and overlooking a grassy Roman site at the back, where children now play) is an unusual bed-and-breakfast house, ideal for families.

Here Tony and Lydia Hollis cook their guests' breakfasts (and service their rooms), give advice on sightseeing, then depart to their own home close by. But there is a fully equipped kitchen which guests are then welcome to use to prepare other meals, if they do not wish to go to Chichester's many restaurants and cafés. Unlimited tea etc. is provided. Guests can also use sitting-room and back garden (with fruit trees), glimpsed in the drawing. It is almost like being in a home of your own, with complete freedom.

rear view

The furnishings, though homely, have individuality. Family antiques mingle with Russian folk art, local paintings (you may meet the artist) with soft furnishings made by Lydia – who has a flair for re-using old fabrics and lace in new ways.

For some older guests, the ground-floor bedroom and shower are particularly convenient.

(Other entries describe Chichester and its environs.)

Reader's comments: The Hollises are so kind and helpful.

The following facts have been supplied by the owners:

Bedrooms There are 4 rooms, which include single, double and family rooms. Bed-and-breakfast costs from £10 (per person). There are reductions for stays of 4 nights or more.

   Some if not all of the rooms have the following amenities: central heating; washbasin, double-glazing, shaver-point; TV (colour), armchairs; views of garden; choice of duvets or blankets; tea-making facilities; door keys. Iron available.

Public rooms There are 2 sitting-rooms, with central heating, books, magazines, local guides and leaflets.

Surroundings There is a small garden.

Cars The nearest main road is the A27 from Worthing to Portsmouth.

Wide Lane Cottage, Sway Road, Brockenhurst, Hampshire
Tel: 0590 22296   **H PT ⌂8**

This 17th-century cottage in the heart of the New Forest, where ponies and cattle roam free, is screened by trees and garden from the road. Honeysuckle climbs over the porch, baskets of petunias hang from the wrought-iron balcony of the principal bedroom, and roses climb up the white walls. Inside, the little rooms downstairs are low-beamed, with old panelled doors which have decorative wrought-iron hinges, and chintz fabrics. A log fire crackles in winter: the right setting for hearing about the Wide Lane ghost!

Mrs Moore has provided a ground-floor bedroom for those who find stairs difficult. All the rooms are furnished in simple cottage style, except for the balcony bedroom which is fitted with white-and-gold furniture. Guests are welcome to sit in the sunny garden which has a paved terrace, lawn and rock-garden with two tall and shapely cypresses.

As to meals, everything, is home-made, from (for instance) the creamy onion soup to Black Forest gâteau. With roast beef comes Yorkshire pudding as well as a choice of fresh vegetables; then there is cheese to follow.

The New Forest and surrounding places of interest are described on page 446.

The following facts have been supplied by the owners:

Bedrooms There are 5 rooms, which include double and family rooms. Bed-and-breakfast costs from £14 (per person in a double room) including service and VAT; prices go up in high season. There are reductions for stays of 7 nights or more; and 'bargain breaks' as well.

   Some if not all of the rooms have the following amenities: central heating; washbasin; armchairs; views of garden; balcony; door keys. Bed-boards, hair drier and laundry facilities available.

Meals The dinner menu is fixed price (£8) or à la carte. There is a choice of dishes on the fixed menu, which consists of 4 courses and coffee. Dinner is served at 7 pm. Special diets can be prepared. Lunches and packed lunches can be provided; and snacks at other hours. Morning, afternoon or bedtime drinks (coffee, tea etc.) can be ordered for a charge. Wine and other alcoholic drinks can be brought in.

Public rooms There is a sitting-room with central heating, open fire, TV (colour), books, magazines, local guides and leaflets, indoor games (such as cards). Maps on loan.

Surroundings The grounds consist of ¾ acre of garden. These are available in the neighbourhood: riding, golf, sailing. Cycle hire.

Cars The nearest main road is the A337 from Lyndhurst to Lymington.

Wigham, Morchard Bishop, north-west of Crediton, Devon, EX17 6RJ   *Tel: 03637 350*   **C S X ⛫3**

Young Stephen and Lesley Chilcott gave up teaching careers in Guernsey in order to start a smallholding in Devon. They fell in love with the apricot walls and thatched roof of Wigham and now (along with producing honey, rich Guernsey milk, butter, goat and other cheeses, clotted cream, yogurt, eggs, vegetables and fruit – some of which you can buy to take home) run it as a particularly delightful Tudor guest-house, facing south across a peaceful valley. Beneath may lie more ancient remains for Wigham is a Saxon name, meaning Wig's farm.

The sitting-room is of special interest. Facing the stone fireplace (with original bread oven) is a solid oak screen-wall, while next to a window with leaded panes is another rarity – a cream oven. Warmed by charcoal, this recess in the wall was used for clotting cream, a bowl of which would be kept there at least 12 hours. In some bedrooms you can see the cruck construction of the house (curving timbers supporting the roof, rough-hewn from great oaks). The cobb walls are three feet thick.

For the dining-room, Stephen had a great wainy-edged elm table and chairs specially made. The walls are hung with tapestries – valuable reproductions of mediaeval originals. Opposite the big stone fireplace are glass doors with a fine view beyond, including a distant prospect of Dartmoor's hills.

Bedrooms are prettily furnished in cottagey style and Lesley puts fresh flowers in them; most have low doorways and sloping ceilings. One pair make a good family suite. A small kitchen for guests' use is handy for preparing children's food.

Children, of course, love staying here and encountering the geese and ducks, calves and horses, goats and cows, and rare breeds of pig. Both Exmoor and Dartmoor are near; sandy beaches to north or south can be reached in about three-quarters of an hour, driving along some of Devonshire's loveliest lanes. This is a 'no smoking' house.

The following facts have been supplied by the owners:

Bedrooms There are 8 rooms, which include double and family rooms. Dinner, bed-and-breakfast costs from £21 (per person in a double room) including service and VAT; prices go up in high season; there are 'bargain breaks'.

Some if not all of the rooms have the following amenities: electric heaters; electric blankets; views of countryside/farmland/garden; choice of duvets or blankets; washbasin or own bathroom or shower – some have bidets. Tea-making facilities on request, or tea can be ordered.

Meals There is no choice of dishes on the fixed menu, which consists of 4 courses and coffee. Dinner is served at 8 pm. Special diets can be prepared. Lunches and packed lunches can be provided; and snacks at other hours. Morning, afternoon or bedtime drinks (coffee, tea etc.) can be ordered for a charge. Non-residents are not admitted to the dining-room. Wine and other alcoholic drinks can be ordered.

Public rooms There is a sitting-room with open fire, TV (colour), books, magazines, local guides and leaflets, video, radio, record-player and records; bar.

Surroundings The grounds consist of 11 acres of smallholding and garden with heated swimming-pool. These are available in the neighbourhood: riding, fishing, golf, hunting, ponies for children.

Cars The nearest main road is the A377 from Exeter to Barnstaple.

Languages spoken French, German.

Also in this neighbourhood: **Nymet Bridge House** at Lapford, a mediaeval guest-house where Mrs Cullimore provides a four-course dinner, bed-and-breakfast inexpensively (tel: 03635 334).

Please check prices before booking, and whether there has been any change of ownership (or cook!)

Windrush House, Hazleton, west of Northleach, Gloucestershire, GL54 4EB *Tel: 0451 60364* C(12) ⌗5

After Mr Harrison retired from business, he and his wife Sydney extended their 1960s home of Cotswold stone in order to turn it into a small guest-house. This was only a few years ago, but already many visitors have been back several times. The greatest attraction is Mrs Harrison's outstanding cooking. Not only is everything impeccably prepared – vegetables delicately sliced and lightly cooked, bread home-baked, breakfast orange juice freshly squeezed, kippers brought from Craster – but she has a repertoire of imaginative dishes that puts many an expensive restaurant in the shade. Visitors sink back into deep velvet armchairs after dinner to argue amiably about which are her best dishes: the nettle soup, generously laden with cream? her pigeon pie or jugged hare? the nameless confection of rum, chocolate and cream with macaroons? hake in a rich, lemony sauce? (All her sauces are light and delectable.) With your breakfast porridge you will be offered whisky. And all the food is served on Royal Worcester porcelain.

The Harrisons are modest, unassuming people whose only aim is to make their visitors feel at home. The friendly welcome is manifest the moment you arrive – a free glass of sherry awaits you in your room, and the two dogs are dismissed if you happen not to like dogs. There are about 20 moderately priced wines to choose from.

As to the house itself, this is furnished with much attention to comfort, and in tranquil colours. All the rooms are immaculate, and the furnishings (conventional in style) are of high quality. The

473

house stands in a quiet spot some 500 feet up in the Cotswold hills, where the air is bracing and the views are of far fields and grazing sheep. It is on the outskirts of a rambling village of old stone farmhouses with a small church nearby – part of it pre-Norman.

Hazleton is close to beautiful Northleach, which has a mediaeval church of great splendour; Cirencester, a lovely market town with the outstanding Corinium museum, crafts, another church as grand as a cathedral and a great park; Burford and Cheltenham, with all the elegance of a spa, particularly at the Montpelier end of the great Promenade (another good museum and fine church). The beauty of the Cotswold hills needs no describing, nor its showpiece villages like Bourton-on-the-Water, Bibury and Stow-on-the-Wold. There are Roman remains, butterfly and bird gardens, folk and farm museums, wildlife parks, stately homes and gardens, castles, abbeys and good walks. (There is more about this area on page 57.)

Readers' comments: Food absolutely outstanding, even for a spoiled Swiss! Absolute calm. First-rate; inventive menu; highly recommended. Excellent food and genial hosts.

The following facts have been supplied by the owners:

Bedrooms There are 4 double rooms. Bed-and-breakfast costs from £13 (per person) including VAT. There are 'bargain breaks'.
   Some if not all of the rooms have the following amenities: central heating or electric heaters; electric blankets, washbasin, shower and wc, shaver-point; radio, armchairs; views of countryside and garden; door keys. Breakfast in bed is available.

Meals The dinner menu is fixed price (£10 or £11.50). There is no choice of dishes on the menu, which consists of 4 courses and coffee. Dinner is served at 7.30 pm. Packed lunches can be provided. Morning, afternoon or bedtime drinks (coffee, tea etc.) can be ordered for a charge. Wine and other alcoholic drinks can be ordered. Sunday lunches in winter only.

Public rooms There are 2 sitting-rooms. The following are available in one or both of them: central heating, open fire, colour TV, books, magazines, local guides and leaflets, indoor games (such as Scrabble), piano, record-player and records.

Surroundings The grounds consist of an acre of garden.

Cars The nearest main road is the A40 from London to Wales.

Please check prices before booking, and whether there has been any change of ownership (or cook!)

**Winnall Cottage Farm, Easton, east of Winchester, Hampshire,
SO21 1DQ** *Tel: 0962 54184* **C D X #11**

There are few places where flocks of free-range hens are kept on a
commercial scale. This is one of them, and the sound of much
contented clucking from the field facing the house is one of the
pleasures of staying here. Among the chickens ponies graze.

An avenue of beech trees leads to the house, which is furnished
in an attractive style: big orange checks, for instance, on bedspreads and curtains; and pine furniture that includes a built-in
closet concealing tea-making facilities. In the well-equipped bathroom (with bidet) there are pine furniture fitments with louvred
doors. Only breakfast is served by Jean Wheeler, and there is no
sitting-room for guests – though they can sit in the garden.

Footpaths take you all the way into historic Winchester if you
want a change from driving (a 20-minute walk), where the
immensely long Norman cathedral, surrounded by lawns, dominates the city. Its interior is rich; elaborately carved chapels,
splendid tombs and wall-paintings all contribute to its grandeur.
Every period of architecture is represented in the streets; there's a
leisure centre; and there are fine walks beside the River Itchen.

All around is rolling countryside. Easton is one of the prettiest
villages along the rural Itchen valley. You can eat here – or, even
better, drive a little further to the ancient and characterful Bush
Inn at Ovington, where the food and setting are both outstanding.
The River Itchen (a clear stream, best seen from the road to the
south of it) meanders on its tranquil way as it has done for
centuries: fords, watercress beds, mills, flint-walled and thatched

cottages dot the maze of little lanes around it. Alresford is a delightful little town; Hinton Ampner a secluded village with fine views – just one of many beauty-spots in the lovely Hampshire landscape. A steam railway is another attraction.

The following facts have been supplied by the owners:

Bedrooms There are 2 double rooms. Bed-and-breakfast costs from £8 (per person) including service and VAT.

   Some if not all of the rooms have the following amenities: central heating or electric heaters; electric blankets, washbasin, shower, own bathroom and wc, shaver-point; TV (colour), armchairs; views of countryside and garden; tea/coffee-making facilities; door keys. No smoking.

Meals Packed lunches can be provided.

Surroundings The grounds consist of 14 acres of pasture, orchard and garden (all available to visitors). Cycles for hire.

Cars The nearest main road is the A31 from Winchester to Alton.

If you prefer to stay at an inn, the **The Plough** (tel: 096278 537), at Itchen Abbas on the north side of the river, has rooms that are spick-and-span – it is run by Henry and Pam Charles. Kingsley stayed here while writing *The Water Babies*; now frequented by anglers, so trout is often on the menu.

Woodstock House, Charlton, north of Chichester, West Sussex, PO18 0HU   *Tel: 024363 666*   C(9) S ⊞5

Once, the premier hunt of England was based at this tiny hamlet in a particularly picturesque Downland valley – or, as a poet of 1837 put it:

> In this sweet vale by hill and downs enclosed
> An age ago, Diana fixed her court.

The flint-walled houses you see were once stables and kennels: all now 'listed', for this is a conservation area. The Palladian folly, Fox Hall, was the Duke of Richmond's hunting lodge (now, restored and well furnished by the Landmark Trust, it can be rented for self-catering holidays). The hunting coats were blue, with gold braid and tasselled caps.

Quiet Woodstock House, too, was largely built in the 18th century with local bricks and flints. Tony and Jocelyn Fowler have furnished the comfortable sitting-room (it has a log fire) with well-chosen fabrics and antiques; the beamed dining-room with leather-upholstered chairs and cream paint on the old stone walls. Bedrooms are more simply furnished; and, if you want tea-making facilities, 50p a day is charged (per head).

There is a pretty little walled garden, with fish-pool and a table tennis room at one end.

For dinner, I enjoyed a gratin of prawns and mushrooms cooked by Jocelyn, steak-and-kidney pie, and a nutty meringue glacé.

The local preoccupation with horses is still strong. There is horse racing and dressage at Goodwood (less than a mile away) and polo at Cowdray. Many people staying at Woodstock House are, however, more interested in the lovely natural harbour at Chichester, and the sailing there; or in its Festival Theatre (early suppers for theatre-goers can be provided). Also in the neighbourhood: the Weald and Downland Open Air Museum (of historic buildings salvaged), half a dozen mansions and castles and many fine gardens, hill and woodland walks, the finest yew forest in Europe, Pagham Harbour nature reserve and Arundel wildfowl gardens, and Roman palaces at Fishbourne and Bignor.

Reader's comments: We stay here frequently: friendly welcome, informal comfort and good cooking.

The following facts have been supplied by the owners:

Bedrooms There are 11 rooms, which include singles and doubles. Bed-and-breakfast costs from £17 (per person in a double room) including service and

477

VAT; prices go up in high season. There are reductions for stays of 2 nights or more; and 'bargain breaks' as well.

Some if not all of the rooms have the following amenities: central heating or electric heaters; washbasin, shower, own bathroom and wc, shaver-point; armchairs; views of countryside/farmland/garden; tea/coffee-making facilities (extra); door keys.

Meals The dinner menu is fixed price (£9). There is a choice of dishes on the fixed menu, which consists of 4 courses. Dinner is served at 7.30 pm. Packed lunches can be provided. Morning or afternoon drinks (coffee, tea etc.) can be ordered for a charge. Wine and other alcoholic drinks can be ordered.

Public rooms There are 2 sitting-rooms etc. The following are available in one or more of them: central heating, open fire, TV (colour), books, magazines, local guides and leaflets.

Surroundings The grounds consist of a courtyard garden. These are available in the neighbourhood: golf, riding, sailing, wind-surfing, squash, tennis.

Cars The nearest main road is the A286 from Midhurst to Chichester.

Closed to visitors We are not open from November to February.

Woody Bank, St Lawrence, west of Ventnor, Isle of Wight, PO38 1XF *Tel: 0983 852610* C(5) **D PT S ⬚4**

This 1840 house is set among terraced gardens on a steep slope leading down towards the sea – one of many such mansions which wealthy Victorians built along a coast they called 'the English Madeira'. In its grounds are mimosa, figs, vines and palms.

Christine and Bob Tindall (formerly journalists) have furnished the sitting-room in high Victorian style; but the dining-room is in

complete contrast – orange tablecloths complement orange-seated bamboo chairs and the sliding glass walls can be opened wide to the garden. The cellar-bar, too, opens onto the garden. Bedrooms vary greatly in size and style: the best has fine walnut beds and a huge mahogany wardrobe, plus capacious armchairs from which to enjoy the sea view. Bedrooms at the front have a sea view; those at the back overlook a road (little used at night) and a nature reserve.

As to dinner, there are choices at every course – lentil soup or egg bouchées, for instance; venison or mullet with anchovy sauce; queen of puddings or bananas in rum-and-lemon sauce; cheeses.

St Lawrence has not only the tiniest church in England (12th century) but another with exceptional pre-Raphaelite stained glass. It has a tropical bird park, glass-making studios, and a network of undercliff footpaths among rocks where subtropical plants grow wild, with small bays and coves down below. There is more about the Ventnor area elsewhere in this book.

The following facts have been supplied by the owners:

Bedrooms There are 9 rooms, which include single, double and family rooms. Bed-and-breakfast costs from £15 (per person) including service and VAT; prices go up in high season. There are reductions for stays of 2 nights or more; and 'bargain breaks' as well.

Some if not all of the rooms have the following amenities: central heating or electric heaters; electric blankets, washbasin, shower, own bathroom and wc, shaver-point; radio, TV (colour or b&w), armchairs; views of sea/countryside/garden; choice of duvets or blankets; orthopaedic mattress or bed-board; tea/coffee-making facilities; door keys. Breakfast in bed is available.

Meals The dinner menu is fixed price (£8.50). There is a choice of dishes on the menu, which consists of 4 courses and coffee. Dinner is served at 7 pm. Vegetarian or special diets can be prepared. Lunches and packed lunches can be provided; and snacks at other hours. Morning, afternoon or bedtime drinks (coffee, tea etc.) can be ordered for a charge. Non-residents are not admitted to the dining-room. Wine and other alcoholic drinks can be ordered.

Public rooms There are 2 sitting-rooms etc. The following are available in one or both of them: central heating, open fire, TV (colour), books, magazines, local guides and leaflets, indoor games (such as board games and cards); bar.

Surroundings The grounds consist of an acre of terraces. These are available in the neighbourhood: golf, riding, sailing, fishing, wind-surfing.

Cars The nearest main road is the A3055 (coastal road round island).

Languages spoken Some French.

Closed to visitors We are not open from November to February.